CONTENTS

PAGE	NO.		PAGE	NO.	
010	001	MEGU New York	110	042	Château Restaurant Joël Robuchon
014	002	MEGU Midtown	114	043	LE CAFÉ de Joël Robuchon
018	003	GLAMOROUS192	116	044	DBL
022	004	CLUB BACH	118	045	DEAN & DELUCA AOYAMA
026	005	COTTON CLUB	120	046	ISLAND VEGGIE Hawaiian Veggie Style
028	006	clotho	122	047	CHOiCE!
030	007	WYNDHAM the 4th	124	048	国会中央食堂
032	008	D			
033	009	club TSUKI	128	049	伊勢丹新宿本店本館 再開発
034	010	HARRY'S BAR	140	050	AOYAMA Francfranc
035	011	Sonoma Wine Garden	144	051	NAGOYA Francfranc
			146	052	Samantha Thavasa ロッテ百貨店本店
038	012	W Hong Kong	147	053	LOVE SWEETS ANTIQUE 青山店
046	013	ANA CROWNE PLAZA KYOTO	148	054	boutique by Shanghai Xintiandi
048	014	CHAPELLE DES ANGES	152	055	cagi de rêves
050	015	ARFERIQUE SHIROGANE	154	056	couronne
052	016	O.M.CORPORATION	158	057	AUDEMARS PIGUET AP TOWER
054	017	Future Plaza of Fantasia	160	058	RESONA BANK Tokyo Midtown
056	018	Residence "S"	164	059	TOKIA
058	019	Residence "M"	166	060	K-two AOYAMA VADI
066	020	Residence "CT"	168	061	K-two AOYAMA LU D0RESS
068	021	Brillia ARIAKE Sky Tower	169	062	BRILLIAGE
070	022	FIELDS Office Lobby	170	063	Takano Yuri BEAUTY CLINIC Shinjuku
072	023	SAN-EI Faucet Osaka Showroom	171	064	KENZO DENTAL CLINIC
074	024	INITIAio Nishiazabu	172	065	嵐電 嵐山駅
075	025	SELLTS LIMITED OFFICE			
076	026	SUNRISE	180	066	松菱
077	027	Residence "T"	184	067	Tse Yang
078	028	GLAMOROUS co.,ltd.	188	068	郷屋敷
			192	069	月の家
086	029	LA FÊTE HIRAMATSU	194	070	Photogenic
092	030	OCEAN ROOM	196	071	お茶屋 まん
096	031	華都飯店	198	072	村田みつい
098	032	THE ST. REGIS OSAKA La Veduta	200	073	二織
100	033	THE ST. REGIS OSAKA Rue D'or	201	074	尾崎幸隆
102	034	HAJIME	202	075	aqua london
103	035	SAVOY	203	076	IT'S
104	036	sinamo	204	077	KEN'S DINING Nishiazabu
105	037	熱烈食堂 HEP ナビオ店	206	078	Salon á dîner Galerie
106	038	ひつまぶし名古屋備長 池袋パルコ店	208	079	NARCISUS
107	039	神戸・六甲道 ぎゅんた ルミネ新宿1	210	080	1967
108	040	Hamac de Paradis 寒梅館			
109	041	へちま	220	081	COOL

English Index: please refer to pages 218-219.

GLAMOROUS
PHILOSOPHY

N° 1

欲望の案内人として。

「人間の心理というか本能というか。レストランでもクラブでも、欲望に訴えるものをデザインしている。物欲、食欲、性欲。みんなの欲を満たすための道筋をサポートするのが、僕の役割だと思っている。商業空間、プライベートなレジデンス、パブリックスペース、いろんなカテゴリーごとにデザインの思考方法は変わるけれど、『欲を満たす』という根本のスタンスは変わらない。こういう雰囲気のレストランで食事をしたら美味しいでしょう？ こんなバーへ行ったら、お互いに気持ちよく合意の上でその先へと進めるでしょう？ 例えばホテルに行くとしたら、もちろんそのホテルは機能性に満ちていて、プライバシーもしっかり確保されている。朝を迎えて、こんな素敵なモーニングが食べられるカフェもあるんですよ、さあ、どうぞ。え？ 洋服をプレゼントしたい？ ならば良いデパートメントストアがあるんですよ！ 僕は、そんな案内人のようなことをしているんだと思っている。

そのためには、まず僕が遊ばなきゃいけない。自分でお金を使ったときに初めて、費用対効果は分かるもの。浴びるようにシャンパンを飲んできたし、買い物を存分に楽しんでいるっていう自負がある。欲しいものには、だいたい値段がついているから、自分のお金で払ってきた。なにも高いものが好きな訳じゃなくて、C級グルメも大好きだし、超一流のフレンチだって食べたい。最先端の都市部にいたと思ったら、翌日には何もないような自然の中にいる。そのどちらも好きなんだよね。自分自身のライフスタイルが、デザインの振り幅になっているんだと思う。日本の純和風の旅館にも本当の居心地の好さを感じるし、ファイブスターのホテルだって大好き。人は、本当にいいと思わなければ絶対にリピーターにはならない。身をもって知っているからこそ、ディテールまで徹底して欲望を満たすようなデザインを考えている」

Guiding Desire.

"Whether the design is for a restaurant or a club, I try to reach deep inside the human psyche and instinct, to create something that speaks to the audience's desires: materialistic desire, sexual desire, and desire for food. My job is to guide my audience, and to satisfy their needs and wants. Although my thought process and methodology change depending on the type of project—commercial space, private residence, public space—my stance on satisfying my audience's desires remains the same.
Doesn't the food taste great in a restaurant with this atmosphere? Wouldn't it be easier to make a move at a bar like this? If the situation requires a hotel, I assure you that it is designed with utmost functionality and privacy, with a great café for a morning after breakfast. Need to find a gift? Here is a great department store! I believe that this is the kind of 'guiding' I do with my work.
To do this, I have to explore and play myself, because I must first spend the money to truly understand its cost-effectiveness. I've had bottles of champaign and enjoyed a lot of shopping. There was always a price tag on the things I wanted, and I've paid for them from my own pockets. That's not to say that I only prefer expensive items; I can enjoy both street food and French cuisine at the same time. I am standing in an ultramodern city today, but tomorrow I might find myself in the middle of nowhere. And I enjoy both of these places. I believe that my lifestyle creates the depth in my designs. I can feel truly comfortable in an old-fashioned, authentic Japanese *ryokan*, but I also like five-star hotels. I can personally identify with the fact that customers will never become loyal, unless they are truly impressed—which is why I'm constantly trying to create designs that can completely satisfy my audience's desires, down to the last detail."

N°001
New York/USA
Mar.2004

MEGU New York

歴史ある建築の壁面に手を加えることなく、「本当の日本の美しさ」を表現したかったのだと、森田は語る。磁器を交互に積み重ねて大きな"日の丸"を造り出す、あるいはアンティークの着物で天井を飾る。金細工や漆、さらには浮世絵。古今を問わず、トライベッカの歴史ある空間を彩るのは、誰もが頭に思い浮かべる繊細で美しい"日本"だ。そして、日本を象徴する色である赤を用いて、店内に統一感を演出していく。太陽が生み出す、さまざまなグラデーションや繊細さが赤には含まれている。もちろん、梵鐘や氷の仏陀など、豪奢なサプライズも忘れない。神秘の国、日本の美でニューヨークを飾った。

Morita explains that he wanted to reveal "true Japanese beauty," without having to disturb the historical architecture. Stacking porcelain to portray the rising sun. Decking the ceiling with antique *kimono*. Gold work, lacquer, and *ukiyo-e*. This space within a historic TRIBECA building is embellished with the consistent and timeless style of "Japan" and its intricate beauty. The symbolic color of the red sun unifies the interior with delicate gradations. Of course, the extravagant surprises of the Buddha ice statue and the *bonshō* are not to be forgotten. New York has been adorned with the allure of mystical Japan.

N°002
New York/USA
Apr.2006

MEGU Midtown

『MEGU New York』から、およそ2年後に完成したミッドタウンの2号店。劇場のような光と影を意識したデザインの要となっているのは、懸案材料でもあった超高層タワーを支える巨大な柱。手彫りのウッド・ビーズで日本の家紋をあしらい、ランプシェードを模すことで、外観へもアプローチするアイコンとなっている。瀧と鯉の描かれた浮世絵、倉科昌高氏による虎や雉の壁画、さらには雲海が映されたパネルが、多様な光によって照らされる。和のモチーフをいかに落とし込むのか。森田が挑戦したバランスは素材の違いにも表れる。黒御影石やトラバーチンなどの床材、あるいは黒切子のシャンデリアやオイルランプによって空間に表情の変化を付けることで自然な動線を作り出している。

This Midtown restaurant was completed two years after "MEGU New York." The centerpiece of this dramatic mix of light and shadow, are the monolithic support columns that pierce the towering skyscraper. Imitating lampshades through the use of hand-carved wooden beads imprinted with a Japanese family crest, the columns are transformed into an exterior visual. Elaborate light captures a complex menagerie, including an *ukiyo-e* of waterfall and carp, Masataka Kurashina's wall painting of tigers and pheasants, with a backdrop of panels portraying an endless sea of clouds. The theme embraces Japanese motifs, and Morita's challenge is also apparent in the balance of different materials. The space is directed with dynamic expression, a natural flow created through a combination of black granite and travertine floors, with a cut-glass chandelier and oil lamps.

N°**003**
Nagoya/Japan
Mar.2005
GLAMOROUS192

2005年「愛・地球博」で誕生した192日限定のディスコ。1990年代のバブル感と2005年の時代感を繋ぐために、あるいは郷愁や憧れを紡ぐためにこの"箱"に必要とされたのが、ラグジュアリーさだった。レザーのロングソファに真っ赤なバーカウンター。天井からは、オリジナルデザインのシャンデリアスタンドが目映く煌めいている。大粒のスワロフスキーがランダムに配され、パープルのカーペットが敷かれた空間。チェアのバックに記された「GLAMOROUS192」の文字は、それらすべての象徴と呼べるかもしれない。非日常を演出するための、あるひとつの方法論が、時代を席巻したディスコには詰まっている。

This 192-day disco was created as part of the EXPO 2005 AICHI, JAPAN. To connect the modernism of 2005 with the nostalgia of the buzzing 1990s, this "box" was festooned with luxury, with leather chaise longues and a crimson bar counter. Custom-made chandelier stands animate the ceiling with sparkle and glimmer. It is a space covered in purple carpet, randomly implanted with large droplets of swarovski crystals. The theme of this place is perhaps symbolized by the word "GLAMOROUS192" imprinted on the back of each chair. A specific methodology to create a unique and sensory experience has been established inside a disco: the epitome of a bygone era.

N°004
Osaka/Japan
Apr.2009
CLUB BACH

圧倒的なラグジュアリー空間を演出するためには、繊細な手さばきが必要となる。例えば、エレベーターホールで待ち構える扉。独特の表情のモアレを生み出すために、ファブリックを重ねてガラスで封印している。あるいはメインホールの壁面は、ブロンズフィニッシュのステンレスと数十万個のクリスタルという異なる素材を組み合わせたパネルで覆い、さらにブロンズミラーをランダムに配している。女性を美しく見せるために白い大理石を選び、ダウンライトで柔らかなハレーションを起こす。そういった緻密な計算の上に、シルクスクリーンアートが埋め込まれ、全身にクリスタルを纏った馬が鎮座している。ラグジュアリーは、細部に宿る。そして、圧倒的な存在感を放つのだ。

Delicate handling is key in staging an irresistibly luxurious space. For example, the door that awaits in the elevator hall is covered by a layer of fabric, sealed behind glass to create a complex moiré pattern. The wall surfaces of the main hall are encrusted with bronze stainless steel panels, with thousands of crystals randomly interrupted by pieces of bronze mirror. The downlight creates a soft halation on the white marble, a material chosen specifically to illuminate women. Silkscreened artworks are carefully positioned on top of this meticulous calculation. In the center of the space, a horse, clad in crystals, breathes quietly. Luxury lies in the details, exuding its utmost presence.

N°005
Tokyo/Japan
Nov.2005
COTTON CLUB

1920年代にNYでもっとも輝いていた伝説のナイトクラブを現代の東京に蘇らせたいというオーダーに、ライヴハウスというよりも「艶のある社交場」という提案で返した。シアーカーテンで仕切られたホワイエから、照明の落とされた客席へ少しずつ向かう高揚感。ライヴ中の一体感とプライベートを同時に成し得た、絶妙な距離の客席。ライティングはまるでステージから直接光が落とされているよう。エレガンスであることを追求し、計算し、辿り着いた空間。ライヴという非日常の化学変化を楽しむためには、「快適さが重要」だと森田は言う。生前、デューク・エリントンやキャブ・キャロウェイがステージを披露した夢の舞台は、新たな装いへと生まれ変わったが、巨人たちの伝説や息吹は今も変わらずに伝えられている。

In response to the client's request to recreate a legendary 1920s New York night club, Morita responded with a proposal for an alluring place for socialization. Starting from the foyer separated by sheer curtains, the thrill gradually heightens into the dimly lit seating area. The seats are arranged with delicate balance, preserving just enough privacy against the immediacy of the live performance. The lighting is like a stream of brightness pouring directly from the stage. This space is the result of an endless pursuit of elegance. For one to enjoy the extraordinary experience of a live performance, "the place must be comfortable," explains Morita. The dream stage, where Duke Ellington and Cab Calloway once proved their mastery, has transformed its facade, but the vigor of the legendary giants still carries on.

N°006
Tokyo/Japan
Sep.2007
clotho

会員制のバーに必要とされるもっとも重要な要素は、特権性だろう。その特別感を強調するために森田が考えたキャッチーな仕掛けのひとつが、エレベーターホールの3枚の隠し扉。専用のIDカードをかざしたときにだけ本当の扉が開かれるという仕掛けを作っている。あるいは、アートギャラリーのようにアーティストの作品で壁を埋め尽くすのも同じ発想から生まれたものだろう。森田が注目するイタリア人アーティスト、カルロ・ピエローニ氏のポップな作品を落ち着いた配色の中に浮かび上がるように構成している。作品と森田の演出に共通するのは、遊び心。大胆な提案はむしろ、会員制だからこそ可能なチャレンジだったかもしれない。

Exclusivity. That is the most important element of a private club. To emphasize this point, Morita constructed three hidden doors inside the elevator hall as part of his many catchy installations. The guests must use their ID cards to open the correct door. The concept of exclusivity also inspired Morita to cover the walls with works of art, simulating an art gallery. Vibrant artworks by Italian artist Carlo Pieroni, one of Morita's favorites, stand out from a palette of muted colors. The common thread between Morita's design and these artworks is the sense of play. This bold proposal was made possible precisely because the club is exclusive to those who understand it.

WYNDHAM the 4th

N°007
Hong Kong/China
Jan.2012

香港ランカイフォン中心部にある雑居ビル。架空の王「Wyndham 4世」のプライベートギャラリーという設定で、空間は統一されている。そのためには、場所や時代に対する固定概念をいかに剝ぎ取るかが、デザインの基盤となる。黒御影石のカウンターの背後には、剝製さながらのロープで形作られたモーツァルト氏の熊と鹿。あるいは佐竹穣氏による艶めかしい女性を描いた壁画のようなシルクスクリーンアート。無国籍性のために森田がチョイスした作品には、時代を跨ぐ普遍性があるのだろう。ビルの4階でありながら、テラスと室内が共に20坪という希有なシチュエーション。森田はシックなトーンで統一することで連続性を作り、階上の古びたビルさえも、趣ある演出へと変化させた。

This project is located in a mixed-use building in central Lan Kwai Fong, Hong Kong. The setting of this design is a private gallery for an imaginary king, Wyndham IV. Stereotypes toward particular cultures, locations, and times must be stripped for one to fully realize this theme. Mozart Guerra's lifelike bear- and deer-head rope sculptures peer from behind a black granite counter, while Joe Satake's silkscreen portrayals of sensual women create a fresco effect. Morita chose these artworks based on their universality, which renders a sense of statelessness. Although located on the fourth floor, the space is a rare mixture of the terrace and the indoor space, each with sixty-six square meters. Limiting the palette to a series of chic tones, Morita successfully transformed a worn-out building into a tasteful stage.

N° **008**
Tokyo/Japan
Jan.2012

D

約8坪という限られた空間を優雅に演出するために用いられたのが、ガラスの中に封印されたドレープ状のチェーン。カウンター席の背面に、あえてゆとりをもたせた表現を採用することで、限定されていながらも余裕ある空間へと変貌させた。それはバーという場所の特性を引き出すものかもしれない。ゲストとバーテンダーとの適度な距離感、あるいは関係性を作り出すキッカケにさえなっている。落ち着いた間接照明も、このドレープが効果的に作用している。壁際の唯一のテーブル席には、取り外し可能なシャンパンクーラーを設置。シックながらも使い勝手の良いバーは、森田の理想のひとつなのだろう。

To encapsulate this twenty-six-square-meter space in elegance, Morita enclosed draping chains inside panels of glass. By deliberately placing metaphors of looseness behind the counter seats, the space, although limited, is transformed into a generous one. This also pulls out the distinctive characteristics of the bar, creating a comfortable distance between the guest and the bartender. The draping of the chains also transforms the indirect lighting into a soothing ambience. The one and only table positioned against the wall is equipped with a removable champagne cooler. This chic yet practical bar is a representation of Morita's ideals.

N°009
Tokyo/Japan
Dec.2007

club TSUKI

銀座8丁目という土地柄に合わせて、コンセプトは「ラグジュアリーでエレガント」。エントランスから誘うように階段にはカスタム・ペイントが施され、真っ黒な世界から店内へ入ると一転、明るくナチュラルな空間が広がっている。バカラ社のシーリングライト「ファントム」171台が、まるで踊っているかのように天井を彩っている。壁面のウッドによって落ち着いた空間を演出しつつも、オリジナルの巨大なシャンパン＆ワインセラーは、圧倒的な存在感で高揚感を煽る。キャンドルを埋め込んだような照明のインスタレーションは、時間と共に徐々にキャンドルが短くなっていくのだという。光で"遊ぶ"仕掛けが幾通りも実践されている。

To match the glossy district of Ginza 8-Chome, the concept behind this project is one of luxury and elegance. Stairs are custom painted to draw guests to the entrance, the blackened world quickly shifting to a well-lighted natural interior. The ceiling is covered with a swarm of 171 Baccarat Fantôme lights. While the wooden wall surfaces create a calm ambience, the custom-made champagne and wine cellars ignite excitement with their unavoidable presence. The lighting installation simulates burning candles, with an effect that shortens the candle length over time. Tricks of playing with light are executed in a variety of ways.

N° 010
Kobe/Japan
Aug.2001

HARRY'S BAR

黒で統一された世界に浮かび上がる、白木のカウンター。木という素材が持つポテンシャルを際立たせるのは、実はこんな演出なのかもしれない。カウンターの背面には、燃え上がる炎と氷のコントラスト。まぎれもなく「本物」である。黒い空間の中に用いる自然素材。ラウンド型の半個室に用いられている革もまた、自然素材である。森田が人工的なマテリアルを多用するというイメージは、まったく正しくない。森田がデザインに用いるそのほとんどは自然素材なのだ。マテリアルに纏わりついている凡庸なイメージを、いかに引き剥がしていくか。思想の一端がつまった、黒い夜の空間に仕上がった。

The bare skin of the wood counter floats amidst a world of black. This might be the perfect staging ground on which to test the true potential of wood materials. The contrasting imagery of ice and burning fire dominates the wall behind the counter. Both of these are unmistakably real. Natural elements are placed inside a black space. The leather used in the round half-private rooms is also an example of a natural material. The common notion that Morita overuses artificial materials is completely mistaken. In truth, nature comprises most of Morita's palette. The challenge lies in removing the stereotypical mediocrity associated with these materials. The resulting effect is that of a dark, black evening, a reflection of Morita's philosophy.

N° 011
Santa Monica/USA
Aug.2010

Sonoma Wine Garden

店のストーリーを紡ぐアイコンを象徴的に使うのは、森田が得意とする手法のひとつだが、この「Wine Garden」では、ワインの銘柄が書かれたボックスの蓋を天井から吊している。一見チープな印象を与えてしまいそうだが、反復というもうひとつの森田らしい手法を使い、壁面にもワインボックスの蓋を用いることで価値の転換がなされている。さらにワインボトルで作られたシャンデリアなど、徹底して「ワイン」の場所であることを伝える。空間を彩るだけでなく、客へ話の種を提供し、店全体が「ワイン」を楽しむ雰囲気に包まれていくことになる。

One of Morita's signature techniques is to use symbolic icons that reveal a business' story. In the case of this Wine Garden, box lids imprinted with wine labels were hung from the ceiling as part of the overall design. Although this might have given off a somewhat cheap impression, Morita applied repetition, another one of his signature techniques, by echoing the iconic lids on the wall surface to twist the meaning of this otherwise humble item. The concept of wine is further stressed through the use of chandeliers made of wine bottles. The resulting space surpasses that of a merely well-decorated interior; it is a space entirely dedicated to enjoying wine, sprinkled with thoughtful hints for conversation.

光でデザインする時間軸。

「デザインにおいてもっとも重要な要素は"光"だと、僕は思っている。朝昼晩の時間軸のデザインは、ライティングによって左右される。顕著なのが、24時間の時間軸で考える必要のあるホテルやレジデンスかもしれない。朝、いかに清々しい光を取り入れ、逆に真昼には強すぎる光をいかに和らげるかを考える。夕方から夜へと続くムードのグラデーション。もしも物件が地下にあったなら、朝昼晩と光を変える。なぜならば、光は、人間の本能に訴えるものだから。
同じように、テクニカルな意味でデザインする際に重視しているポイントを挙げるなら、素材の選び方。できるだけフェイクは使いたくない。もしも制限があって、本物の木を使うことができず、木目調のプラスチックを使わなければいけない状況があったなら、例えばアーティストの倉科昌高さんに木目を描いてもらう。そこまですれば、フェイクの素材さえも本物になるから。
レジデンスの場合はまず、いかに機能的で、リラックスできるかを考える。無駄なデザインはしない。でも、ハッピーなデザインはところどころに。自分がゆっくりと過ごすような寝室や書斎は静かなデザインで、でも、友だちを呼んだときに、『こんなリビングに住んでんのー!』っていう"おもてなし"の部分にはサプライズを入れていく。それが住宅における基本的な考え方。いや、実はほとんどの物件に共通の考え方なのかもしれない。プライベートの空間は、素に返れるように徹底的に機能面を重視している。密室のトイレは、住宅でも、オフィスでも、商業施設でもとても大切。機能とサプライズ。それが、僕がいちばん大事にしている"おもてなし"に繋がっているんだと思う。僕は、できるだけ陰に隠れて人が喜ぶ姿を見ていたいんだけど、実は人の注目を集めたいタイプでもある。そんな両極性のある性格が、この仕事には向いていたのかもしれないな」

Designing Time with Light.

"I believe the most important element in design is *light*. Light is what determines the timeline of the entire day and night. This becomes most obvious in hotel and residential designs, when I have to think in a 24-hour timeline. For these projects, I need to consider how to incorporate fresh light in the morning, and how to soften the sun in the afternoon. I create a gradation of ambience, from twilight to darkness. For projects located underground, I control the lighting depending on the time of day, because light is an element that speaks to human instincts.
In a more technical sense, I consider the choice of materials equally important. I try to avoid using 'fake' or synthetic materials. If, for some reason, I'm required to use plastic instead of real wood, then I'd ask an artist like Masataka Kurashina to draw wood grains on them. If I go that far, I can transform this 'fake' material into a new *authentic*.
For residences, I first consider how functional and relaxing the space can become. I don't design excessively. But I sprinkle my projects with some happiness. I keep the private bedrooms and offices tranquil and serene, but I also try to inject some surprise into the entertaining areas, so that my clients can impress their friends. That's my basic philosophy on residential design. In fact, my thoughts are the same for almost all of my projects. I keep the private spaces thoroughly functional and down to earth. For this reason, private bathrooms are always important, whether in residences, offices, or commercial facilities. My concept of hospitality is based on functionality and surprise. Most of the time, I'd rather hide behind a wall and watch my audience from a distance, but I also want to stay in the center of the crowd. Maybe this two-sided personality is what qualifies me for my work."

N°012
Hong Kong/China
Aug.2008

W Hong Kong

"都会のオアシス"というストレートなホテルの役割を、デザインに落とし込むこと。森田が目指したのは、「森」でホテルを彩ることだった。自然の表情を抽象的なフォームに転換し、ホテルの随所に配置する。例えば、小枝で作ったガラスボックスが、ファサードの特徴となる、といった具合。あるいは1階から全階を貫く柱は、木の根を想起させ、SPA「bliss」階段脇のガラス玉は、まさしく恵みの雨を表現している。何よりインスピレーションを受けているのは、自然の力強さなのだ。ただ優しい空気を充満させるのではなく、時に驚きを与えてくれるエネルギー。ホテルは、癒され、力をチャージする場所であることが、デザイン・コンセプトの根幹になっている。

The challenge was to incorporate the straightforward function of the *urban oasis* into the design. For this project, Morita aimed for a hotel embroidered with elements of the forest, by converting natural expressions into abstract forms. The facade is characterized by a glass box made of small twigs, to name an example. A supporting pillar runs through the floors to resemble the roots of a tree, while the glass droplets that decorate the stairs of SPA "bliss" simulate fallen raindrops. The powerful force of nature is the greatest source of inspiration. It is the energy that not only fills the air with a healing ambience but also animates us with surprise. The very basis of this design concept is that a hotel is, first and foremost, a place for resting and recharging.

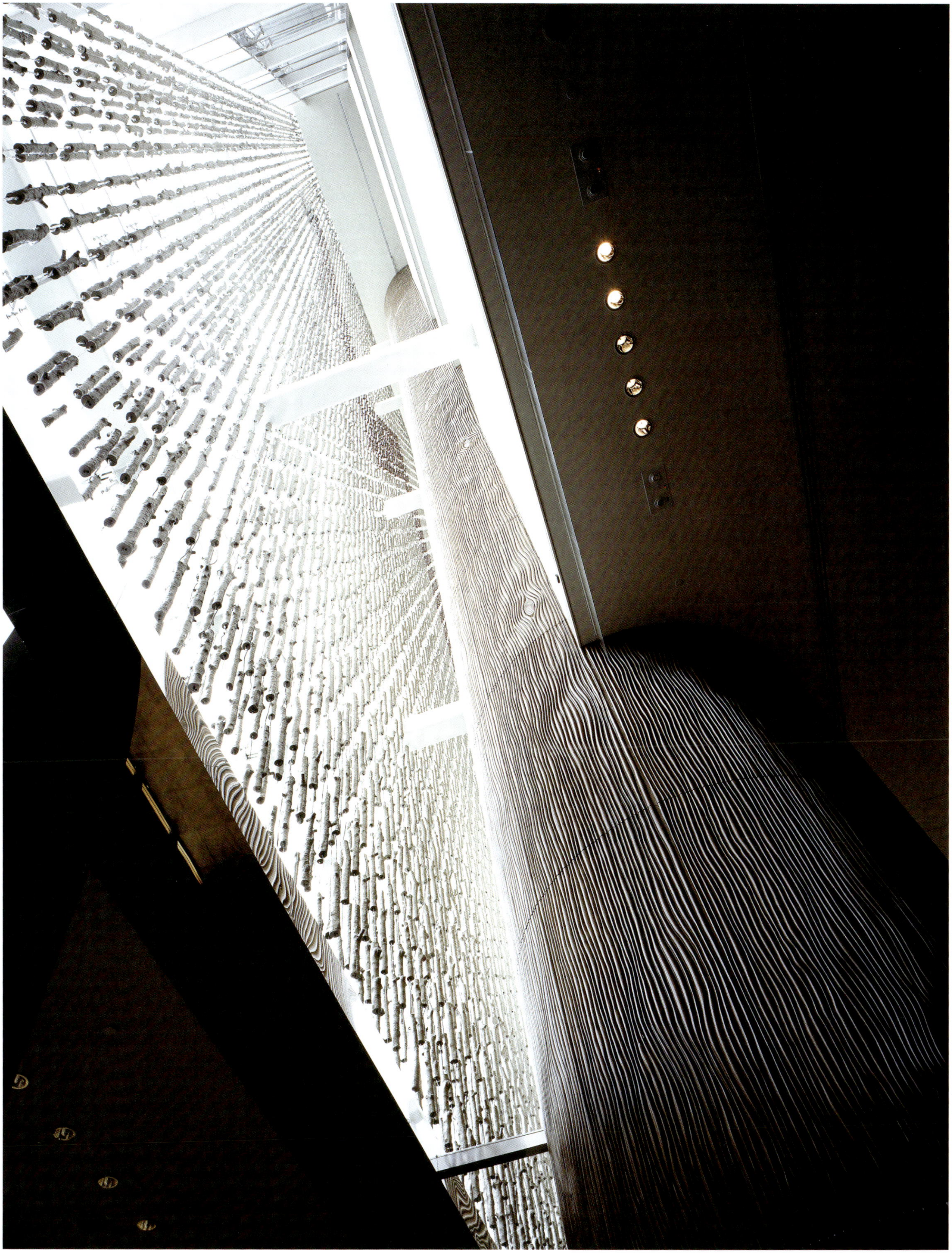

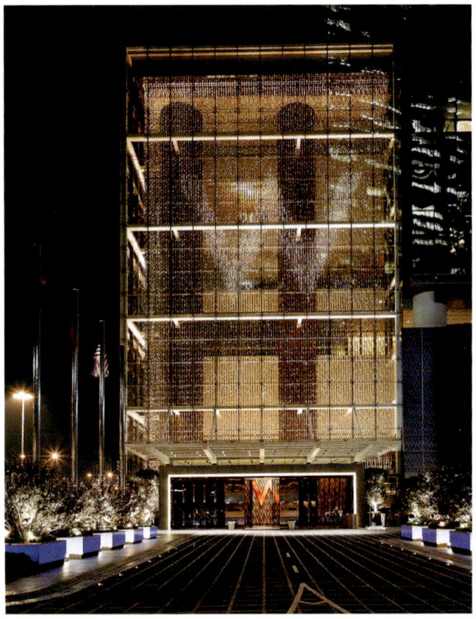

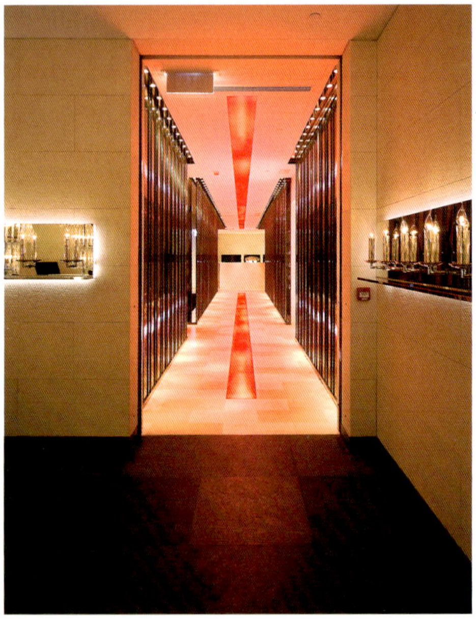

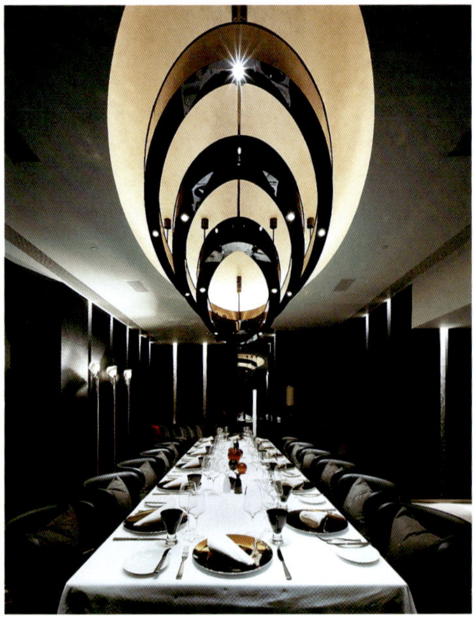

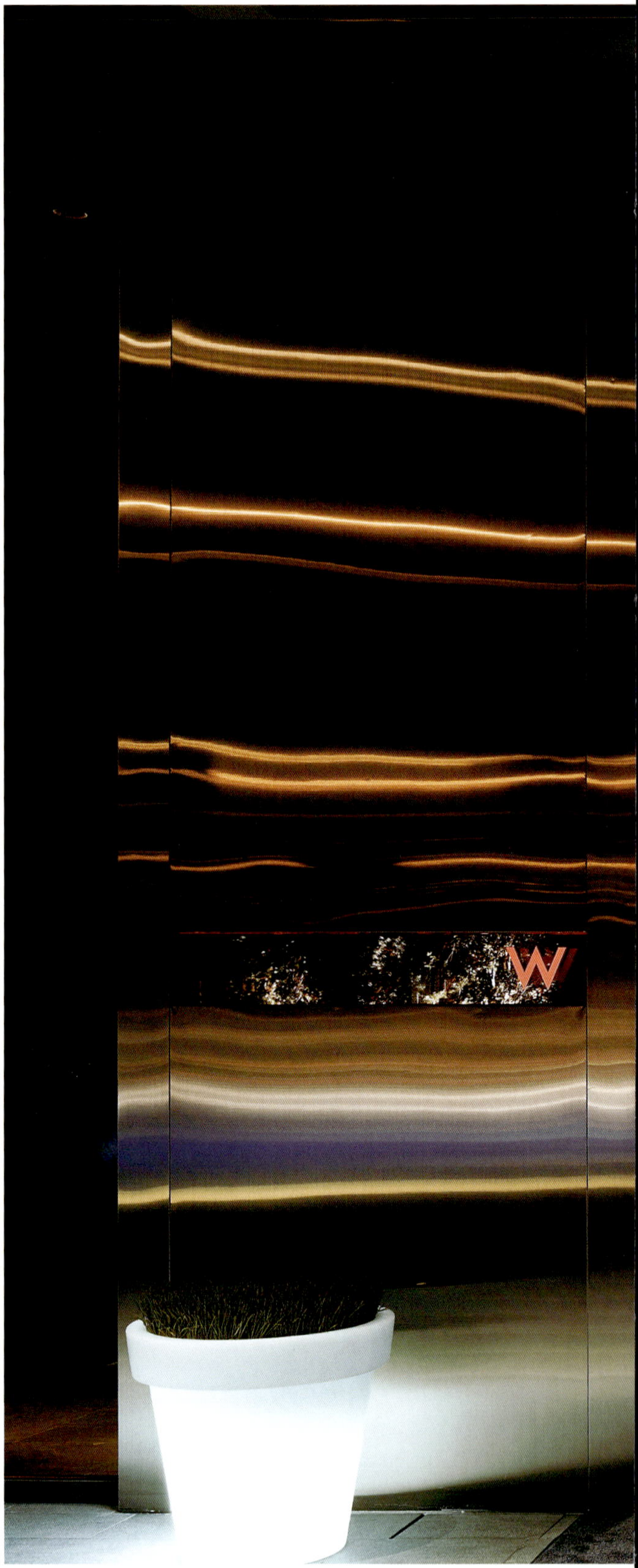

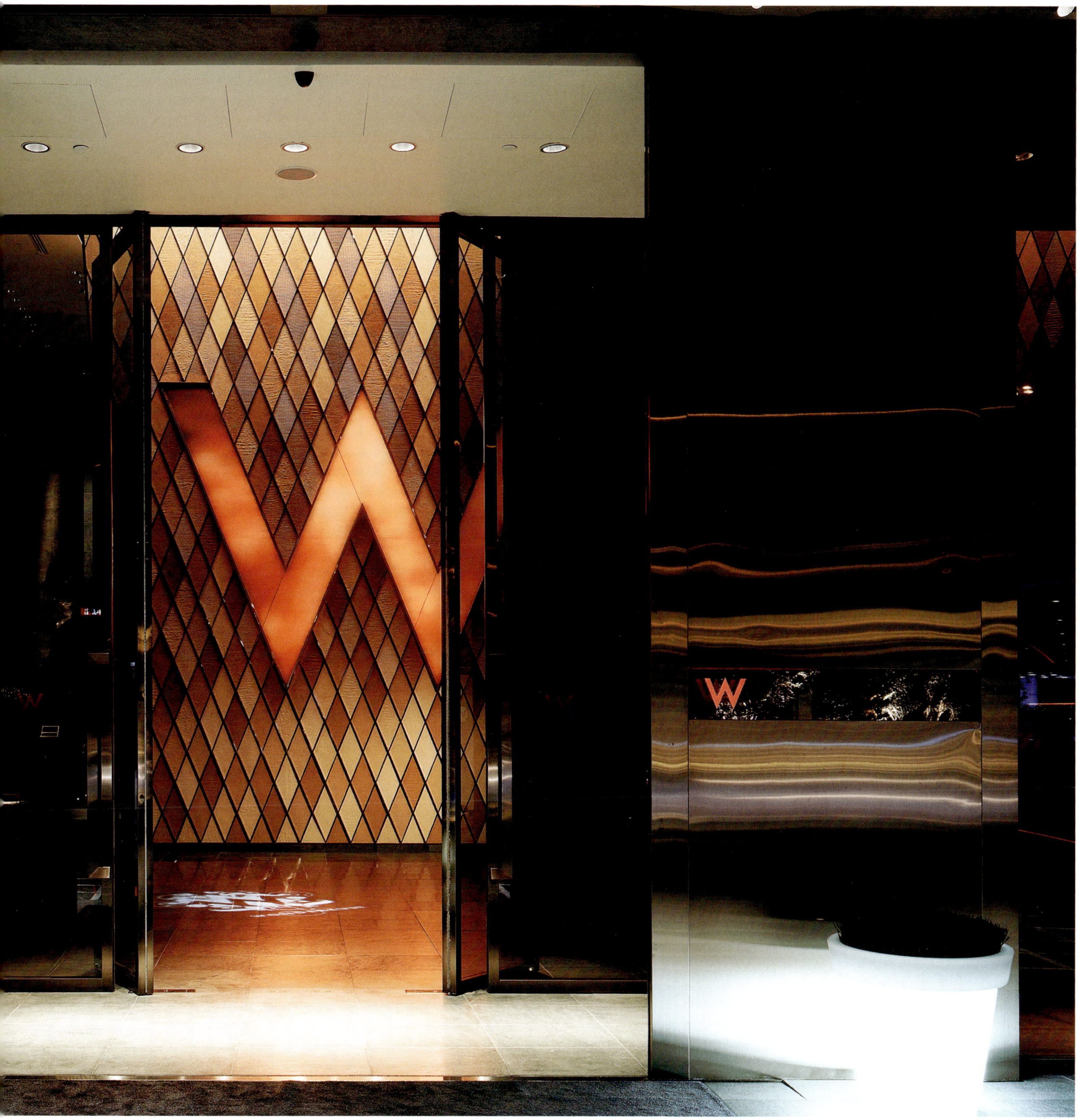

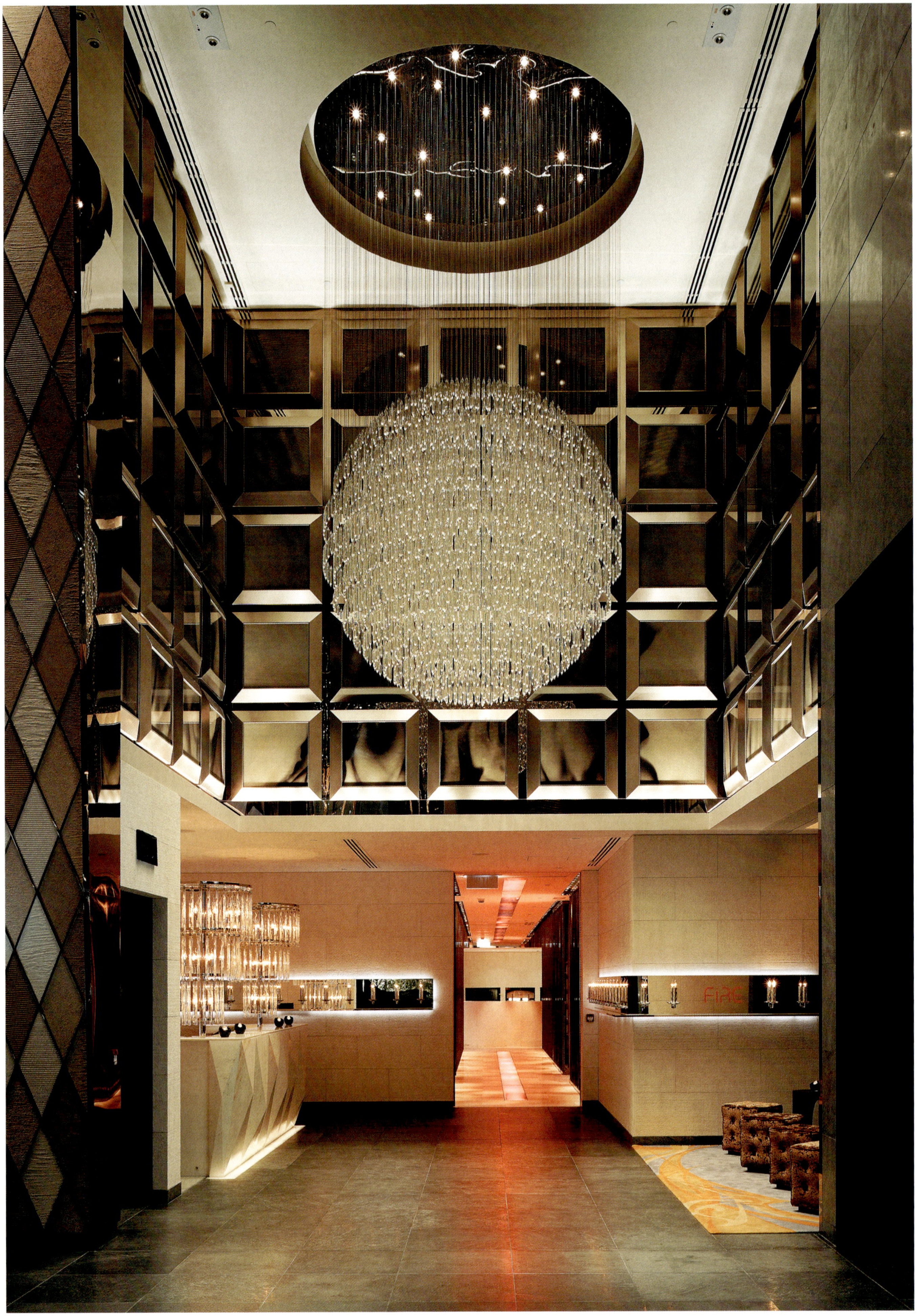

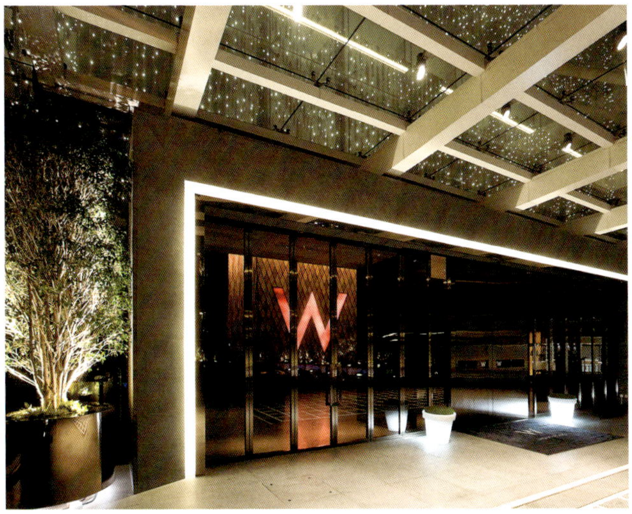
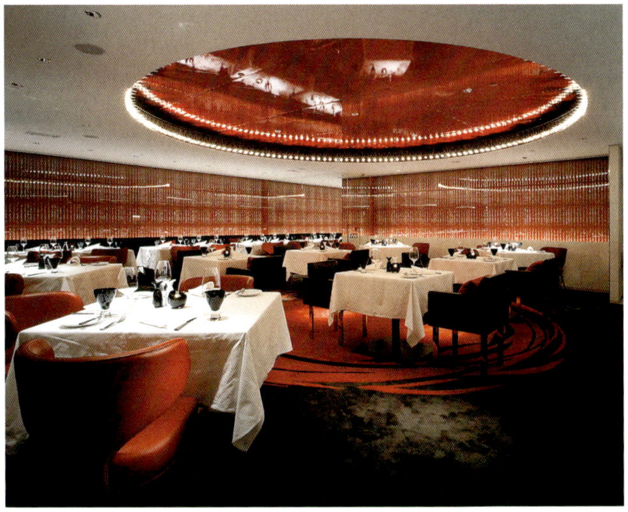
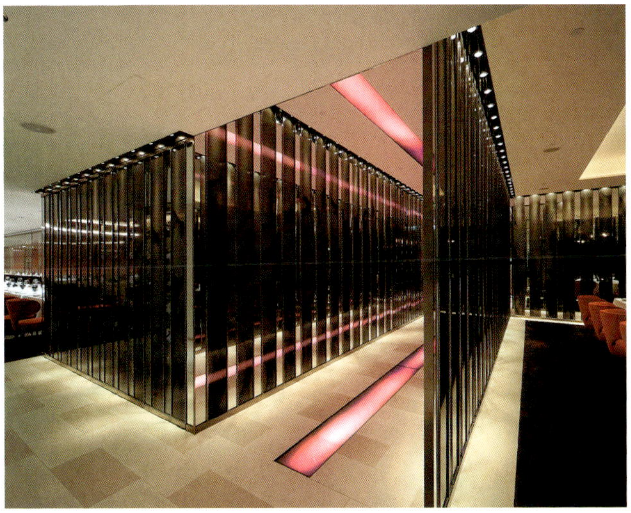
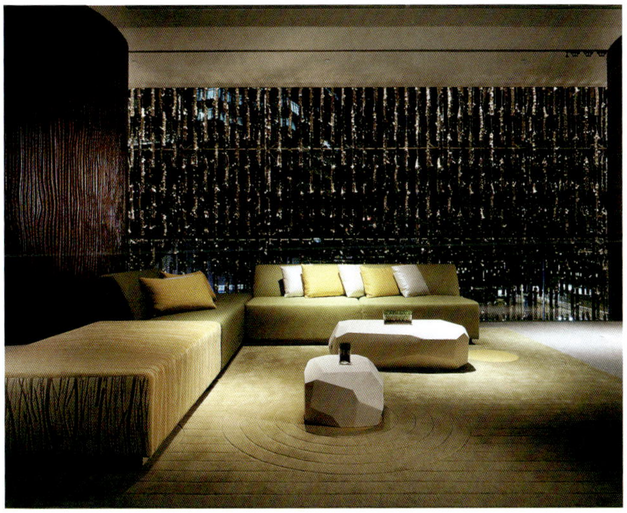
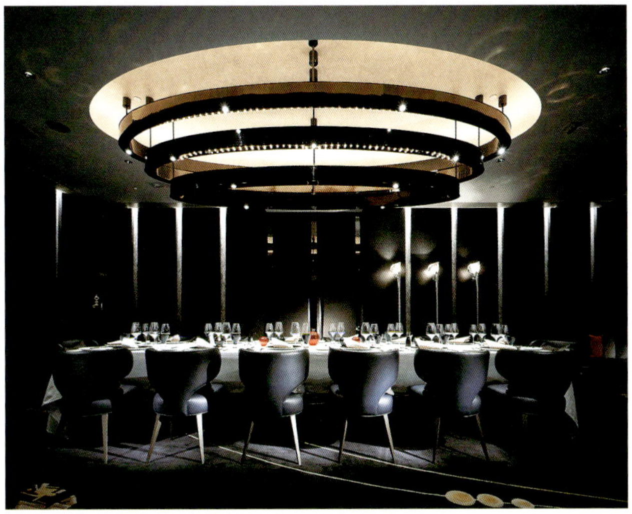
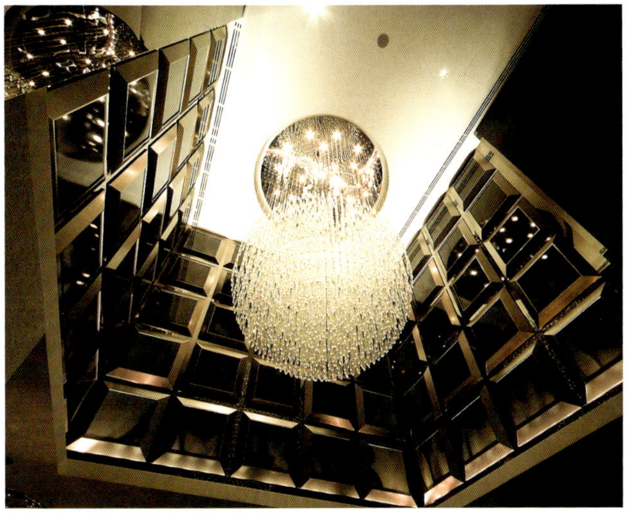

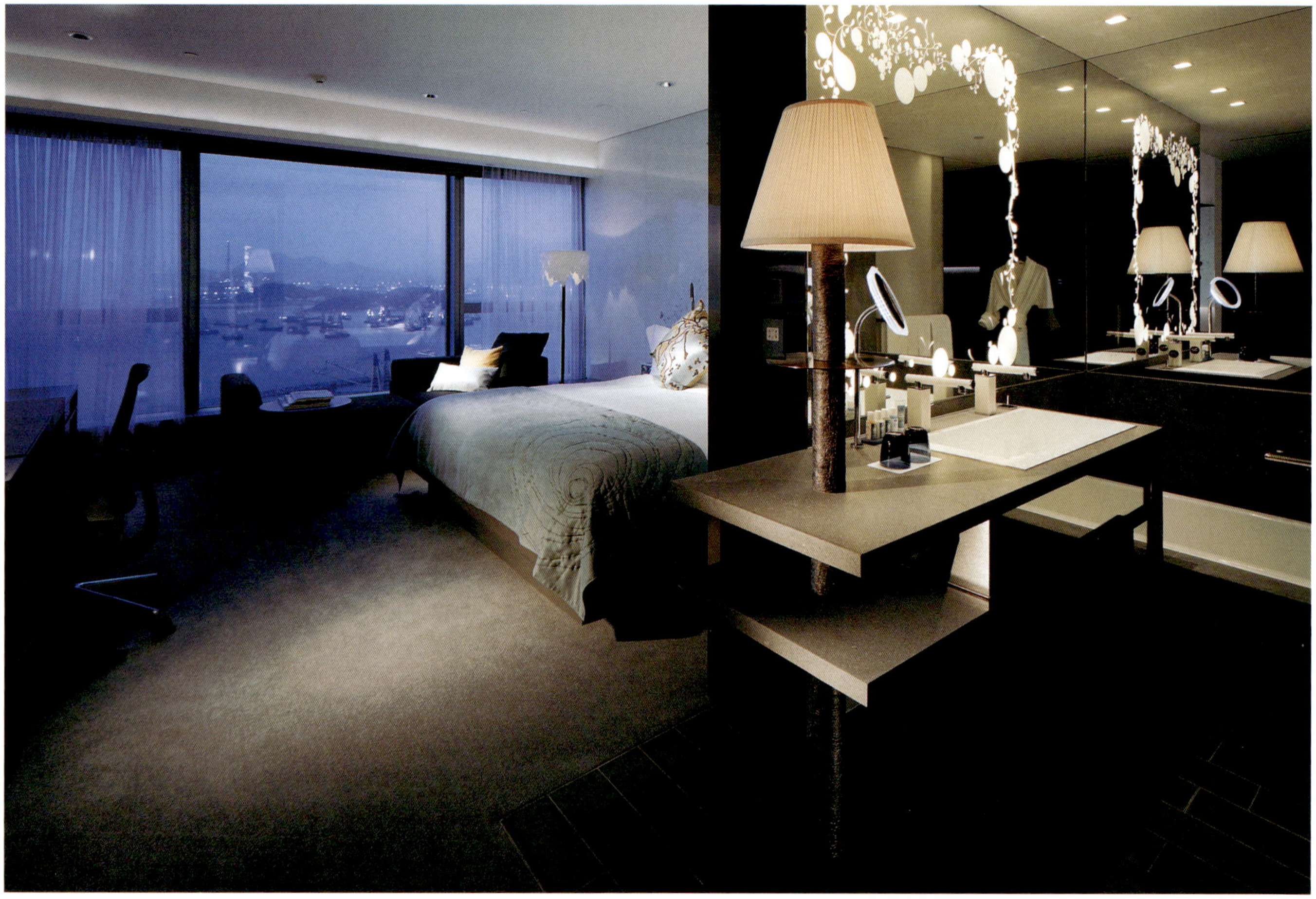

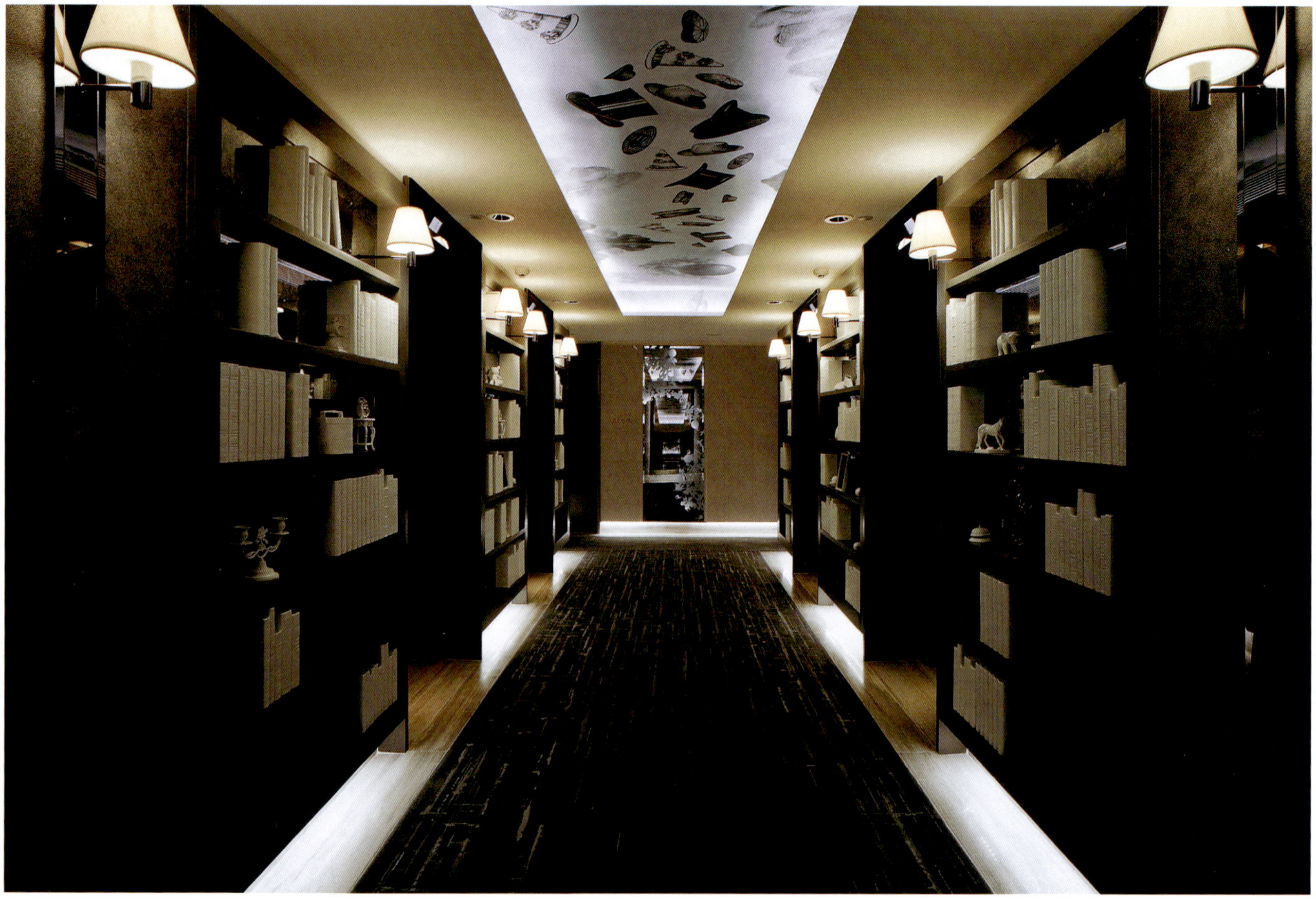

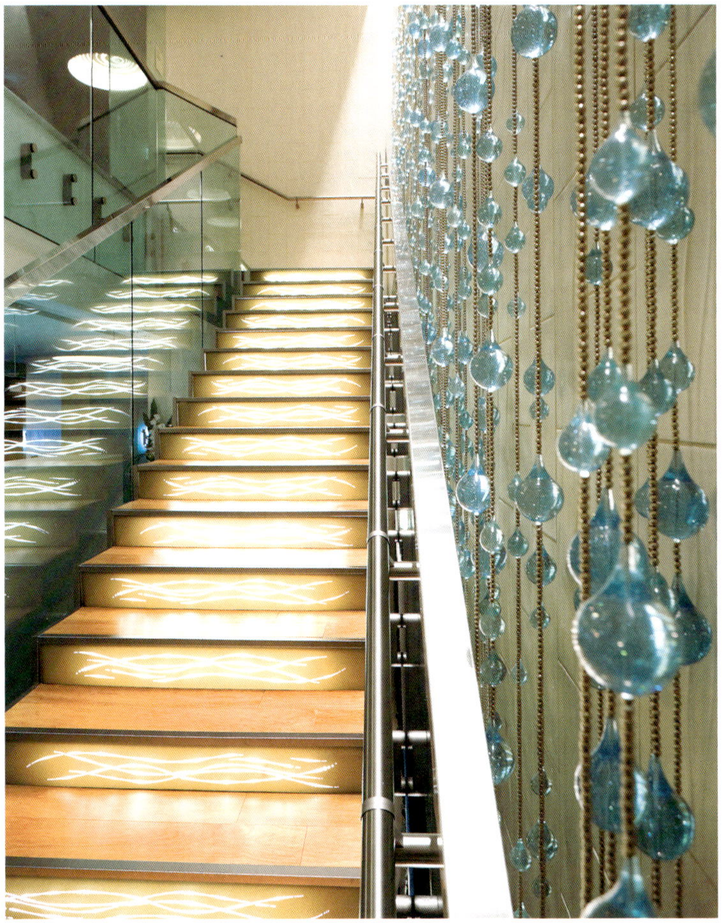

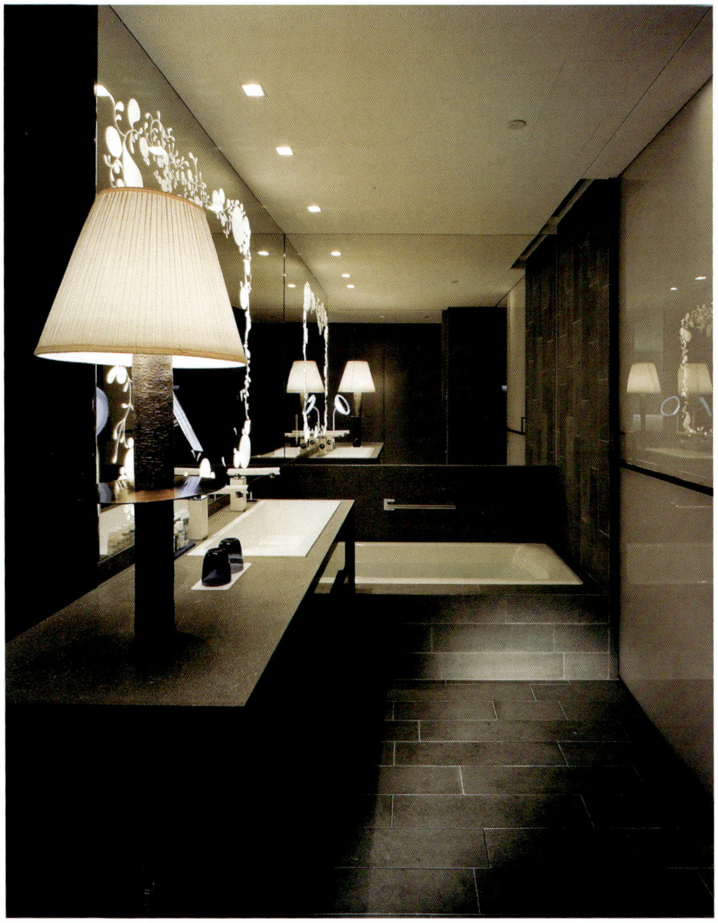

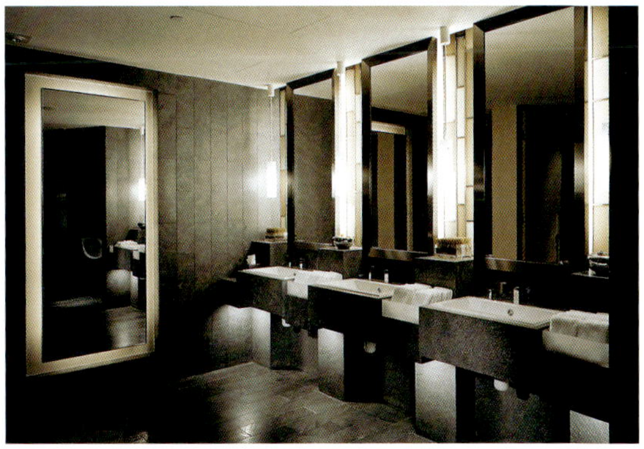

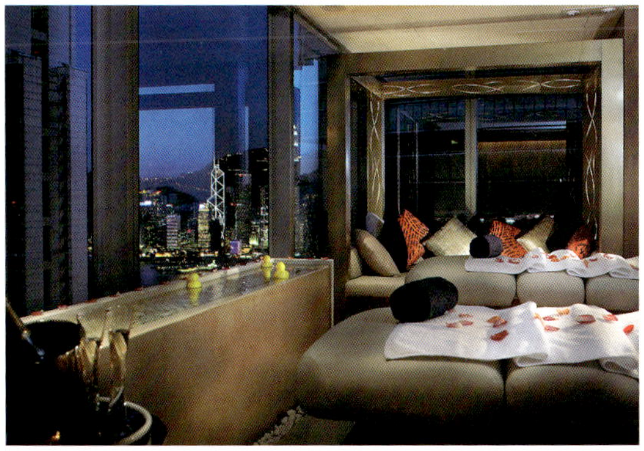

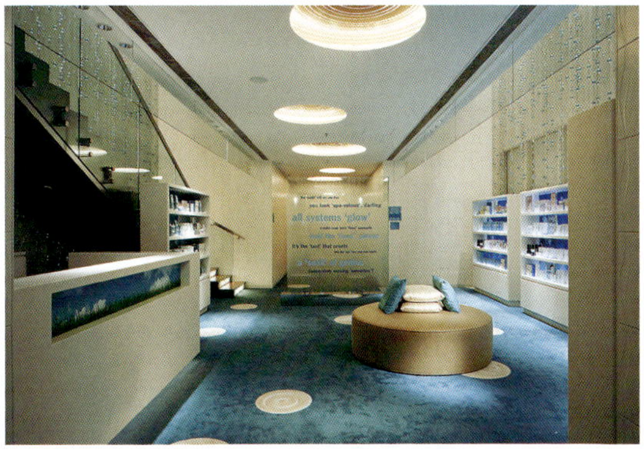

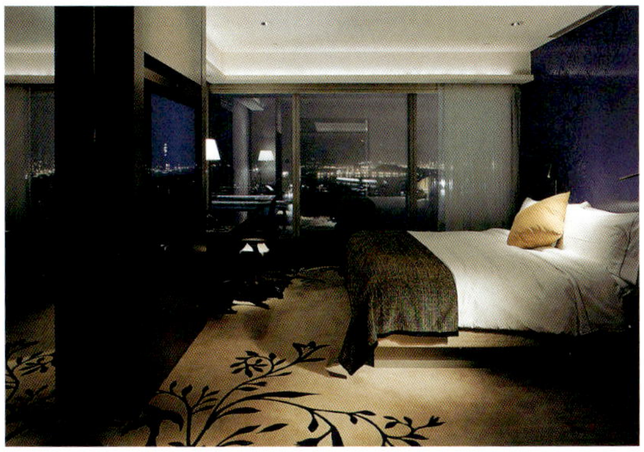

N°013
Kyoto/Japan
Dec.2012

ANA CROWNE PLAZA KYOTO

二条城を眺める京都らしいシチュエーションを快適に過ごすために、邸宅のような温かみのあるデザインを施した。木製のパネルがエントランスからゲストルーム内部へと続き、ミニバーやテレビボードなど、ホテルに必須の機能も包み込んでいる。木パネルの組み合わせは、和の空間にリズムを生む。また、まるで木立のように降り注ぐ月明かりをイメージし、空間を仕上げた。ベッドサイドには、伝統的な陶芸の技術を用いるアーティスト・近藤髙弘氏の『ミスト』が配され、別名・銀滴彩と呼ばれるこの作品は、まるで火の中から生み出された水のような、鮮烈なイメージを与えている。

The hotel is designed with the warmth of a home, where guests are able to enjoy a time of comfort against Kyoto's scenic backdrop of the Nijo Castle. Wooden panels continue from the entrance to the guestrooms, enveloping essential hotel functions such as the minibar and television board. The composition of the wooden paneling creates rhythm in a quintessential Japanese interior. The space is finished with beams of light meant to resemble that of the moon. Traditional ceramic art by Takahiro Kondo is placed at the bedsides, a series of works entitled "Mist" that illustrate vivid imagery of water born of fire.

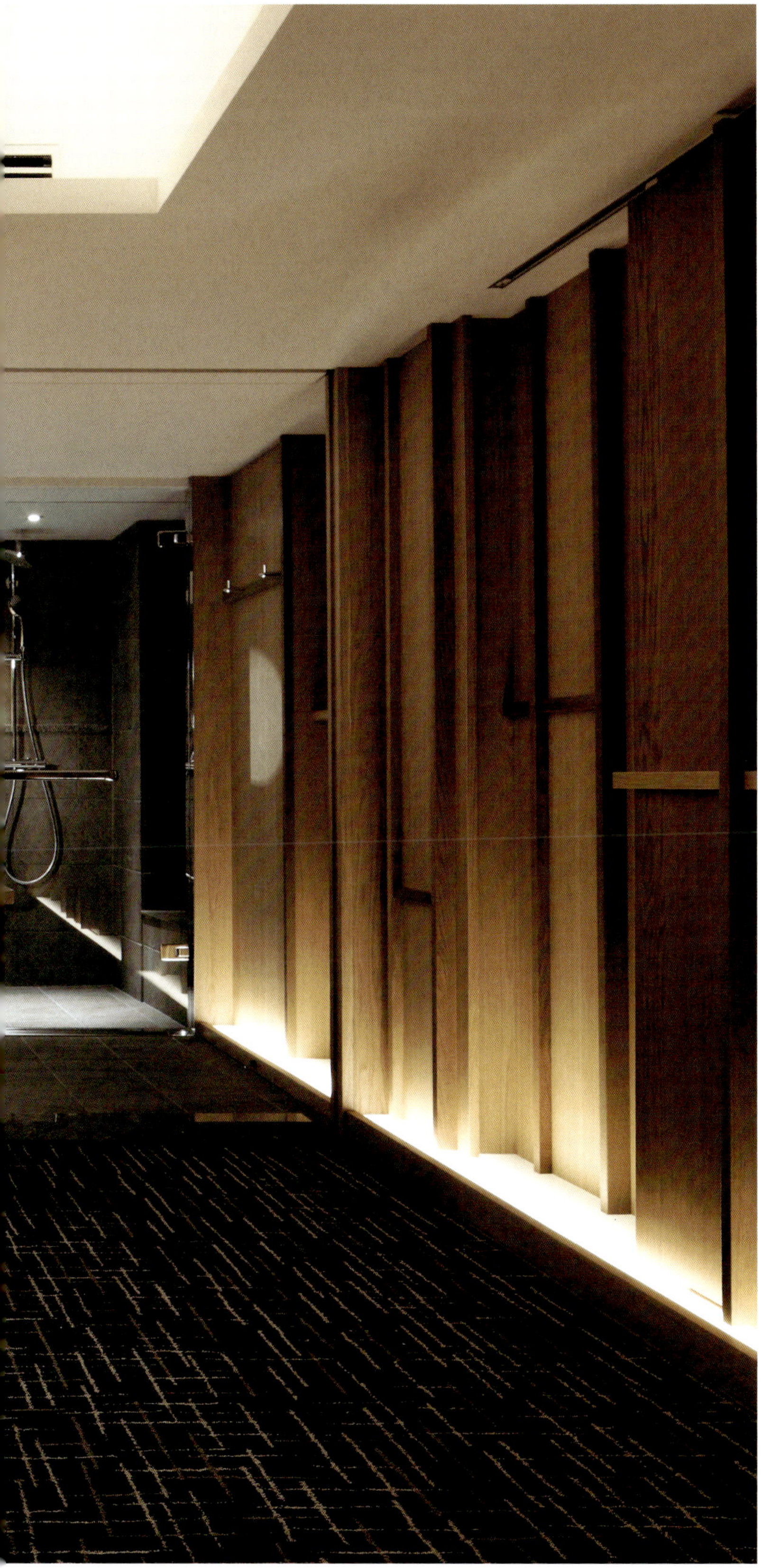
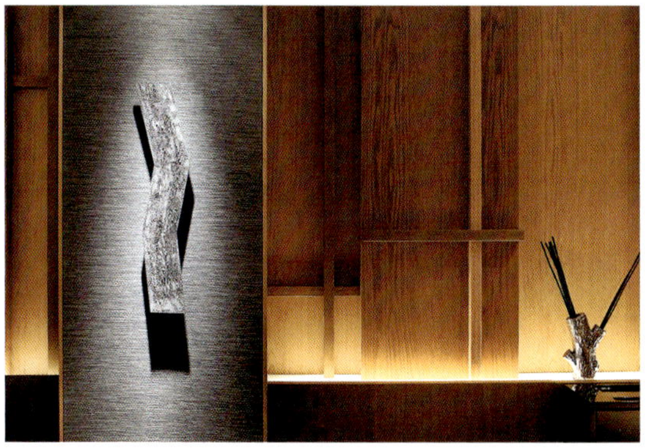
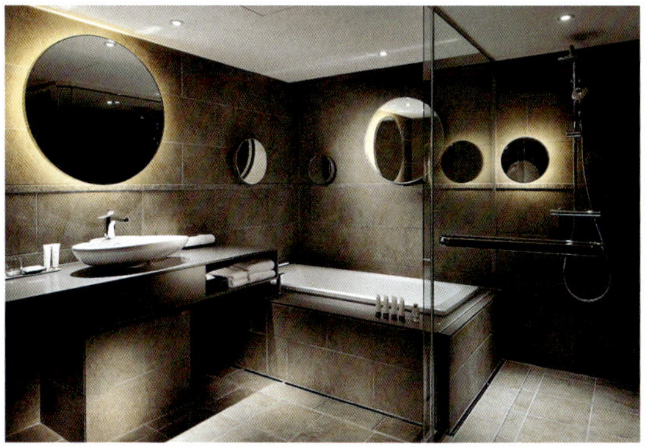
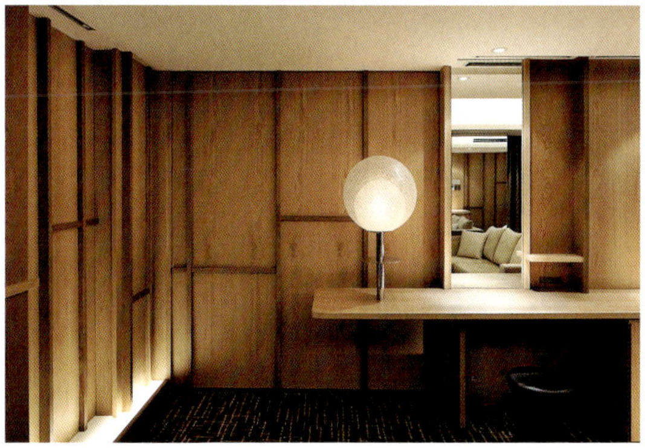

N° 014
Nagoya/Japan
Mar.2009
CHAPELLE DES ANGES

イタリアの丘陵地に立つ街並みをイメージして作られた結婚式場をいかにクラシカルに、かつモダンに見せるのかが、デザインのソースとなっている。花嫁のヴェールから着想した紋様が、大理石モザイクの通路や重厚な門構えに施され、礼拝堂へのアプローチから、その内部への動線に統一感を持たせている。さらに礼拝堂内へ踏み入れば、天高7mの贅沢な空間をより厳かに見せるカーテン状のパイプ。アーティスト・近藤髙弘氏による十字架が空間を引き締め、厳粛さと華やかさという、式場に求められるふたつの要素を成立させている。

The design source of this project lies in the challenge to create a classical yet modern venue out of a wedding hall, originally built in the style of the Italian countryside. The marble mosaic portrays a pattern inspired by a wedding veil, embellishing the aisles and the entrance gate to create a unified flow from the approach through to the chapel's interior. Inside the chapel, a curtain of pipes emphasizes the seven-meter ceiling with increased dignity. Artwork of a cross by Takahiro Kondo pulls the interior space together, unifying the seriousness and splendor of the wedding hall.

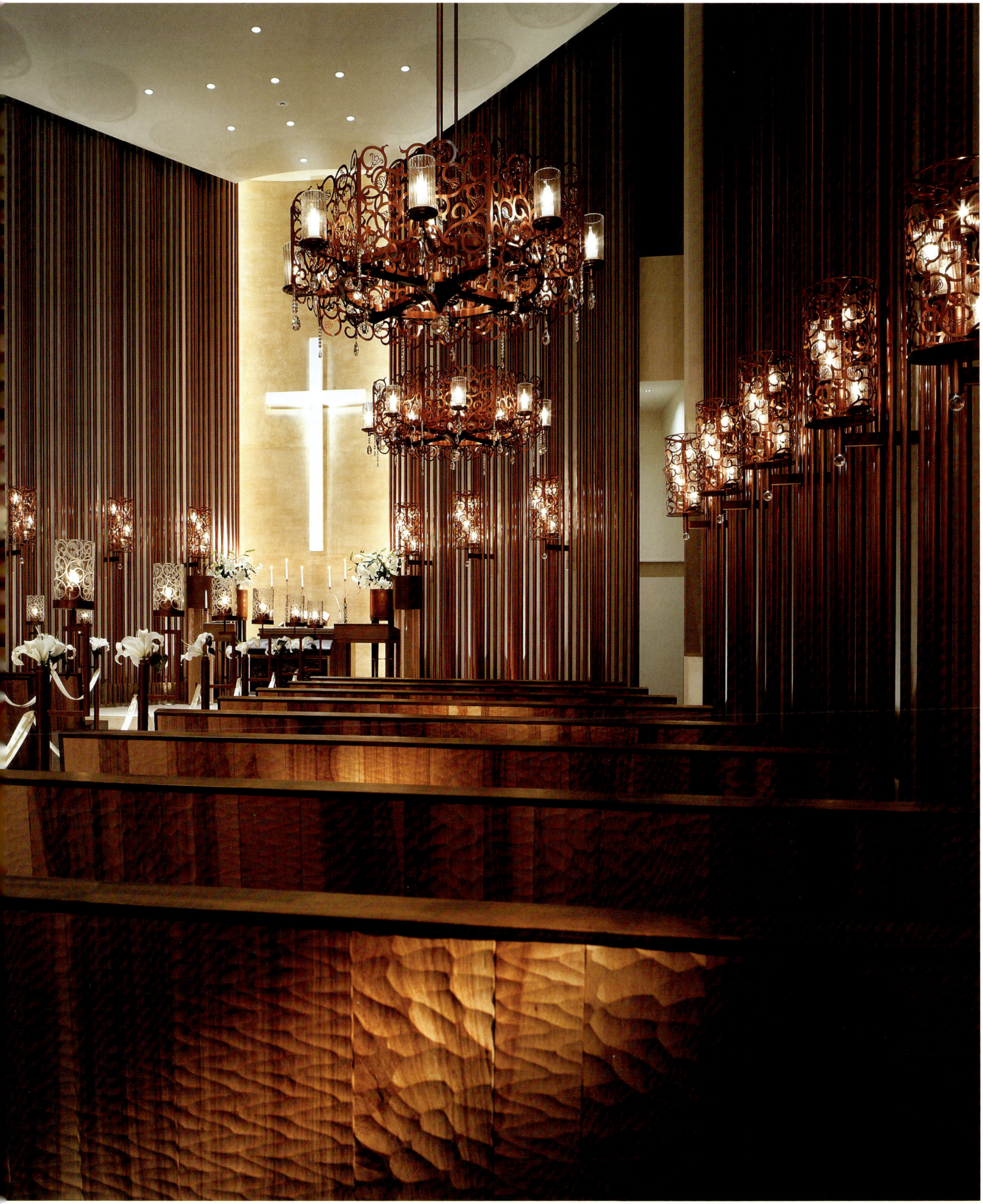

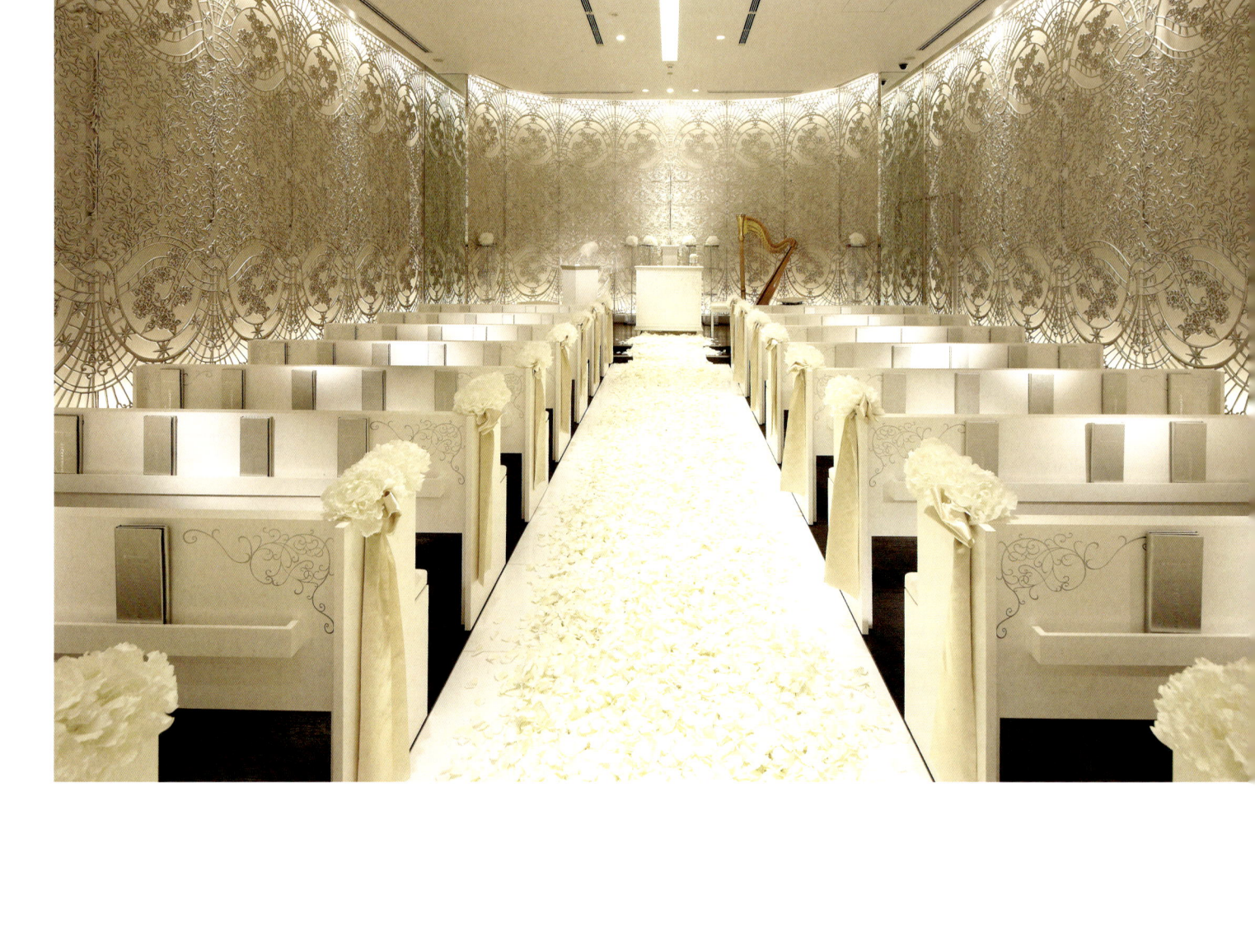

N°015
Tokyo/Japan
Jan.2011

ARFERIQUE SHIROGANE

森田のインテリアデザインには、キーとなるイメージが存在することが多々あるが、このクライアントの場合には、ベルとレースがそれだ。アプローチ、メインフロアにあしらわれたウェディング・ベルのモチーフ。チャペル内を飾るレースは、施設そのもののコンセプトを示しているよう。細やかで、上質で、可愛らしい空間のためにキーとなるエッセンスを抽出する。カットミラーで幾重にも反復し、特別な一日に期待する来場者を祝福する。グラマーではなく、ロマンティックで可愛らしいデザインにも、実は森田の思考がはっきりと表れている。

Morita's designs are often characterized by his use of iconic images. For this particular client, he used the image of a bell and lace. Motifs of a wedding bell appear in the approach and the main floor, while layers of lace frame the interior of the chapel as if to signify the very purpose of the facility. Essence is extracted to create a delicately fine, sweetly pleasant atmosphere. Through the use of cut mirrors, the imagery was infinitely replicated to celebrate those who arrive for the ceremonious occasion. Morita does not limit his philosophy to the glamorous, as revealed by this romantic and sweetly designed space.

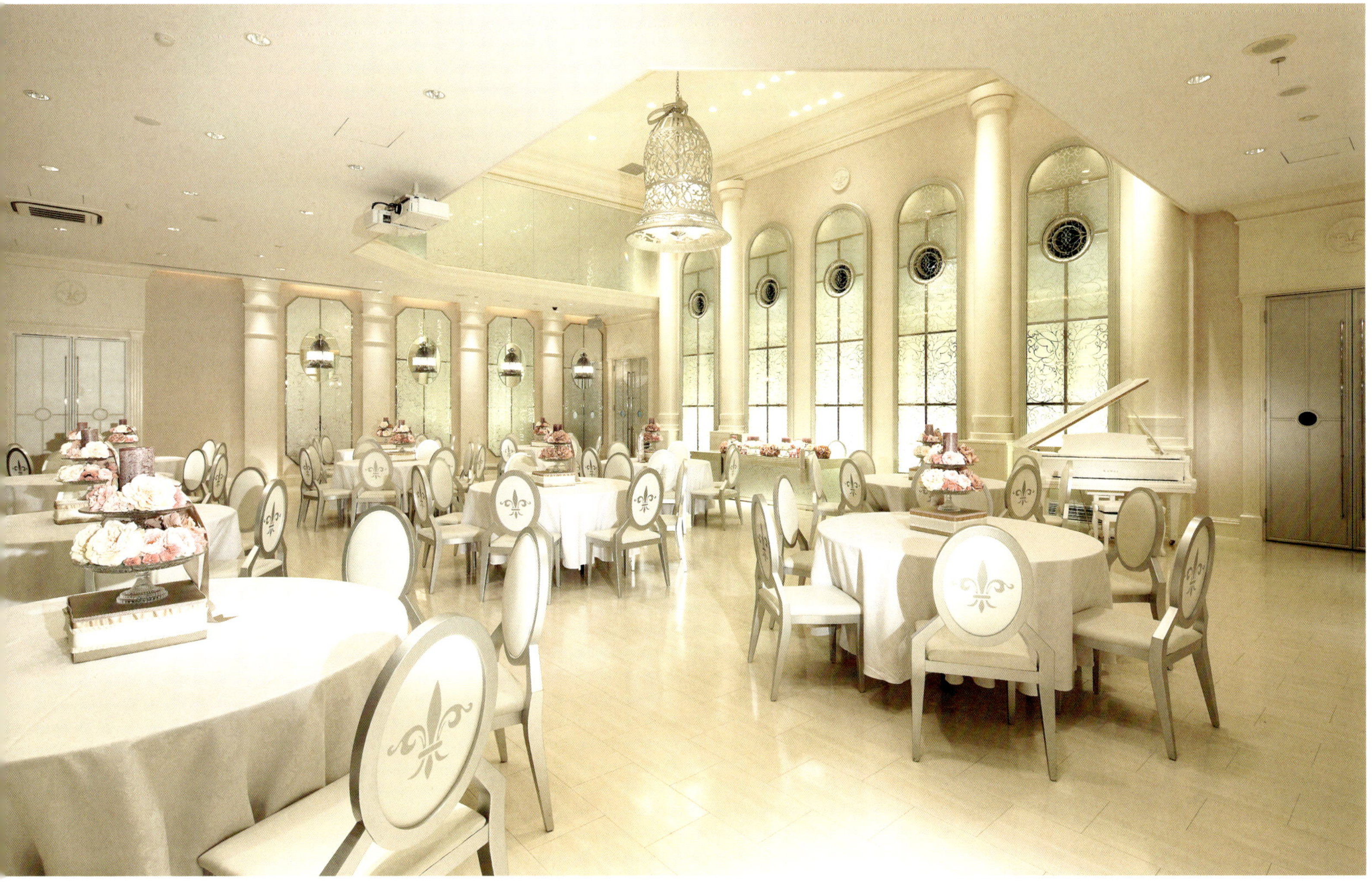

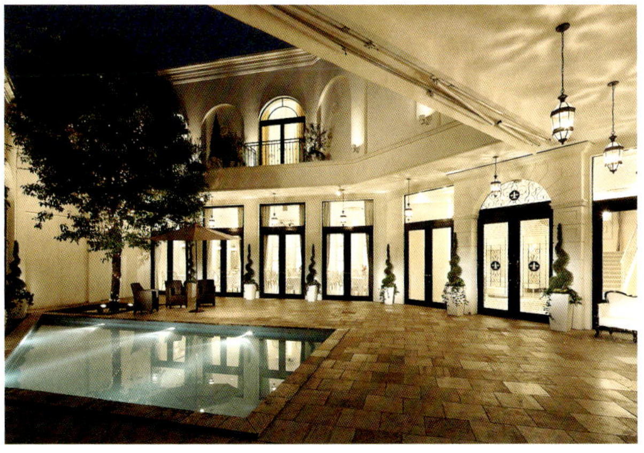

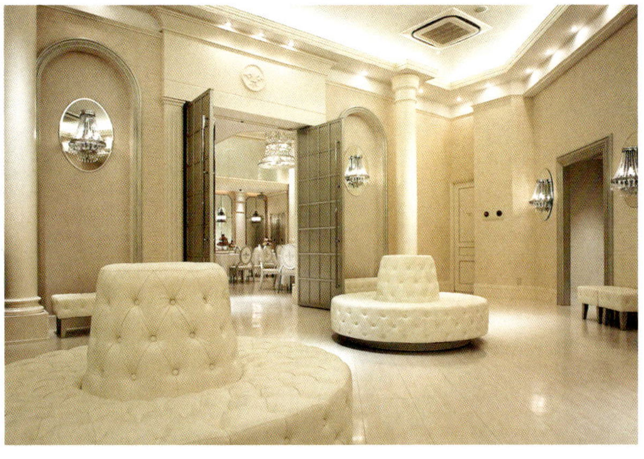

N°016
Osaka/Japan
Apr.2006

O.M. CORPORATION

「自然に囲まれた環境を」というオーナーからのリクエストに対して、木のビーズを多用したデザインで応えている。ファサードにはカーテンとして、エントランスではウッドシリンダーとして使用。「不動産会社という堅いイメージの職種をいかに温かく柔らかな印象へと変化させるのかに気を配った」と、森田は言う。連なった木のビーズは、日中には陽射しを浴びて緩衝材に、夜間には間接照明によって光がこぼれる設計に。ファサードから内部へと連続するマテリアル、様式を用いることで統一感を生み出している。ミーティングスペースでは、「緊張感を解放し寛ぎの空間を提供する」という目的を、テーブルの中にテーブルがあるかのような遊び心に落とし込んでいる。巨大な家具も、もはや森田のひとつのアイコン的存在となっている。

In response to the owner's request for an environment surrounded by nature, Morita created a design filled with wooden beads. These beads, used as curtains for the facade, are also echoed as wooden cylinders in the entrance. "I wanted to change the rigid and formal image of the real estate company into a warm and inviting one," explains Morita. Chains of wooden beads block sunlight during daytime and diffuse the indirect lighting to create an evening ambience. A continuation of material and style from the facade to the interior fuses the entire space into a unified whole. The meeting space was designed to provide a place for relaxation, with the playful illusion of a table inside a table. Enlarged furniture has now become one of Morita's design staples.

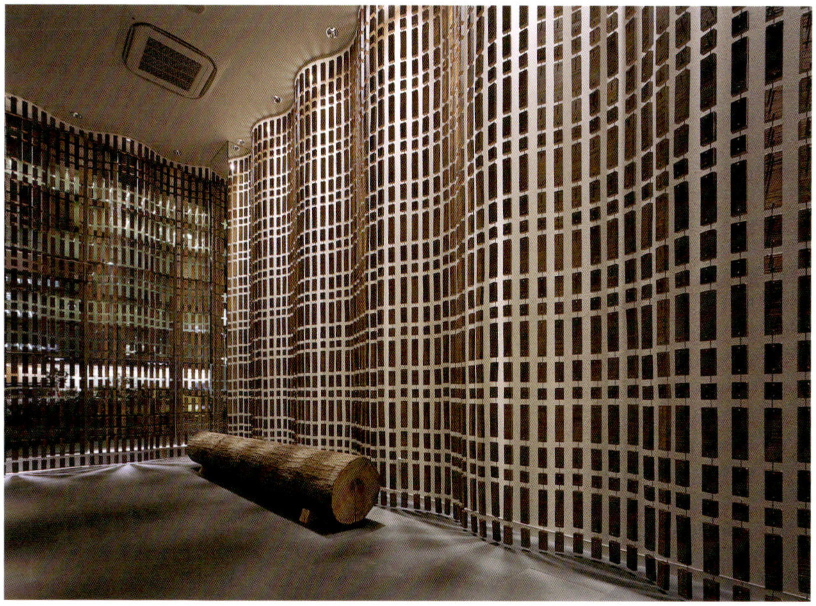

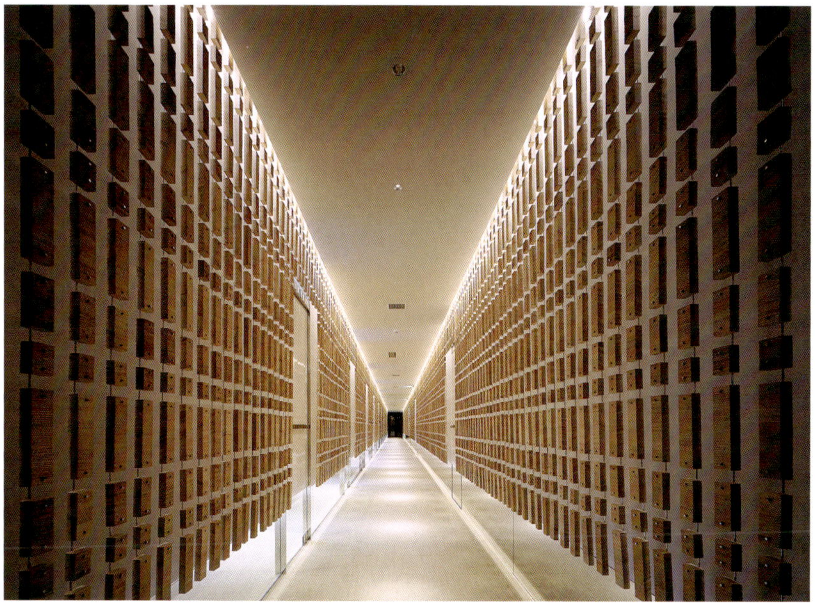

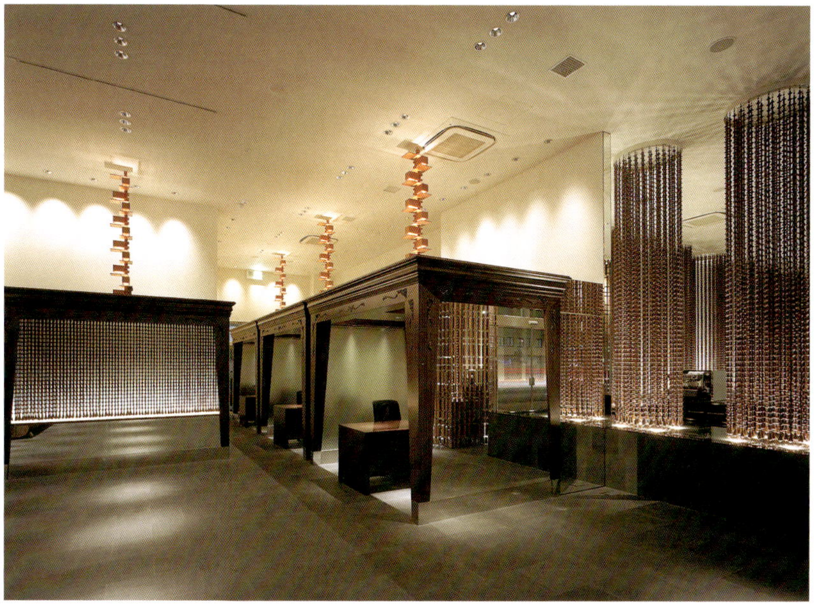

N°017
Chengdu/China
Oct.2012

Future Plaza of Fantasia

エントランスホールとリフトロビーの内装には、大地がうねるような造形を用いた。素材は、石。柔らかさと力強さという双方向のイメージを抱かせることを可能にしている。さらに石が途切れる"亀裂"部分であるリフトロビーはシャープなガラスに囲まれた場所。ガラスパターンはそのまま階上に引き継がれ、2階のモチーフのひとつになっている。試みたのは、「自然とハイテクの融合」だった。石とガラスという極端な素材のチョイスもさることながら、直線を多用したデザインを施すことで、逆に有機体として構造物を捉えることになっている。動きのある直線と反復するイメージ。パブリックスペースだからこその挑戦と言えるかもしれない。

Undulating shapes characterize the interiors of the entrance hall and the lift lobby. The material: stone. These waves portray a contrast between the curved softness and intensity of nature. The lift lobby, signifying a crack in the stone, is a space surrounded by sharp glass. The glass pattern continues above as part of the motifs that adorn the second floor. This is an experiment in fusing nature with advanced technology. Through the clashing of stone with glass and the heavy layering of straight lines, the design captures the structure as part of an organic body. Dynamic lines and looping imagery. This public space is indeed a perfect setting for such a challenge.

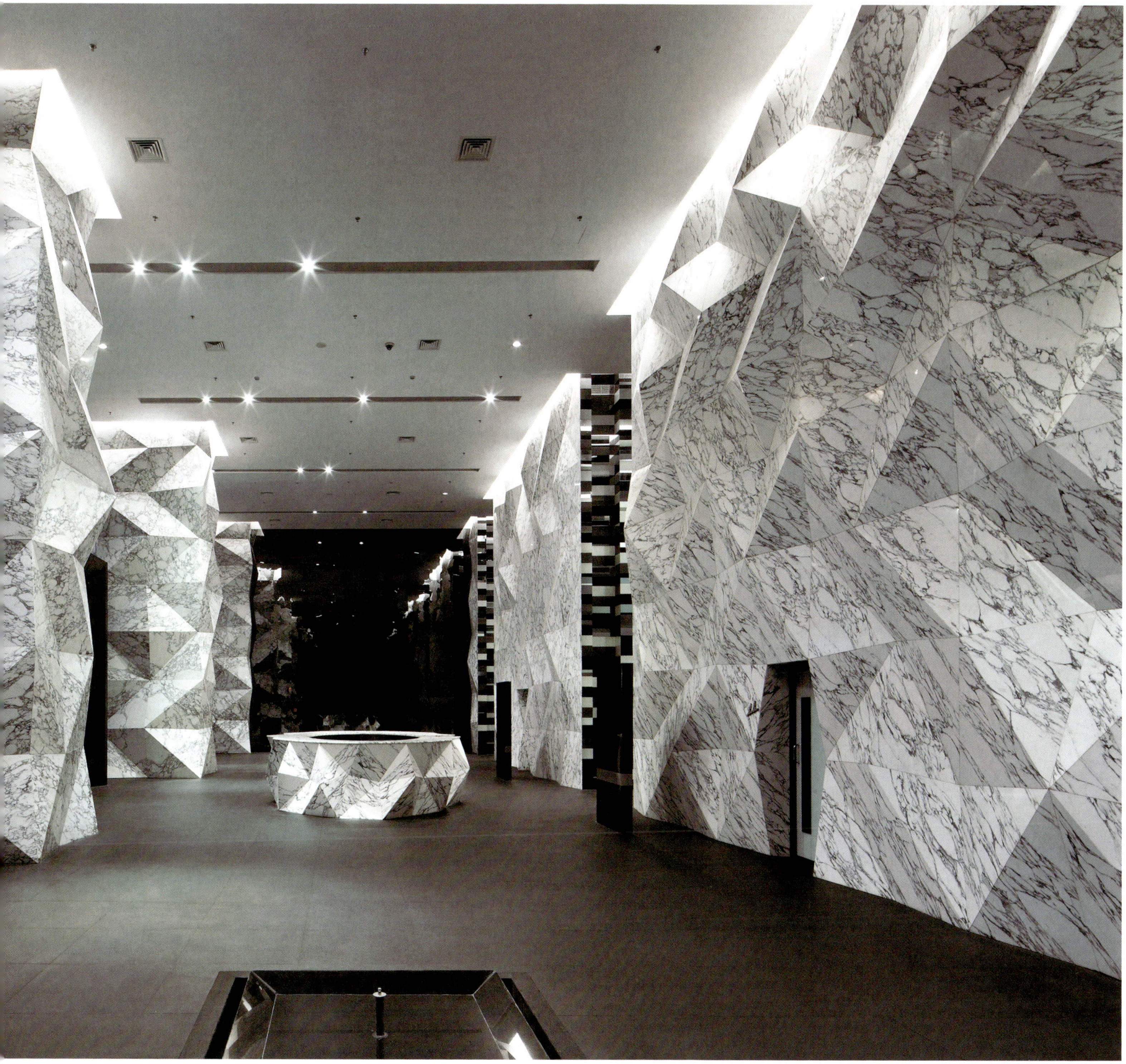

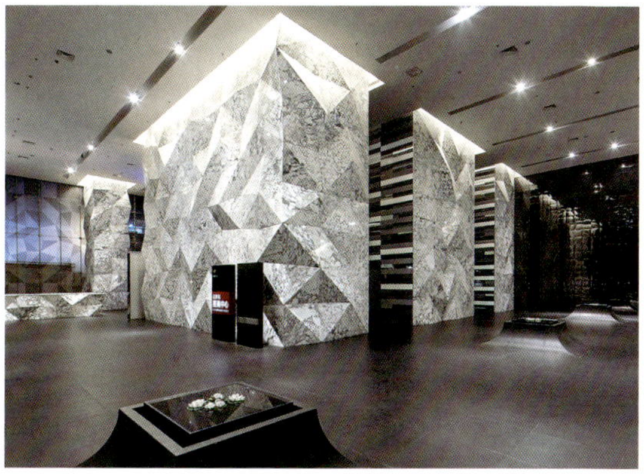

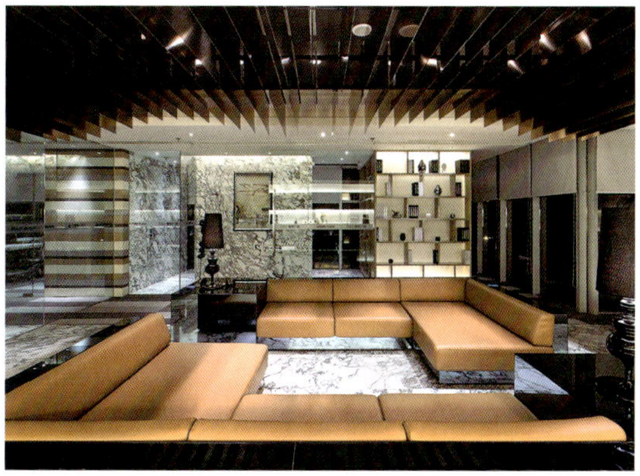

N°018
Hyogo/Japan
Aug.2011

Residence "S"

1000坪を超える広大なロケーションに建てられた全室南向きの明るい邸宅に似合う「シンプルなデザイン」が、クライアントからの依頼だった。エントランスからテラスまで抜けるよう扉を作らずに、森と海を眺める動線を確保すること。室内と屋外テラスの素材を合わせて内外の境界を取り払うこと。いくつかの要件を積み重ねて実現したのは、自然を感じることのできる家。まるで教会のようなウッドパネルの張り合わせと、そこに設置された下からの間接照明が、夜間も柔らかい空気を作り出す。自然光と照明が、いかに時間を受け渡していくのか。光と時間の移ろいを味わうことのできるデザインとなった。

For this bright house with southern exposure, standing on a spacious location of over 3,300 square meters, the client requested a simple design. The list of conditions included: to preserve the open feel of the entrance and the terrace; to maintain the flow of the forest and ocean views; and to combine materials to integrate the indoors with the outdoor terrace. The result is a house where one can feel close to nature. The church-like wood paneling, illuminated by indirect lighting, creates a comfortable ambience that continues through to the evening hours. The essence of the design lies in this smooth transition between natural and artificial lighting. The result is a design that allows one to appreciate the changing of both light and time.

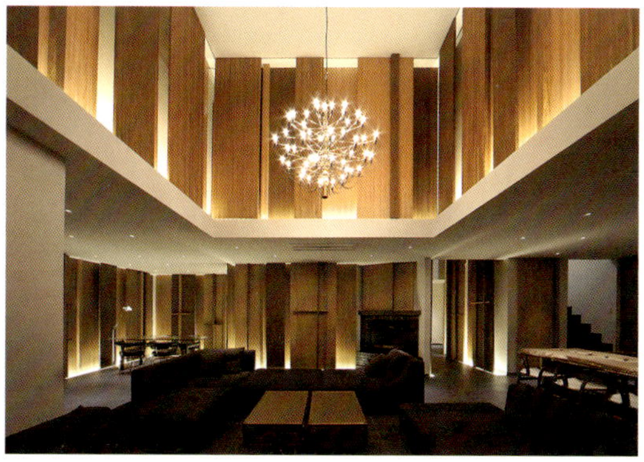
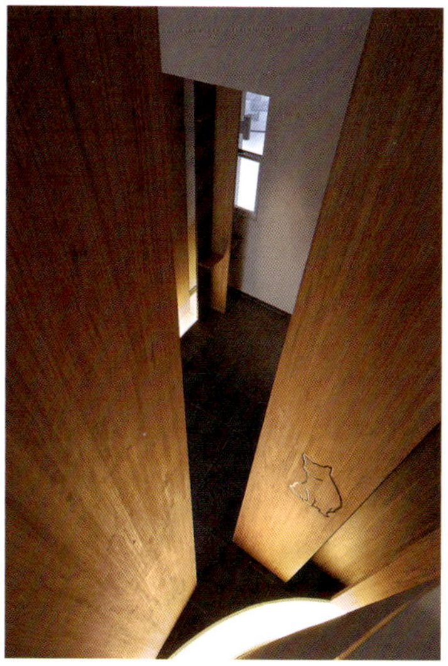
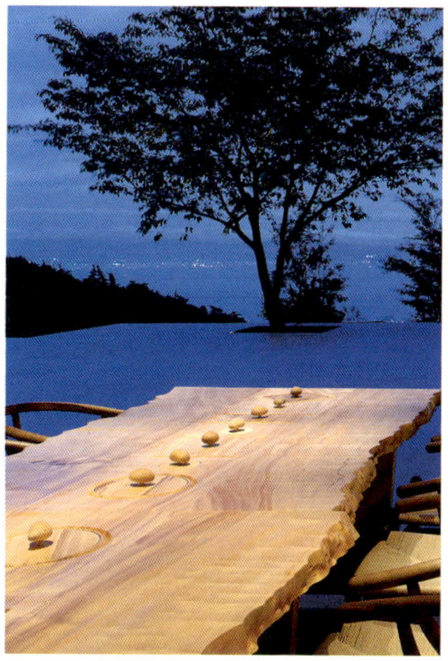
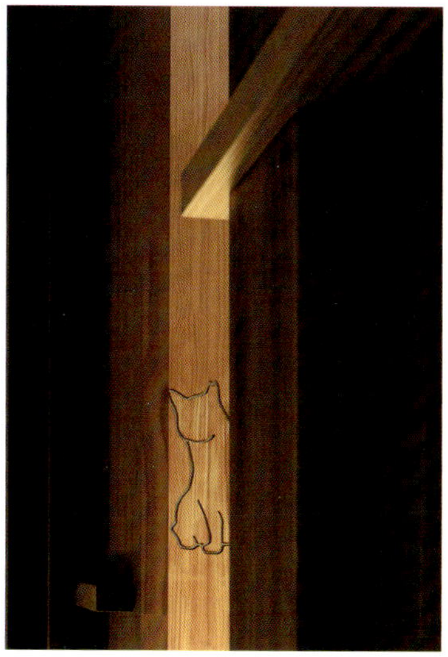
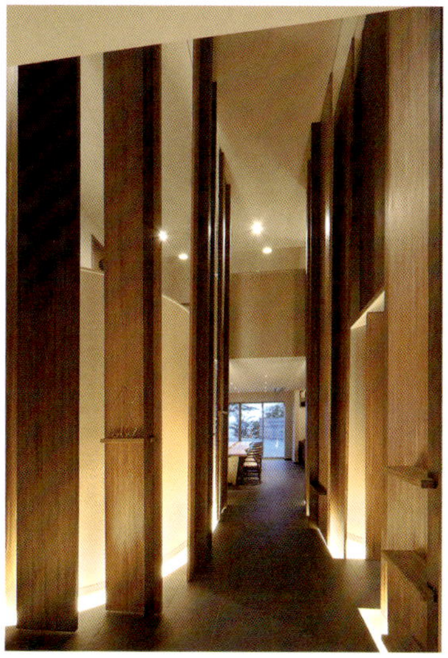
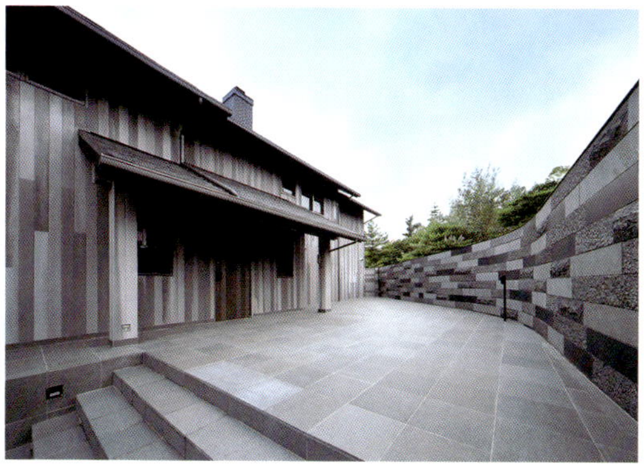
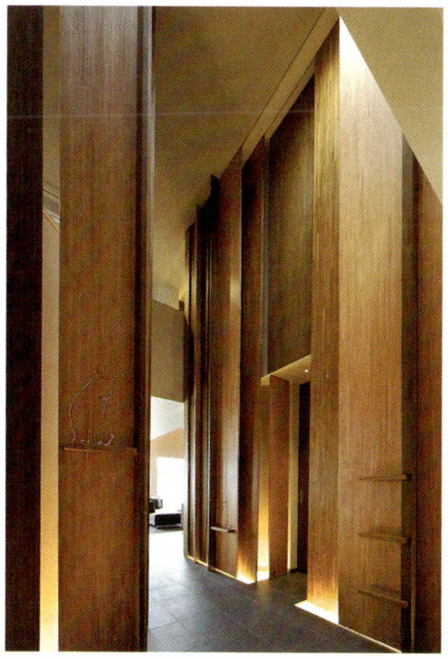
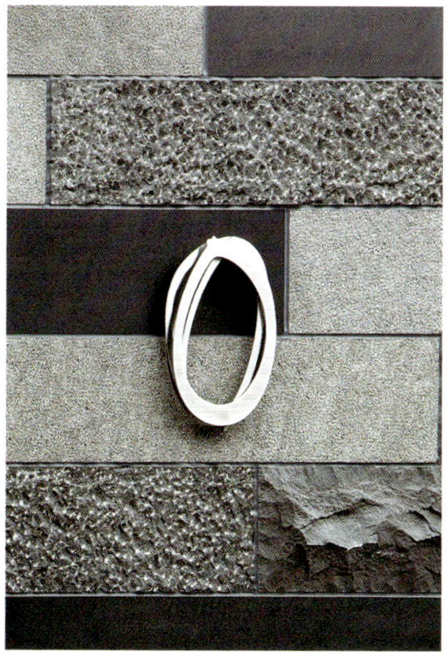
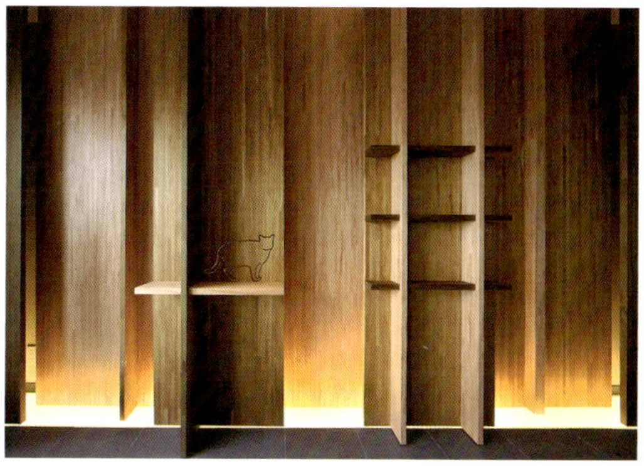

N°019
Tokyo/Japan
Jul.2007
Residence "M"

自分のための空間である森田の自邸は、「ウチのお姫様に似合うものを」というシンプルな動機から作られている。落ち着いている部屋は色数を減らし、客人をもてなす空間はエレガントに。コンセプトが明確にあるわけではなく、むしろ主役は自分たちが持っていたアート作品。例えばエルメスのスカーフを額装して壁に掲げている。古くから集めたもの、新しく手に入れたもの。いかにアートを飾るか、あるいは収納するかを考えて、部屋のデザインが決まっている。アートを愛でるためというよりも、アートと共に暮らすための家。ベッドルームには、やはり天蓋をイメージしたメタルのチェーンによって作られたシャンデリアが設えられている。

Morita's private house is a space entirely for his own. The project began from a simple idea: "a place that suits my princess." Colors are limited in the private rooms, whereas entertaining areas are tailored with elegance. There was no specific concept or theme. In fact, an archive of collected artwork takes center stage. A series of Hermès scarves have been framed on a wall, and the space comprises myriad collected treasures, old and new. The rooms are designed with the specific purpose of properly displaying and storing art. It is a house not for admiring art but for living among it. In the bedroom, a metallic chain chandelier hangs like a canopy from the ceiling.

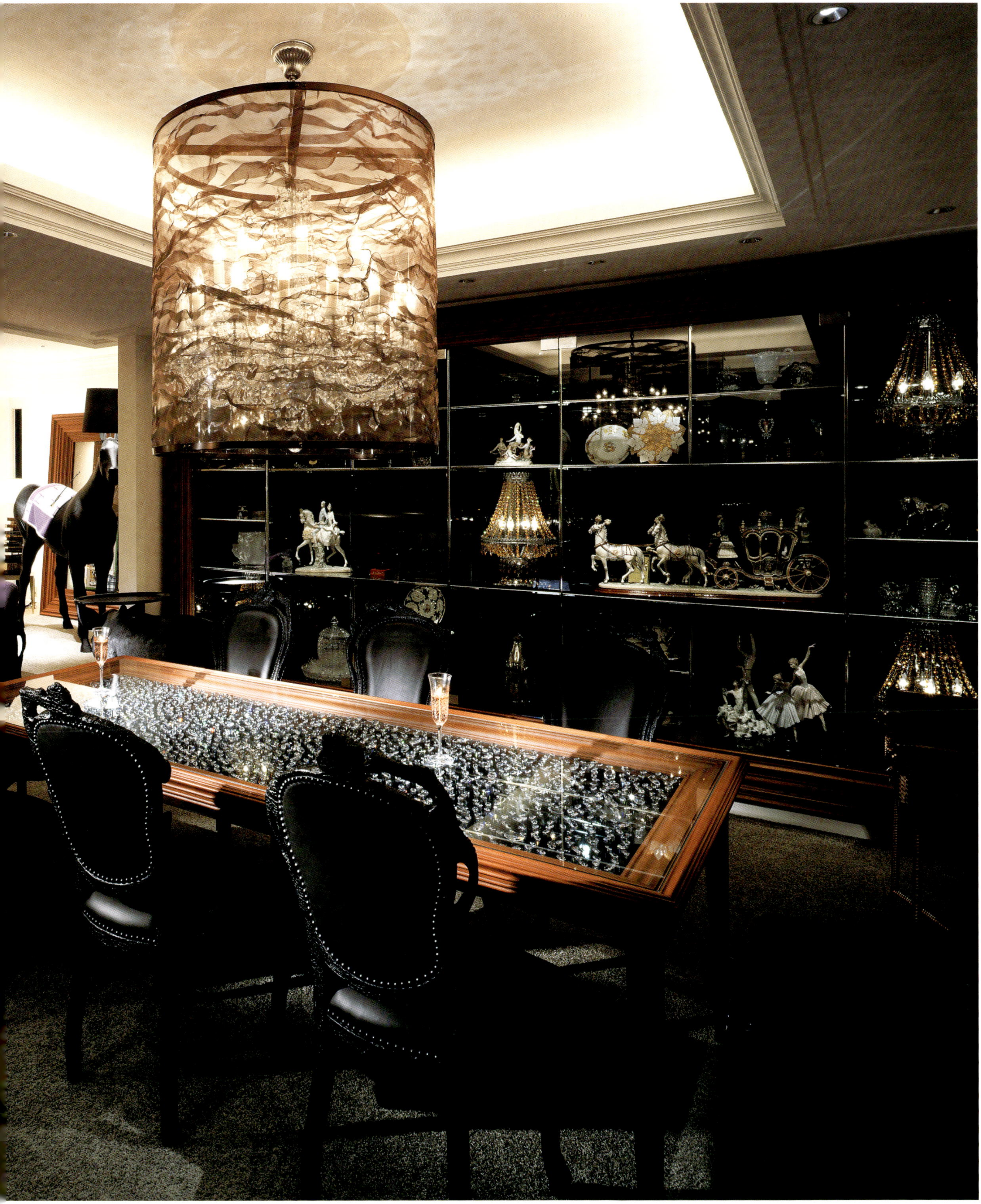

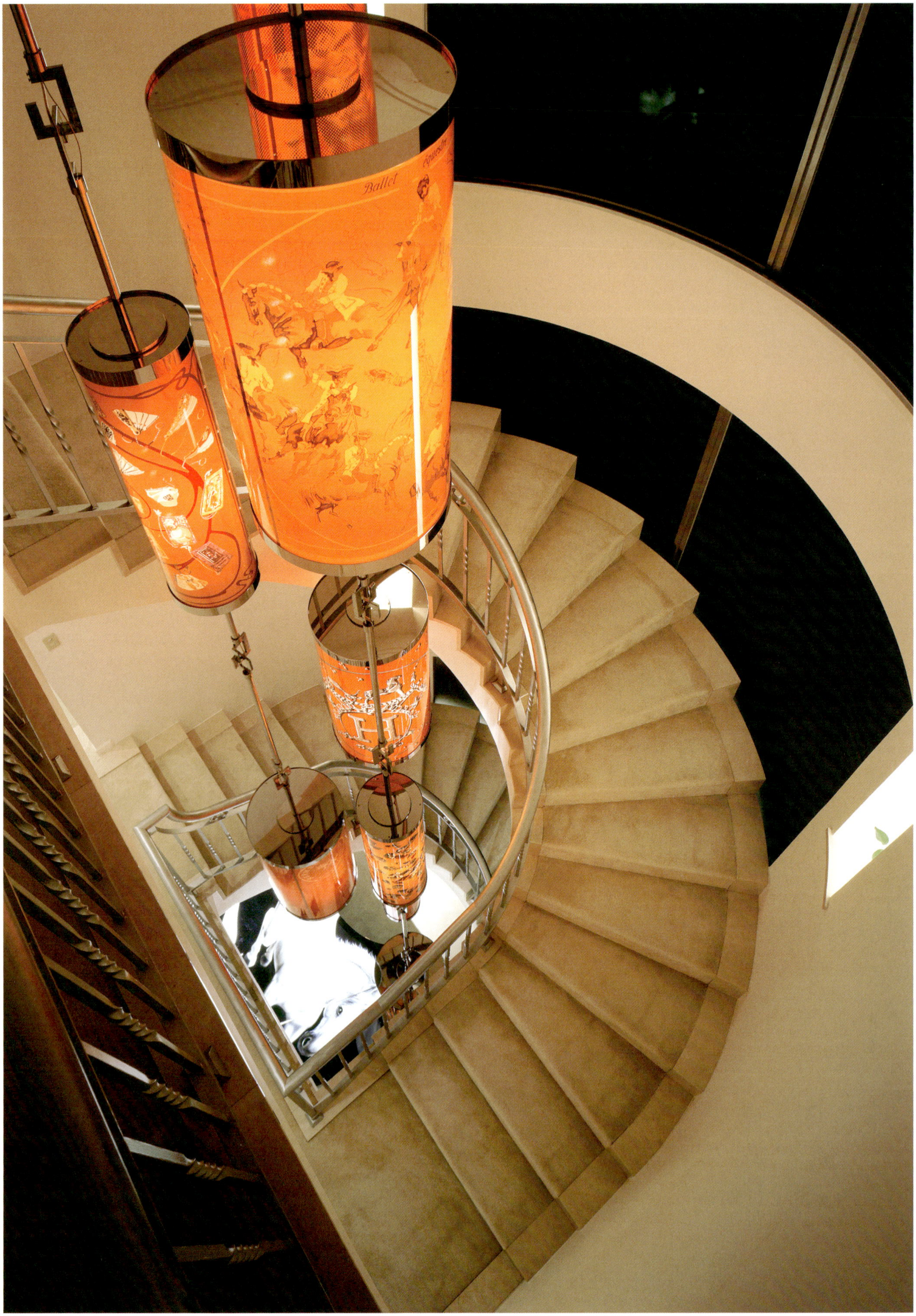
Ballet

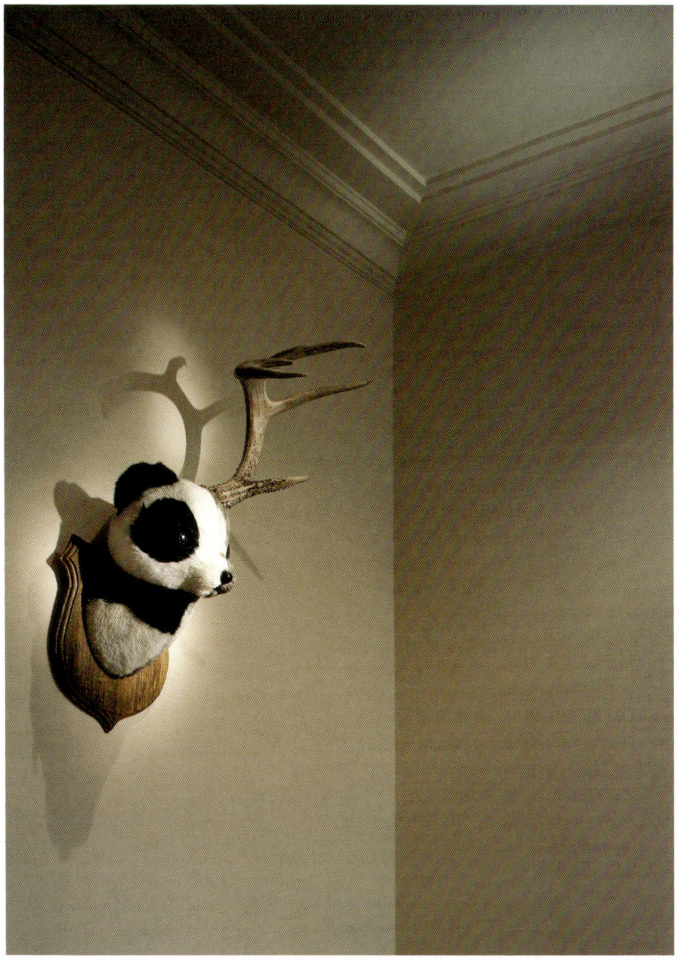

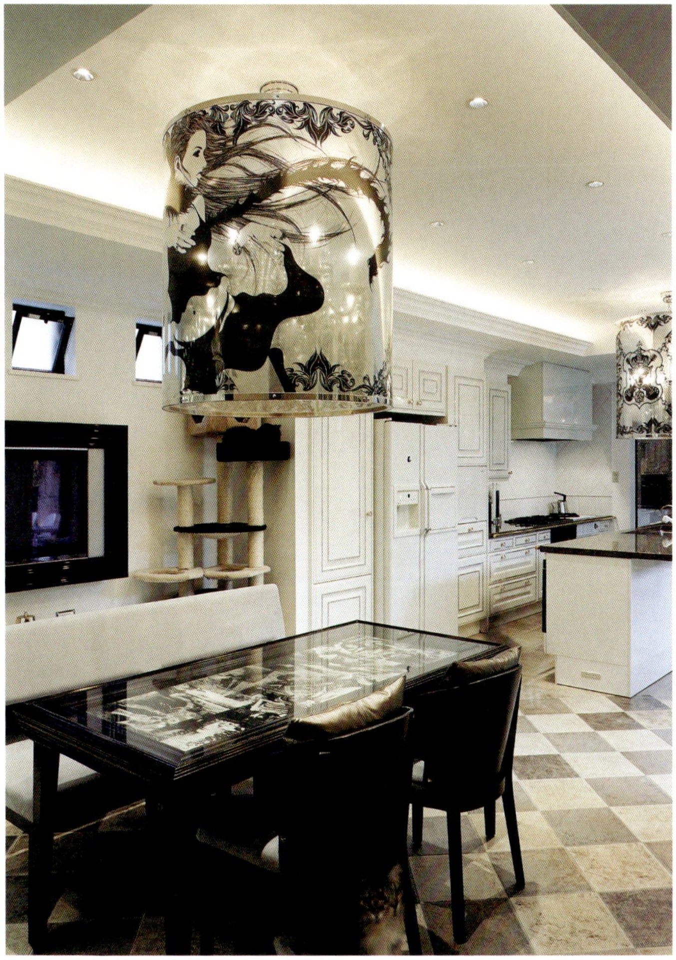

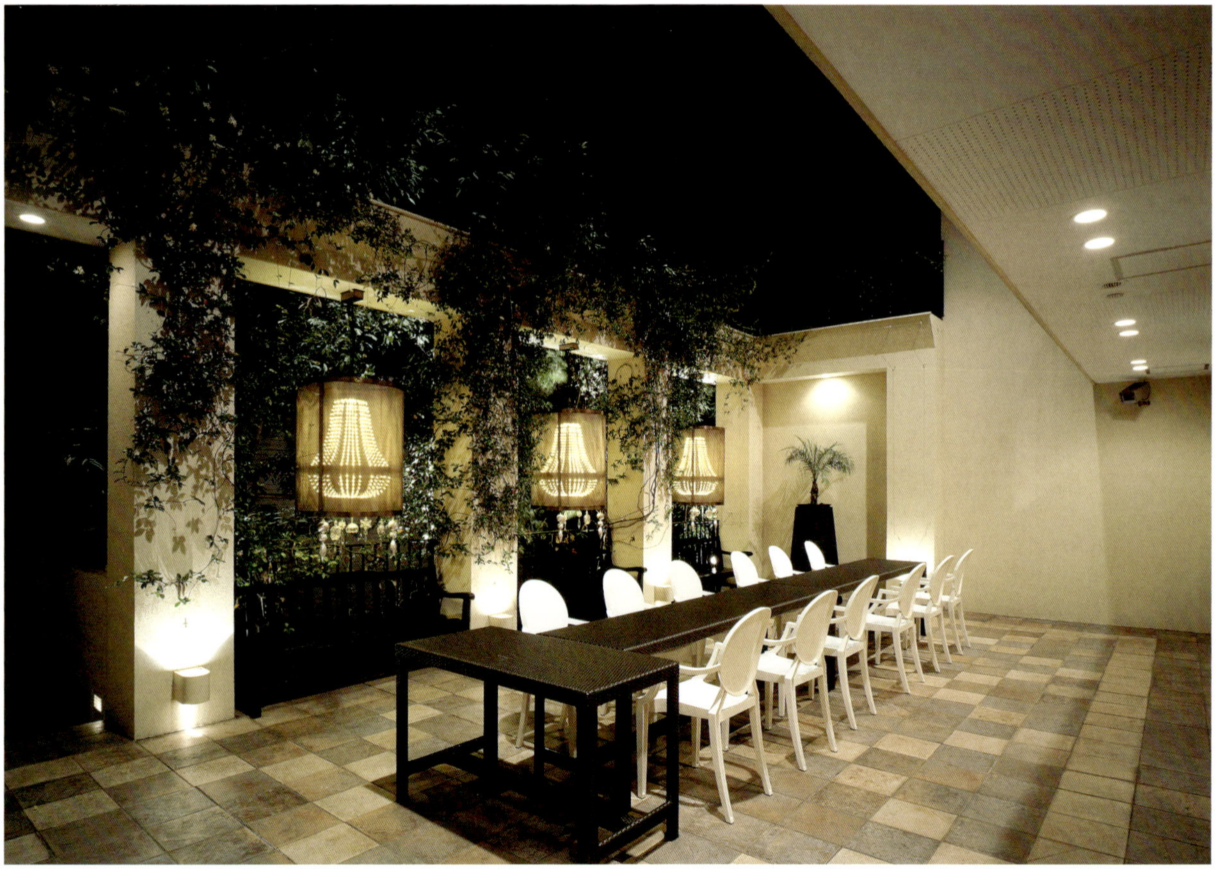

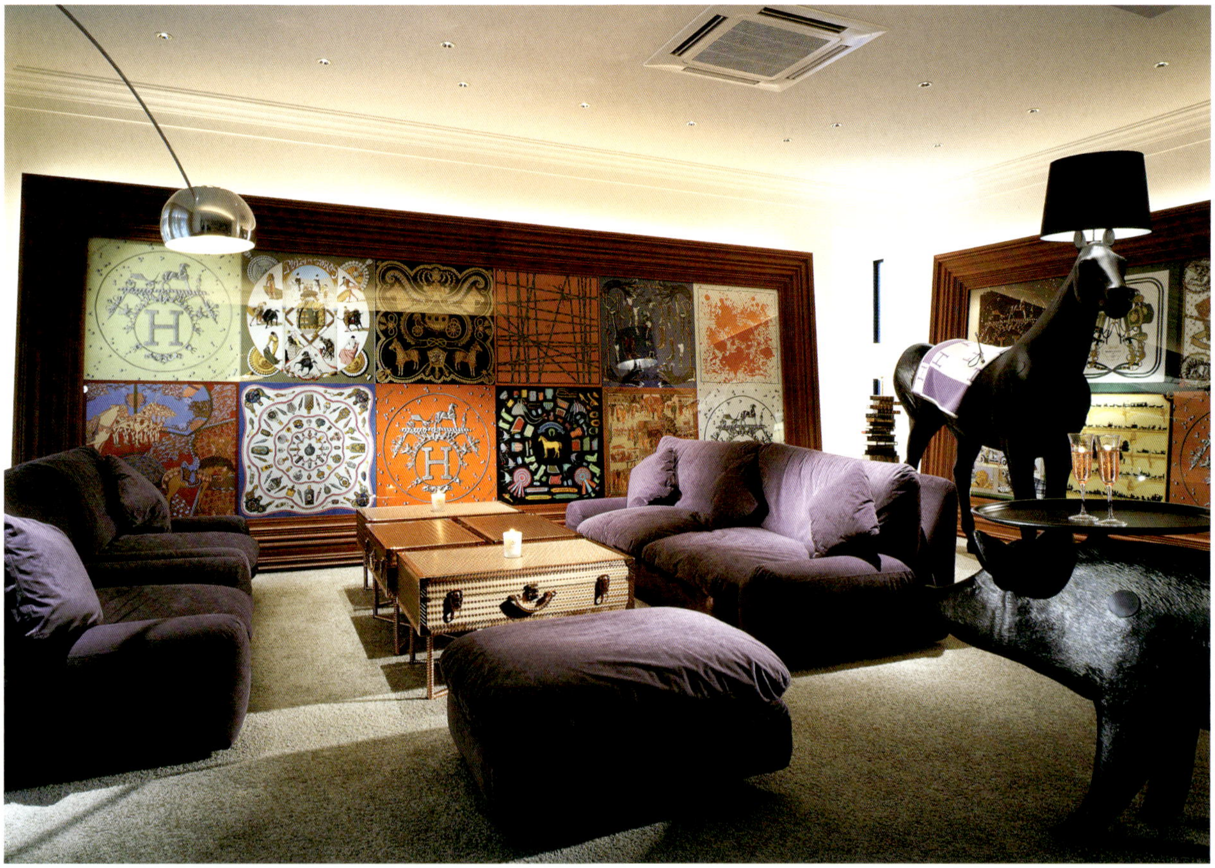

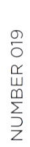

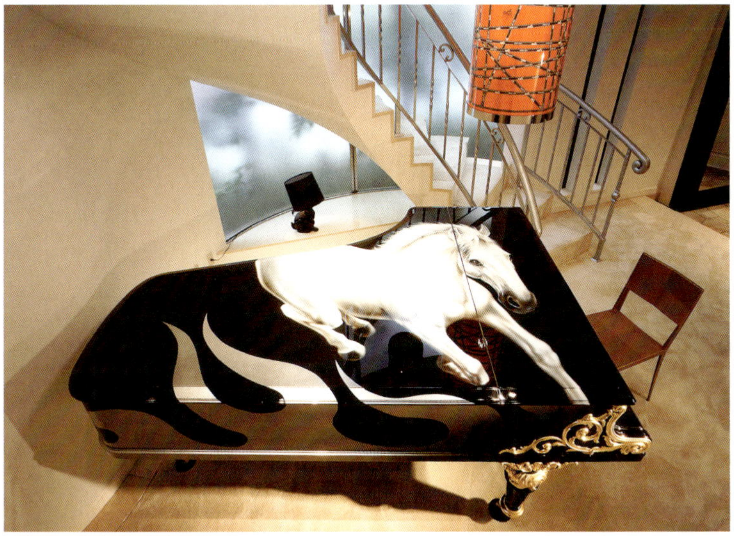
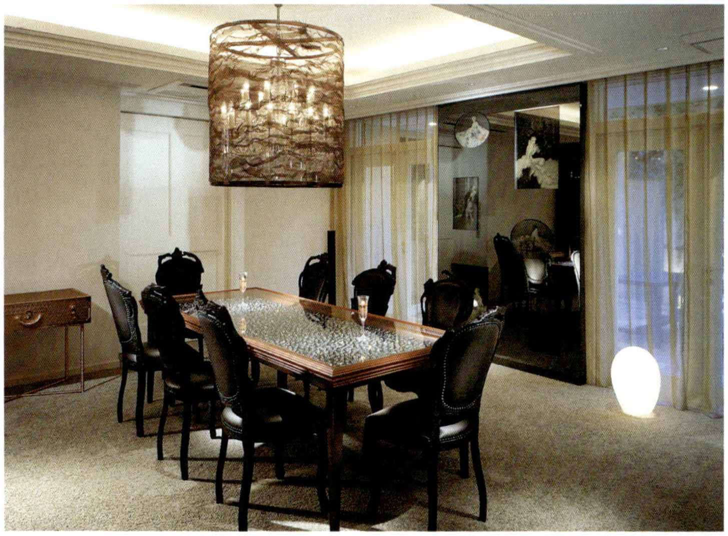
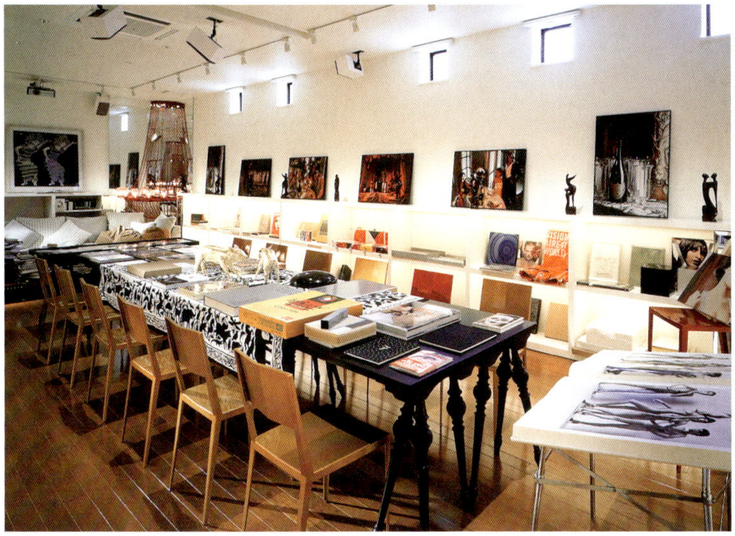
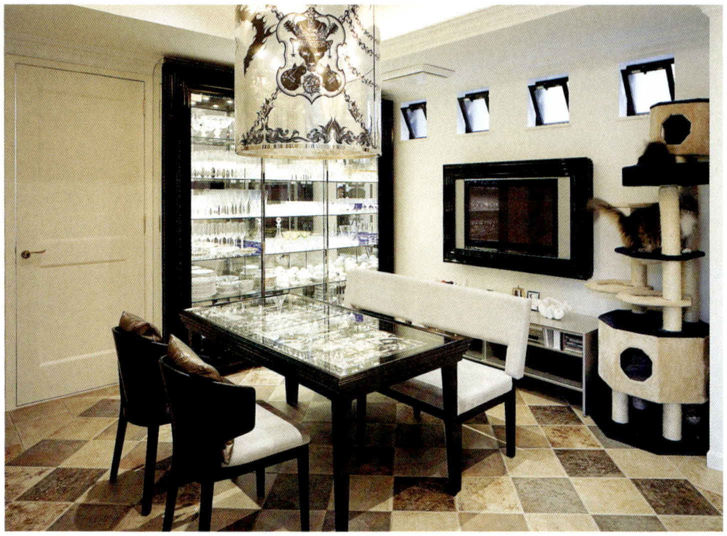

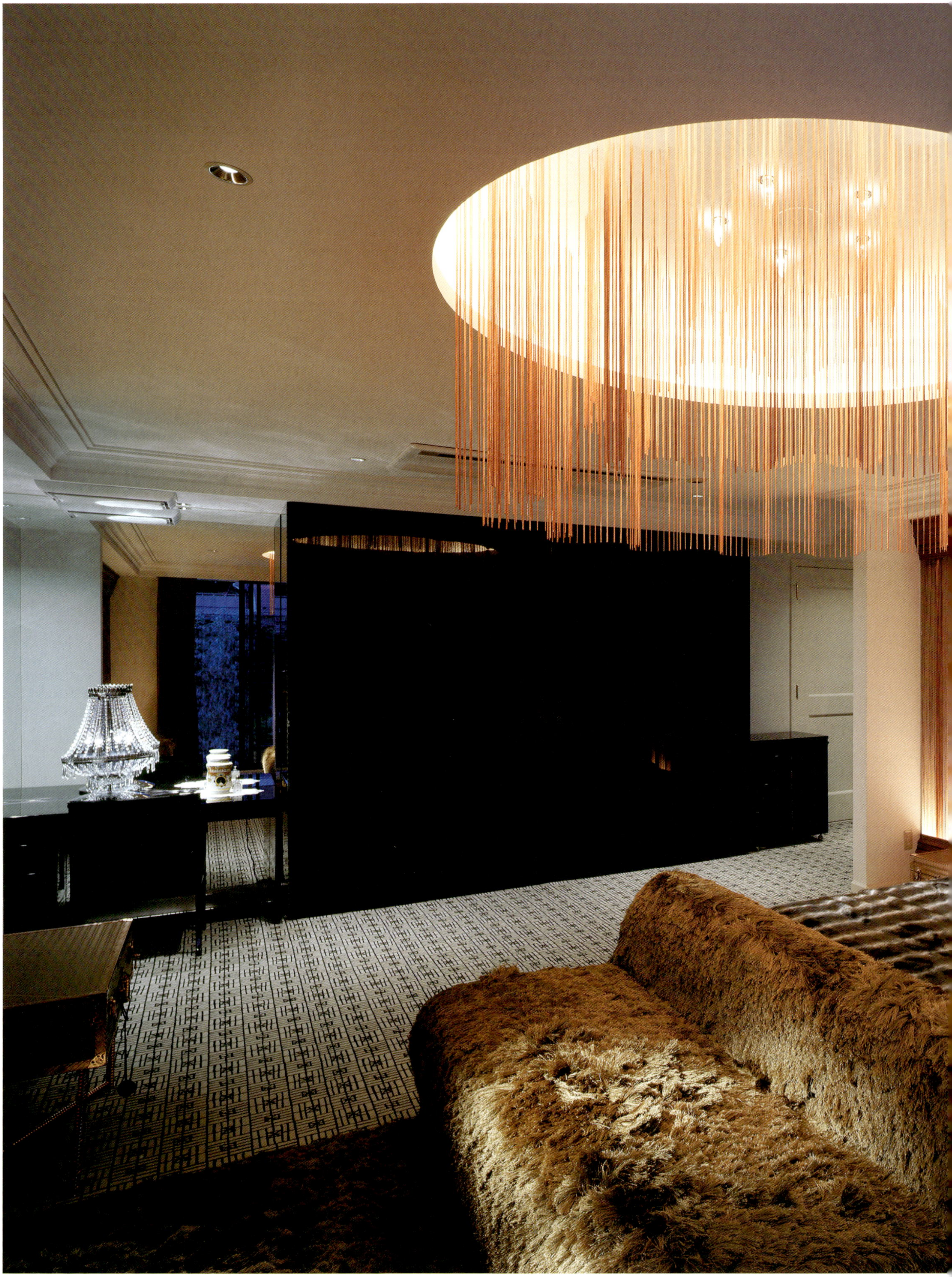

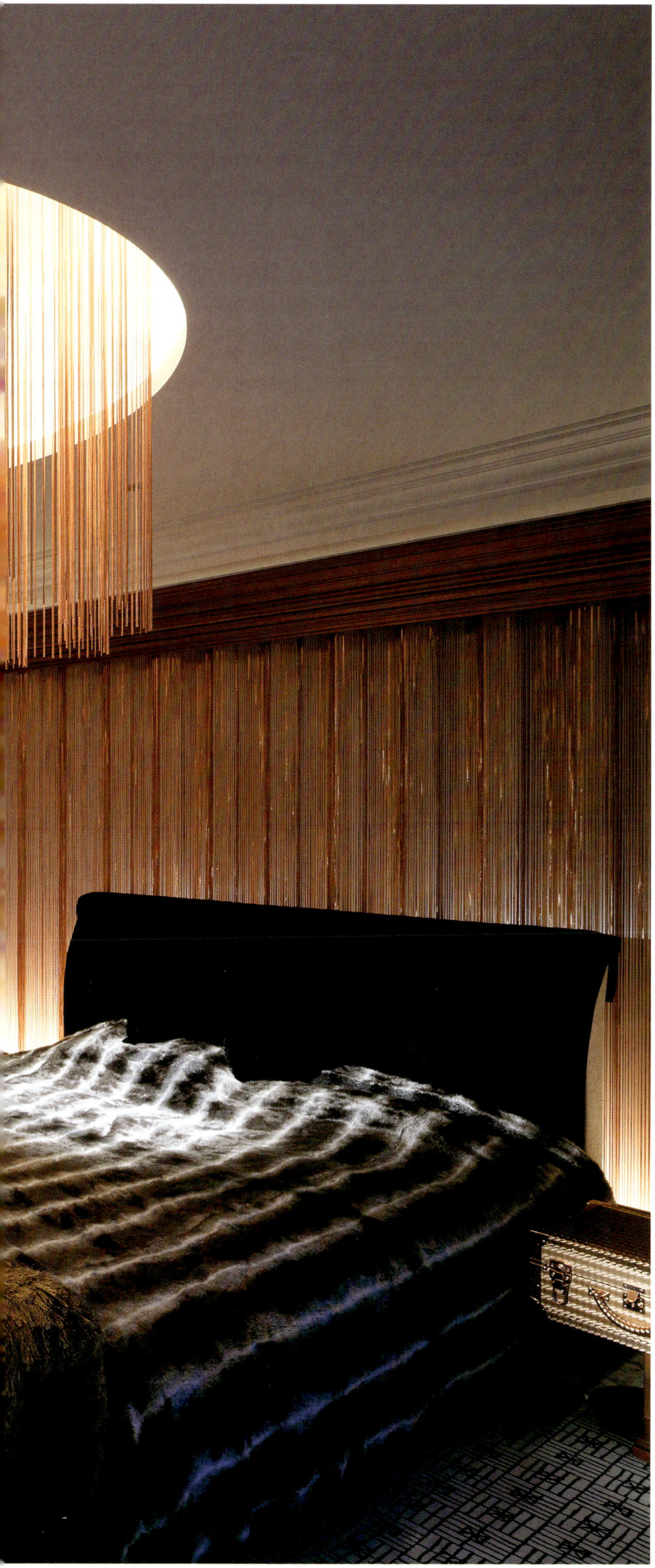

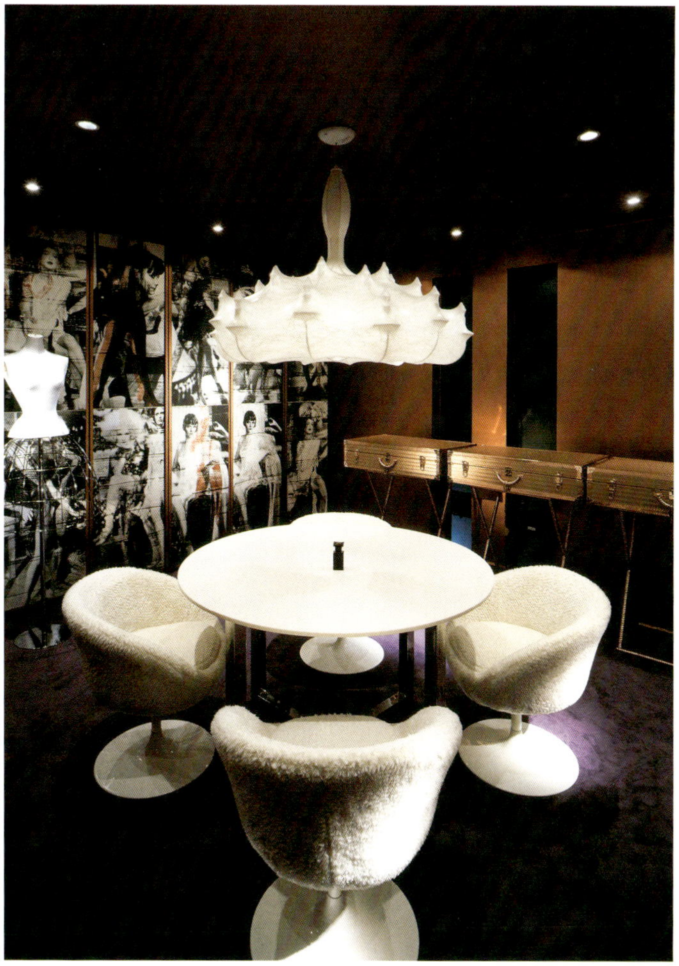

N°020
Hong Kong/China
Jan.2012

Residence "CT"

ジェットセッターである若いクライアントの要望は、「木材を最小限に、現代的な素材を用いること」。森田は、メタルパネルを効果的に使うことを選択する。映り込みによる空間的な広がりを意図すると共に、緻密な凹凸感や色味、テクスチャーの異なるメタルパネルを用いて表情に変化を生み出している。さらに縦のラインを意識させることで、空間にリズムを付けることに成功している。ダイニングテーブルから見える景色は、オリジナルのペイントがメタルパネルの規則性を裏切ることで、さらに変化を生んでいる。超高層ビルという近代的なシチュエーションをより引き立たせる無機質な空間。だが住居であるために、メタルの冷たい印象を払拭する仕掛けを、随所に発見することができる。

The client was a young jetsetter who requested Morita to limit the use of wood in exchange for a more modern choice of materials. Morita chose metallic paneling as his main design element, intending to expand the space with reflections, as well as to create a dynamic range of different textures and shades. Through an emphasis on vertical lines, the space is further styled with a flowing rhythm. The view from the dining table is a striking scene, punctuated by a custom painting that breaks the rule set forth by the metallic paneling. The austere, inorganic space also accentuates the modern location inside a skyscraper. Because the project is a residence, however, it is also sprinkled with techniques to alleviate the cold ambience with hints of warmth.

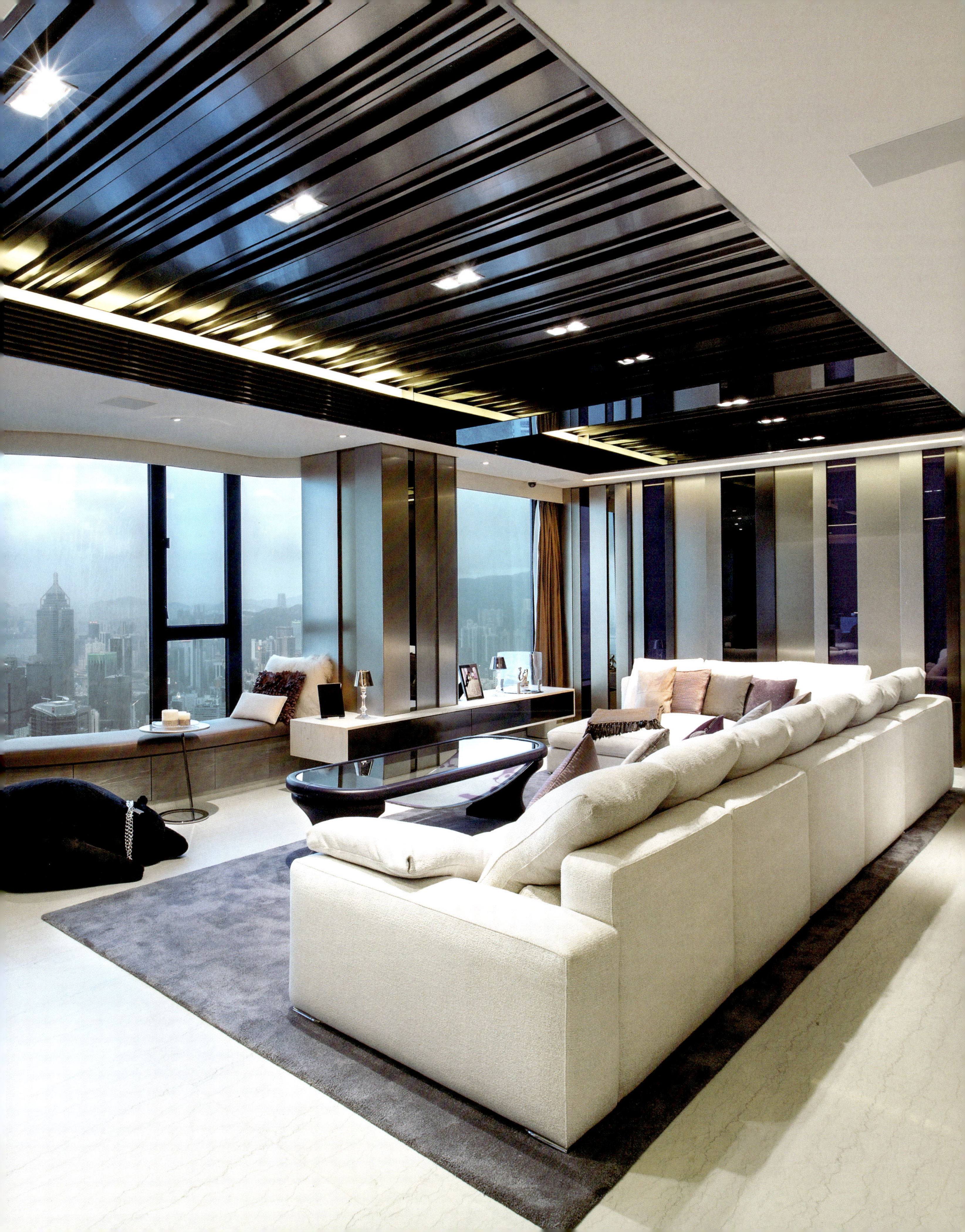

N°021
Tokyo/Japan
Mar.2011

Brillia ARIAKE Sky Tower

役割の異なる各スペースには、それぞれ異なるデザインを施しつつ、共通項としてマンション全体を貫く「モダンミュージアム」というコンセプト。ゆとりと同時に刺激を感じることのできるデザインが、森田に求められた。グランドエントランスから2階へと続く階段は、まるで舞台美術のセットのようにさえ見える。中山ダイスケ氏の作品を収めた額縁、オリジナルの大型シャンデリア。あるいは、レセプションホールに設置された「Book of Look」と名付けられたライトスタンドなど、森田オリジナルのインテリアも多く配置されている。最上階33階では、屏風のような設えのフォトアートがエレベーターホールに、さらに黒御影石を書棚のように仕上げた壁面アートが迎えてくれる。パブリックは豪奢に、プライベートルームはシックに。その対比が、豊かな居住空間を作り出している。

While each space is designed differently according to its unique function, the entire apartment complex is unified through the underlying concept of a modern museum. Morita was asked to combine both relaxation and excitement in his design. The fight of stairs connecting the grand entrance to the second floor exudes a theatrical presence. The space features a framed artwork by Daisuke Nakayama and a large custom-made chandelier. Morita's design also includes his custom furnishings, such as the light stand entitled "Book of Look" inside the reception hall. On the thirty-third floor, screen- like photo art greets the guests in the elevator hall, with surfaces featuring black granite wall art finished in a bookshelf-like style. The design keeps the public space luxurious and the private spaces chic. The contrast between these two characteristics helps achieve a rich and abundant residential space.

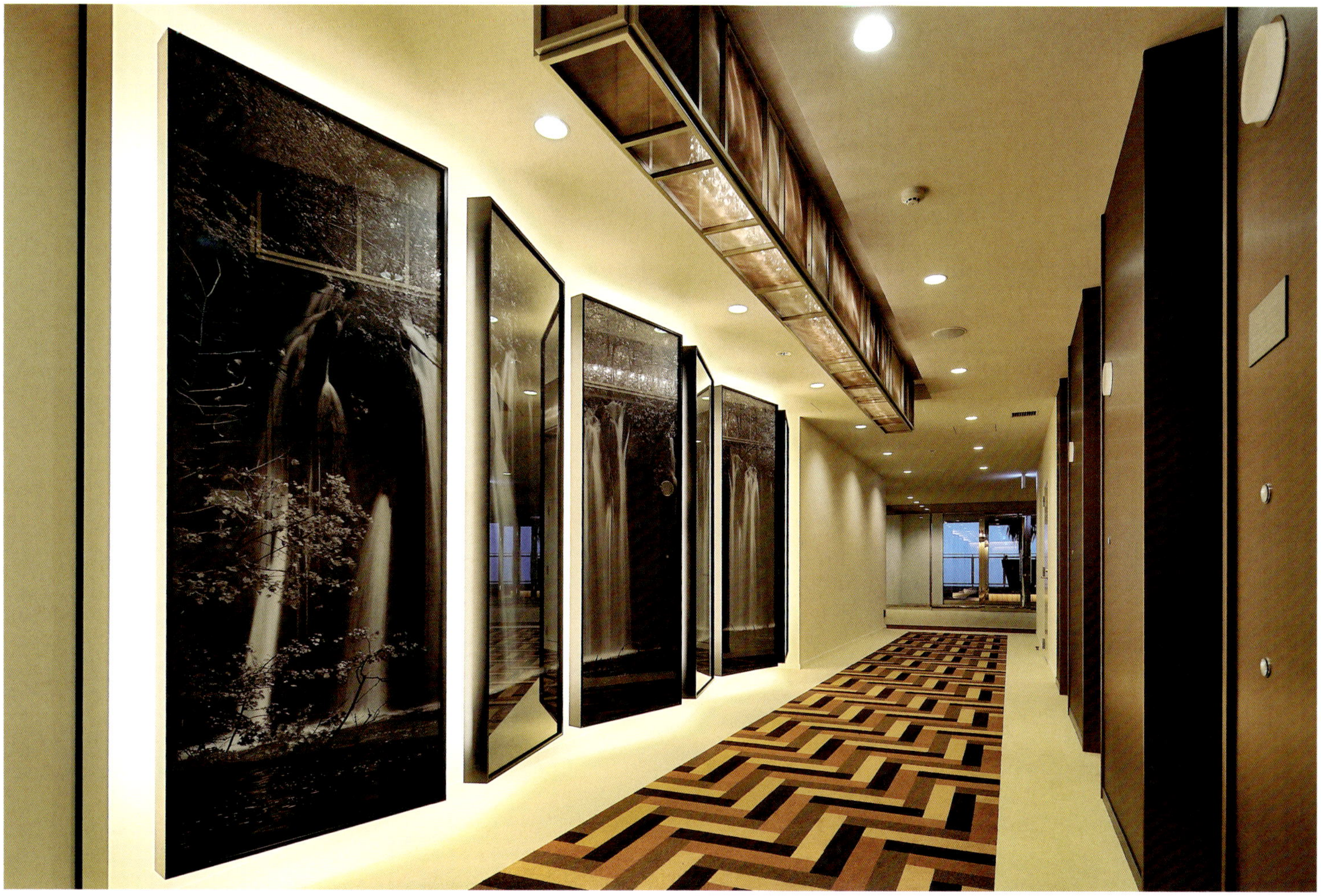

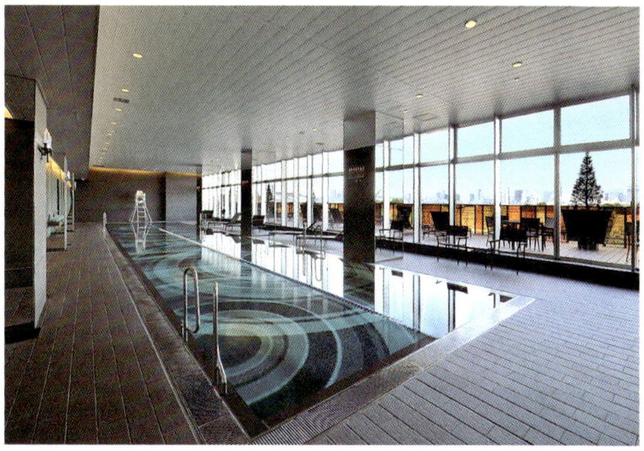

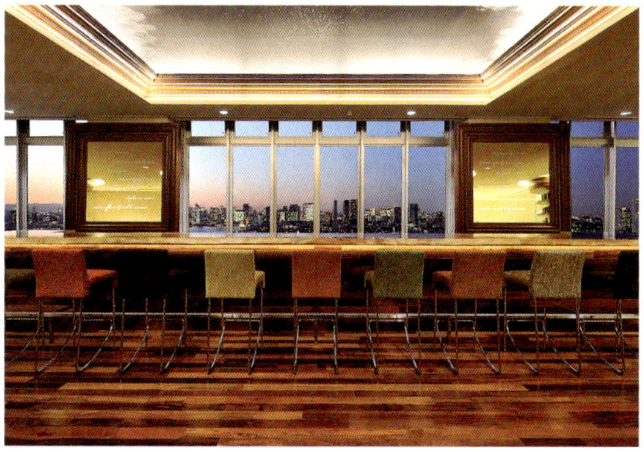

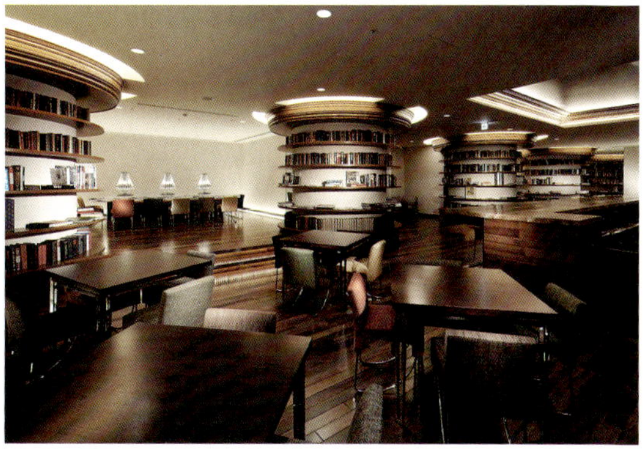

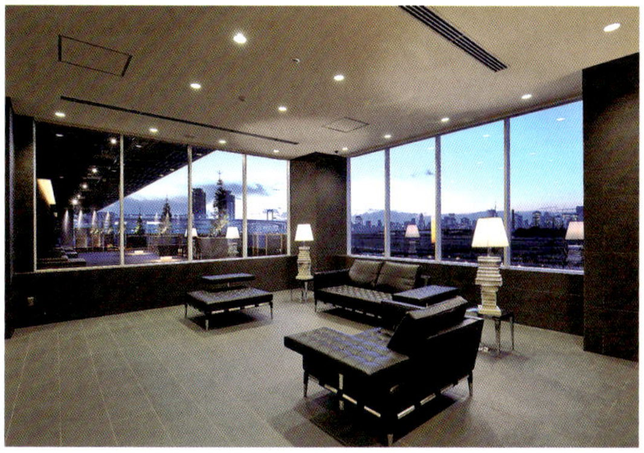

N°022
Tokyo/Japan
May 2012

FIELDS Office Lobby

「創造の場」として、クリエイティビティを刺激するデザインが求められたオフィスのロビーでは、「不思議の国に迷い込んだかのような」と森田が表現するスケールアウトの手法が取られている。オリジナルデザインによる極端に大きなチェアにランプ。人間がそこに立ったときに覚える違和感は、既成概念から外れる面白さへと繋がっていくのかもしれない。軸となっているライブラリーとのサイズ感の妙。オフィスロビーは会社の顔であるという面から考えれば、この大胆とも言える提案も、ある種、企業にとっての意思表明のようにさえ受け取れる。

As a place of creativity, this office lobby was to be designed as a source of inspiration. Here, Morita employed a scaled-out technique, a concept which, he explains, is "like wandering through Wonderland." Chairs and lamps were exaggerated into extreme scales. This sense of incongruity is perhaps what elevates the concept beyond the stereotypical. The contrast against the library creates an interesting sense of proportion. In the sense that the office lobby is the "face" of a company, this daring proposal can even be interpreted as the company's declaration of intent.

MOVIE AND MUSIC
EAT

SPORTS

STORY TELLER

JAPANESE PERSPECTIVE
NATURAL WORLD
SPORTS

EAT

N° 023
Osaka/Japan
Mar.2004

SAN-EI Faucet Osaka Showroom

水回りの商品を中心に提供する企業のショールームの主役は、当然、商品になる。その無機質な主役たちの置かれた場所へ、いかに足を向け、止めさせるかが手腕の見せ所だった。真っ白な中に、黒い箱を作り誘導するかのような空間設計。背面のブラックミラーに商品のみが映り込むことによって、浮かび上がっているかのような錯覚を抱かせる。あるいは、光の道で誘導し、光を遮ることでそれぞれのブースを作るという方法論。「心理的な働きかけ」こそが、森田がデザイナーとしてもっとも重要視している部分だが、この小さな箱の中には、あらゆる「心理的な働きかけ」が詰まっている。だからこそ企業ショールームが、宝石箱のようなキラキラとした印象となっているのだろう。

The centerpiece of this showroom of a water- fixture brand is, of course, the fixture products. The challenge was to draw the visitors into a space where these inorganic objects were displayed. Spatial planning involved the creation of an enticing black box within a vastly white space. Black mirrors in the background create a floating effect, while lighted pathways lead the way, interrupted by booths that segment the light. As a designer, Morita is always careful to reach deep inside his audience's thoughts. Although the scale might be small, this particular project is filled with such considerations. The result is a glittering treasure box, an impression that transcends the limits of an ordinary business showroom.

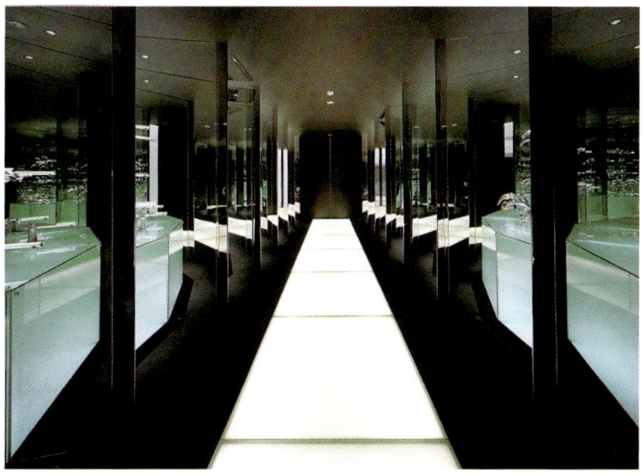
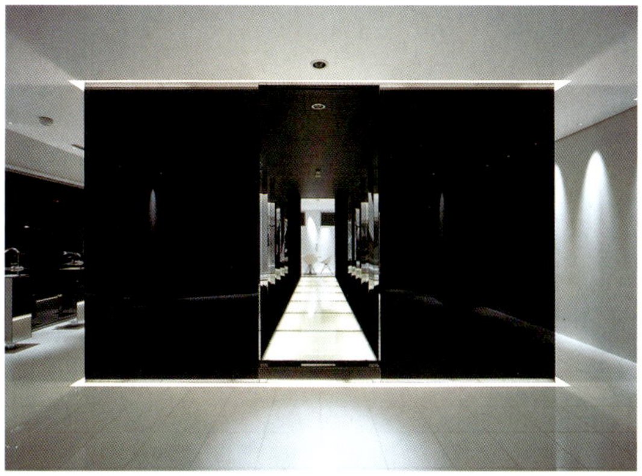
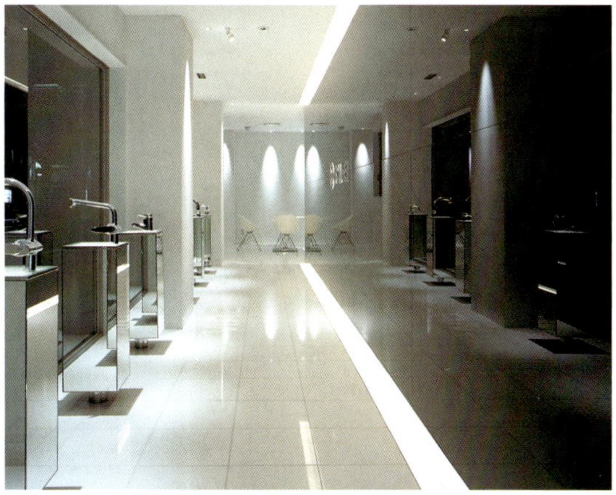
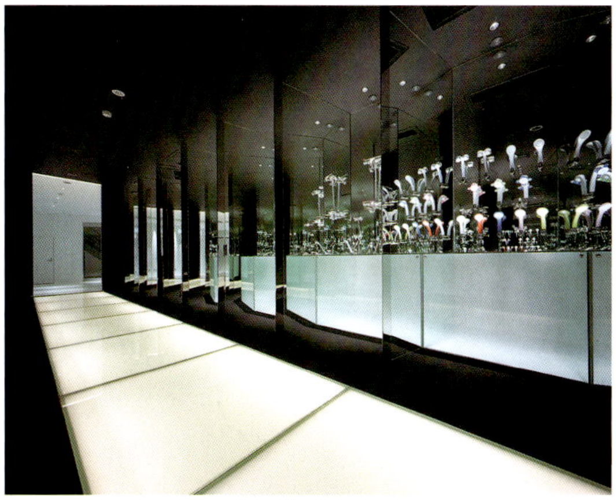
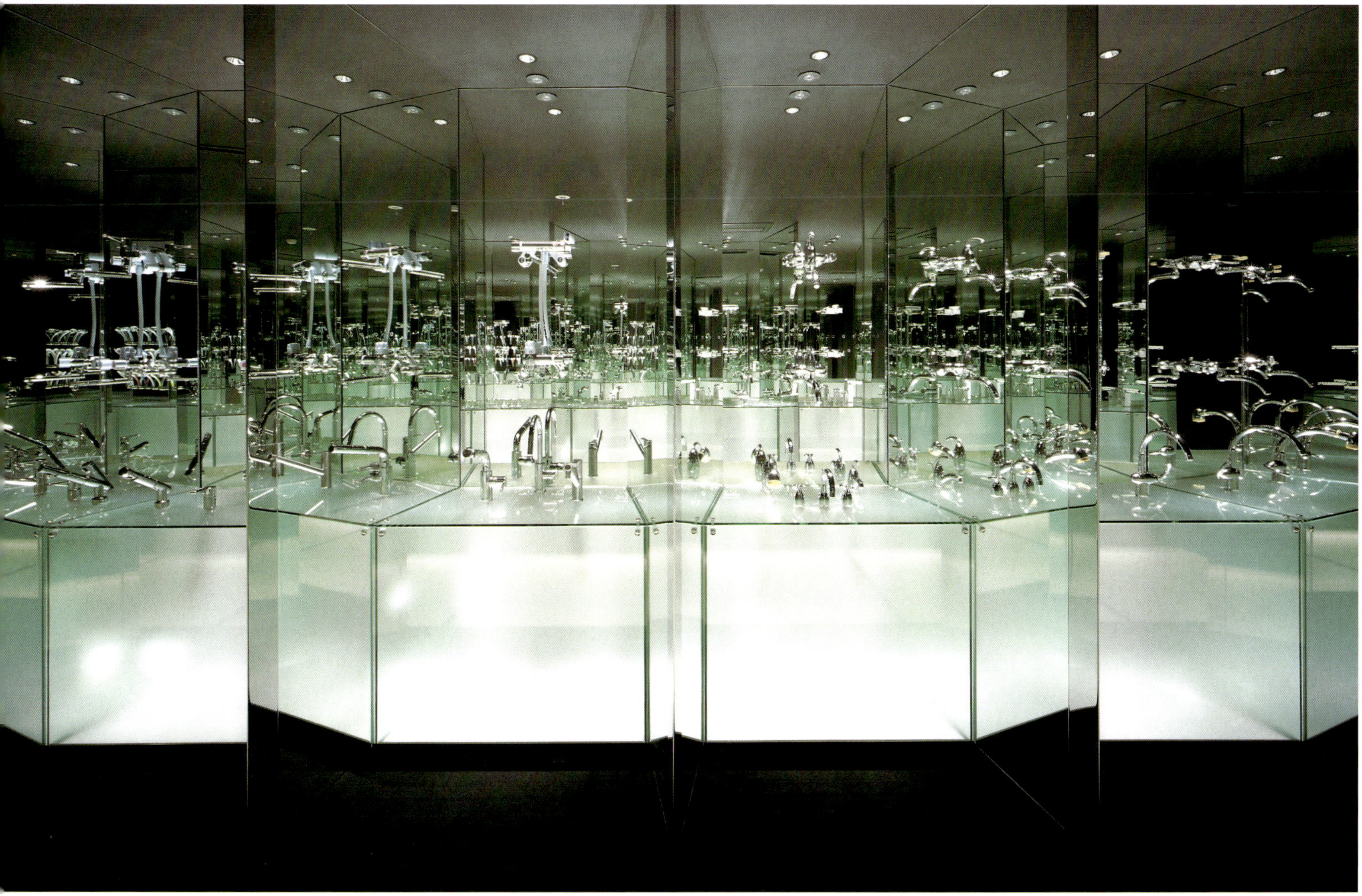

N°**024**
Tokyo/Japan
Mar.2012

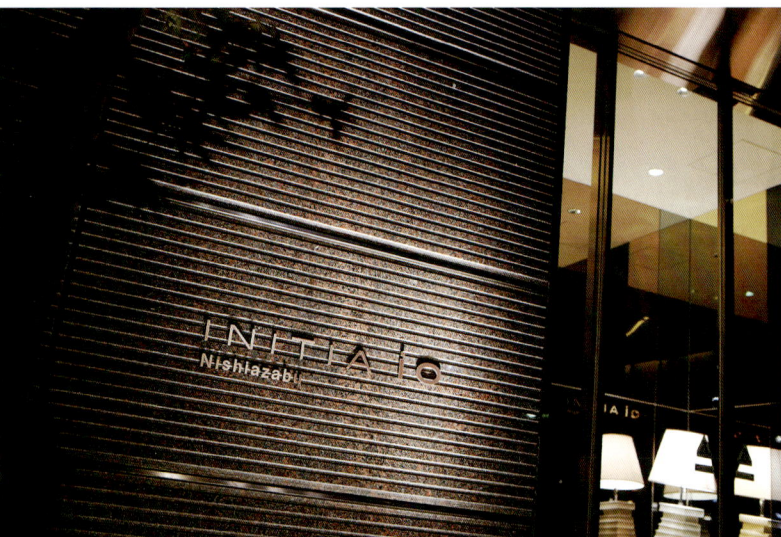

INITIAio Nishiazabu

この西麻布のマンションでは、時代に流されないことをいつも以上に意識したと森田は言う。街に見合った景観を残していくことが、デザイナーに求められる重要な要素のひとつである。強固なイメージのメインアプローチに対して、エントランスホールにはライムストーンをカーテンドレープのように用い、内廊下には温かみのあるウッドをテーマにしたグラデーションを配した。外と内とのバランスは、そのまま、家というものに対する考え方に通じる。住まう人が寛げるような、抱擁感や安心感。外から内へと入り、ゆるやかにスイッチが切り替わるような穏やかさが、マンションのデザインには求められる。

For this apartment in Nishi-Azabu, Morita was careful to keep the design timeless. One of the important tasks of a designer is to create works that blend naturally with the local scenery. As opposed to the unyielding main approach, the entrance hall is designed with limestone to simulate a draping curtain, and the interior hallway is colored with a gradient of warm-toned wood. The balance between the exterior and the interior spaces encompasses the purpose of the house itself: to create a sense of security that embraces the inhabitants. This smooth transition from exterior to interior, and the gradual switching of the mood, is vital in the design of a residential apartment.

N°025
Tokyo/Japan
Nov.2012
SELLTS LIMITED OFFICE

ファッションバッグのブランドのオフィスに求められる開放感を、"白"で表現した。ニューヨークの街角で見られるようなレンガの壁面に、波形のガラスからなる間仕切り、既存の窓部分に埋め込まれた間接照明とドレープの美しいレースカーテン。シンプルな素材、配色ながら、過不足ない雰囲気が抜けの良いオフィスを実現している。また、プレゼンテーションルームは、いかにバッグを引き立たせるかを考えてデザインされている。オフィスフロアのすべての家具の高さが揃えられているために、奥行きを実際以上に感じることができる。ミニマルな表現によって、適度な緊張感が生み出されている。

In this fashion brand office, a sense of openness was achieved through the use of white. The interior is composed of a mix of elements: a brick wall surface similar to those found in the streets of New York, partitions made out of wavy glass, indirect lighting embedded around the original window, and generously draped lace curtains. With the use of simple materials and a limited color palette, the design creates an airy and open office space with balanced ambience. The presentation room is designed to showcase the brand's bags. The furnitures on the office floor are designed with uniform height to emphasize the expansiveness of the sweeping space. A pleasant level of professionalism is being maintained through minimal expression.

N° 026
Osaka/Japan
Apr.2007
SUNRISE

モチーフとなっているのは「木」だ。エントランスのアートワーク、あるいは扉に使われている写真も「森」。オフィスでありながら、さらに「木」「森」を見せるための仕掛けとなっているのが、額縁。アートを囲う額だけでなく、扉、あるいは空間の仕切りに用いられているモチーフでもある。借景という言葉の通り、額縁に収まることで部屋そのものさえ美しい風景に見えてくる。また反対に、ガラス越しの中之島バラ園の広大な景色を活かすために、ミーティングルームのガラス面はできるだけデザインを遠ざけた。アート、部屋、そして風景。異なる存在が、連動するような設え。それは同時に、広がりを生む仕掛けにもなっている。

The motif here, is the tree. The artwork in the entrance, and the photographs that decorate the door, both illustrate the forest. A device that helps portray these "trees" and "forests" while preserving the integrity of the office space, is the framing. The frame does not merely install the art; it is also a motif used in the doors and partitions. As if to borrow from the surrounding scenery, the framing transforms the space into a beautiful landscape. On the other hand, Morita stayed away from over-designing the glass surface of the meeting room to make use of the sweeping views of the Nakanoshima Rose Garden. Art, space, and scenery. This rhythmical symbiosis of distinctive elements also creates the expansiveness of the interior.

N°**027**
Osaka/Japan
Mar.2007
Residence "T"

ファサードからインテリアのすべてを手がけた。「プレイランドのような住まいを」というオーダーに、各部屋の扉に家族写真をアートとして落とし込んだり、アイランドキッチンの背後はウッドの扉を設置したり、森田らしい遊び心で答えている。プライベートリビングには円形の琉球畳を配して寛ぎの空間とし、ゲスト用リビングにはおもてなしとしてホワイトレザーとウッド、さらにゲルマニウムのチェーンを用いた壁面やオリジナルのシャンデリアを設えた。常にゲストが絶えないレジデンスだからこその、驚きのあるデザイン。シンプルでありながら、楽しむための仕掛けが施されている。

The project encompasses the entire site, from the facade to the interior. The client requested a "play-land house," and Morita responded with a playful design exemplified by the family portraits that artfully decorate each door, and a wooden door behind the kitchen island. The private living room is designed as a space for relaxing, with a circular *tatami* mat. The guest living room, on the other hand, is characterized by white leather and wood, wall surfaces embellished with chains of germanium, and a custom-made chandelier. To meet the demands of a residence enjoyed by a constant stream of guests, the design is filled with surprises. While simple, numerous playful devices have been added to the overall design.

N°028
Tokyo/Japan
Jan.2011

GLAMOROUS co.,ltd.

元々は幼稚園の教室として利用されていた物件。天井が低く、水回りも幼児用の設定だった。そのために天伏を除いてスケルトンにし、壁面と天井はベージュに統一した。下地は実にベーシックなもの。圧迫感を避けるために会議室はすべてガラス張り。少しずつ森田の"色"が見えてくる。パーテーションは可動式のものをオリジナルにデザインし、壁面収納にはボルドーカラーのカーテンを採用。少しラグジュアリーな雰囲気が加わったところに、オリジナルのペイントや、各所に置かれたアートで"味付け"をしていく。常にフレキシブルで、パフォーマンスを引き出すオフィスは、森田のデザインの思考が階層となって、はっきりとわかるようになっている。

The property was originally being used as a kindergarten, with low ceilings and sinks built for children. The ceiling panel was first knocked out so that only its skeleton remained, and the wall and ceiling surfaces were painted beige. The base of this design is strictly conservative. Meeting rooms are sectioned with glass to alleviate tension. When the design is viewed in further detail, Morita's style becomes more apparent. The custom-made partitions are removable, and wall shelving is covered with bold curtains. Following a layer of luxury, the design is topped with custom paintings and numerous art pieces. The constantly flexible, high-performing office is a reflection of Morita's design philosophy, a visible layering of his thought process.

GLAMOROUS co.,ltd

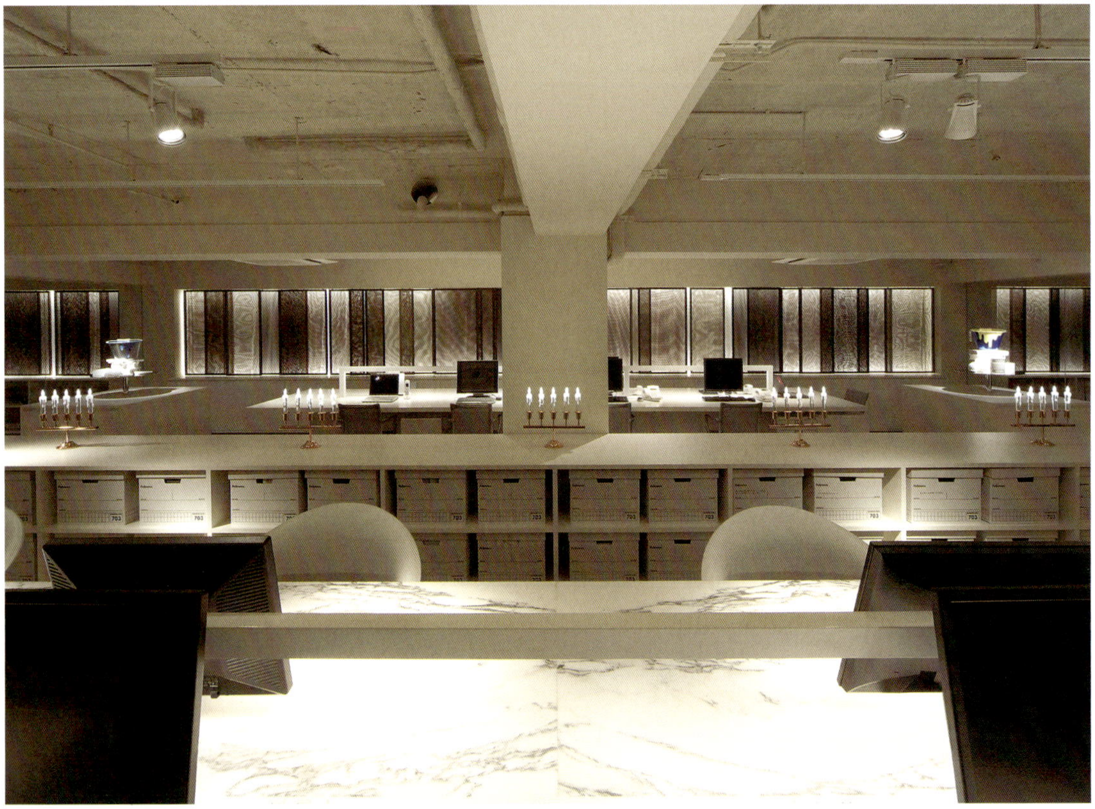

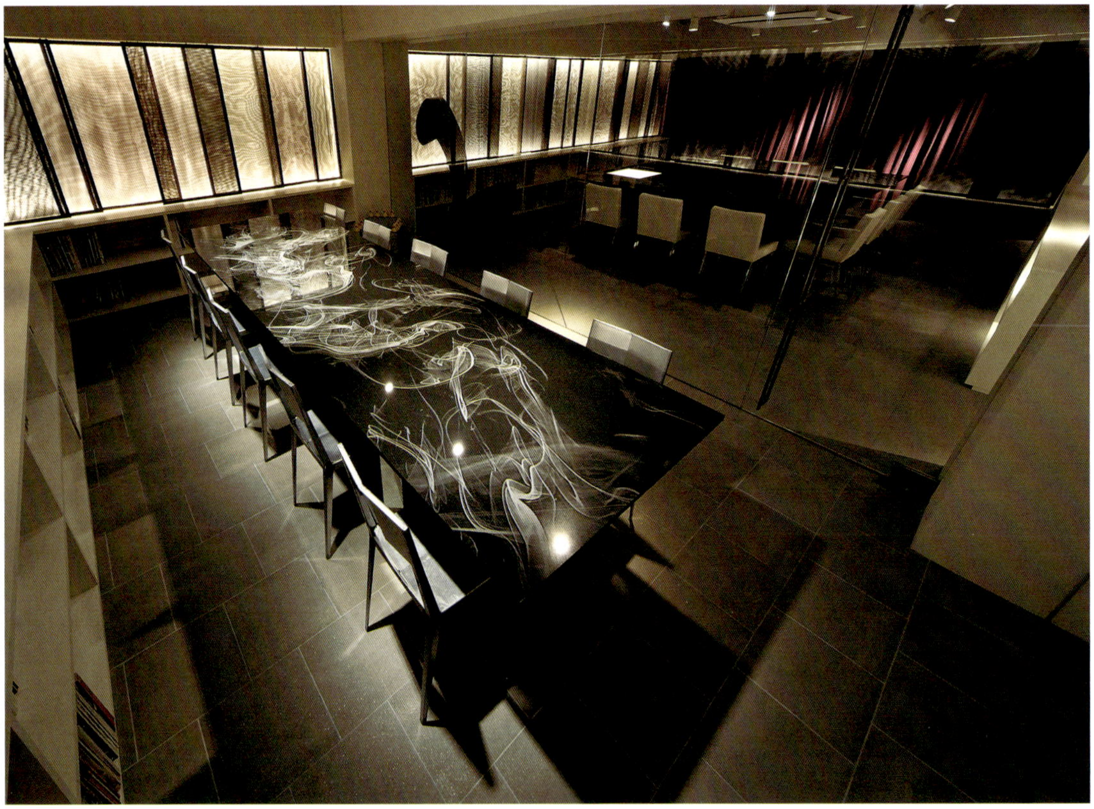

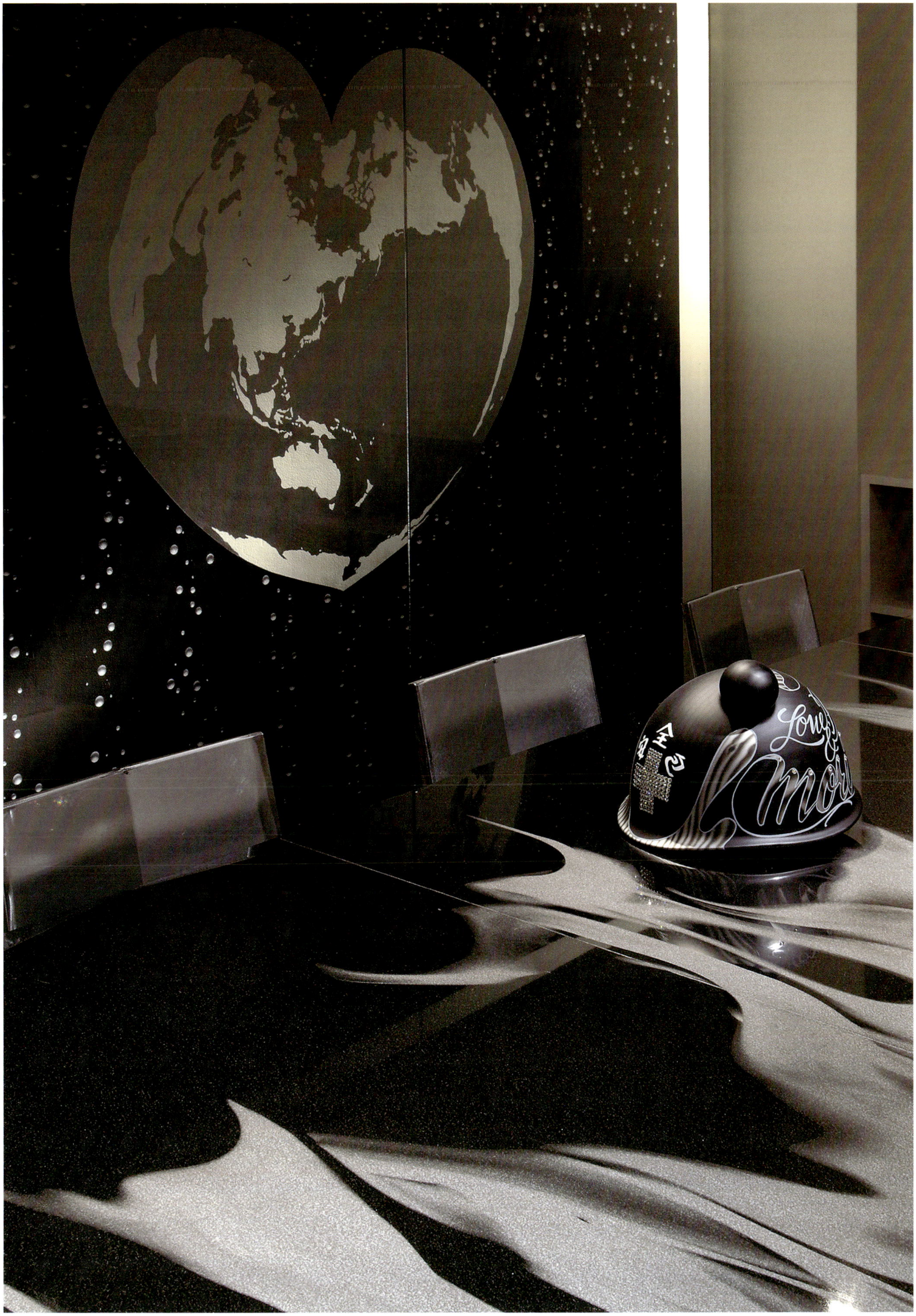

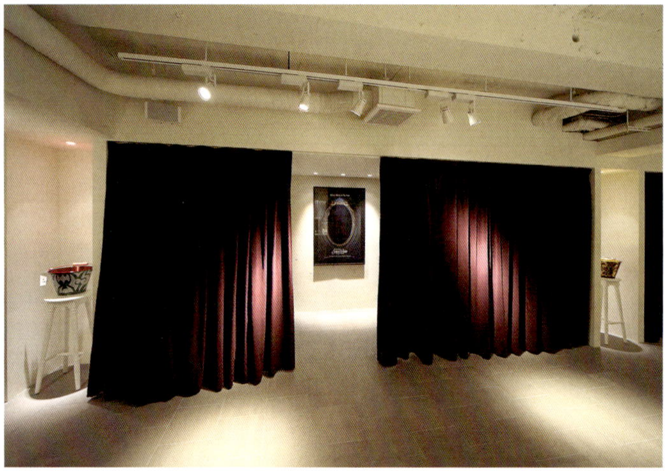

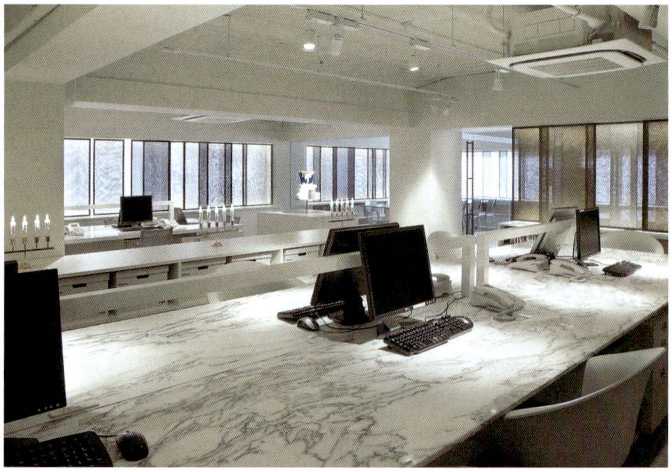

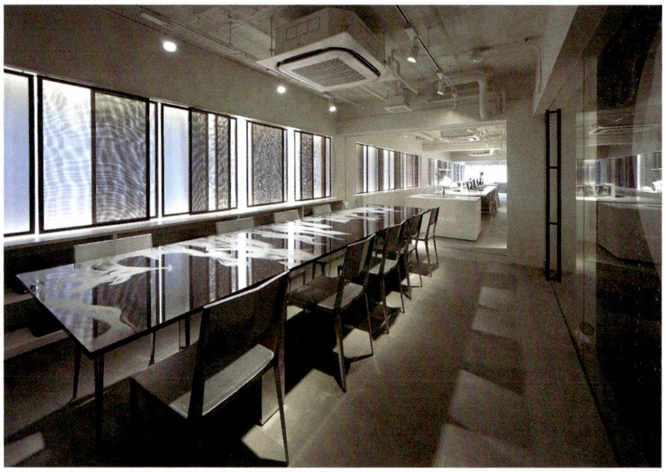

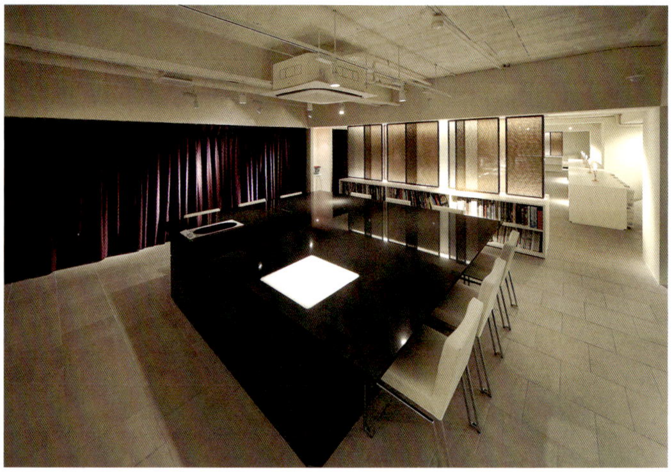

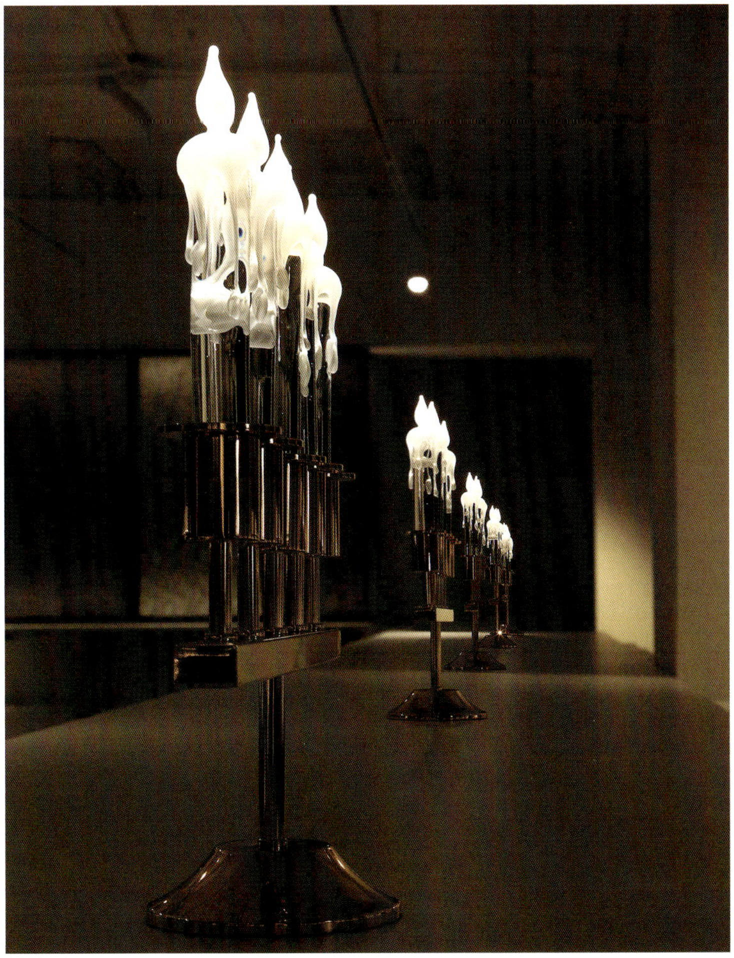
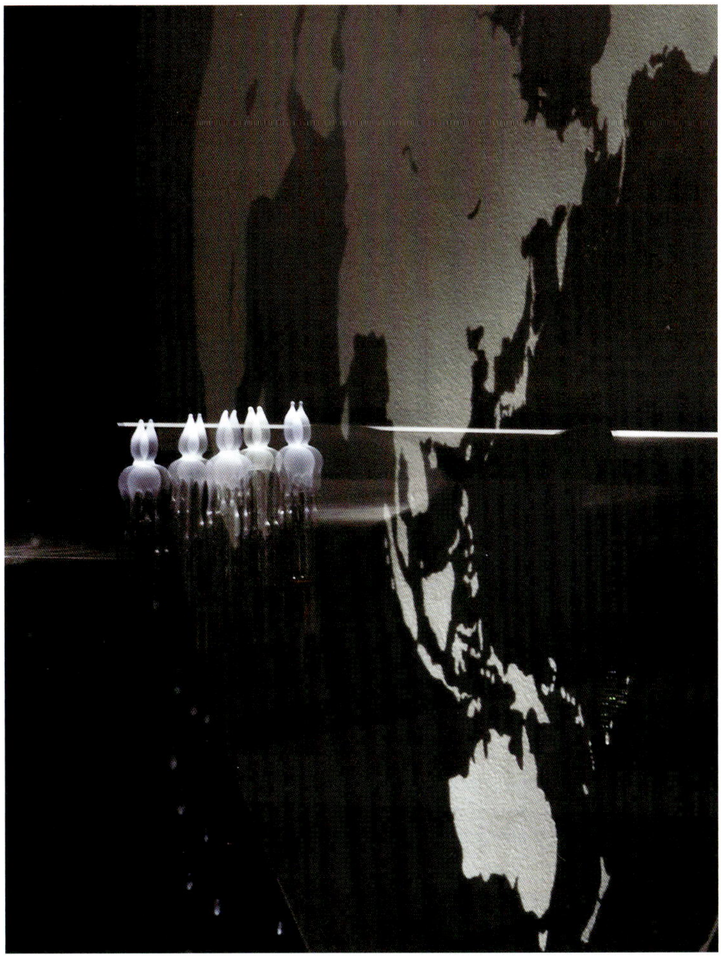
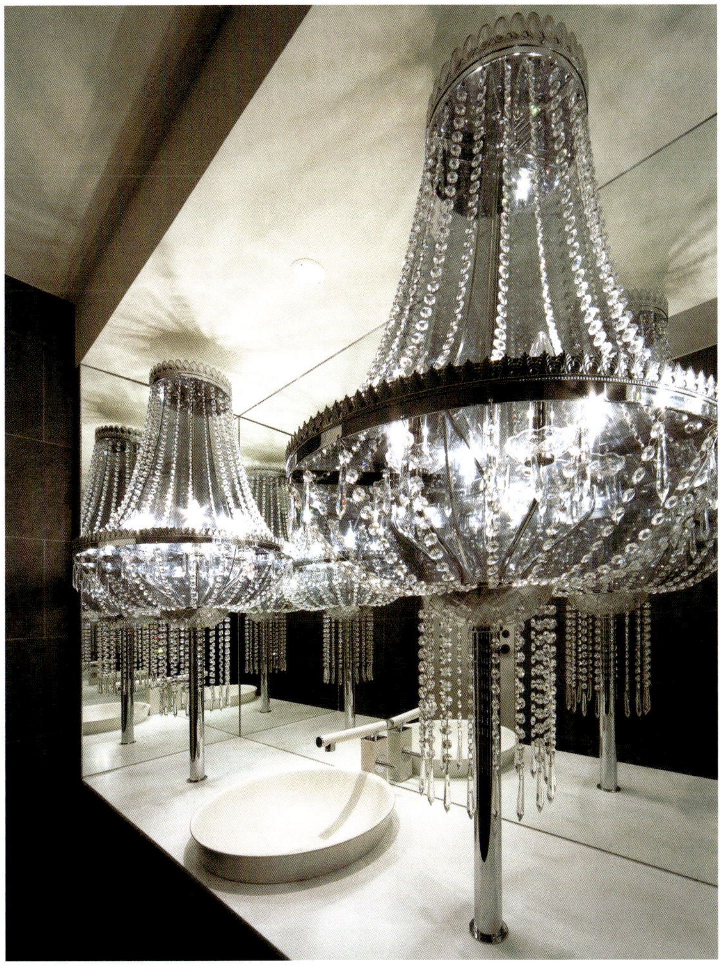

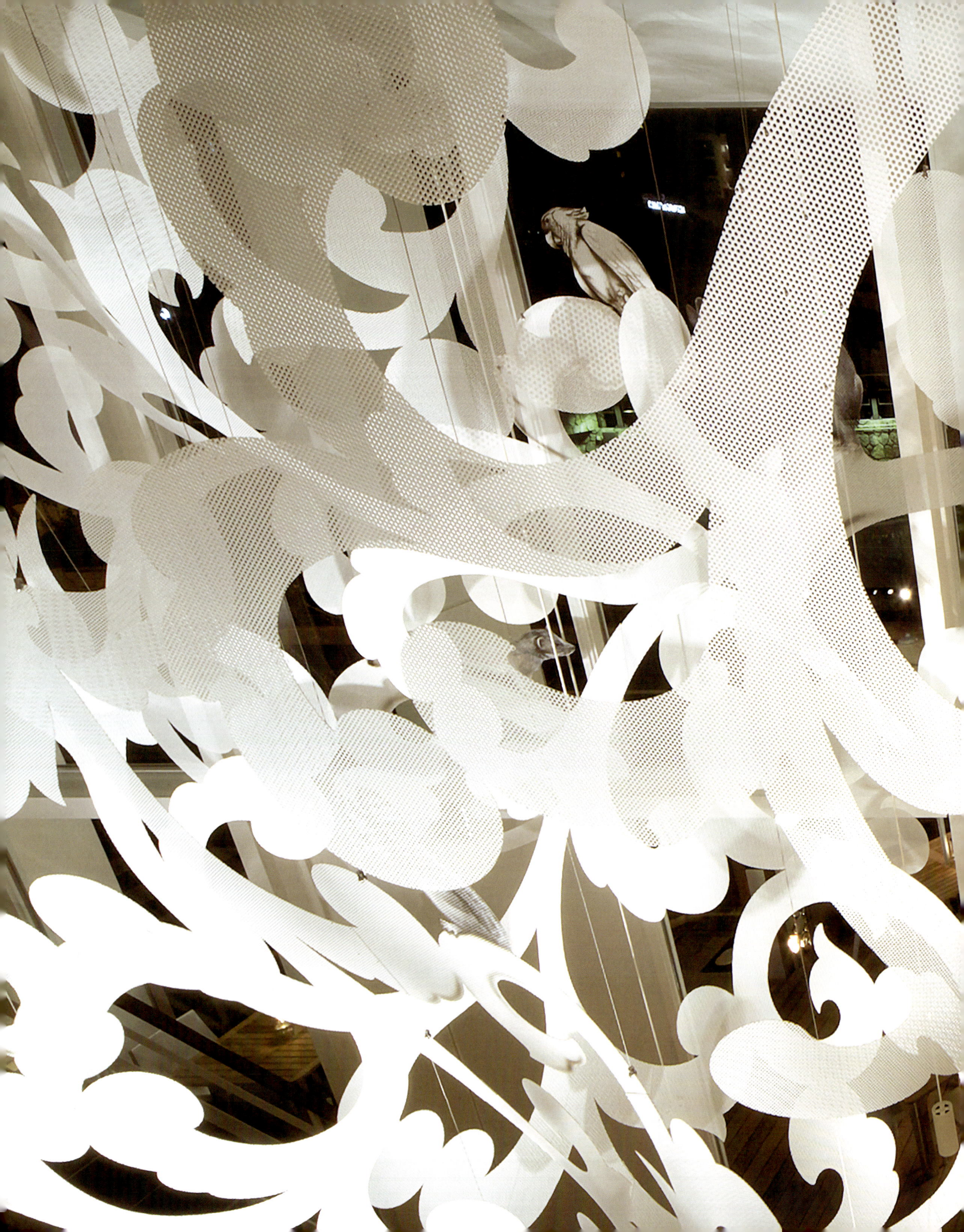

デザインは、メッセージである。

「デザインは、ある意味で、メッセージでもある。すごく直接的な例で言えば、国会中央食堂のリノベーションを手がけたときのこと。昭和よりも以前のイメージを僕は感じたので、まずはライティングを変えようと。蛍光灯を替えて、明るすぎず暗すぎず、いい感じに調整して、照明スタンドに日本の象徴でもある家紋をチャームとして付けた。壁をいじることはできなかったんだけれど、私たちの国にはこんなに素晴らしいところがあるんだよっていう意味を込めて、日本のモノクロームの写真を並べた。改めて、私たちの原点はこういうところにあるんだよって、日本という国を動かそうとしている人たちに伝えたかった。脈々と続く伝統と美しい風景をいつも目にしながら仕事ができるようにって。それが、デザイナーとして僕が果たすべき役割だと思ったから。
レストランのリノベーションも同じように、メッセージを伝えることができると思っている。どうすれば『前の方がよかった』ってならないのかを考えて、以前から通うファンに納得してもらうためにはDNAを引き継ぐことが大切なんだと思う。そのレストランが誇りにしてきたものをデザインの中に織り込むことで、過去と未来が繋がっているっていう安堵感が生まれる。以前の店の良きところを守りながら、新しいエッセンスを入れていく、そのバランスがデザインの肝なのかもしれない。デザインにできることはすごくいろいろあって、そのレストランがどんな歴史を紡いできたのか、あるいは、どんな風に楽しんでもらいたいのか。料理が運ばれる前に、もっと言えば、店に入った瞬間にそのメッセージを伝えることは、デザインの重要な役割のひとつ。それは訪れるお客様だけじゃなくて、そこで働く人たちへのメッセージでもある。あなたの働いている店は、こんなにも素晴らしい店なんですよって、僕はデザインで伝えたいんだと思う」

Design is the Message.

"Design, in a sense, is also a message. A very straightforward example of this is the renovation project I did for the central cafeteria of the National Diet Building. I felt an atmosphere of the pre-Showa era, so the first thing I did was to change the lighting. I changed the fluorescent lights to make them just bright enough, and added a symbolic family crest to the lighting stands. I wasn't allowed to touch the walls, but I hung monochromatic photographs of Japan, to show that our country is blessed with magnificent places. I wanted to remind the very people who run our country, that our origins lie within the places captured in the photographs. My goal was to create an environment where the workers are surrounded by visuals of continued traditions and beautiful scenery. That, I thought, was my role as a designer.
Similarly, I think that restaurant renovations can also carry messages. It's important to preserve the DNA of the original design, so that the fans of the restaurant are not disappointed by the new renovation. By incorporating the restaurant's prided essence into the new design, people are relieved, because they understand that the past is still connected with the new. The balance between preserving the old and injecting the new, might be the key to creating a great design. There is a lot that can be accomplished through design, such as the restaurant's history, and how it wants to entertain the guests. One of my important roles as a designer is to convey the restaurant's message *before* the first plate is served, or even earlier, at the moment the guest enters the restaurant. This message is not only directed towards the guests, but towards the restaurant staff as well. I want to communicate, through my design, that they're working at a magnificent restaurant."

N°029
Osaka/Japan
Dec.2012
LA FÊTE HIRAMATSU

「モダンクラシック」という、相対する言葉がコンセプトである、地上200mに位置するレストラン。360度の眺望からの大阪の街そのものが、ひとつのデザインソースとなっている。例えば、世界初の試みであるシャンデリア型の噴水には、大阪のシンボルとも言える大阪城や中央公会堂がアイコンとなって彫り込まれている。「都会のオアシスだからこそ、豊かな素材を意識した」という森田の言葉通り、レストランのそれぞれには、銀や錫など、実は大阪と深い馴染みのある素材を用いている。さまざまなシーンを施設の中に有する「ラ・フェットひらまつ」の物語性を演出するための答えは、大阪という環境そのものの中にあった。

The restaurant, with the conflicting concept of "modern classic," is located on a floor two hundred meters above ground. Its 360 degrees breathtaking views of the Osaka city are an important source of this design. The chandelier water fountain, the very first of its kind, is engraved with icons of Osaka Castle and Osaka City Central Public Hall. "I wanted to make use of rich materials for this urban oasis," says Morita, who applied silver and tin in the design, materials historically associated with Osaka. The solution to showcase the narrative of the restaurant, a facility that hosts an assortment of scenarios, lies in the environment of Osaka itself.

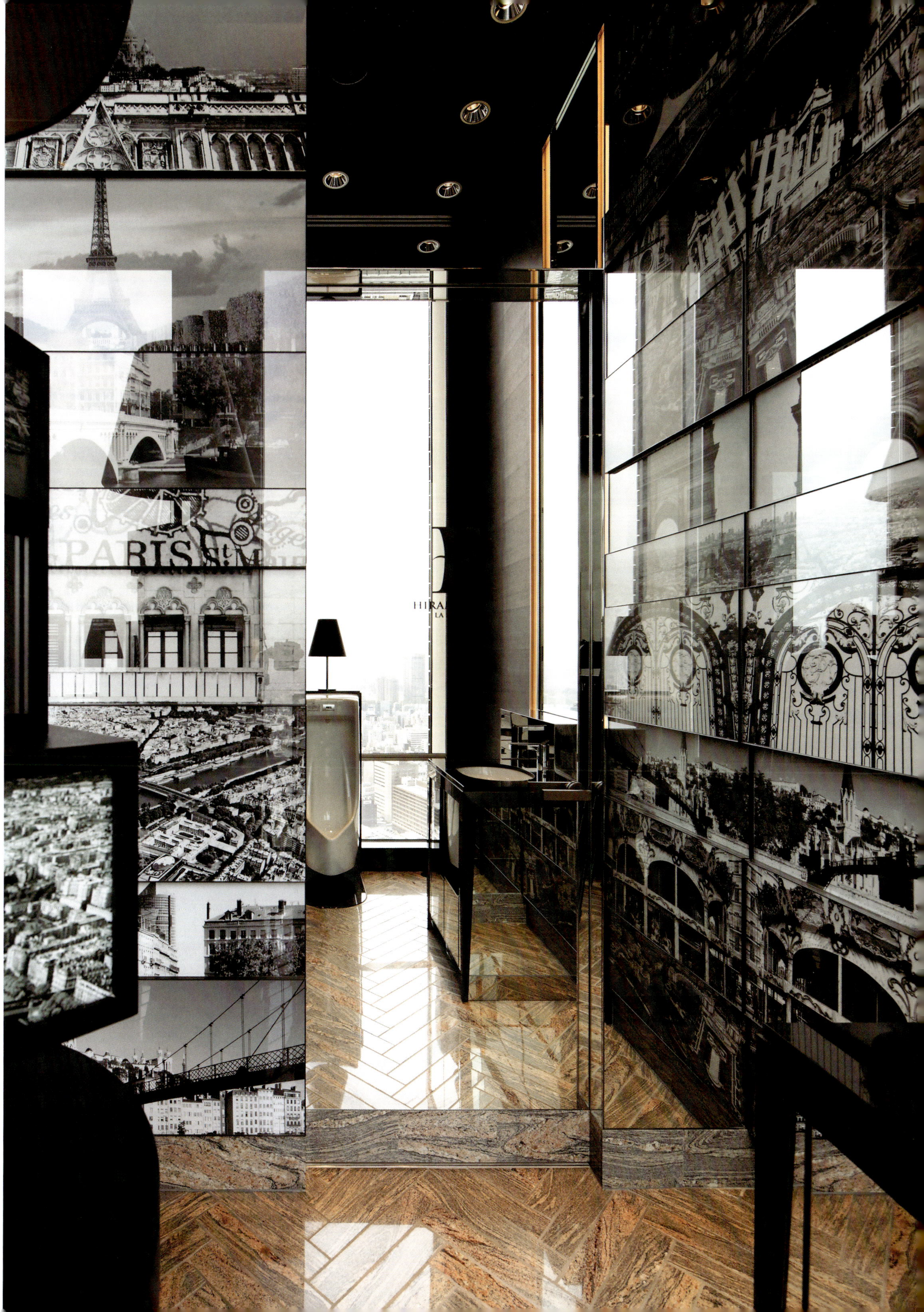
PARIS

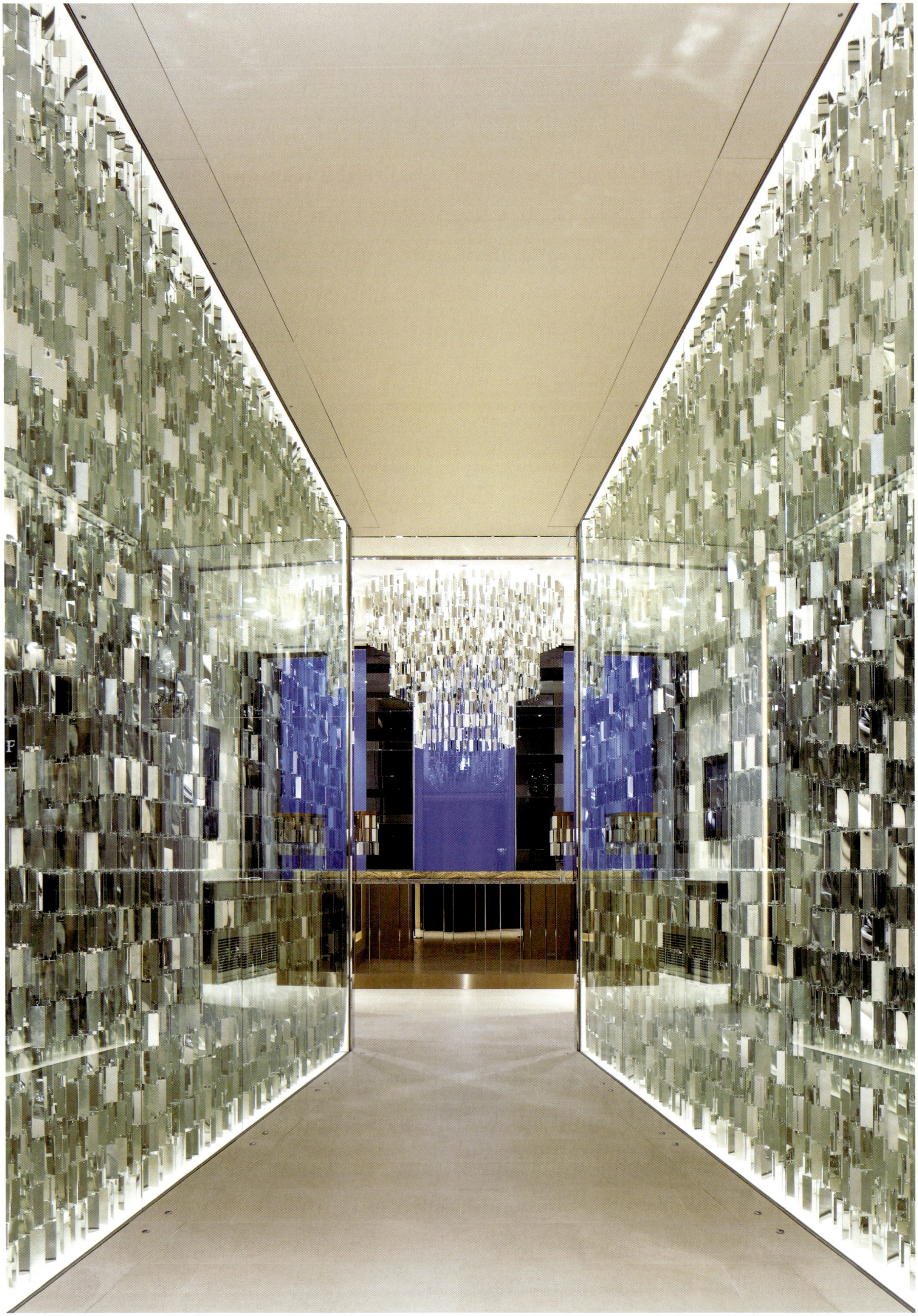

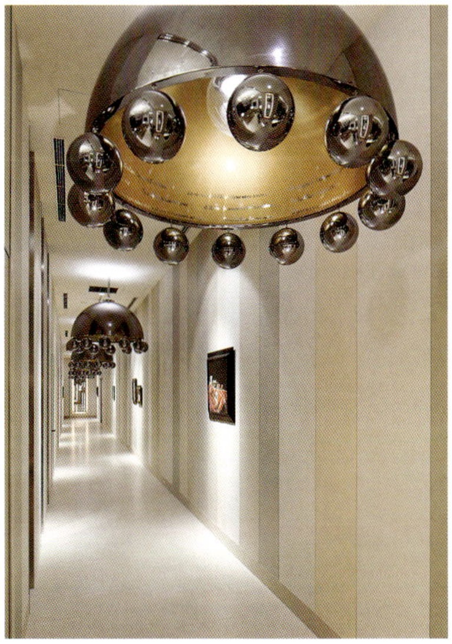

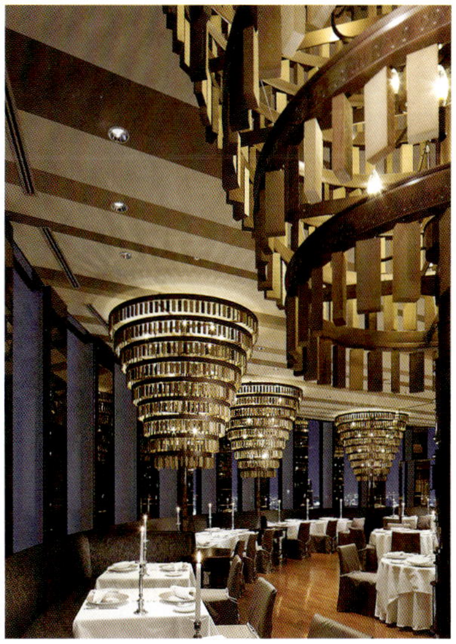

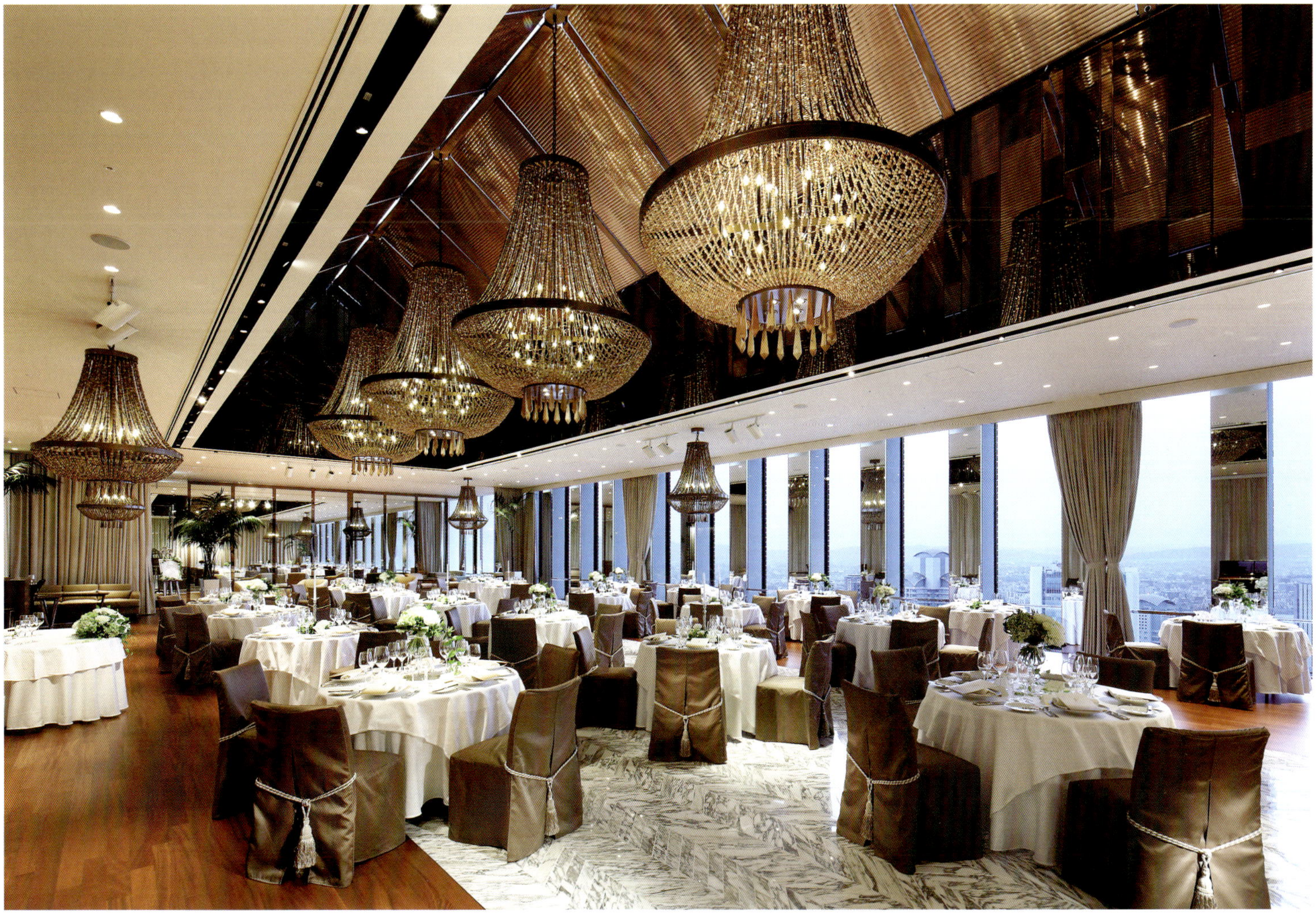

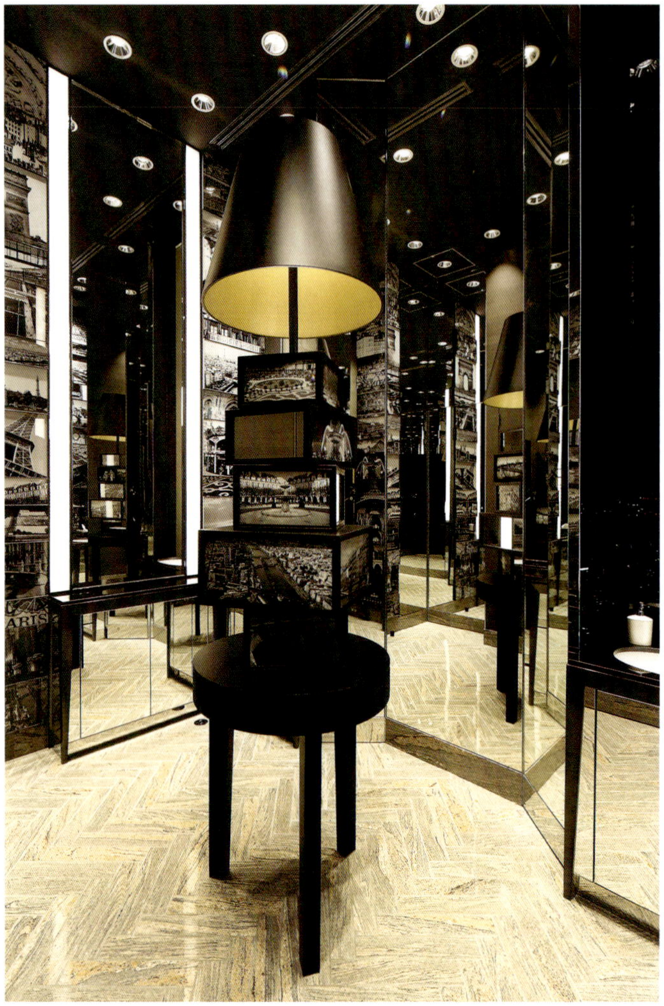

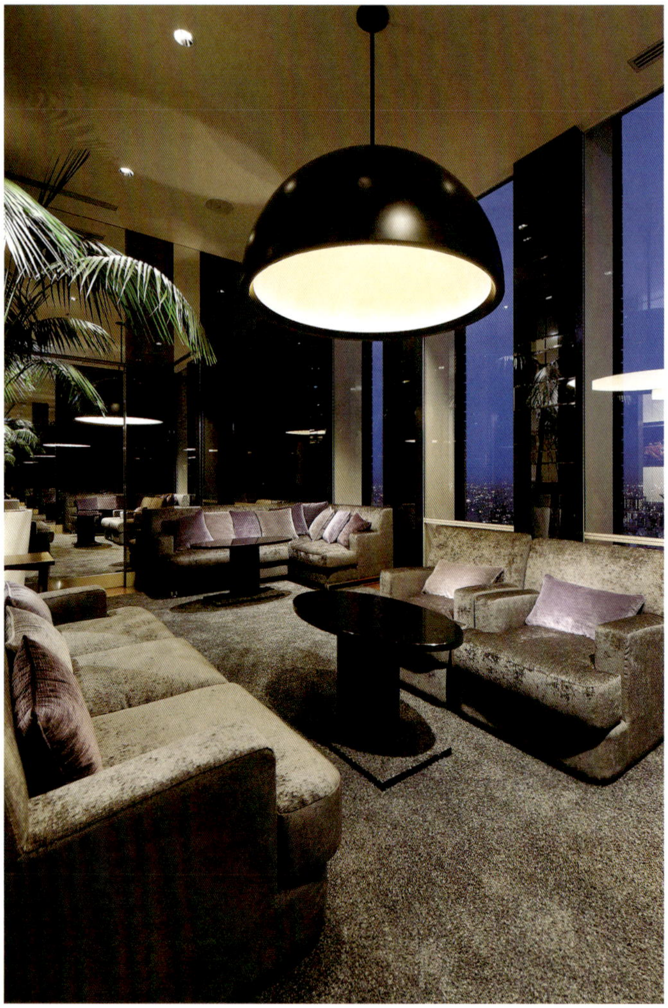

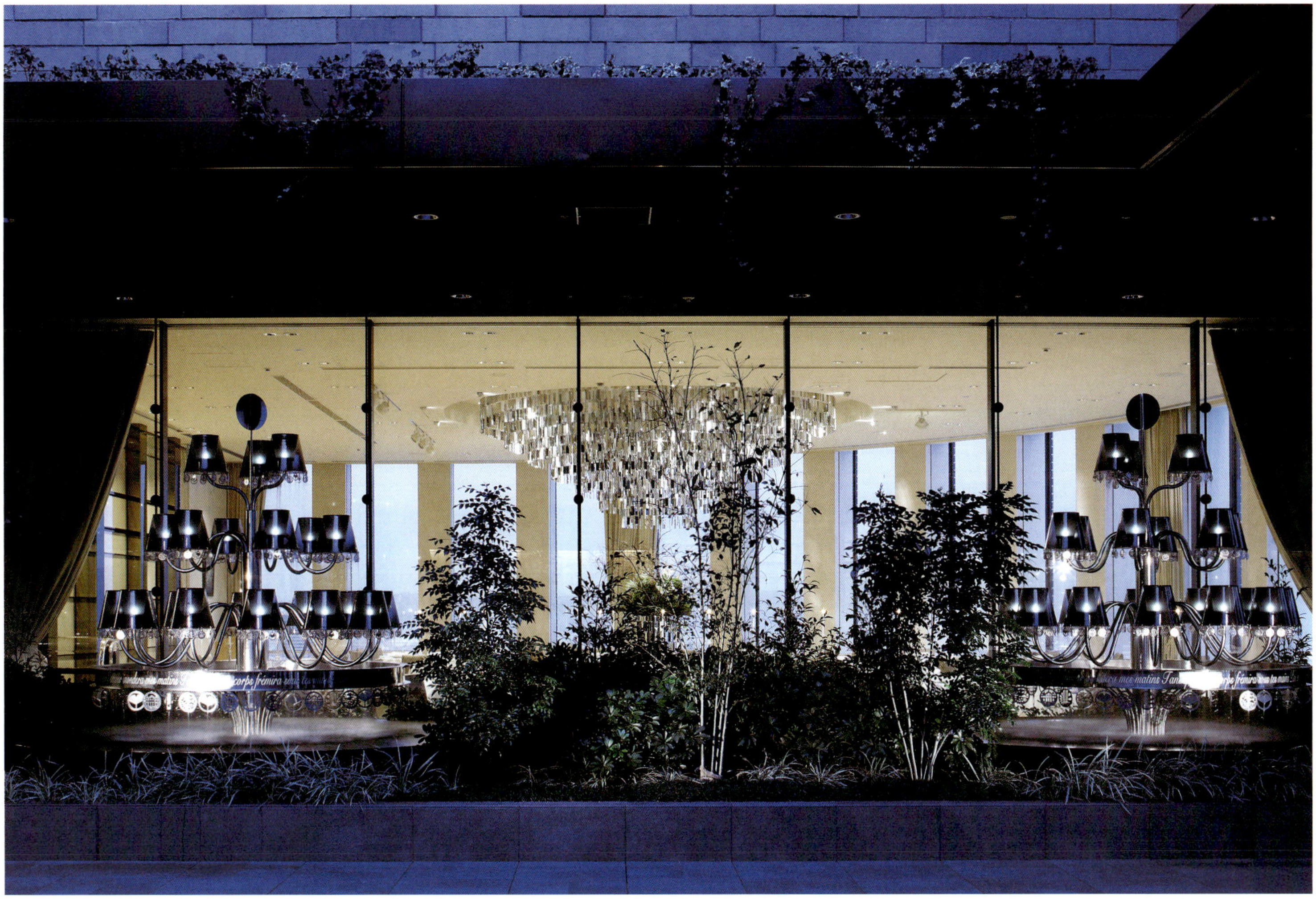

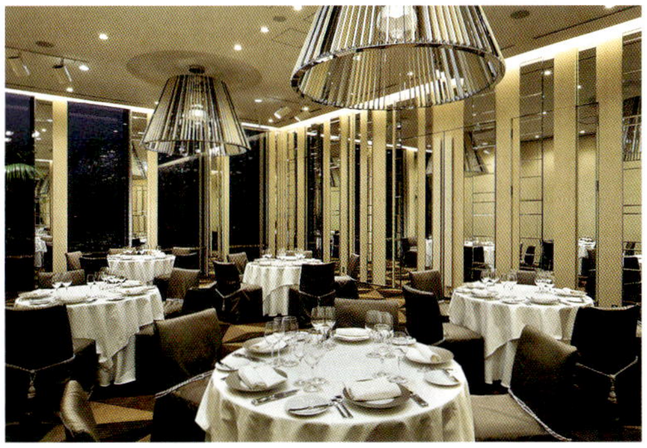

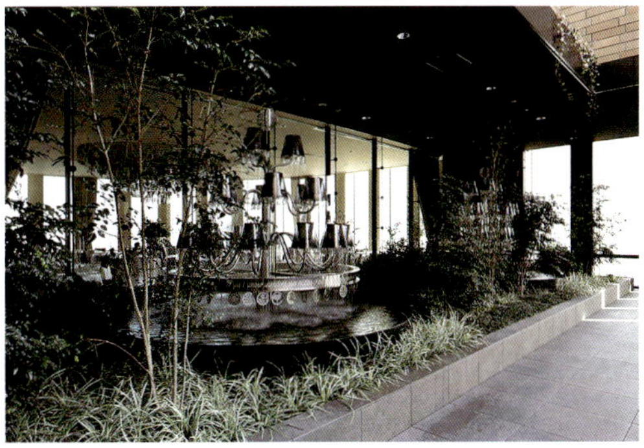

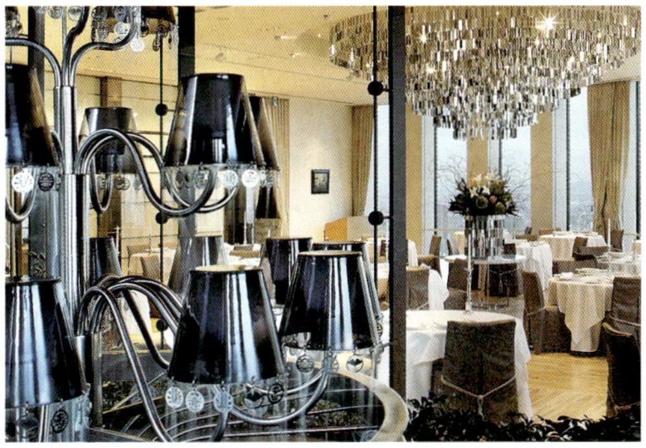

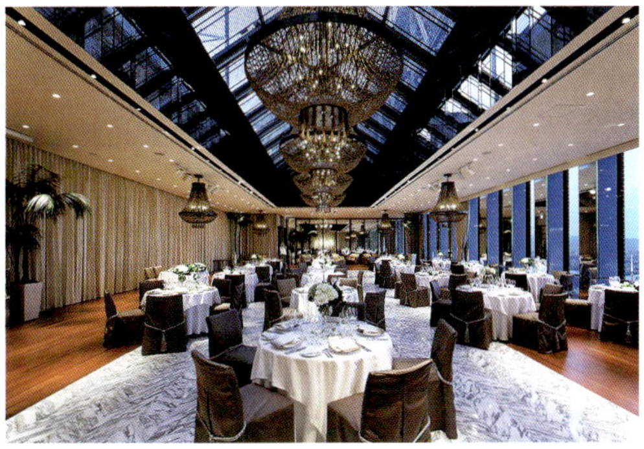

N°030

Sydney/Australia
Sep.2009

OCEAN ROOM

天井に広がる4万個以上ものウッド・ビーズは、「ニュースタイル・ジャパニーズの料理を提供するレストランとしてふさわしい雰囲気」という依頼に対しての回答だった。オペラハウスを眺めるシドニー湾沿いという最高の立地で表現したのは、ウッド・ビーズによるアジアの風と波。オーストラリアのアイコンとのゆるやかな親和性が、室内の雰囲気を軽くしている。ビーズの素材は、桐。軽やかな木材である桐を用いることで、温かみを与えることに成功している。どの位置でも料理やテーブルに座る人が美しく照らされるように照明を計算し、床材をタイルとフローリングに切り替えることで自然なゾーニングを生み出した。大胆で繊細なデザインが、空間を明るくしている。

The ceiling, decked with over forty thousand wooden beads, is the answer to the client's request for an ambience fit for a restaurant serving a new style of Japanese cuisine. The project, located along Port Jackson with a view of the Opera House, portrays the winds and waves of Asia through the use of wooden beads. Displaying a gentle familiarity with Australia's icons, the design brightens the interior ambience. These beads are made of paulownia wood, and the use of this light material adds warmth to the entire design. Lighting has been carefully calculated to perfectly illuminate the guests and their dishes in any seat. The tiled floor switches to hardwood, naturally separating the space into different zones. A bold yet delicate design emphasizes the brightness of the space.

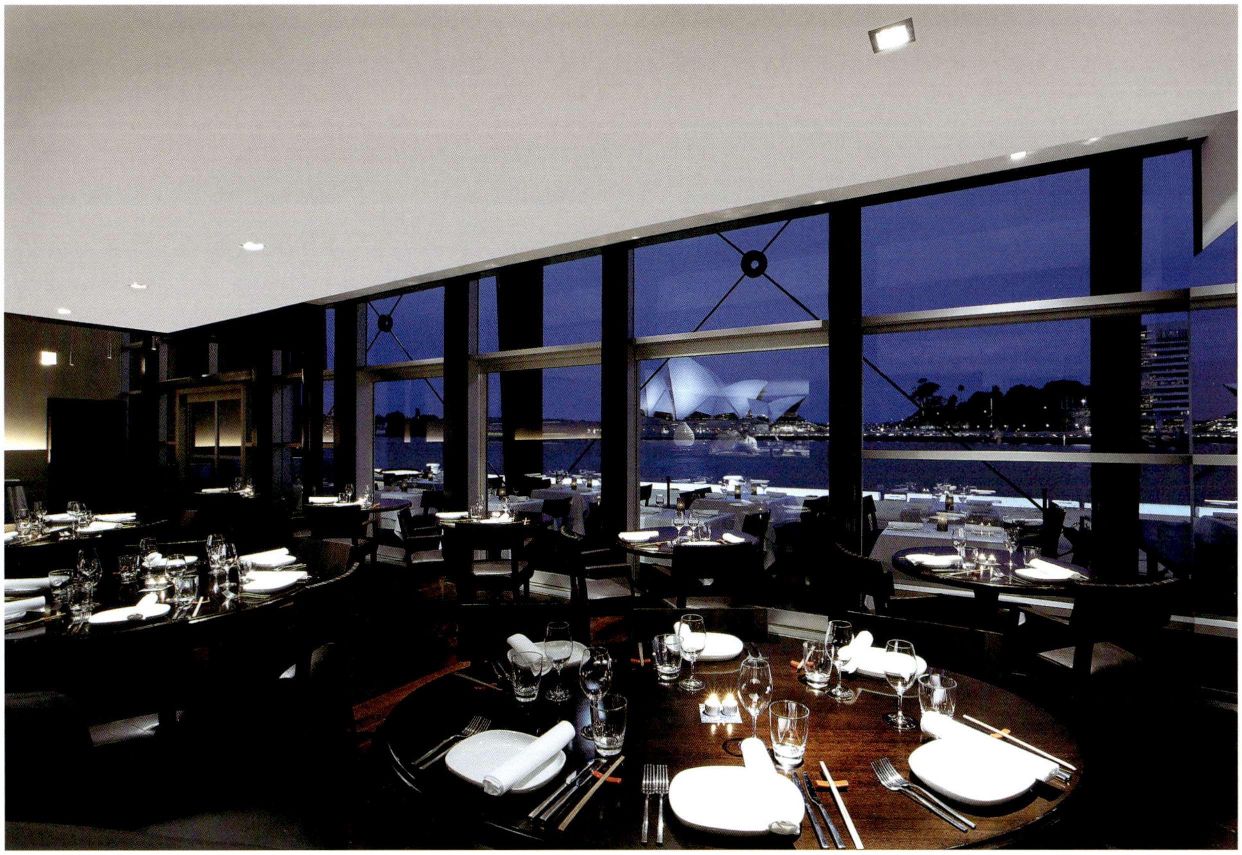

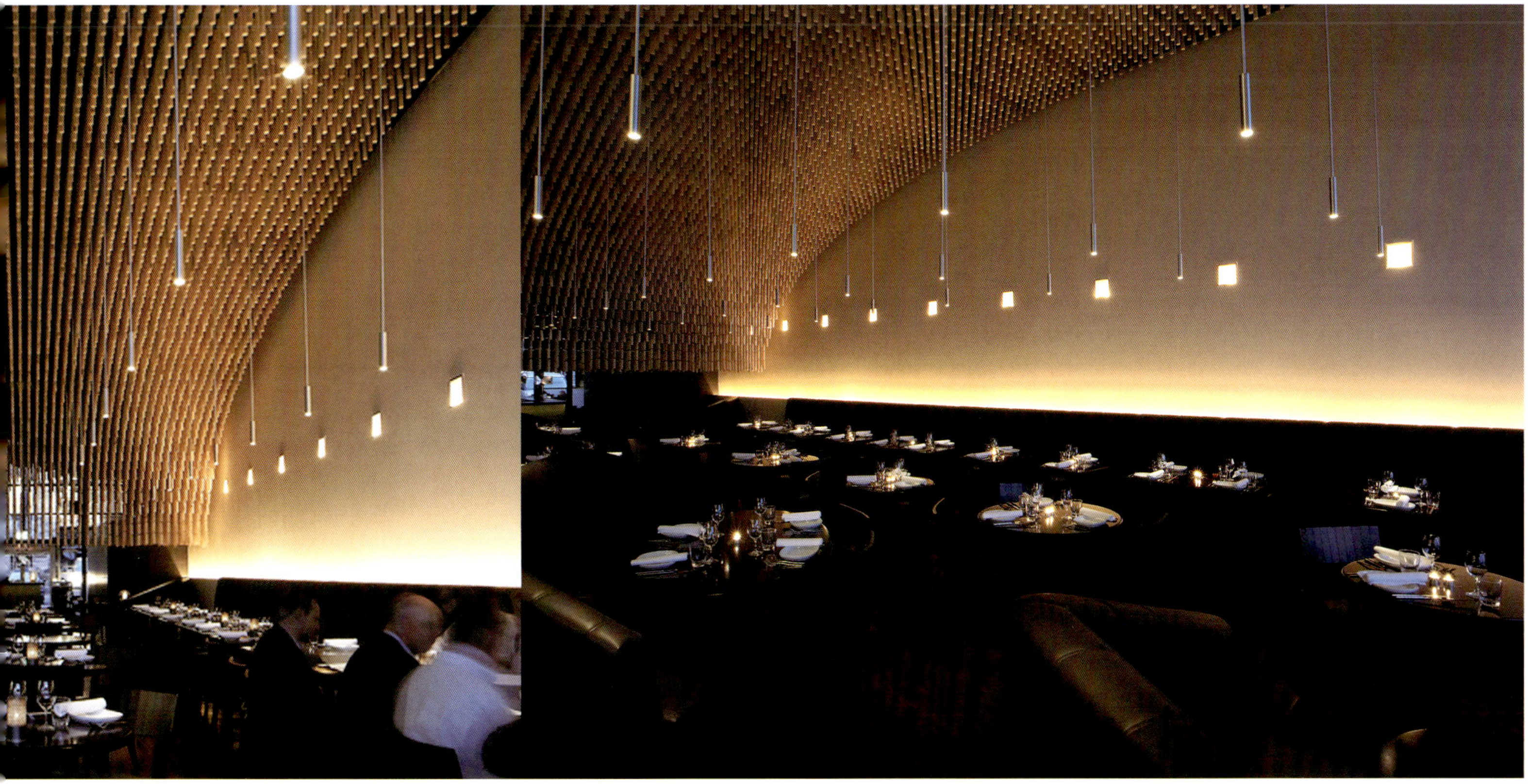

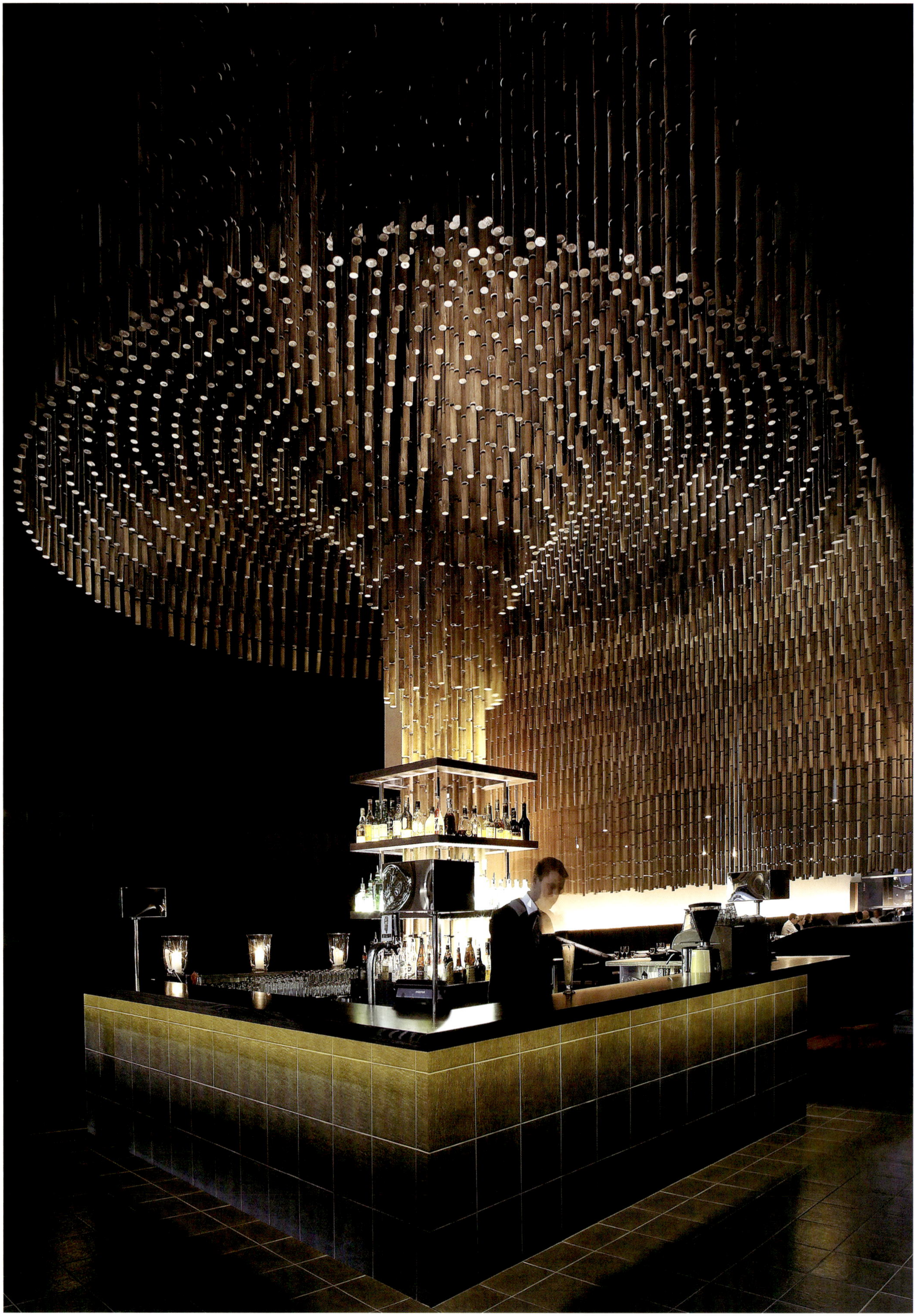

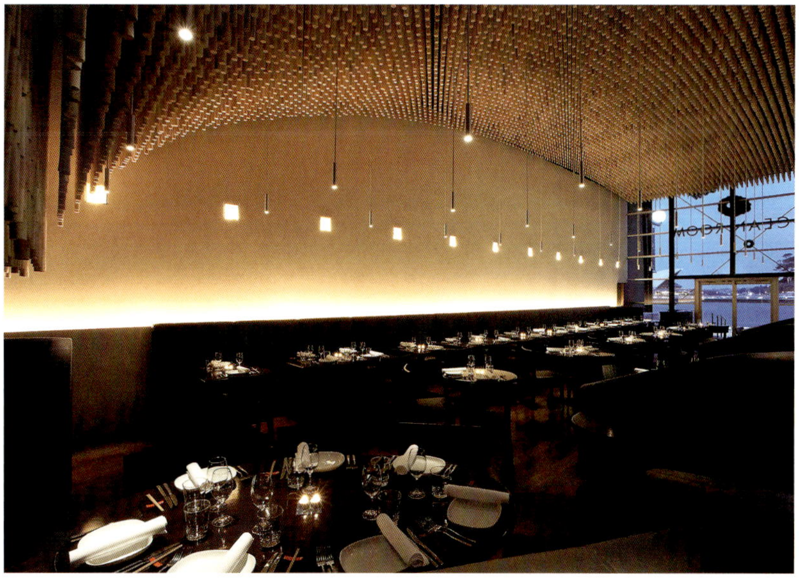

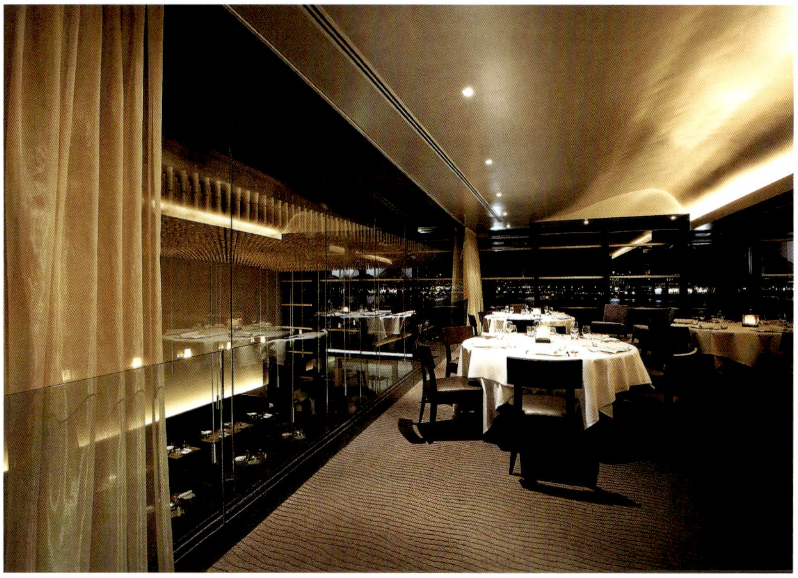

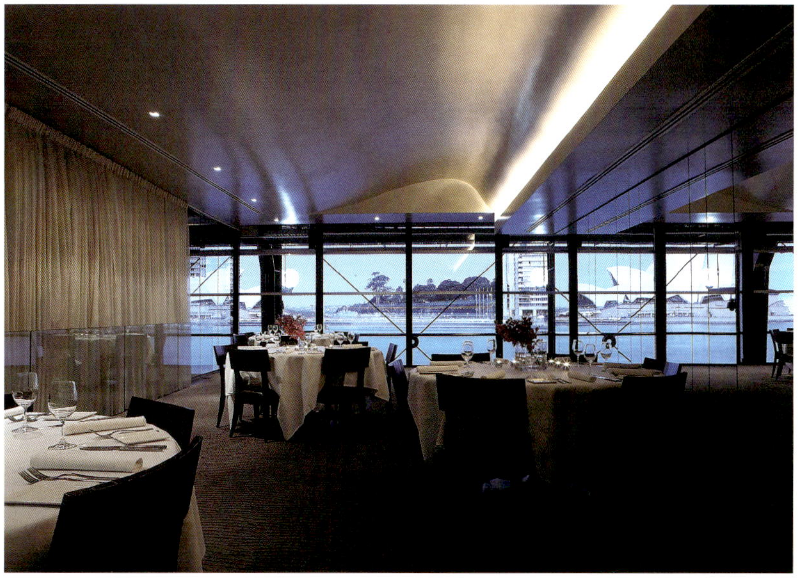

N°031
Tokyo/Japan
Sep.2012
華都飯店

土地に根付いている店の移転に際し、何よりも大切にしたのは「歴史と伝統」だった。馬家一族が代々使用していた屏風にあった翡翠をアンティークの木材に埋め込むこと。あるいは、結び目で表現した「絆」をグラフィックにあしらい、陶器に表現すること。世代を超えて受け継がれる伝統的な料理と異文化の融合という、半世紀愛されてきた店の歴史を新たに紡ぐためのデザインが考えられている。美しいロイヤル・チャイナブルーは、鮮烈な印象と同時に落ち着きを与えるものになっている。もちろん空間をフレキシブルに使うことが可能なデザインは、今後も末永く愛されていく店にとっては必須のもの。機能美こそが、なにより名店には必要なのだ。

In the relocation of this locally rooted restaurant, the most important concern was preserving its history and tradition. Pieces of jade were transported from the family's folding screens and embedded onto an antique wood material. Chinaware was treated with illustrations of a knotted string to graphically portray the family's bond. The design continues the history of a business that has been operating for half a century, fusing an intercultural vibe with traditional recipes. The graceful royal china blue color strikes the viewer with both a vivid impression and cool poise. Of course, the design allows the space to be used flexibly, leaving margins for growth in the restaurant's future. Functional beauty is a vital element of this famed restaurant.

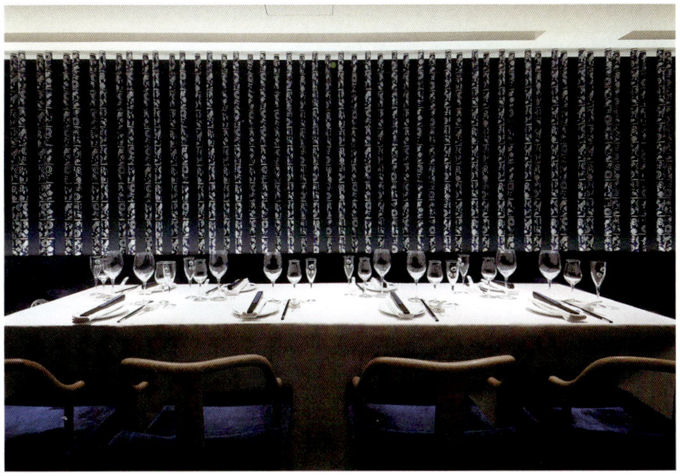

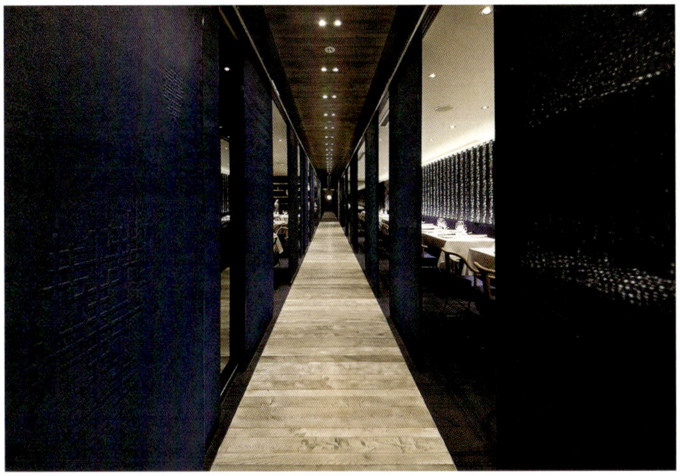

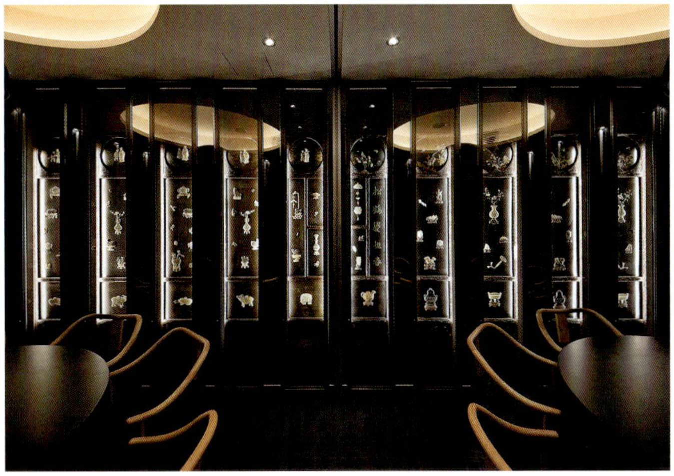

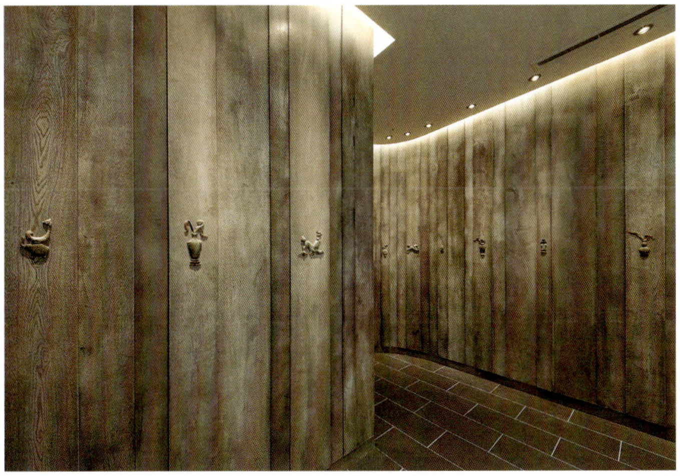

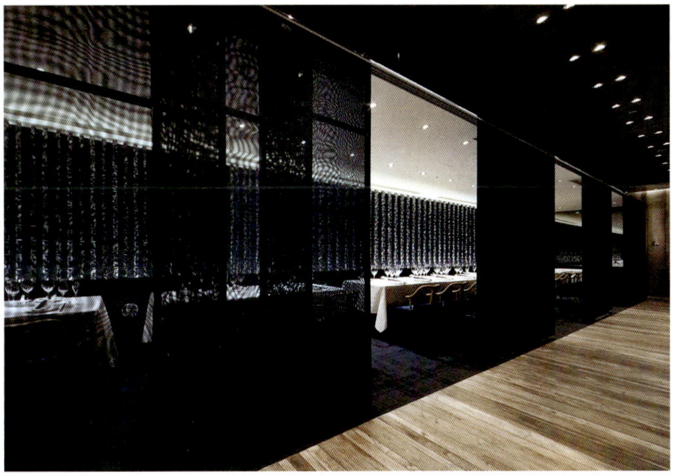

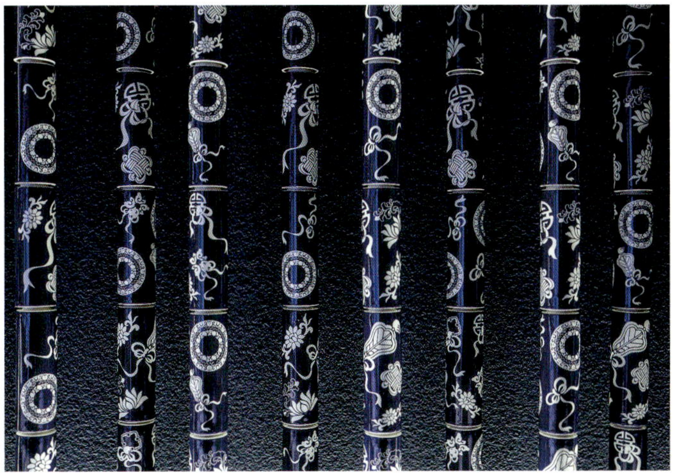

N°032
Osaka/Japan
Oct.2010

THE ST. REGIS OSAKA
La Veduta

テーマは「オール・デイ・ダイニング」。そのために必要なのは過剰に明るい店内ではなく、落ち着いた雰囲気だった。高さのある天井から吊されたモーツァルト氏のシャンデリアは、クラシックな形状ながら、ロープという斬新な素材を用いることで新たな価値観を付与している。テーマとするアート作品がスペースごとに代わり、何度訪れても飽きることのない、"違い"を感じることのできる空間になっている。壁面に掲げられた中山ダイスケ氏の作品は、大阪の街がモチーフになっている。日中にはシアーカーテン越しに柔らかな自然光を、夜にはシャンデリアでムーディーな灯りを。美しい光こそが、最上級のもてなしになる。

The theme behind this project is "all-day dining," calling for a room that was not overly bright, with an ambience of calm and relaxation. Mozart Guerra's chandelier hangs from the ceiling, making an artistic statement with its use of rope and a classical appearance. Each area is characterized by different pieces of art, creating a space in which guests are entertained by the uniqueness of each visit. Daisuke Nakayama's artwork hangs on one wall, portraying the city of Osaka. During the day, natural light illuminates the space through a layer of sheer curtains, with evenings lit by the sensual ambience of the chandelier. Such beautiful illumination is the essence of the finest hospitality.

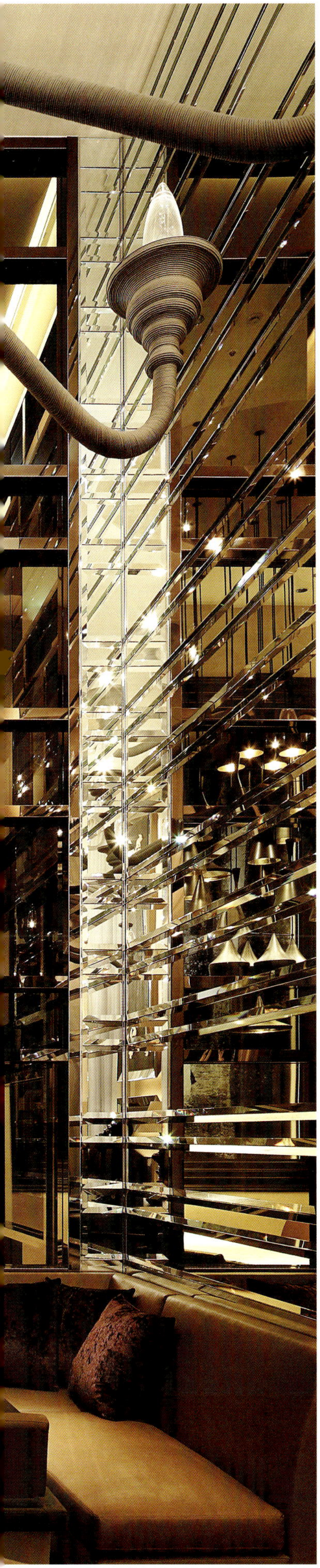
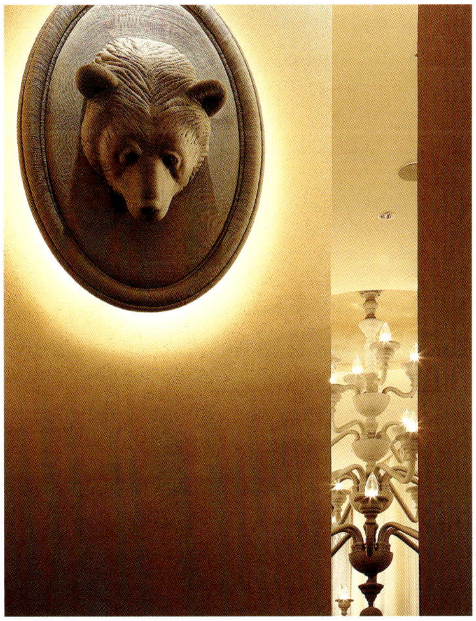
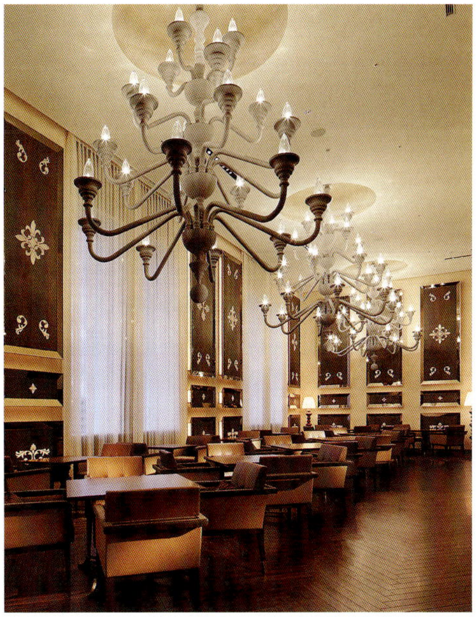
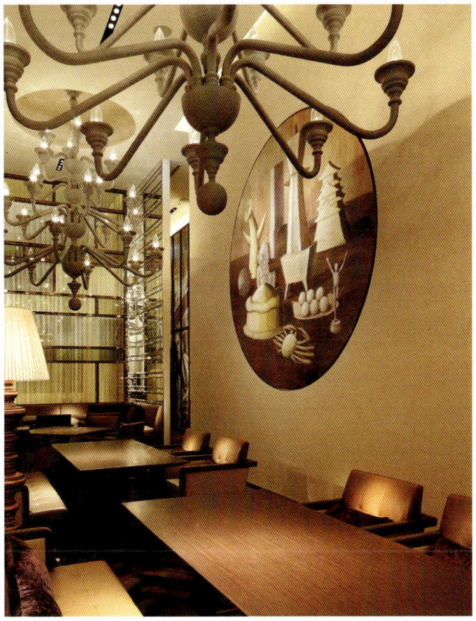
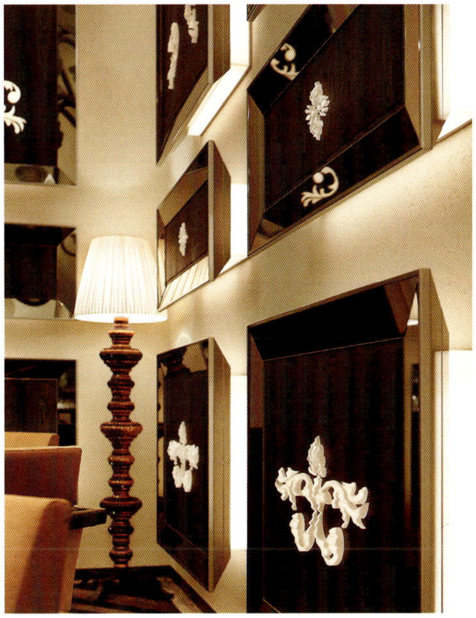

N° **033**
Osaka/Japan
Oct.2010

THE ST. REGIS OSAKA
Rue D'or

これほどまで、壁そのものがアイコンとなっているデザインは珍しいのではないか。吹き抜けには、キッチン雑貨やグラス、ワインボトルなどを陶器であしらった。それは「空間全体を楽しんで欲しい」というメッセージになっているという。ふたつのフロアを繋いでいくのが、階段脇に設定された、フランスの料理用語が刻まれた巨大な壁。開けられたさまざまな形状のブロンズミラーの"穴"は、フォトフレームのように景色を切り取ることを促している。ただ空間を仕切るためだけではなく、効果的に空間を彩ることが「壁」の役目であることを認識させられる。このレストランのすべての壁は、フランスの文化を表す額としてデザインされている。

This design, which transforms a wall into a visual icon, is rare. The open ceiling space is treated with ceramic kitchenware, glasses, and wine bottles, with the intention of creating a space that can be enjoyed entirely. The floors are connected with a great wall that stands adjacent to the staircase, its surface covered in expressions of French cuisine. The bronze mirror is cut in various shapes that capture the scene like small photo frames. As such, the wall is not merely a partition, but an important element that adds character to the space. The walls of this restaurant are designed specifically to frame the essence of French culture.

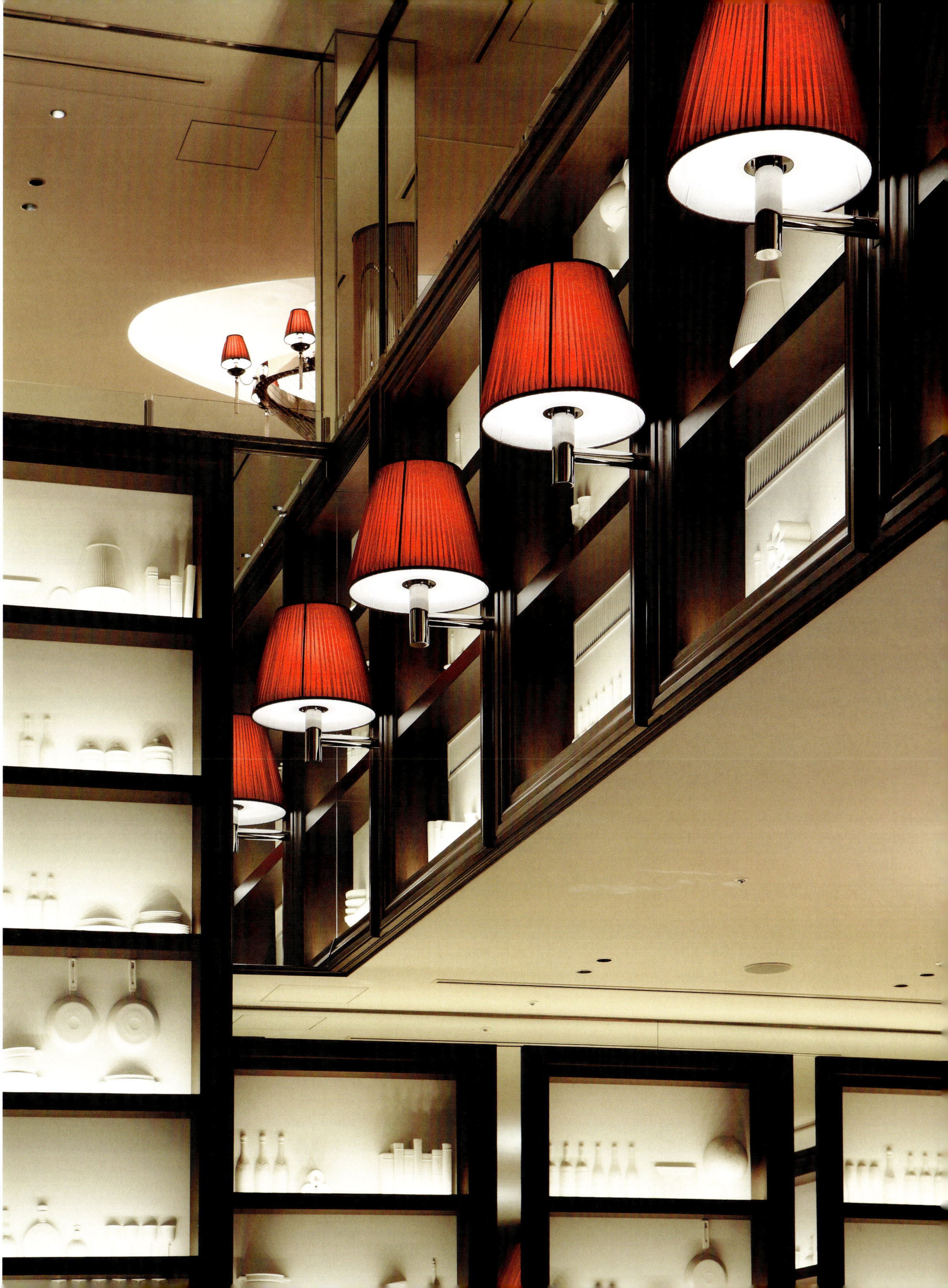

N°034
Tokyo/Japan
Feb.2002

HAJIME

銀座6丁目の裏通りに位置する和食レストランバー。大通りに面した光のラインを辿るうち、導かれるのは、12坪の店内。エントランスから壁に沿った光の帯は、そのまま空中を貫いてカウンターへと到達する。壁面の鏡によって増幅し、自由奔放に空間を占領する光。限られた空間にあえて施した光のラインは、唯一無二の存在感を放ちつつ、奥行きさえも生み出している。逆に、この裏通りの限定空間だからこそ可能な大胆な方法論なのかもしれない。ちなみに、その光のラインは、オーナーの「一行」という名前にも由来しているという。

This Japanese restaurant-bar is located off an alley in Ginza 6-Chome. Following the lights off the main street, the road eventually leads to a space of less than forty square meters. A line of light illuminates the wall from the entrance, cutting through the air to arrive at a counter. The light, amplified by the mirrored wall surface, freely inhabits the space. The contouring line exudes a singular presence, deliberately designed to emphasize the visual depth of the space. This daring methodology may have been possible precisely because the project takes place inside a small space found on the backstreets of the city. By the way, the line of light also signifies the owner's name, *Ikko*, which literally means "one line."

N°035
Tokyo/Japan
Apr.2013
SAVOY

ピザ生地を伸ばすのに使われるホワイトマーブルを用いたカウンターテーブルと壁面のダークグレーの大判タイルの対比が美しい。店の心臓部ともいえるピザ窯は、オリジナルで鍛造した鉄のプレートを市松模様に並べ、鏡面のリベットで留めることでアクセントとした。同じくホワイトマーブルのカウンター席は、一直線ではなく、凹型のようにリズムをつけることで少人数でもグループでも楽しめるよう配慮している。また、呼応するように球体のライトにもマーブル模様を施し、デザインの統一感を強調。白と黒が有機的に"溶け合った"デザインは、シックな印象を与えつつ、ピザ屋らしいカジュアルさも備えている。

The white marble counter creates a beautiful contrast against the dark grey tiles on the wall. The pizza oven, which is the heart of the restaurant, features a checkered pattern of custom-forged iron plates accented with mirrored rivets. Similarly, the white marble counter is designed in a dynamic curve to create rhythm when hosting varying numbers of guests. The white marble is also echoed in the spherical lighting, which ties the theme together. This organic melting pot of black and white creates a chic impression, while simultaneously maintaining the casual pizza-restaurant ambience.

N°036
Kyoto/Japan
Apr.1999
sinamo

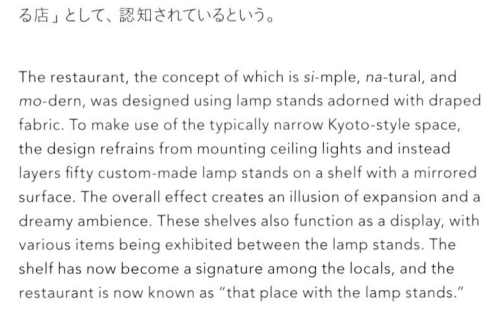

"シ"ンプルで"ナ"チュラルで"モ"ダンという店のコンセプトに合わせたデザインとなるように設置したのは、ドレープが可愛い照明スタンド。京都特有のうなぎの寝床のような細長い空間を活かすために、天井に照明器具は設置せず、壁面にミラーを張り込んで陳列棚に50個ものオリジナル照明スタンドを重ねていった。実際よりも広く感じるという効果と共に、幻想的な空間を演出することに成功している。この棚には、通常は照明スタンドの合間に雑貨が陳列されていて、商品棚としても機能しており、「あの照明スタンドのある店」として、認知されているという。

The restaurant, the concept of which is *si*-mple, *na*-tural, and *mo*-dern, was designed using lamp stands adorned with draped fabric. To make use of the typically narrow Kyoto-style space, the design refrains from mounting ceiling lights and instead layers fifty custom-made lamp stands on a shelf with a mirrored surface. The overall effect creates an illusion of expansion and a dreamy ambience. These shelves also function as a display, with various items being exhibited between the lamp stands. The shelf has now become a signature among the locals, and the restaurant is now known as "that place with the lamp stands."

N°037
Osaka/Japan
Jul.1996
熱烈食堂 HEPナビオ店

「ほら、赤い店」「ああ、中華鍋のライトの店だ」「そうそう、何だか光っている店だよ」。そんな会話が容易に想像できてしまうほど、熱烈食堂は、「分かりやすく、憶えやすく、説明しやすい」のが特徴。真っ赤な店内は、複合商業施設内のレストランフロアにある店舗という条件から導き出されたものだった。視認性を強くして顧客を惹き付け、調理道具を用いてデザインされた照明器具でゲストの印象をさらに強くする。「あ、中華鍋だ!」と驚くゲストの顔が浮かぶようではないか。テーブルのガラス天板に反射する光は、イメージを増幅させる効果も担っている。

A typical explanation of this restaurant would go like this: "It's that red place with the glowing wok." The restaurant is so easily identifiable, easily remembered, and easy to explain. To solve the problem of the restaurant's location, the interior was painted red to outshine competitors on the restaurant floor of a commercial complex. The design attracts visitors with its unmistakable visual elements, with lighting fixtures that borrow from the shapes of cookware. Surprised guests should surely comment on the illuminated wok. The light reflecting off the glass tabletops also amplifies the restaurant's lively image.

N° 038
Tokyo/Japan
Nov.2011

ひつまぶし名古屋備長
池袋パルコ店

供される食事が生まれる過程に、飲食店デザインのヒントを探すことが、ストーリーを生み出すのだと森田は語る。ひつまぶしならば、鰻を焼く際に使う「串」だ。行灯を構成する格子状の桟は、ステンレス製の串。コスト減もさることながら、「鰻を食べるのだ!」という期待感をあおるインパクトも十二分。商業施設の飲食店フロアにあって一際目を引く鰻のオブジェと相まって、食欲をそそる。ひつまぶしを食べるには、ゴージャス過ぎては決していけない。チープ過ぎてももちろん美味しくは見えない。落ち着いて、お櫃に盛られた贅沢なひつまぶしに向き合うためのちょうどよい案配。「串」の演出が効いている。

According to Morita, a story is created when one discovers hints for restaurant design within the process of serving food. In the case of *hitsumabushi*, a local dish in Nagoya, the hint lay in the skewers used for roasting eels. As a result, stainless skewers were integrated into the latticed framing of the lanterns. This design not only reduces cost but enthusiastically encourages guests' appetites for the forthcoming *unagi* dish. The interior design, when combined with a striking eel-shaped sculpture, captures attention on the restaurant floor inside a commercial building. *Hitsumabushi* does not call for over-the-top extravagance. Of course, it cannot look cheap, either. A balanced arrangement allows one to sit down and take a moment to enjoy the delicious indulgence. The "skewers" add an extra spice.

N°039
Tokyo/Japan
May 2012

神戸・六甲道 ぎゅんた
ルミネ新宿1

和のテイストを重視しながらも、モダンなイメージのデザインに仕上げたのは、多くの女性により気軽に鉄板焼きを楽しんでもらえるようにという思いからだった。メニューの木札が入口から誘うように連続して繋がり、店内には竹を用いた照明がやわらかな光でリズムを作っている。各席の腰壁を通常よりも高めに設定することで、視線を気にすることなく食事できるようにと配慮した。複合施設内の店ながら、席ごとにゆるやかに変化があるために、いつ来ても新鮮な感覚を得ることができる。鉄板焼きの賑わう空気に、ほんの少しの洗練を加えることで、より万人に受けるデザインを実現している。

While preserving Japanese tastes, this design was finished with a modern image to attract a wider female audience for enjoying the Japanese griddle cuisine of *teppanyaki*. A series of wooden menu tags continues from the entrance, drawing the guests into an interior illuminated by the soft and rhythmic light of bamboo lighting. The knee walls were measured to stand higher than usual, creating privacy around the tables. For the interior of a restaurant situated within a commercial complex, the space offers refreshing experiences through a gradual yet noticeable change in each of the tables. By adding a hint of refinement in the lively air of the *teppanyaki*, the project achieves a sense of universality in its design.

N°040
Kyoto/Japan
Mar.2004

Hamac de Paradis 寒梅館

同志社大学の学食でありながら、一般の方も利用できるサロン。狙いは、学生と社会人との垣根を越えたコミュニケーションだった。そのために、少人数／大人数を問わずミーティングが行いやすいレイアウト、あるいは会話が弾むようなリズム感ある光が用意された。空間内を回遊するように続いていく照明には、校歌がモチーフとなって刻まれている。また壁沿いには、椅子にもなり、モノを置くスペースにもなるように照明が配されている。柔らかく寛げる空間であることと同時に、多機能であること。レンガ造りの格式高い伝統建築に、ポップで新しい学館内レストラン・カフェを提案している。

While this project is the student cafeteria of Doshisha University, it is also a public salon. The objective was to encourage open communication between the students and the rest of the public. To achieve this goal, tables were positioned so that meetings of all sizes could easily be held, with rhythmical light to inspire conversation. The lighting fixture circulates around the entire space, engraved with motifs of the school song. Additional lighting line the walls, which can also be converted into chairs and spaces for placing one's belongings. The space is designed for both functionality and relaxation. The project proposes a fresh take on the student restaurant-café, built inside the formality of traditional brick architecture.

N°041
Osaka/Japan
Sep.1995
へちま

まるでアートのような「竹籤」使い、壁面の上部から吊して照明を当て、さらに天板に敷き詰めてガラスでフィックスして中からそれぞれに光を照らす。この店を構成するデザイン要素は、「竹籤」と「光」だけなのだ。だが、この縦長の狭小空間に快適さとゆとりを感じられるのは、素材を限定したこと、また同じ素材で違う使い方をしたことの効果による。直線的な光は揺れる竹籤によって表情を作り、生み出された影が空間を和らげる。デザインとはひとつの素材と光だけでも成立することを、この店舗は十二分に教えてくれる。

These strips of bamboo have been made into a work of art. Some hang from the top of the wall surface, and some are spread on tabletops and fixed with illuminated glass. The compositional design elements of this restaurant are limited to these bamboo strips and light. Within the walls of this narrow space, one can feel a sense of ampleness, an effect achieved by limiting the use of materials and echoing them in completely different ways. The linear light creates unique expressions with the swinging strips of bamboo, casting soothing shadows. The restaurant is an example of how design can be achieved through the use of a single material and light.

Château Restaurant Joël Robuchon

N°042
Tokyo/Japan
Dec.2004

どんなシチュエーションの空間であるかを分かりやすく伝えるのが森田の役目のひとつであるが、シャトーをリノベーションした世界最高峰のフレンチレストランでは、色がデザインの鍵になっている。既存の建物を彼らの歴史ごとシャンパンゴールドのガラス内に閉じ込めた『ジョエル・ロブション』。別世界の広がる『ルージュバー』は、ロブション氏のテーマカラーであるルージュになっている。また、カジュアルな雰囲気も併せ持つ空間『ラ ターブル ドゥ ジョエル・ロブション』は、伝統色でもあるパープルで統一した。求められたのは上品であることだが、それだけではない。遊び心と呼ぶには少々強烈な配色も、バカラのシャンデリアや随所に埋め込まれたクリスタルと相まって、独特の優雅さを獲得している。

One of Morita's tasks as a designer is to define and convey exactly what type of situation a space is made for. In the case of the world's top French restaurant with a renovated chateau, color is the essence of design. Joël Robuchon captures its own building and history behind a champagne-gold glass, while the Rouge Bar is colored in Robuchon's rouge. LA TABLE de Joël Robuchon, a space with a more casual ambience, is dressed with a traditional purple. The project demanded a refined grace, but the design transcends this notion. The palette, slightly too bold to be called playful, achieves a distinctive elegance when combined with the Baccarat chandelier and embedded crystals.

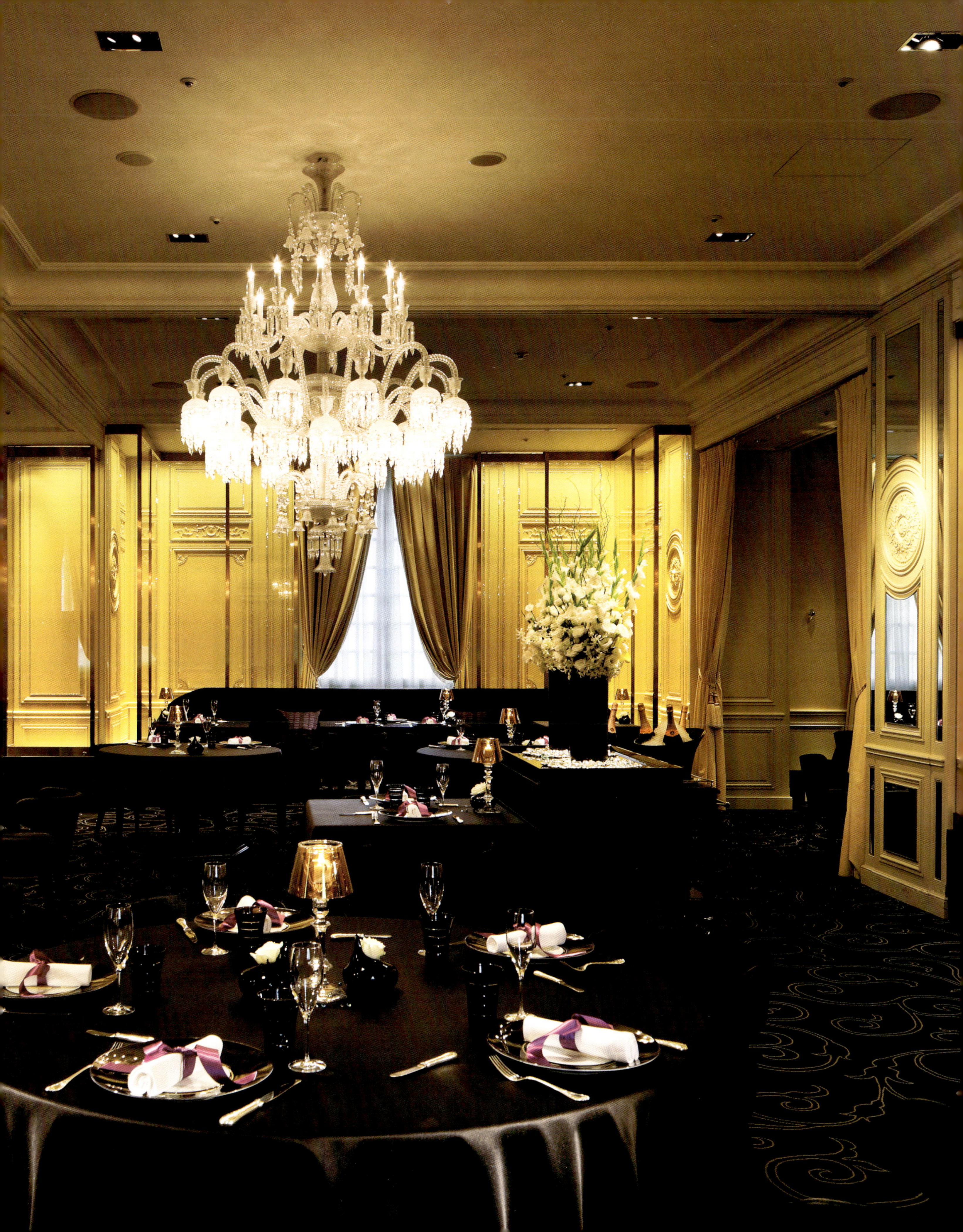

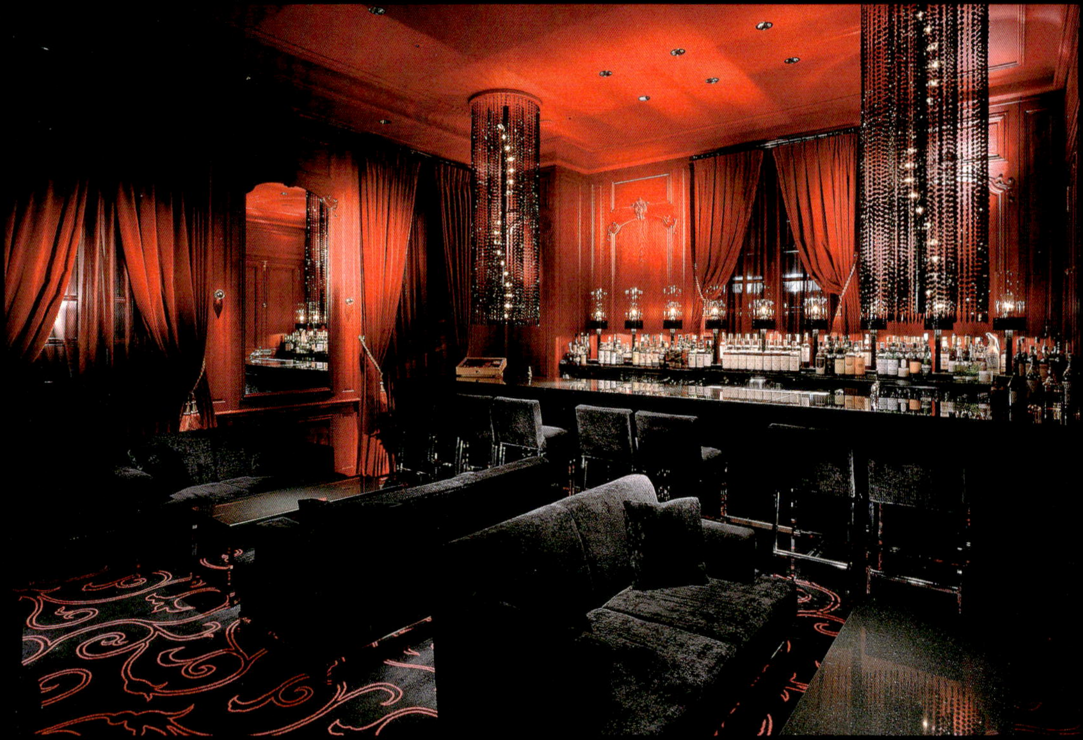

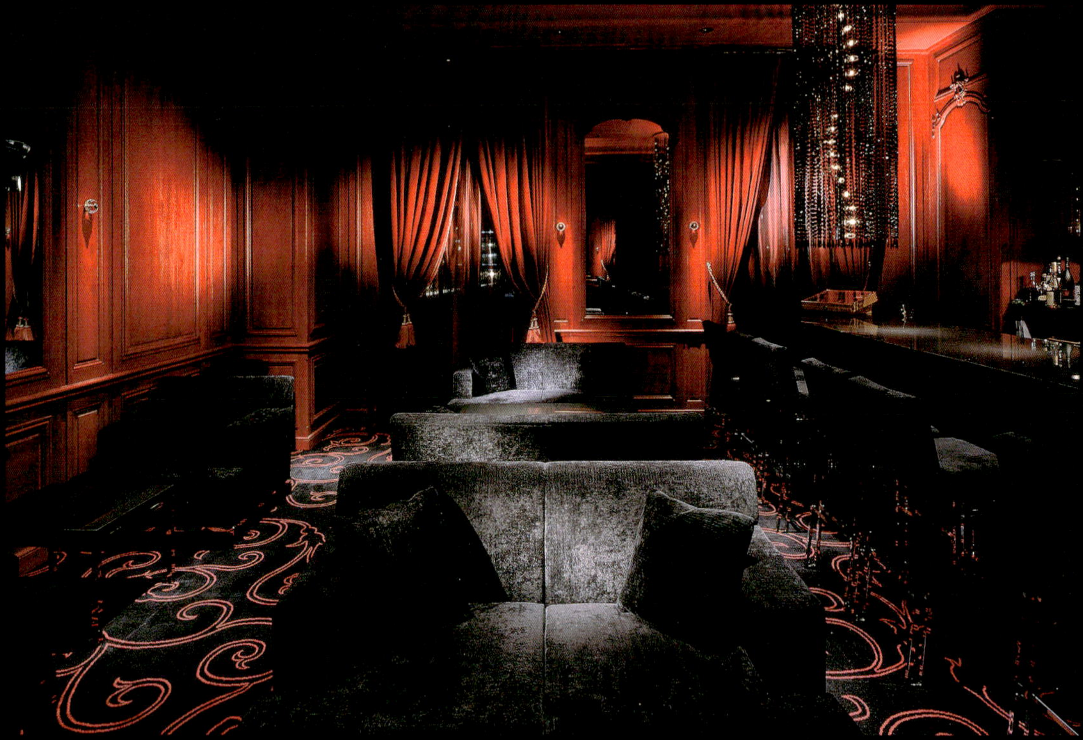

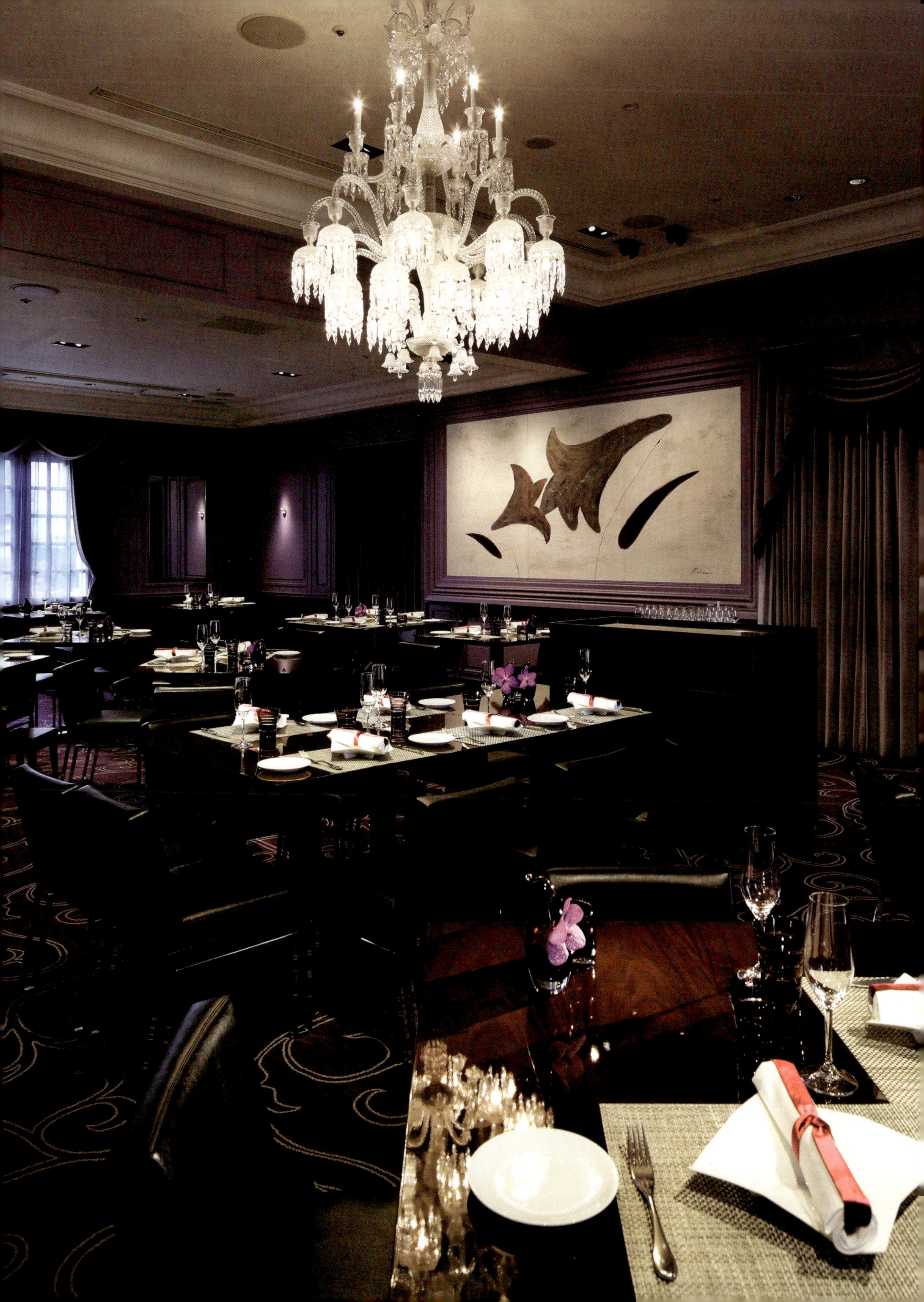

N°043
Tokyo/Japan
Apr.2004
LE CAFÉ de Joël Robuchon

ジョエル・ロブション氏の象徴的なカラーは、赤と黒。炎と大地を意味するこのツートンカラーを基調に、1万個ものクリスタルをドレープ状に配することで、相対するふたつの効果を融和させている。軽やかさとラグジュアリー。あるいは、一流のカフェに求められる機能性と優雅さ。「料理は、愛から始まる芸術である」というロブション氏の言葉は、味わうだけでなく、体感すべきものなのだろう。パティシエの流れるような仕事姿を眺める、まるでプライベートサロンのようなカウンター席。美味しいスイートな時間に浸るためのデザインが施されている。

The colors of red and black are symbolic of Joël Robuchon himself, and this palette is a metaphor for flame and earth. With ten thousand crystals draped over the two-tone palette, this dynamic contrast is thrown into a harmonious relief. The design is that of lightness and luxury, or elegance and practicality, demanded of a first-class café. Robuchon's philosophy that "cuisine is an act of love" suggests an appreciation of experience that transcends the plate. The counter seats offer unobstructed views of the pâtissier's work, as though guests were seated in a private salon. The space is designed to immerse guests in a deliciously sweet time.

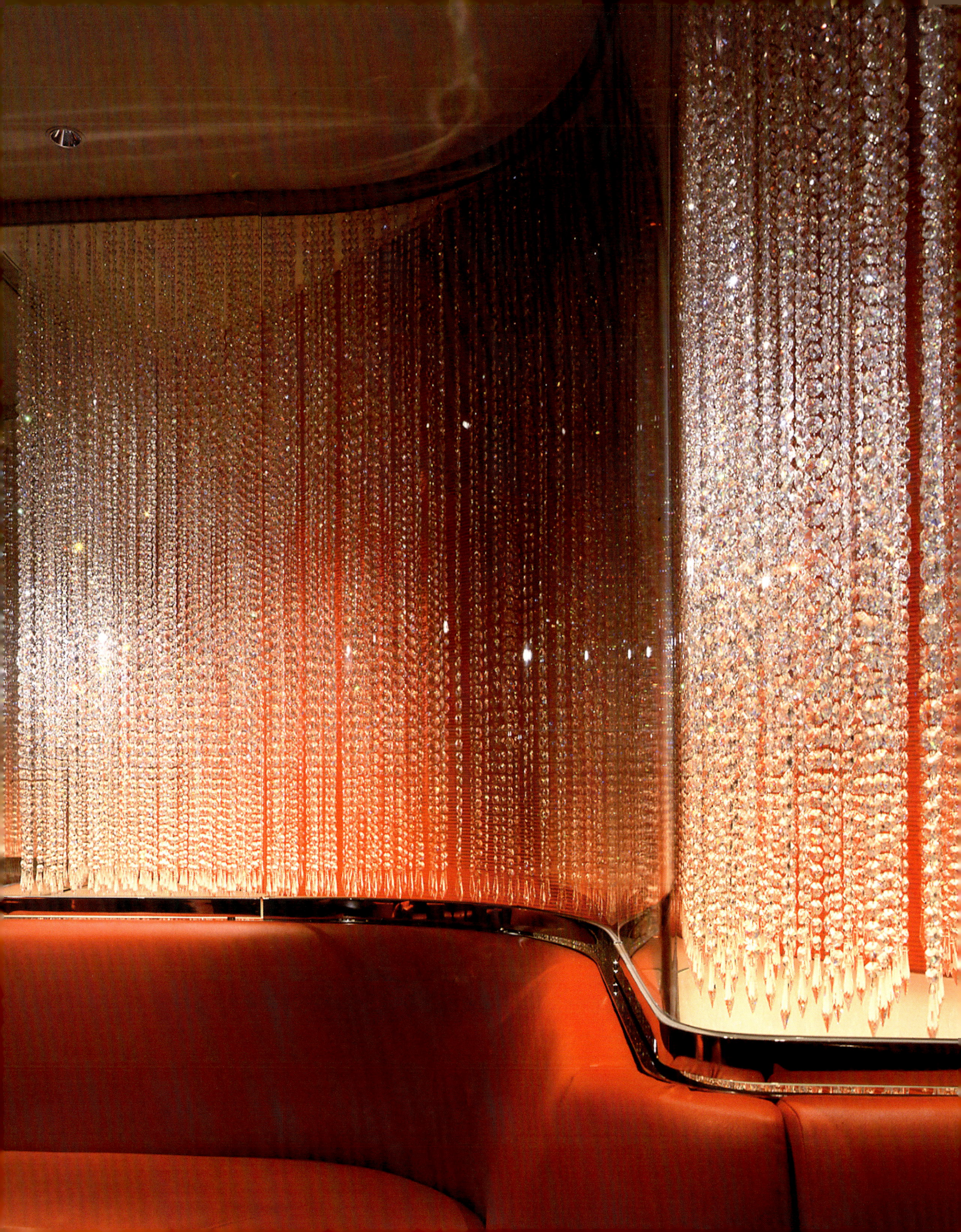

N°044
Osaka/Japan
Mar.2008

DBL

高さ6mの広い天井に揺れるのは、倉科昌高氏による唐草アート。2Dから3Dの世界へと連なるアルミパンチング製の唐草模様は、自然光あるいは計算された調光によって幻想的な影となって映し出される。さらに唐草の背後にはさまざまな動物が隠されていて、「物語の中に迷い込んだかのような」演出となっている。呼応するように2階のバーラウンジには、アイラインに、唐草模様をあしらったオイルランプを包むガラスシェード。唐草という同一のテーマを用いながら、1階と2階でまったく違う表情に性格付けている。空間を仕切るのは、物理的な構造だけでなく、素材や色、あるいは光であることが、森田のデザインからは伝わってくる。

Works of *karakusa* art by Masataka Kurashina sway in arabesque from an expansive six-meter ceiling. The coiling pattern on perforated aluminum flourishes as it grows into a three-dimensional world, casting shadows under the illumination of both natural and controlled lighting. Camouflaged by the arabesque, a menagerie of animals hides in the background, luring guests into a storybook atmosphere. In the second-floor bar lounge, the pattern is echoed onto the glass shades of the oil lamps. Although the theme of *karakusa* remains, the pattern evolves into completely different expressions on the first and the second floor. Morita's design exemplifies how a space can be partitioned through the controlled use of material, color, and light, without having to rely on physical structures.

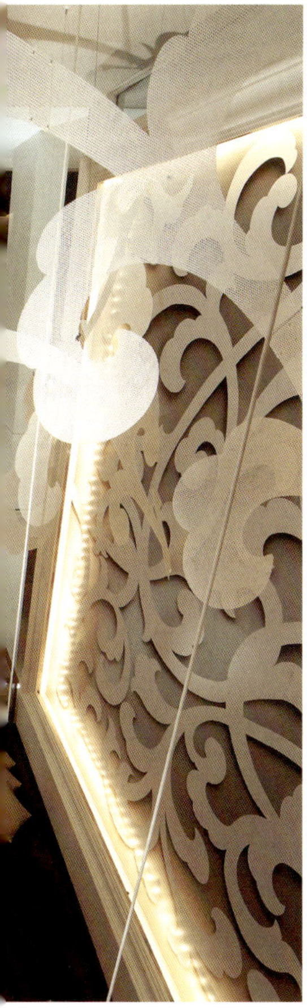
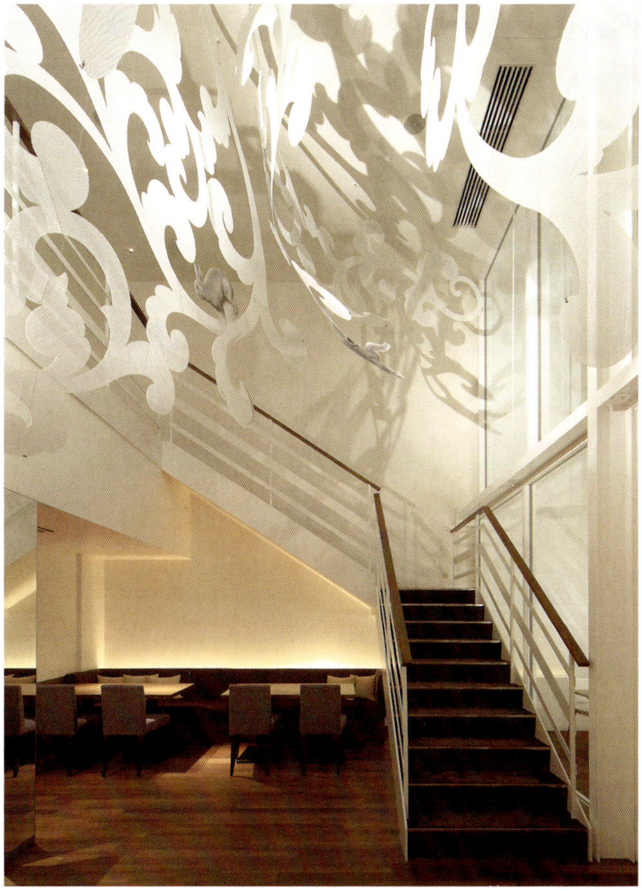
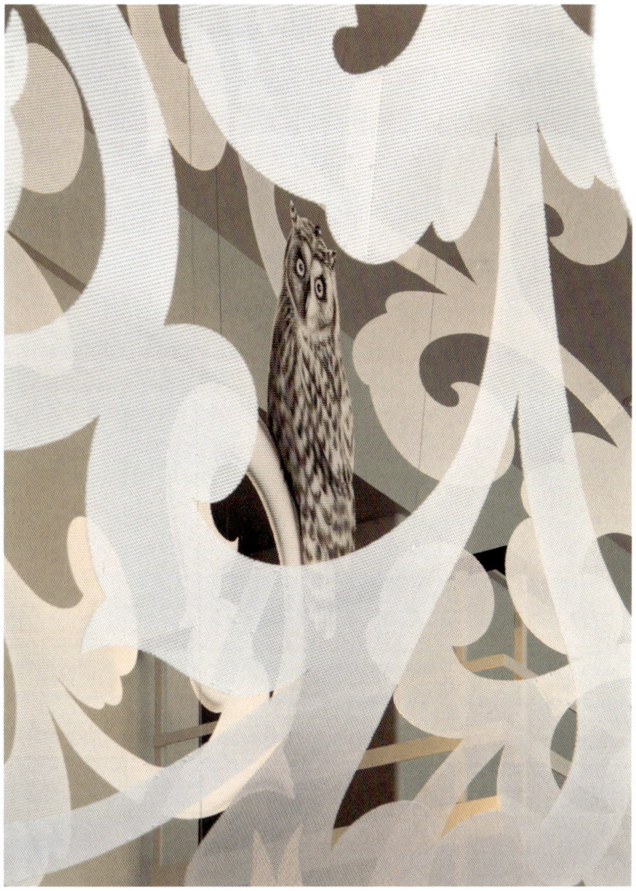
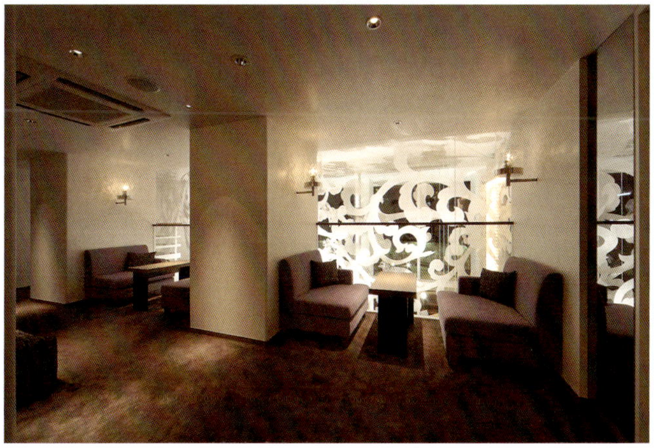

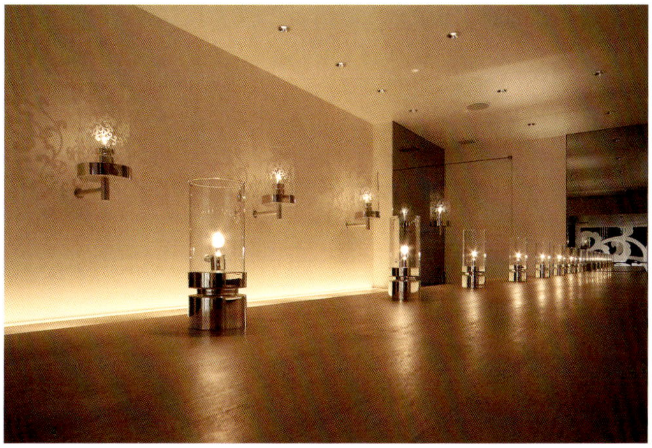
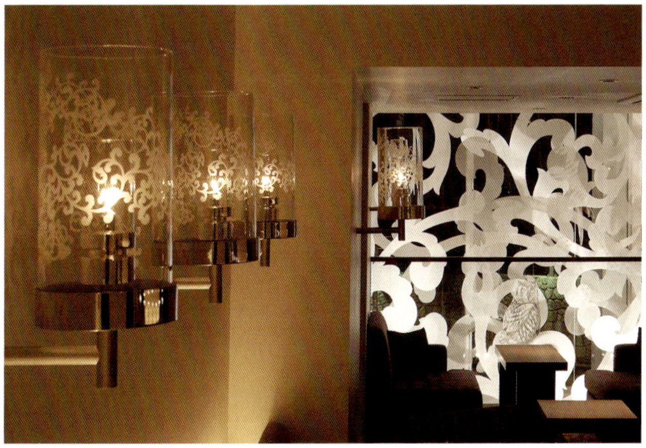

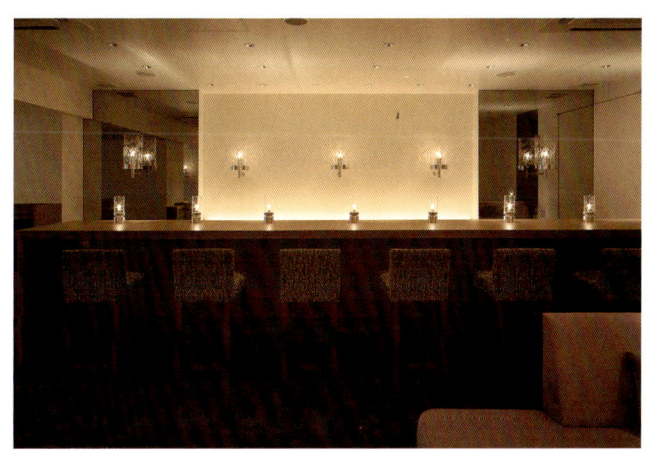

N°045
Tokyo/Japan
Dec.2005
DEAN & DELUCA AOYAMA

多数の店舗を展開する「DEAN & DELUCA」では、強烈なデザインを提示することはできないが、メッセージ性の強いファサードなど、森田らしさが随所に見える店舗となった「DEAN & DELUCA AOYAMA」。ロゴの名前が入ったバッグをモチーフとしたライト、あるいはシルバーの天井は、華美ではなくとも、記憶に残る強さを持っている。その「記憶に残る」という効果こそが、外苑西通りと青山通りの交差する一等地に構えるカフェに求められたものだった。あの場所には「DEAN & DELUCA」があると知らしめるためには、適度に品がよく、適度に強いデザインが必要だった。そのバランスこそが、この店舗のデザイン、最大の特徴だろう。

Although it is difficult to be daring when working with a fully developed brand such as DEAN & DELUCA, Morita's work for DEAN & DELUCA AOYAMA is interspersed with his signature style, including an evocative facade. The light fixtures with logo motifs and the silver ceiling may not be dazzling, but they carry enough power to leave a memorable impression. This was precisely the goal for a café that stands on one of the busiest intersections of the prime Aoyama area: to create a place that remains in memory. For DEAN & DELUCA to establish its presence, the design needed to be reasonably refined and tolerably bold. The balancing of these two elements is what characterizes the design of this project.

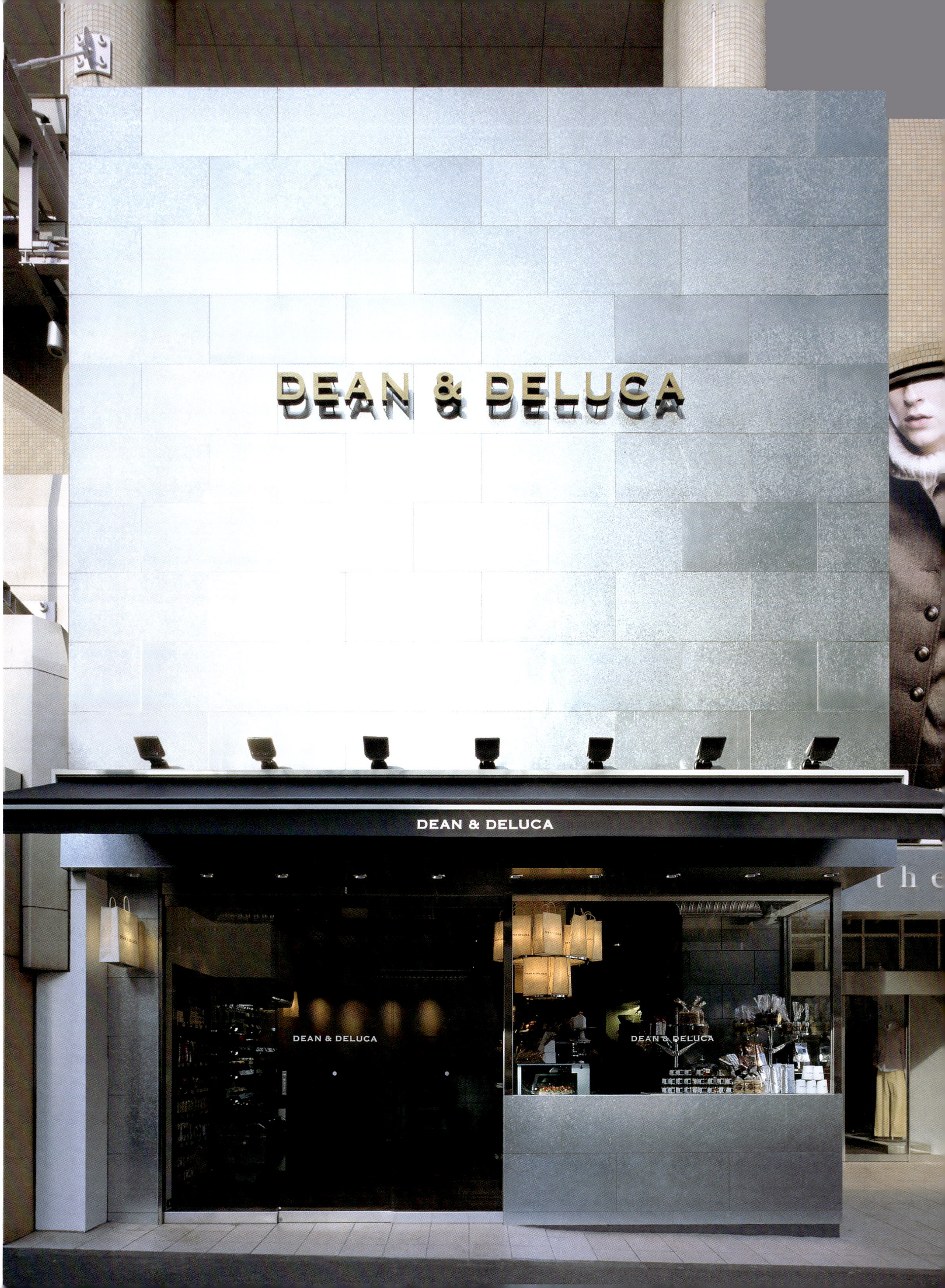
DEAN & DELUCA
DEAN & DELUCA
DEAN & DELUCA
DEAN & DELUCA

N°046
Tokyo/Japan
Oct.2011

ISLAND VEGGIE
Hawaiian Veggie Style

「偉大な生命」という意味を含むマクロビオティックのレストランでは、当然ながらデザインにおいても同様の思想が求められる。そのために用いたのは、長く愛されてきた、時代を含んだアンティークの家具。棚や看板に手を加え、新たな素材ではなし得ない温もりを店内に宿らせている。グリッドによって扉ひとつひとつを仕切ることで、新たな価値観さえ付与されている。シャンデリアの瀟洒なイメージの強い森田だが、ニュートラルなデザインでも根本が変わることはない。店のコンセプトを体現するという意味においては同じ地点からスタートしていると言える。ハワイアン・マクロビオティックの店舗にも、森田らしさが垣間見えるのだ。

One of the philosophies of this macrobiotic restaurant is the importance of the *great circle of life*. The design for this project, therefore, also had to agree with this concept. In order to accomplish this, Morita used a set of lovingly maintained antique furniture. Modifying the shelving and the restaurant sign, the space carries an air of warmth unattainable through modern materials. Using a grid to frame the doors, the design even ventures into the idea of finding a new sense of value. Although known for his stylish chandeliers, Morita's roots remain in this neutral design. In fact, both Morita's ideals and those of this restaurant share a common starting point: to bring to life the concept behind the business. Even within a Hawaiian macrobiotic restaurant, hints of Morita's style can be found.

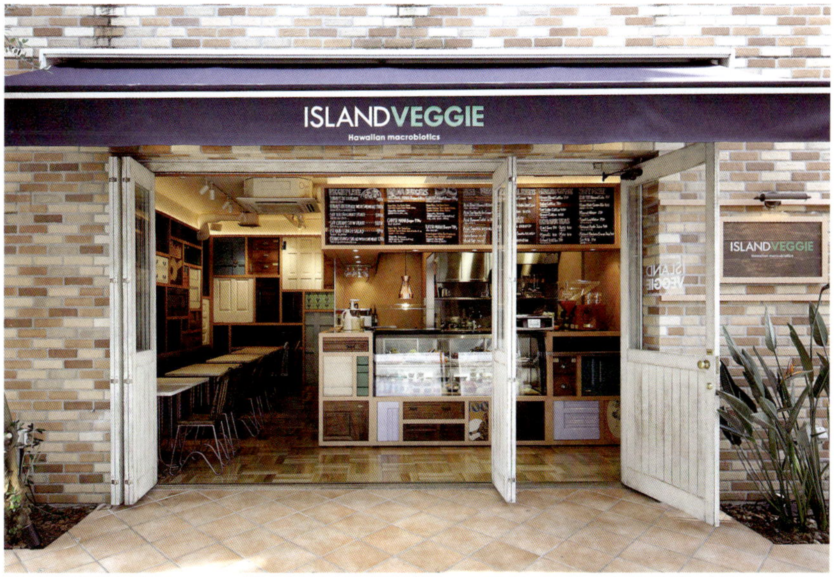
ISLANDVEGGIE
Hawaiian macrobiotics

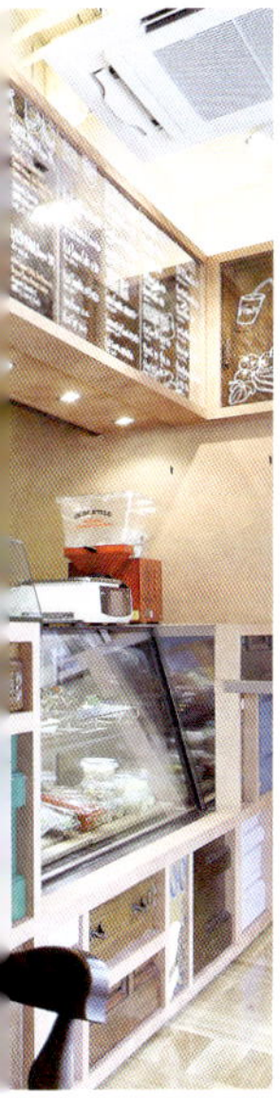

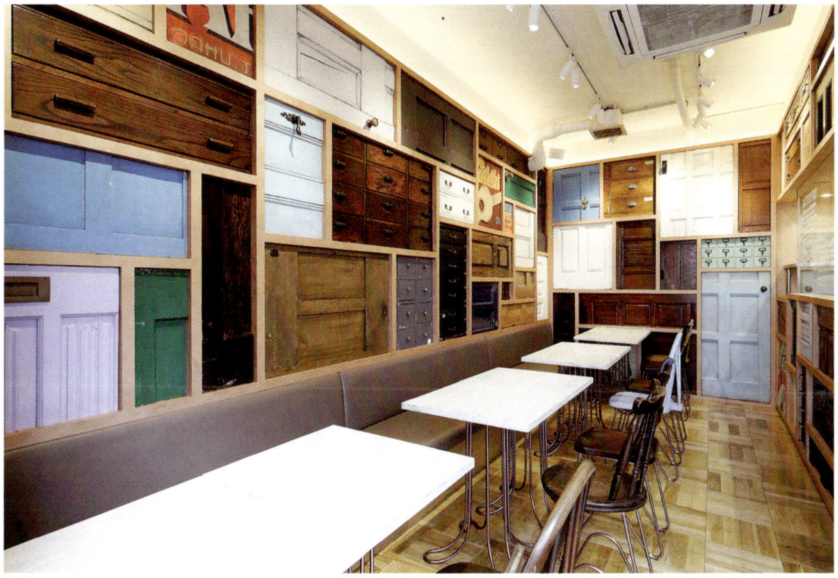

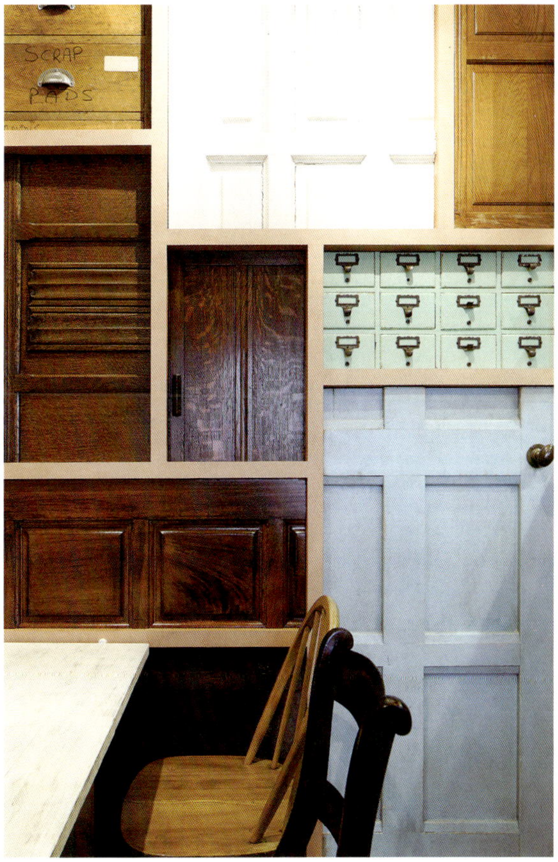

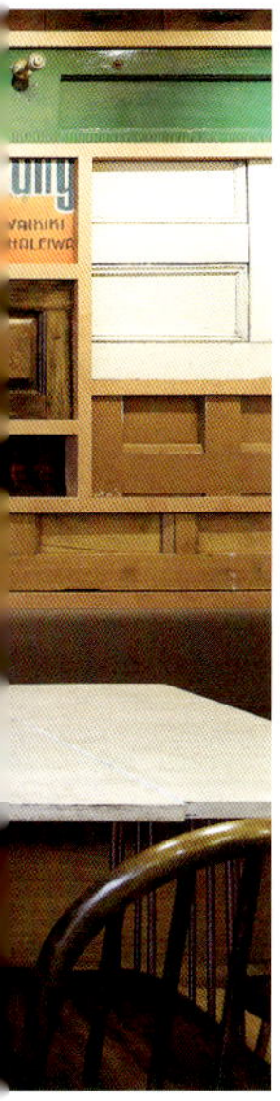

N°047
Tokyo/Japan
Apr.2010

CHOiCE!

ビルの3階にありながら、開放感に溢れるカジュアルダイニング最大の特徴は、昼と夜とで表情がまったく変わることだろう。広いテラスの自然光の入るシチュエーションであることも魅力のひとつだが、バーとなる夜の間接照明によって、ガラリと空気が変わる。昼夜どちらにも対応することが、デザインには求められた。森田が表情の違いを反映させる素材として選んだのは"土"だった。左官職人の久住有生氏を起用し、変化をつけた"土"でカウンターを彩った。独特の黄土色は光に照らされて、空間を柔らかく包み込む。光を反射させるために何を選ぶのか。素材とは、デザインの根幹をなすものでもある。

This open and airy casual dining restaurant located on the third floor is characterized by its dramatic shift from daytime to evening atmosphere. While the large terrace offers ample sunlight, the air suddenly changes as the space transforms into an evening bar with indirect lighting. The project demanded a design that responded to both of these contrasting situations. As a solution, Morita chose the element of earth to reflect these different expressions. Master plasterer Naoki Kusumi surfaced the counter with a variety of plastered earth, and the uniquely radiant yellow ochre blankets the space with velvety warmth. The key here lay in the choice of material used to catch and reflect light. Material is what holds the very foundations of design.

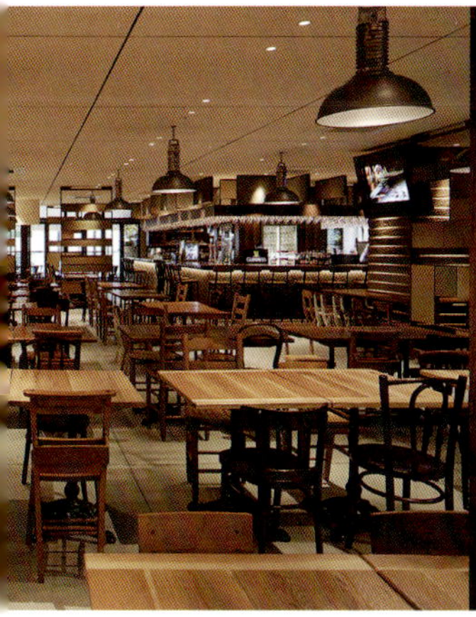

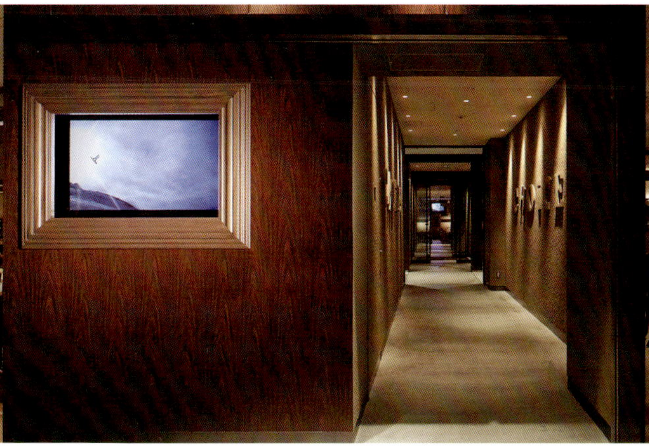

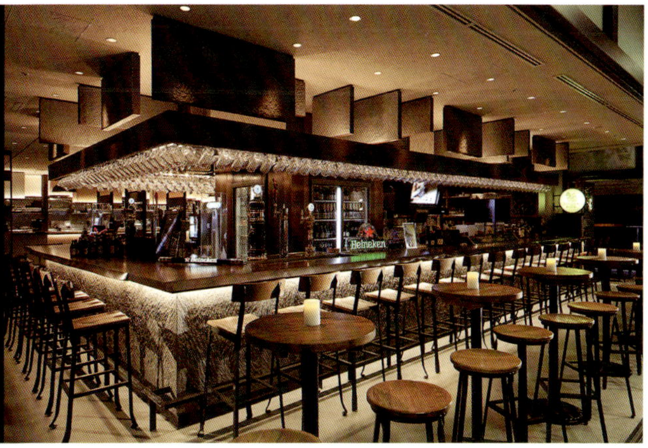

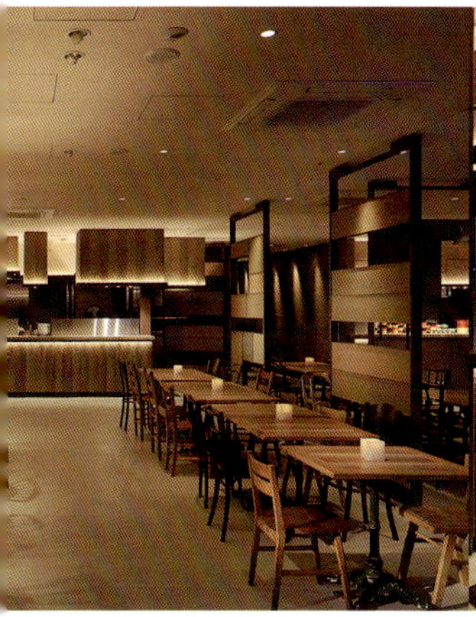

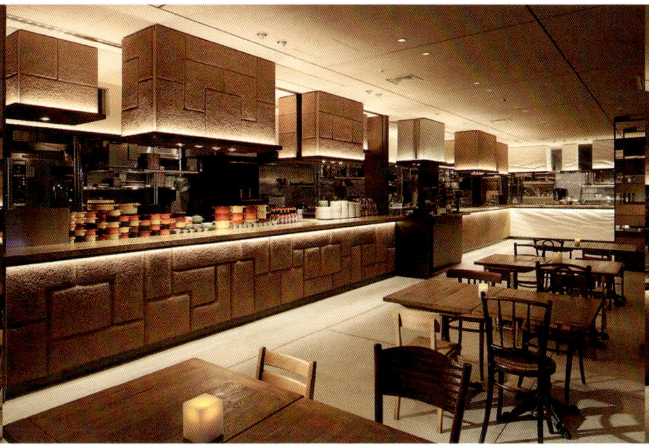

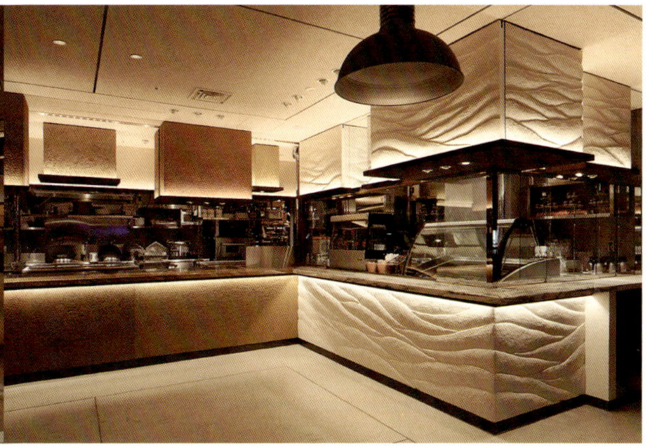

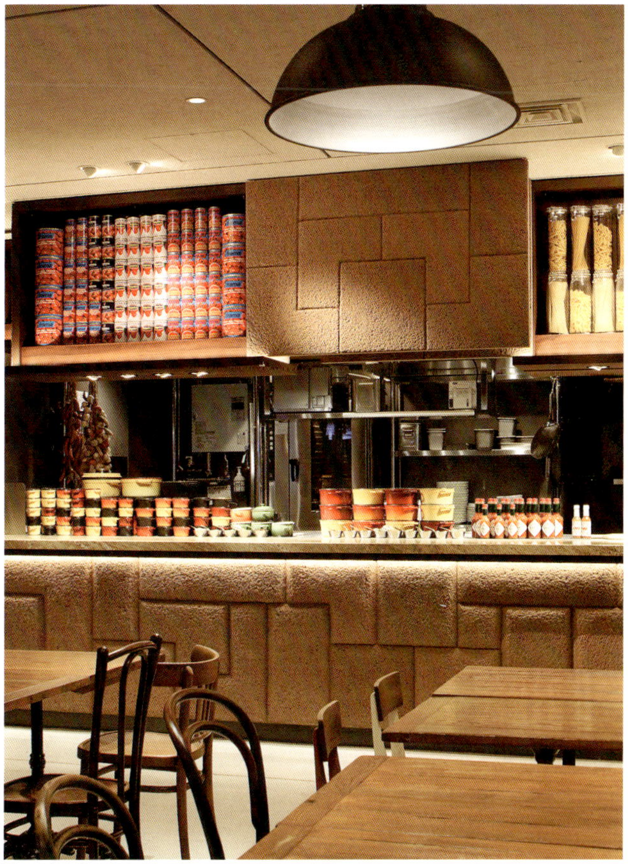

N°048
Tokyo/Japan
Jun.2012

国会中央食堂

デザインはひとつのメッセージでもある。特に限定的な機能を持った空間ならば、そのメッセージの強さこそが、コンセプトの根幹をなす。国会中央食堂という一般人の入ることのできない場所を森田が手がけたことの意味はなんだろう。「日本の将来を牽引するための力の源、休息の場として活用してもらいたい」という思考からスタートしたという。日本の象徴たる「家紋」をモチーフとした照明、壁面に収められた四季折々の日本の写真。日本という国を導くために、何を思い、考えて欲しいのか。まるで一般人の"代弁者"のように、デザインに込められているのは、日本を統べるための美意識だろう。明るく誇り高い食堂になっている。

Design is a kind of message. Especially for a space with strictly defined functions, the concept must be based on its persuasiveness. What does it mean for Morita to work on this private cafeteria found inside the National Diet Building? The process began from his thoughts on creating a source of inspiration for leading the future of Japan, as well as a place of relaxation and rest. The lighting is adorned with motifs of a quintessentially Japanese family crest, while the walls are covered with photographs capturing Japan throughout its changing seasons. The key lay in directing the thoughts and inspirations of those who run the country. Like a spokesperson, the design is coded with an aesthetic sensibility fit for leading Japan. The result is a bright and dignified cafeteria.

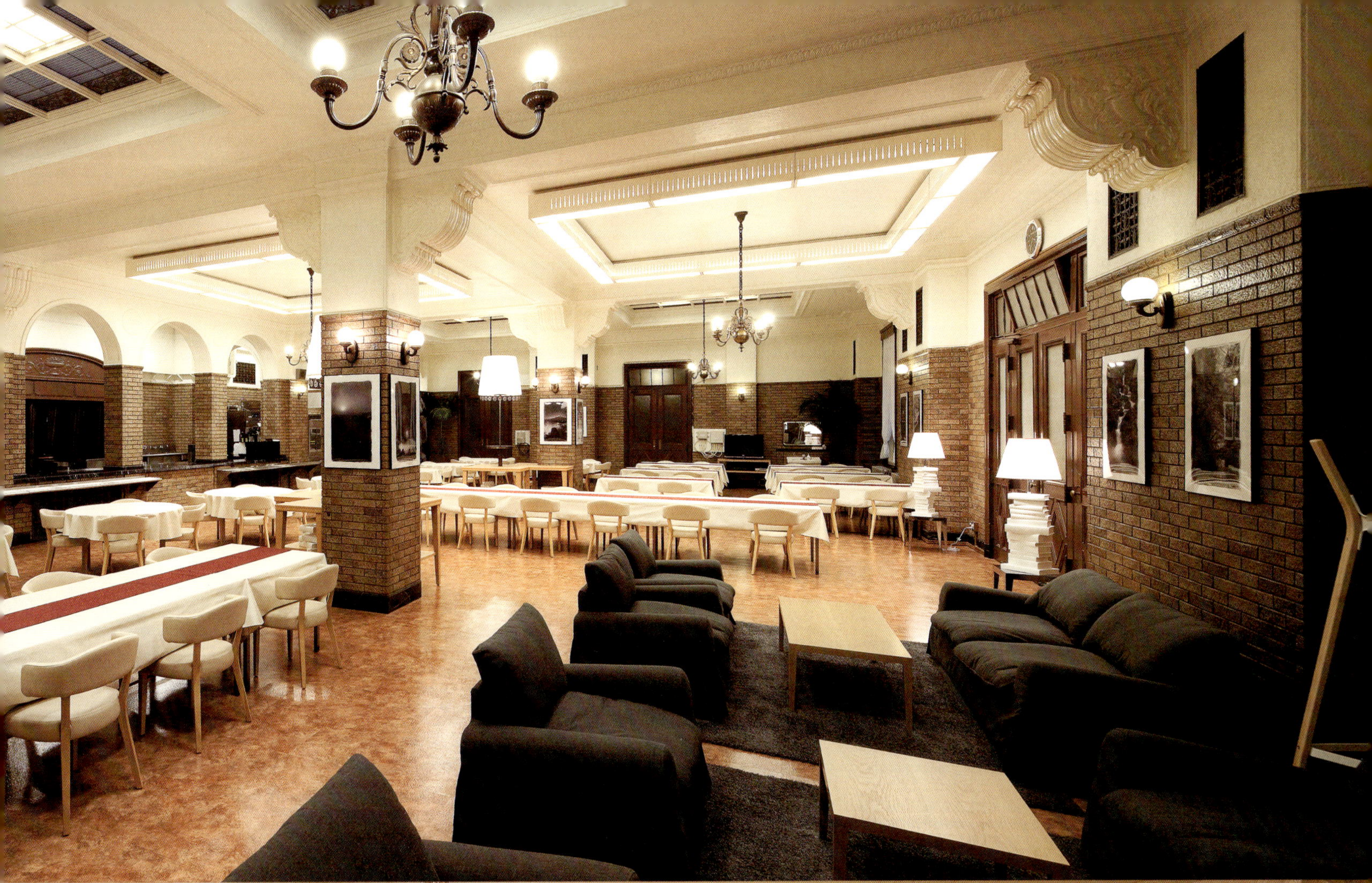

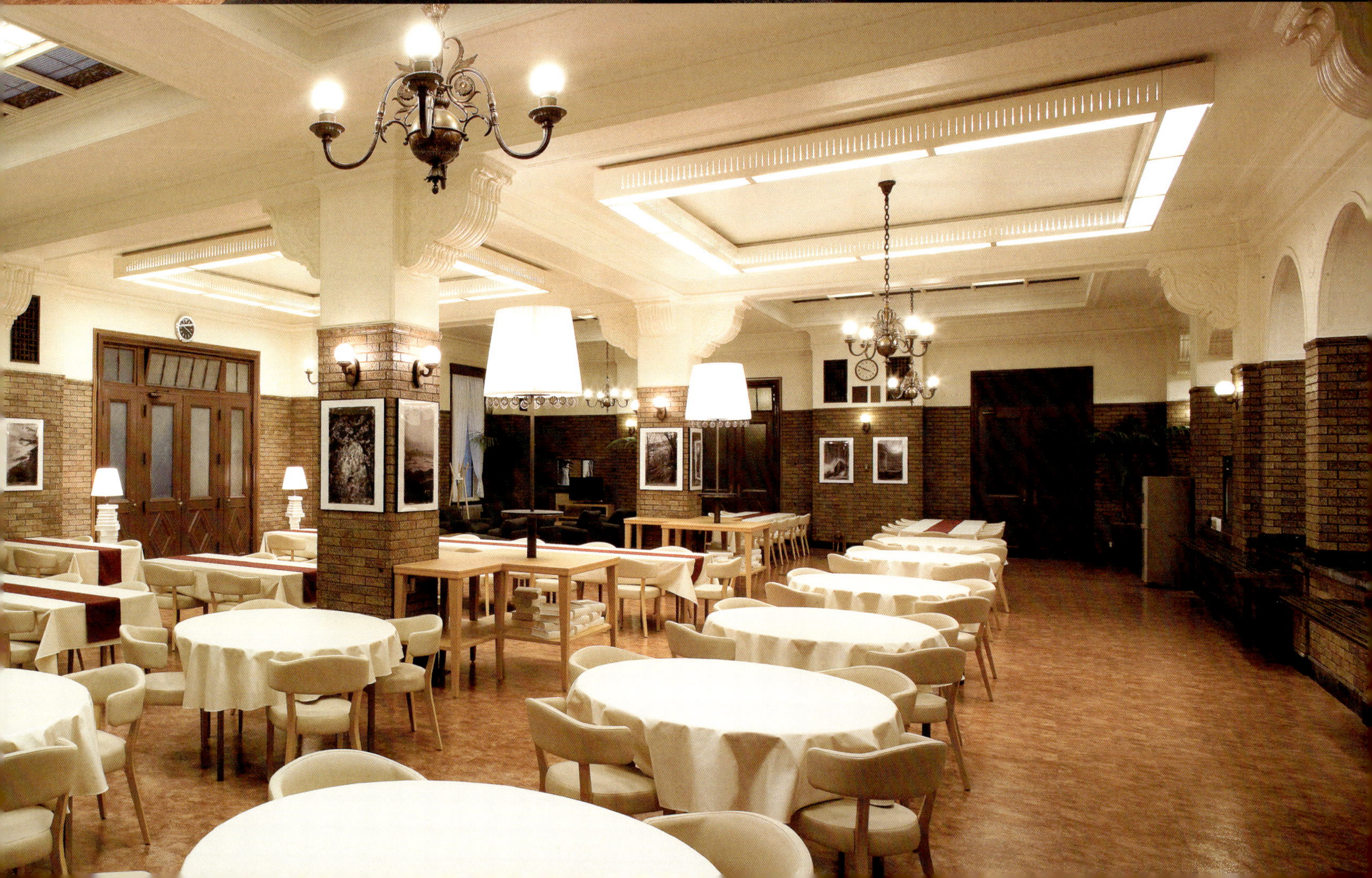

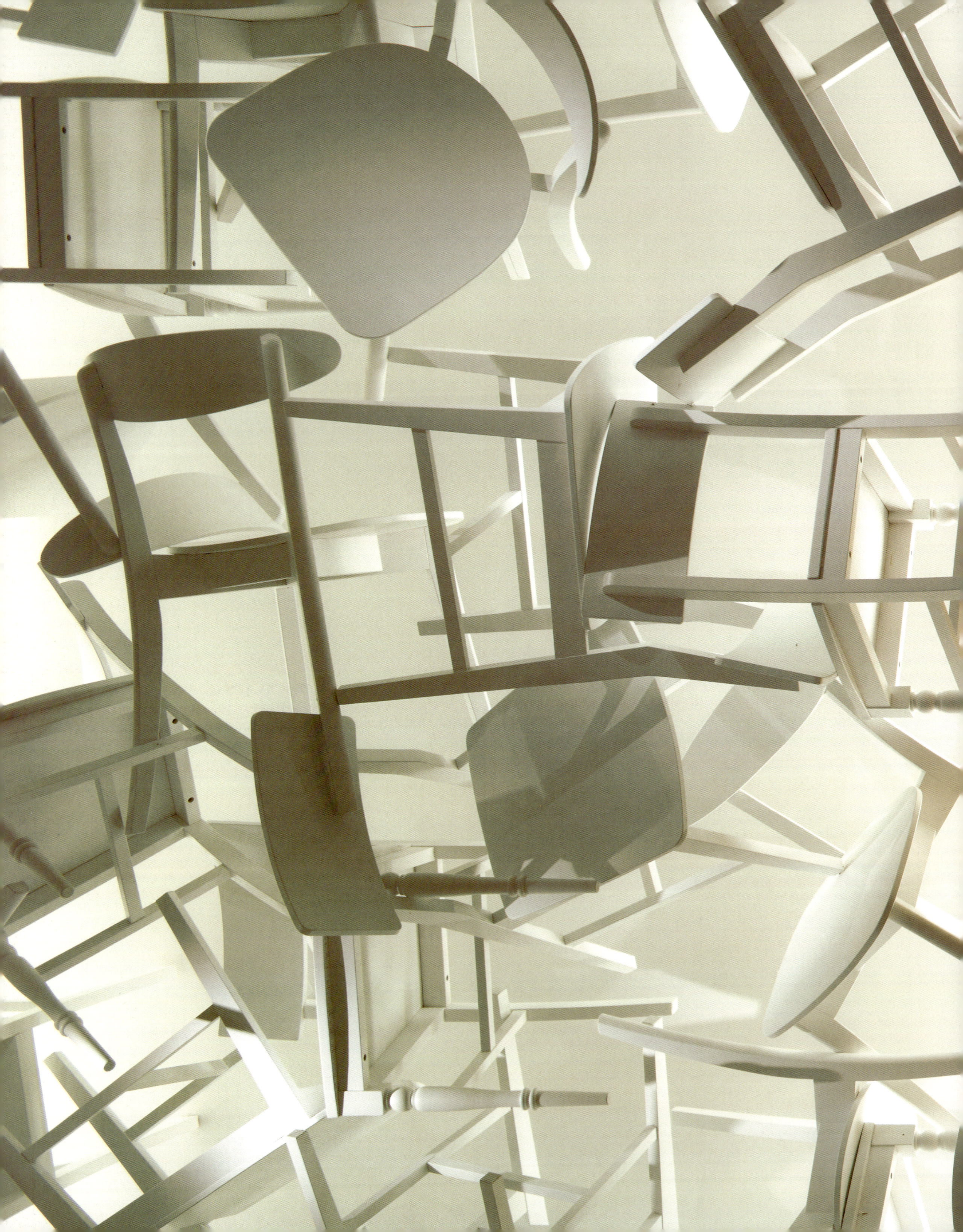

すべては、妄想から始まる。

「プランを考えるときには、すべて妄想からスタートする。例えば、大好きなモデルのヘレナ・クリステンセンとは、何度も何度も脳内デートをしている。彼女に『モリタ、今度、東京に行くんだけど、どっかある？』って言われたときに、『ないから、じゃあ、作ろうか！』って。そうやってプランを作り始めている。カーラ・ブルーニなんて、サルコジより知っている。妄想の世界でだけど。女性に限らず、男性との関係だって同じこと。身近な友人との普段の会話の中にだってヒントは沢山あって、『最近、こういう店ないよね』、『じゃあ、作ろうか』って。
僕のデザインに説得力があるとすれば、それはストーリーがあるからだと思う。妄想から生まれるストーリーもそうだし、その店が持っている歴史を繋げるっていうストーリーもある。コンサルティングのようだと言われるのは、ストーリーを紡ぐ作業こそがデザインの根幹だと思っているから。色や形の話から入るのかと思いきや、まず歴史や働き方の話をするから驚くクライアントもいる。
3年近くかかった伊勢丹の場合も、半分はデザインに入る前の話。このロン毛の眼鏡のことを信じてもらうために、いかに自分が世界中で買い物をしてきたのかを話した。お客さんの目線で、『こんなモノがあったら喜ぶのに』『男性が女性の売り場に行きづらい』と、思っていることを伝えて、それからパークというエスカレーターの周囲を広場にするアイディアを見せていく。『シャツを買いにきたのにマカロン買っちゃった』とか『食品を買いにきたのにアート買っちゃった』とか、ワクワクする出会いを提案して、実現できたんじゃないかと思っている。食べて感じるもの、音楽、アートや匂い、デパートは五感で感じるもの。そして、『これをプレゼントしたいな』と第六感を働かせる場所でもある。五感＋シックスセンス。そこまで妄想して、デザインはスタートする」

Everything Starts with Daydreams.

"When I think of a plan, I begin by daydreaming. For example, I've been on countless imaginary dates with my favorite model, Helena Christensen. She's the one who would ask me, 'Are there any good places in Tokyo, Morita?' to which I'd reply, 'No, but let me make one!' That's how I start planning. I think I know Carla Bruni better than Sarkozy—in my head, that is. My so-called 'relationships' aren't just with women. I'm often inspired by conversations with my closest friends. They would say to me, 'It's hard to find a good place these days,' to which I would say, 'Then let's make one.'
If my designs are actually convincing, then it's because they are based on stories. By *stories*, I mean narratives that arise from daydreams, or scenarios that convey the history behind a particular business or store. People often say that my work is similar to consulting, because I believe the foundations of design lies in the process of storytelling. Some of my clients are surprised when I begin to talk about their history and their business, instead of about colors and shapes.
The project with Isetan, for example, took almost three years, half of which was spent on the process *before* design. I talked about how much shopping I'd done around the world, just to prove to them that I'm more than just a guy with glasses and long hair. I first told stories from a customer's point of view, making comments like: 'I would want to see this product here,' and 'It's hard for men to go into the women's section.' I then proposed ideas to create open spaces around the escalators called 'park.' I think I succeeded in endorsing new and exciting encounters in which people would say to each other: 'I got these *macarons* instead of a shirt.' or 'I bought this piece of art while shopping for groceries.' A department store touches on all five senses, with food, music, art and scent. It is also a place that affects the *sixth* sense, where the customers are tempted to buy gifts for their loved ones. Five senses, plus the sixth sense. That's how deep I daydream to start the design process."

N°049
Tokyo/Japan
Mar.2013

伊勢丹新宿本店本館 再開発

近年の代表作とも言える巨大プロジェクト。その規模もさることながら、五感＋シックスセンスへ訴えるデザインという森田の理念が凝縮されている。伝統的な価値を持つ建築内において、新たな価値を創造すること。建築家・丹下憲孝氏と共に、そのために森田が考えたのは伊勢丹をファッションミュージアムと捉え直すことだった。エスカレーターを中心に「PARK」と名付けた回遊式のスペースを確保。「PARK」から各店舗へアクセスし、また「PARK」へと戻る構造は、ルーヴルやメトロポリタンなど、世界の名だたるミュージアムと共通している。シャツを買いに来た客がジュエリーを持ち帰るような、バッグを買いに来た客がアートを手に取るような、驚きある体験を引き出したかったと森田は言う。シックスセンスとは、体感以上の幸福なムードのことでもある。そのための大胆で繊細な仕掛けが、フロアごとに隠されている。

This project is one of Morita's more recent masterpieces. Its impressive scale aside, this project extracts Morita's ideology in creating designs that embrace all five senses *and* the "sixth" sense into one whole. The challenge is to establish new meaning within traditional architecture. In collaboration with architect Noritaka Tange, Morita redefined Isetan as a new fashion museum. A strolling area called PARK was created around the escalators. As in many of the world's renowned museums, the space is structured so that PARK acts as a central area through which stores are accessed. Morita's intention was to create surprises so that one might pick up jewelry while shopping for clothes, or take home a work of art instead of buying a new bag. The "sixth" sense also relies on the atmosphere of happiness. Each floor is embedded with numerous bold yet delicate devices to evoke this ambience.

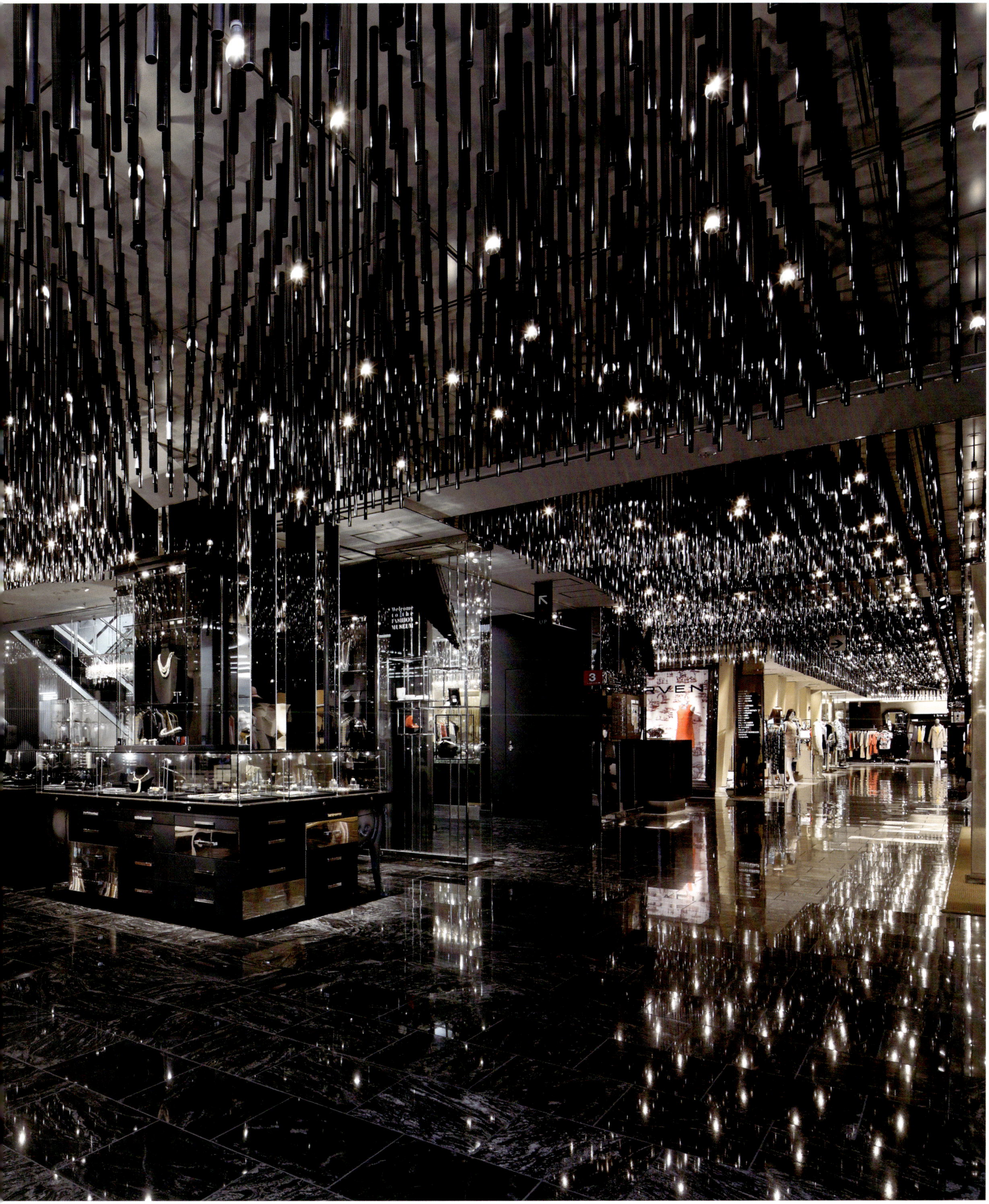
Welcome
to the
FASHION
MUSEUM
3
RVEN

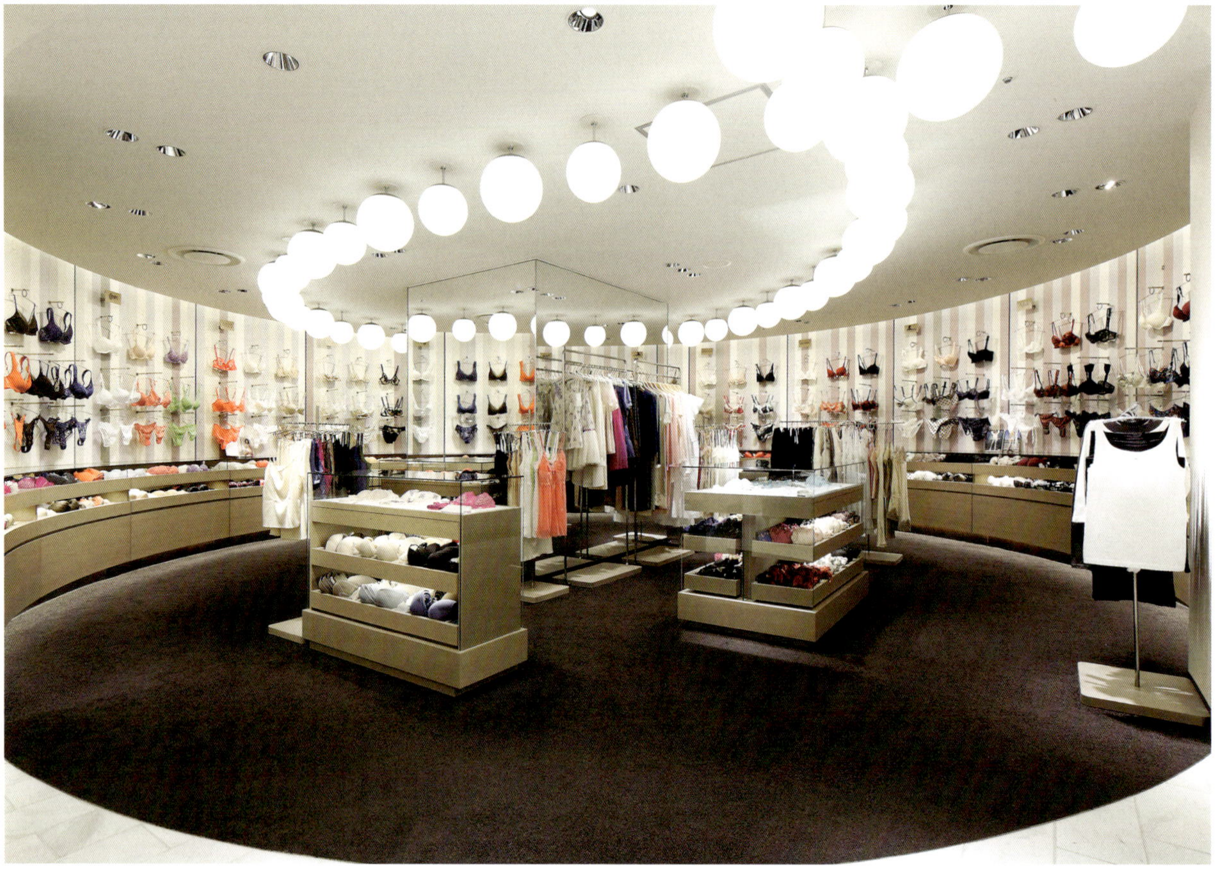

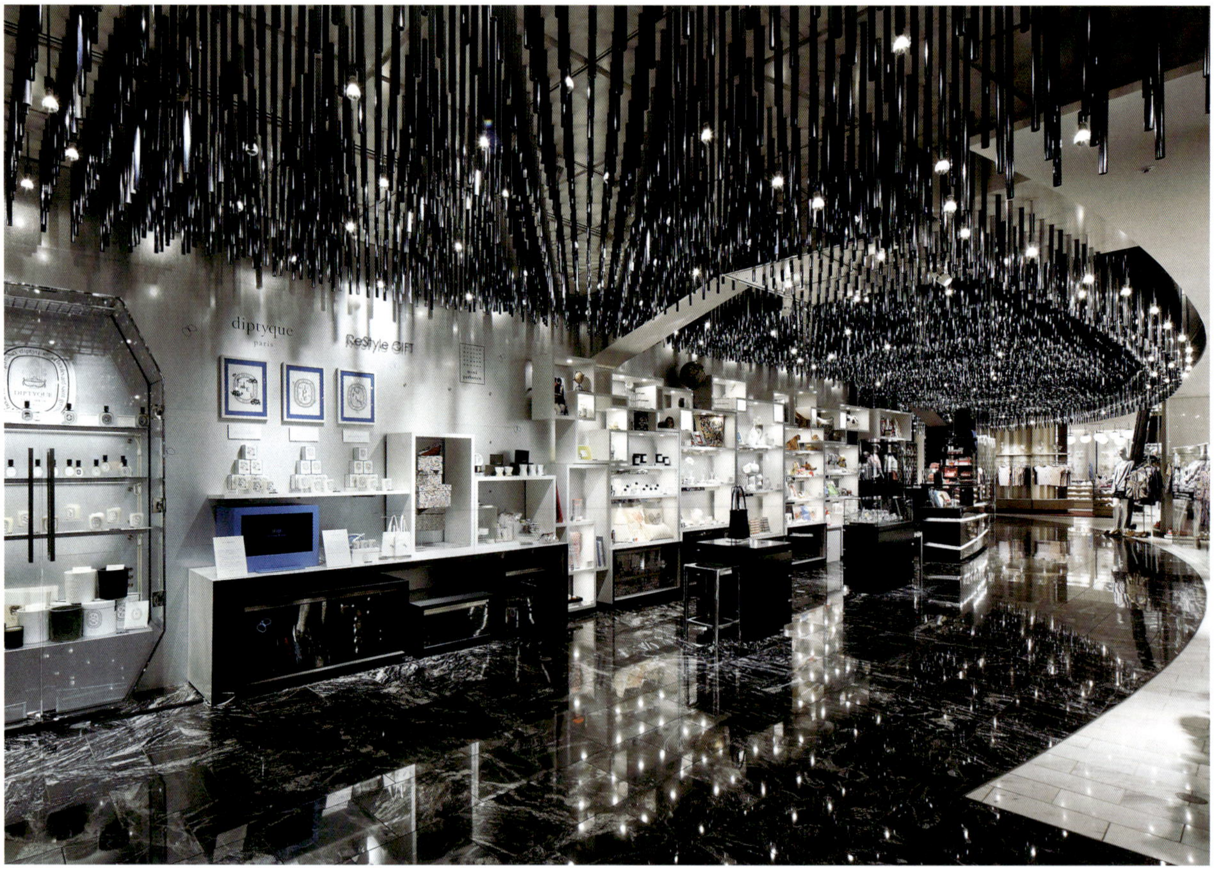
diptyque
paris
ReStyle GIFT

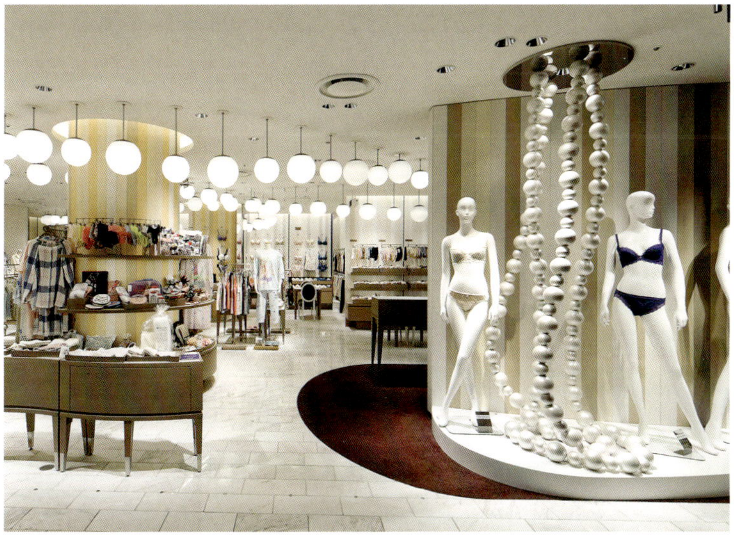

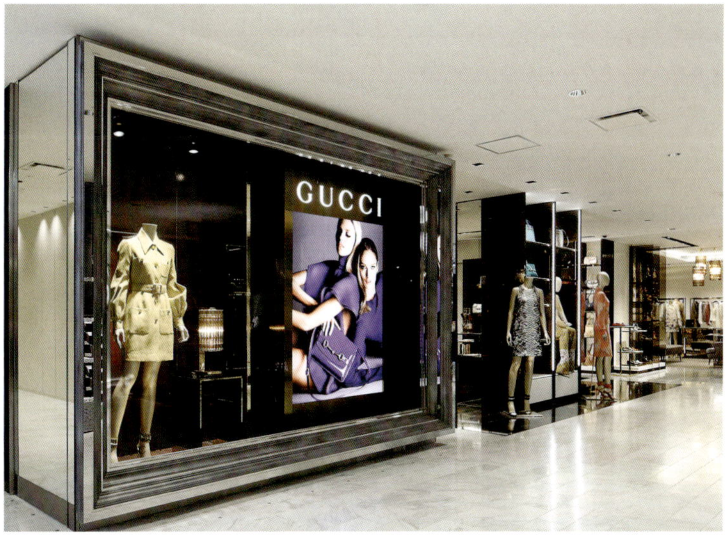
GUCCI

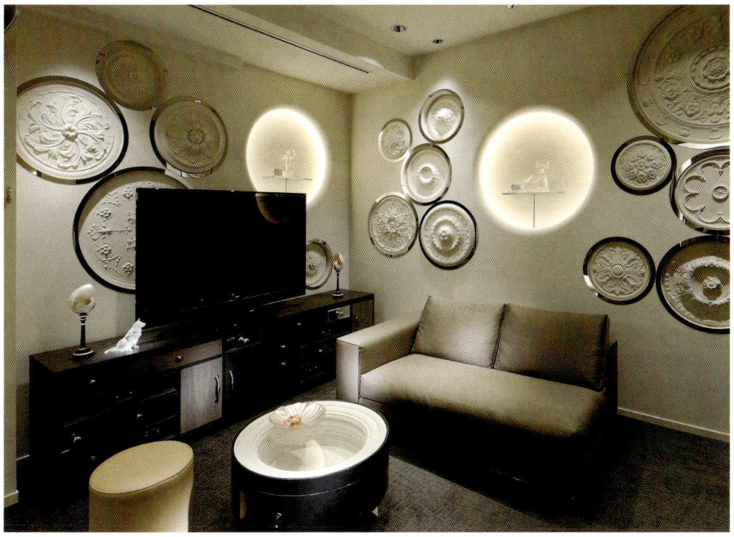

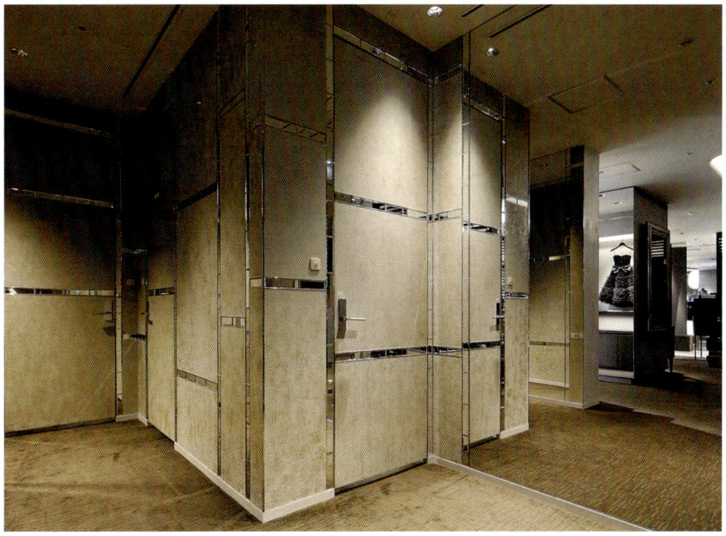

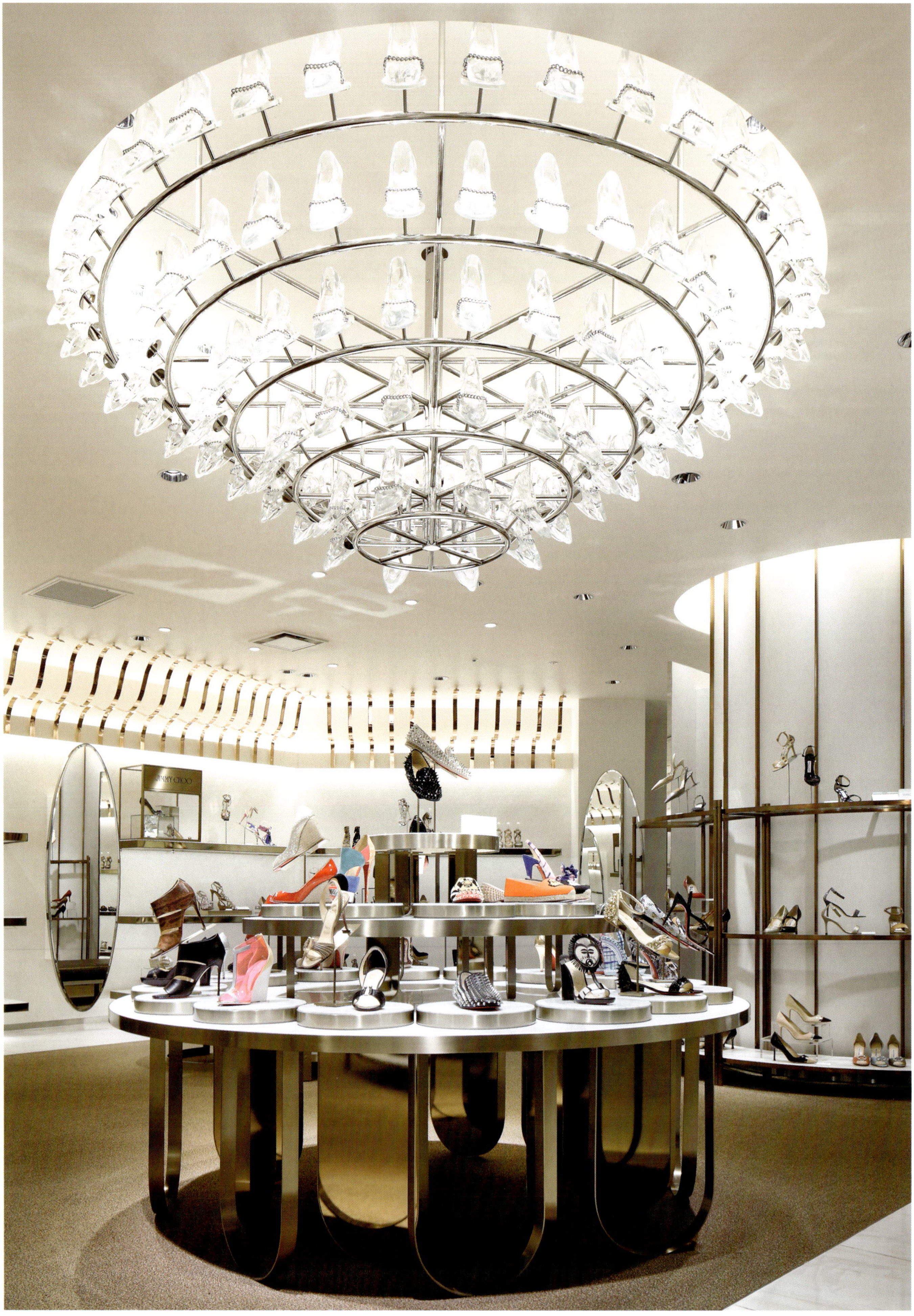

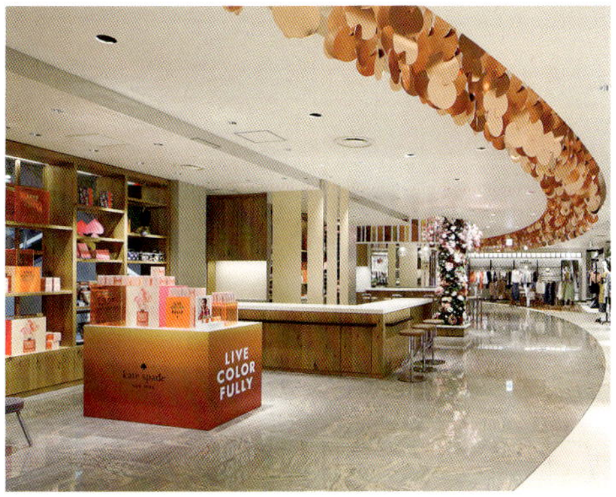
LIVE
COLOR
FULLY
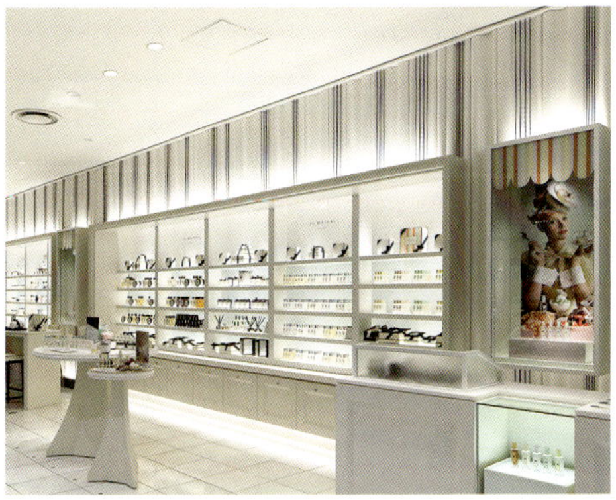
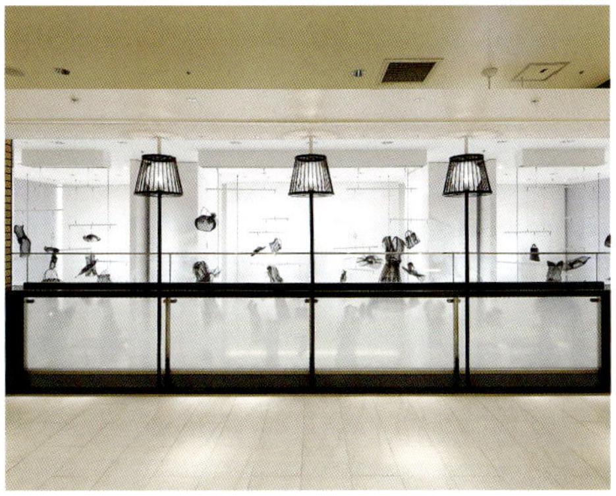
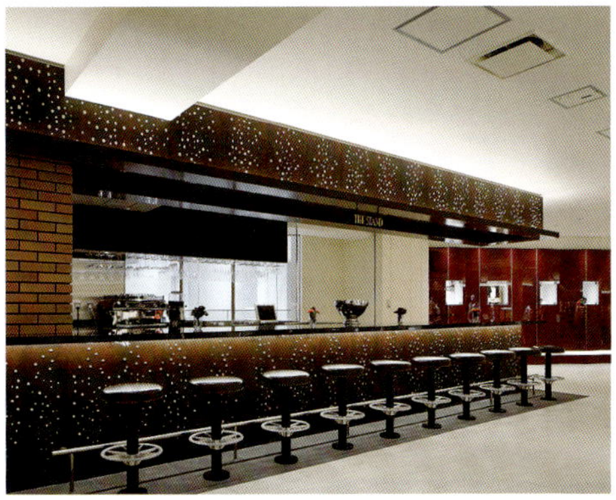
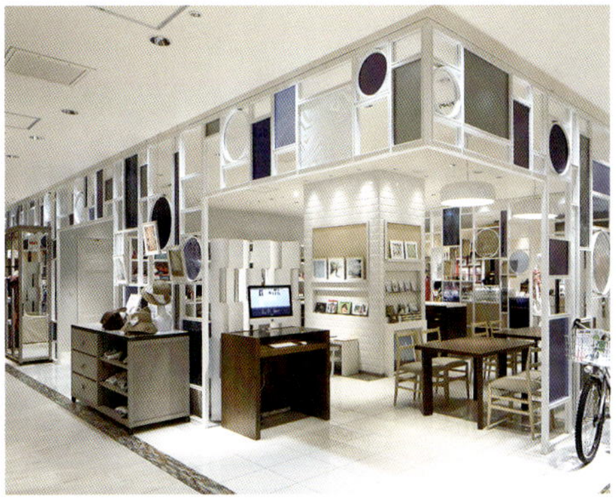
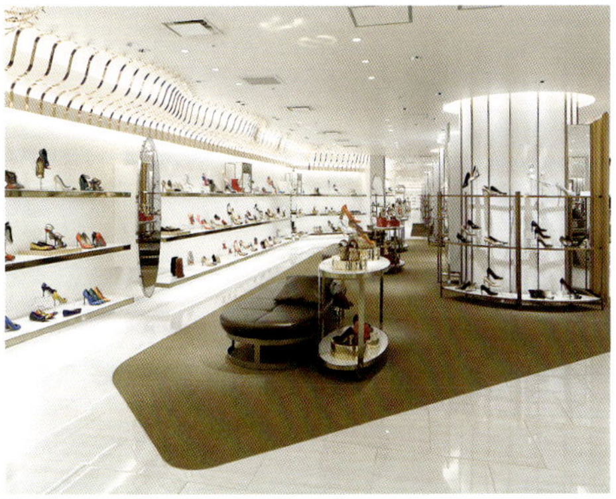
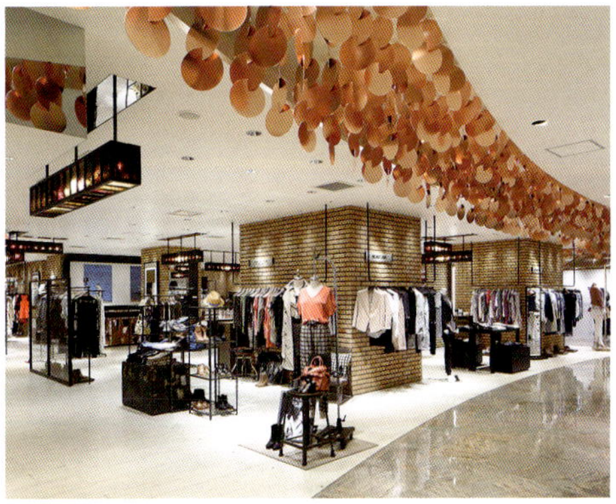
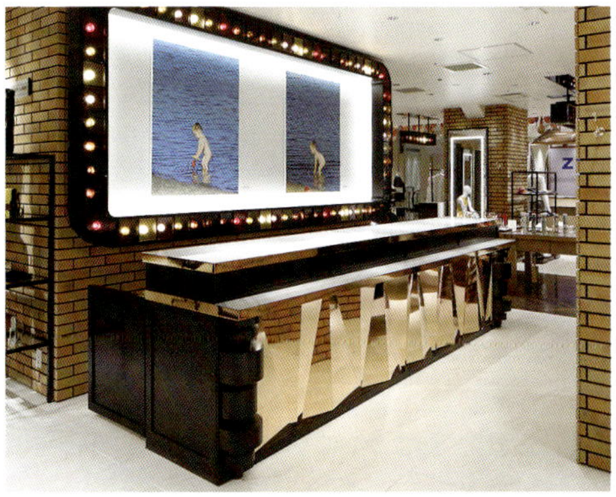
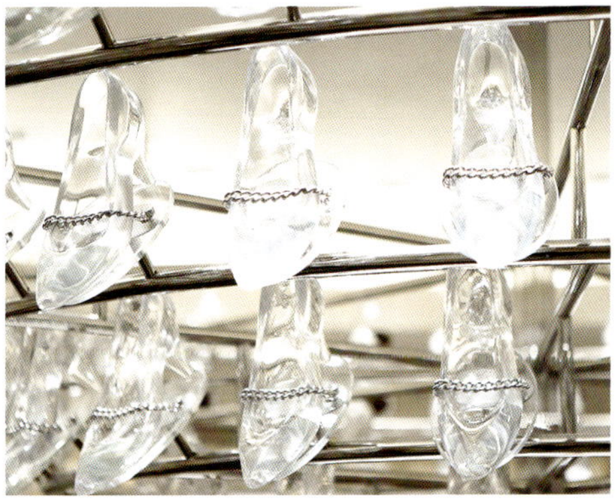
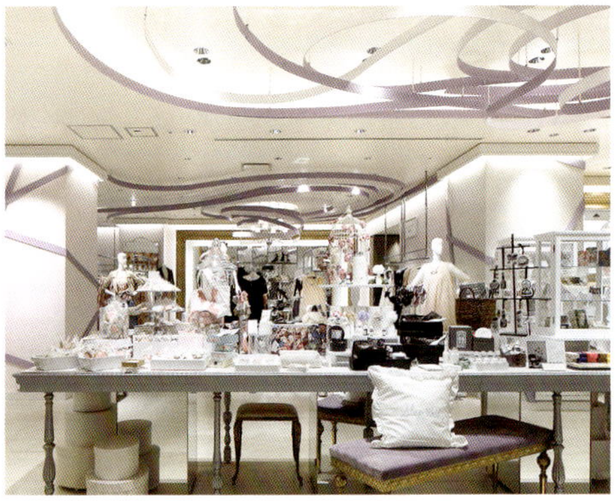

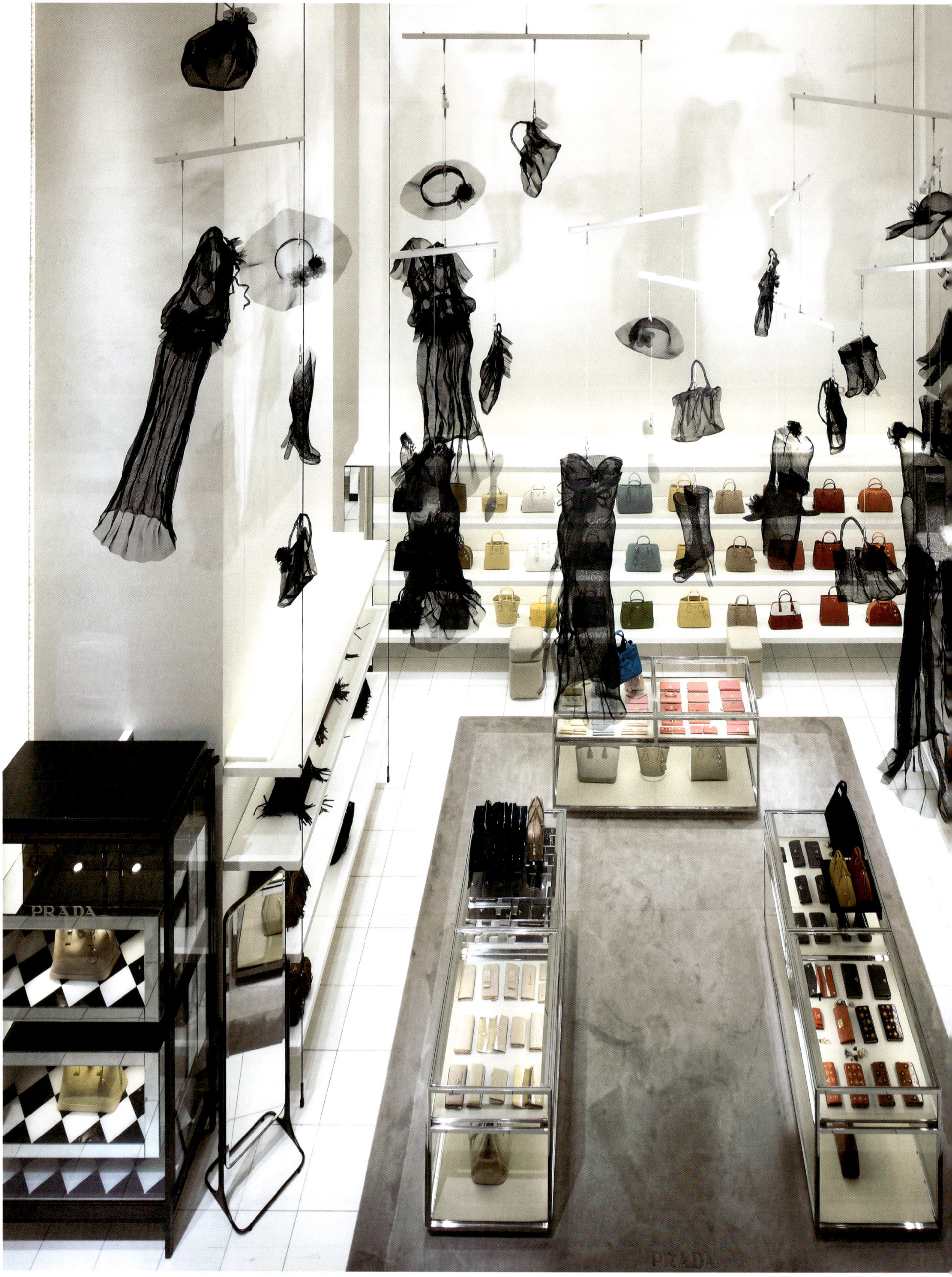
PRADA
PRADA

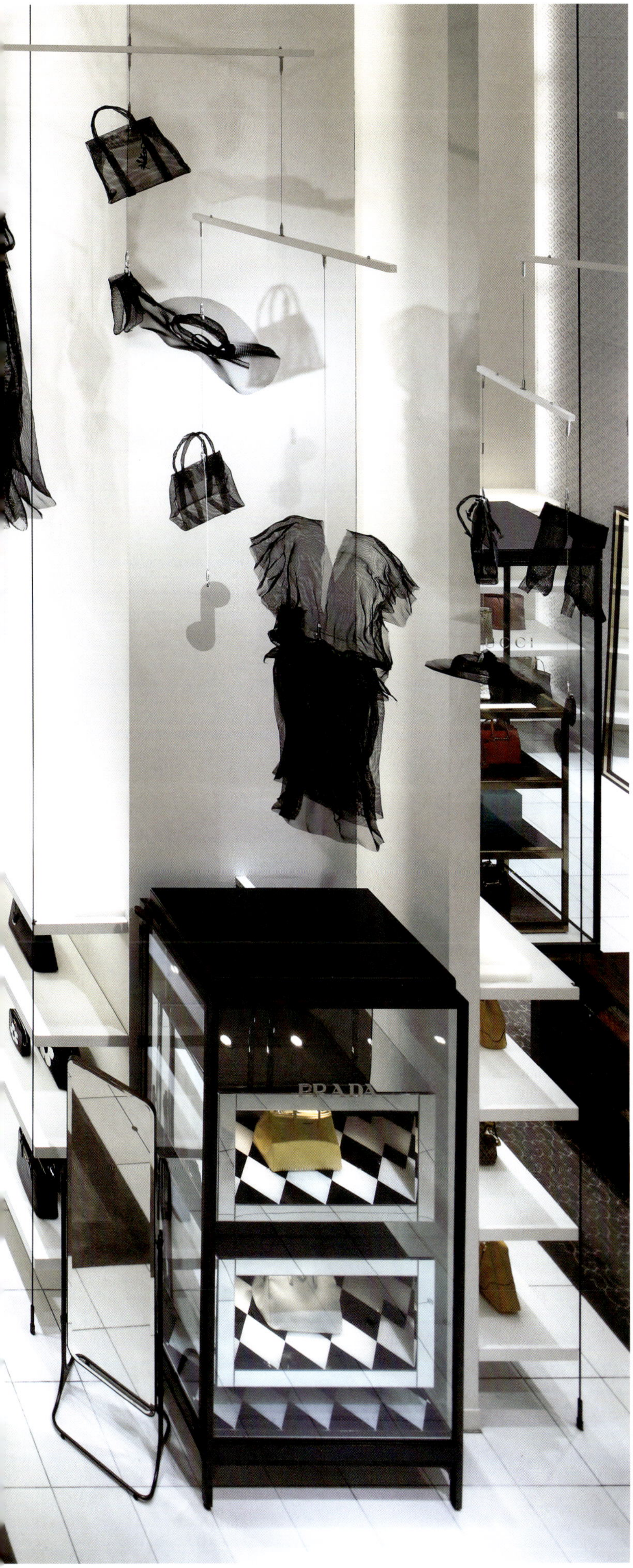
PRADA

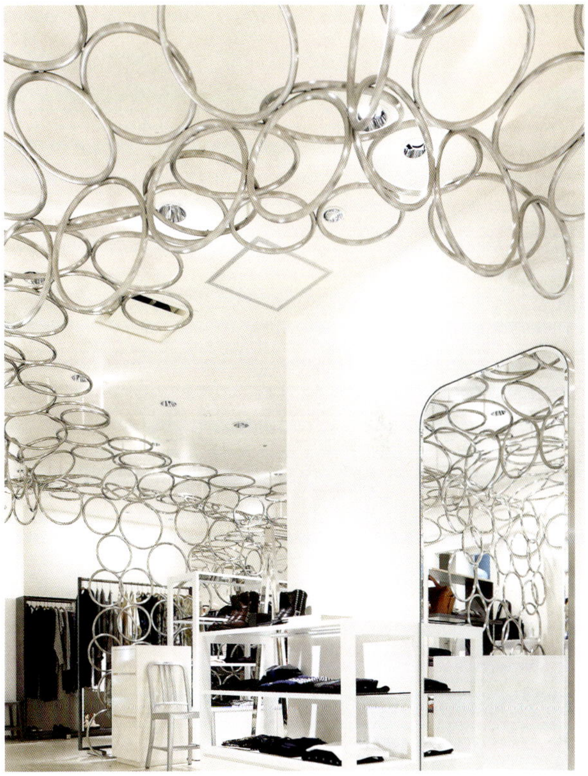

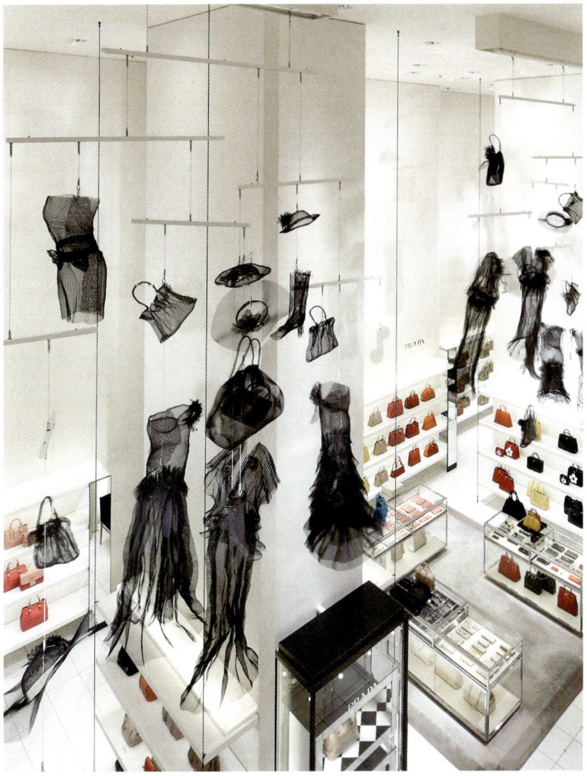

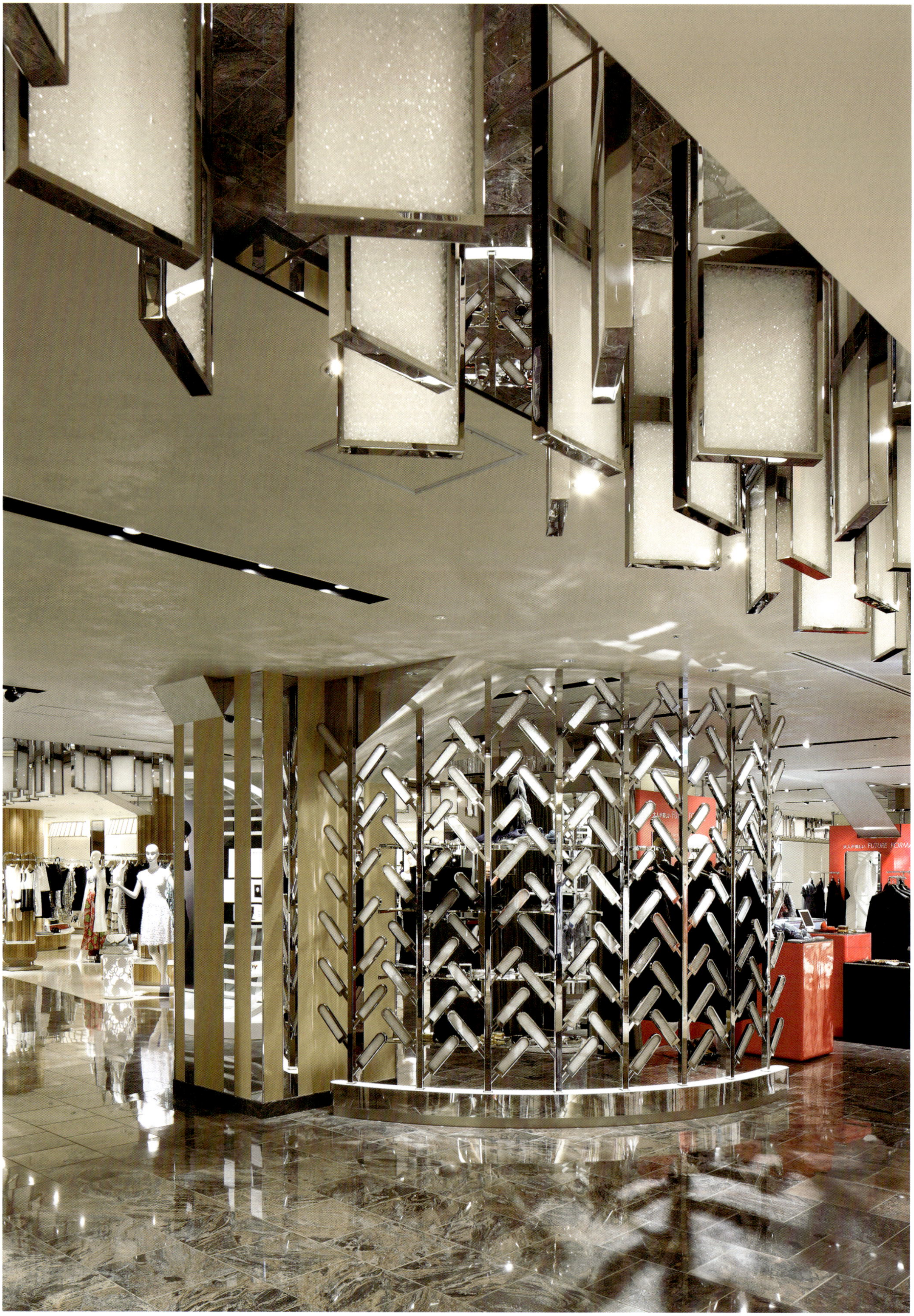

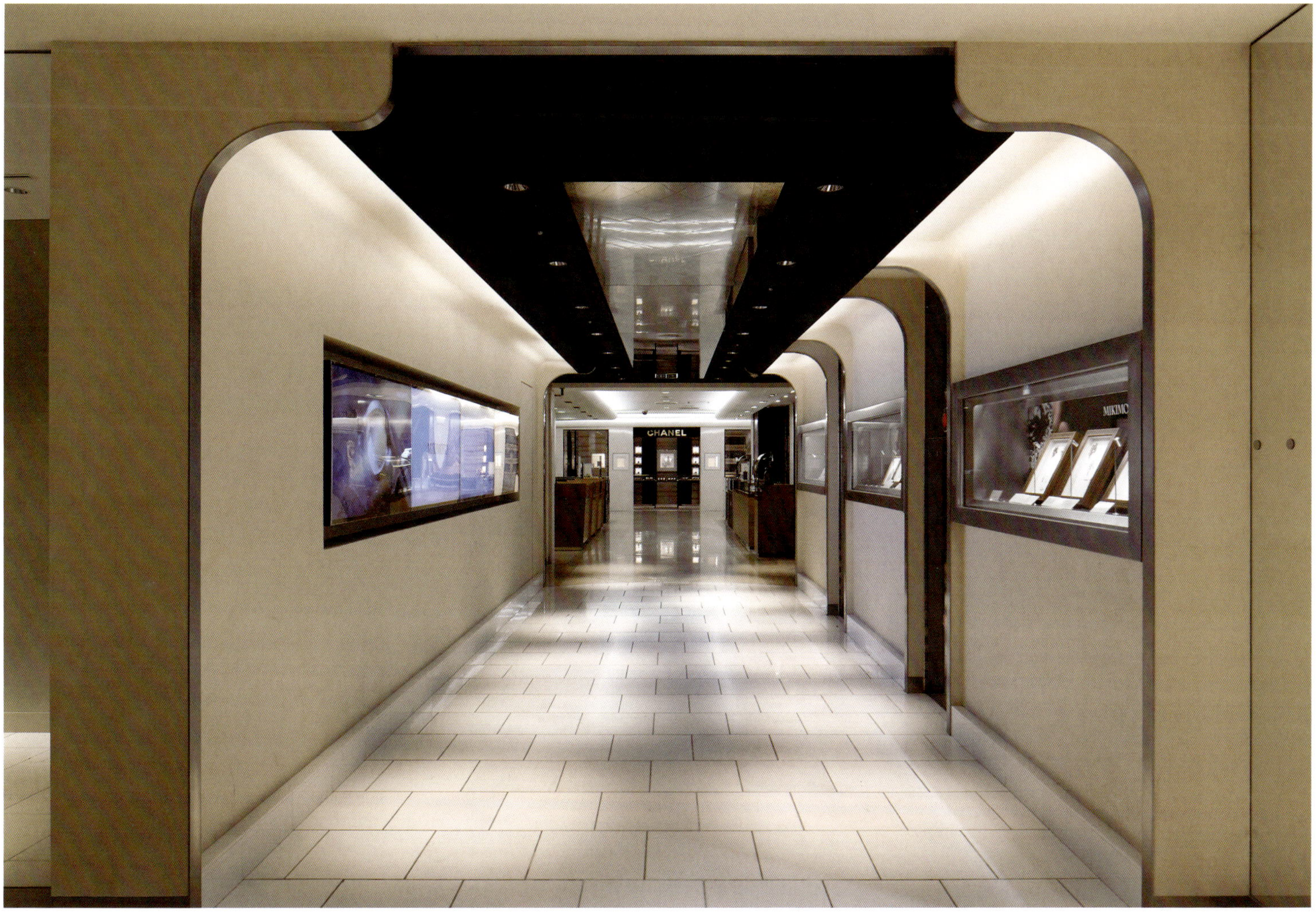
CHANEL

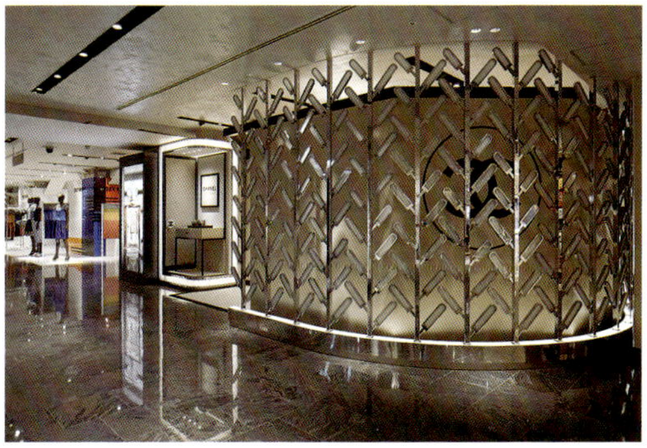

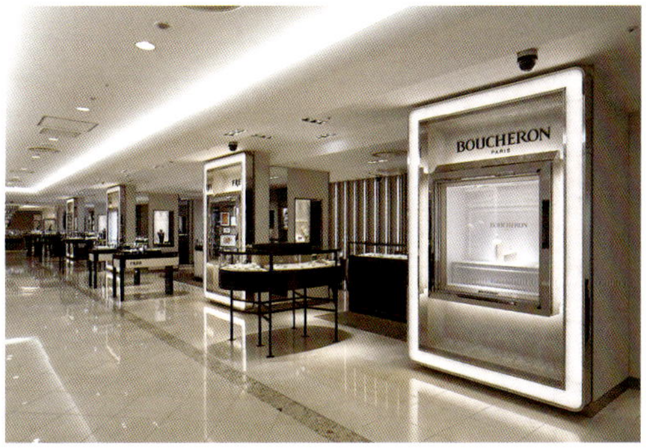
BOUCHERON

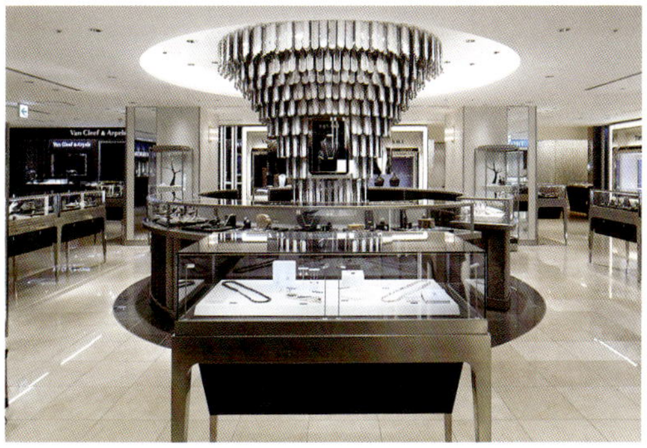

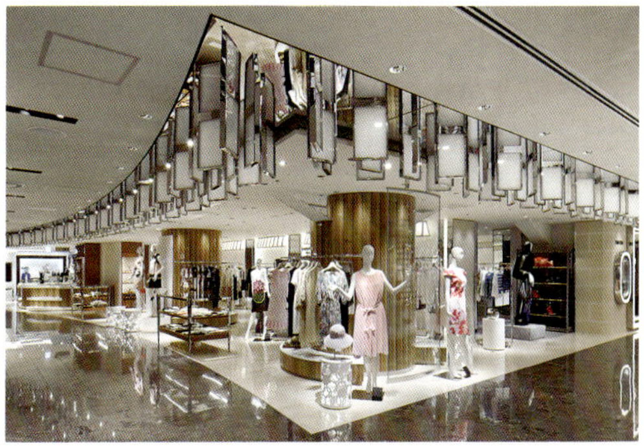

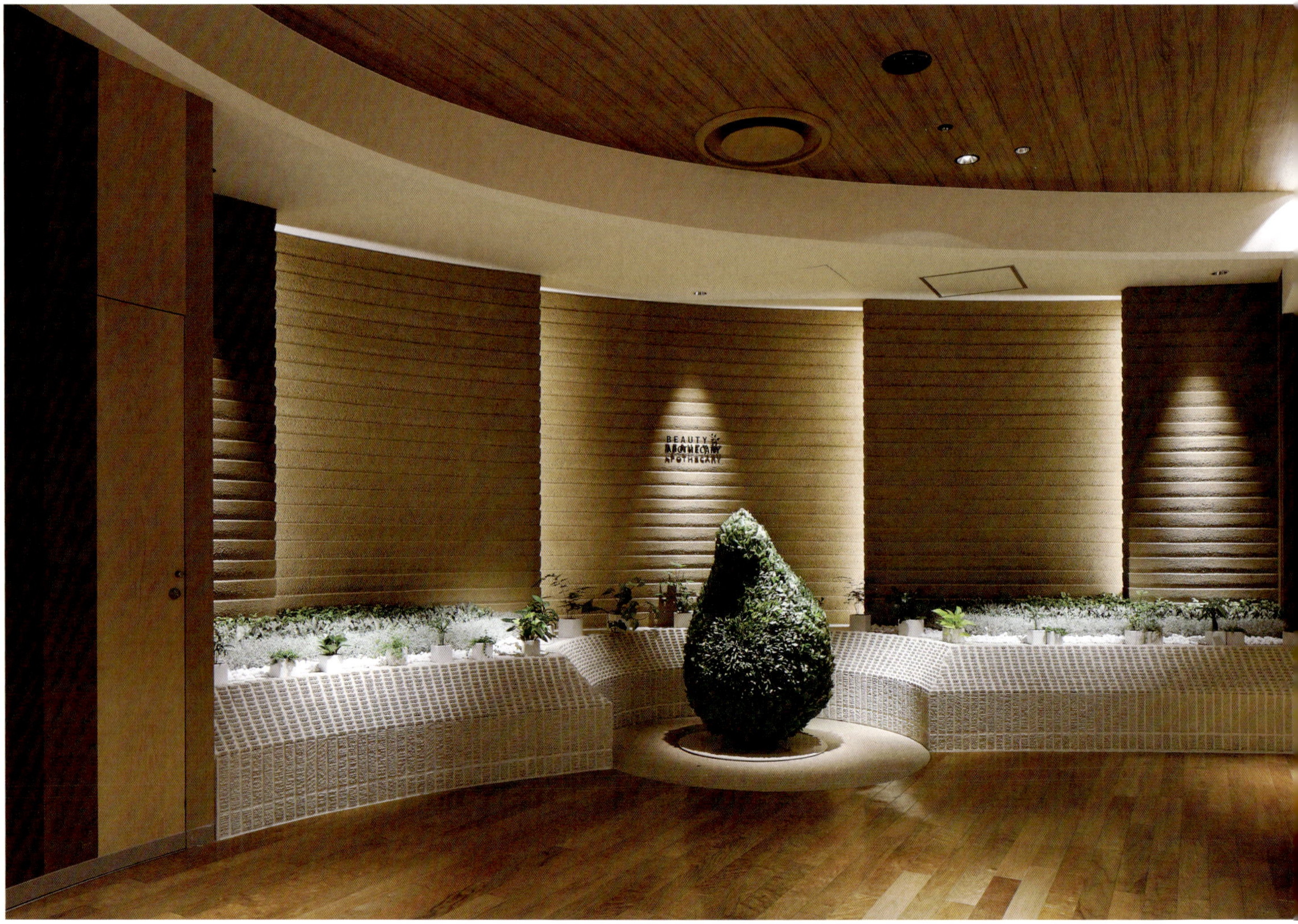

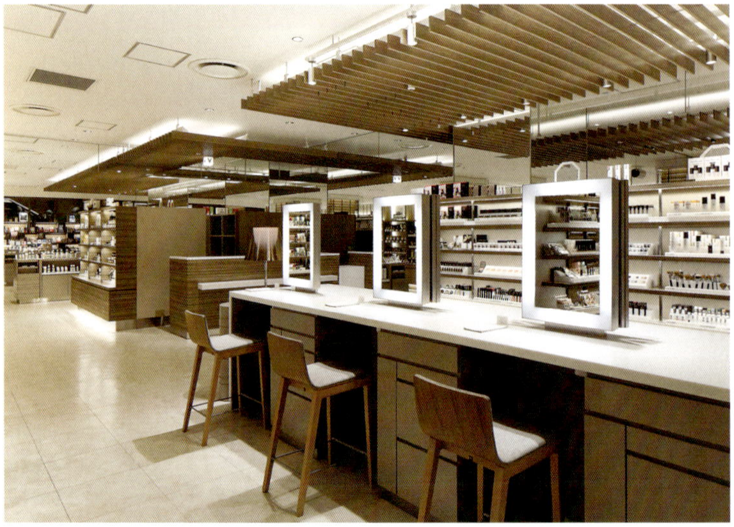

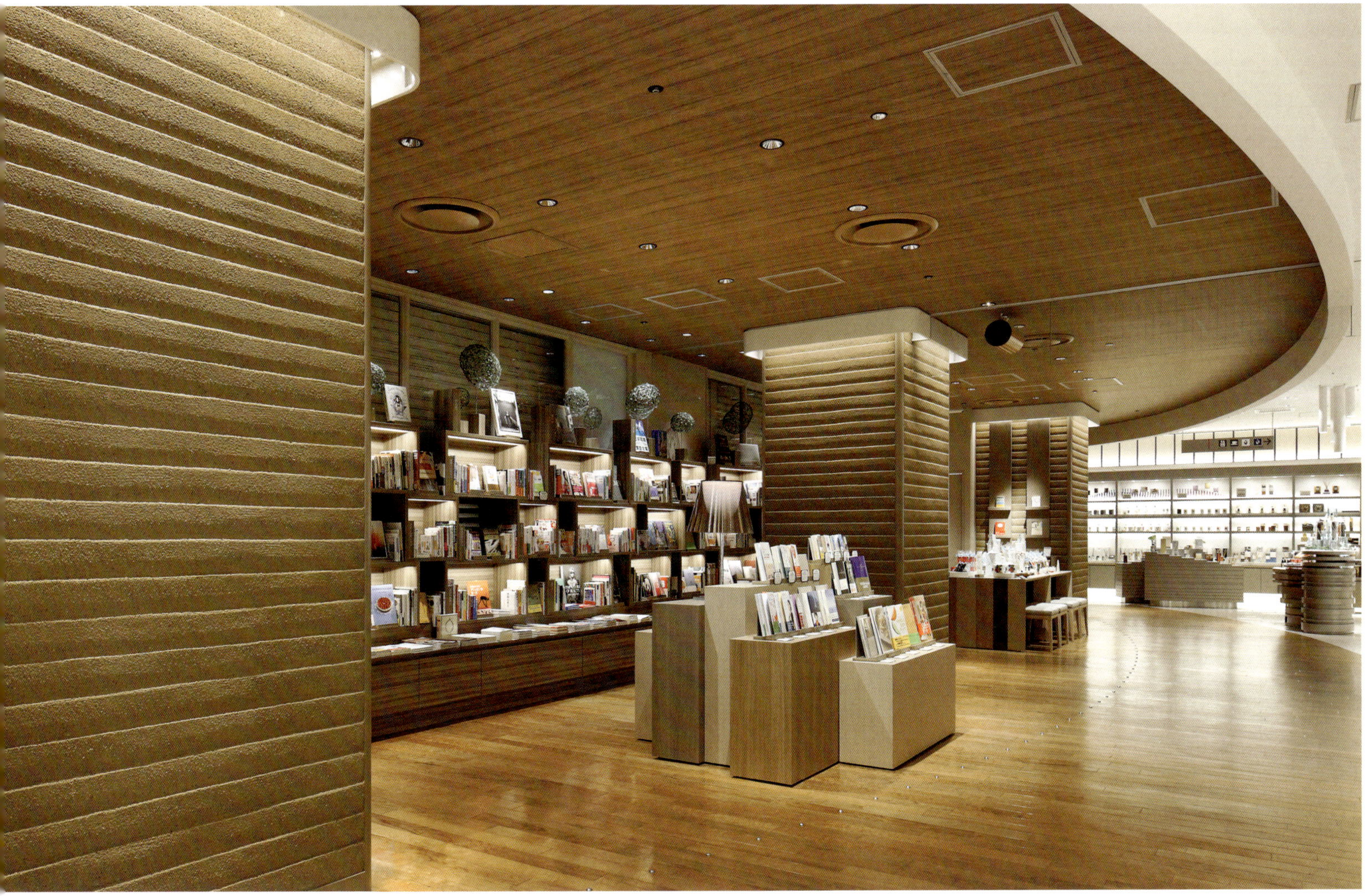

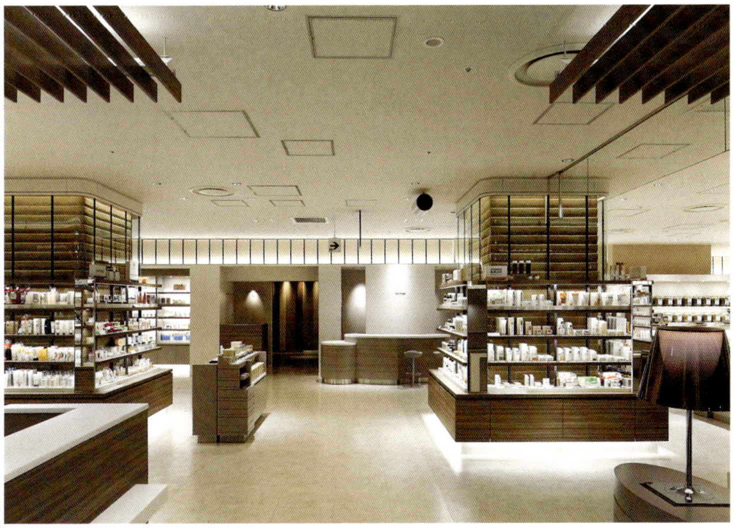

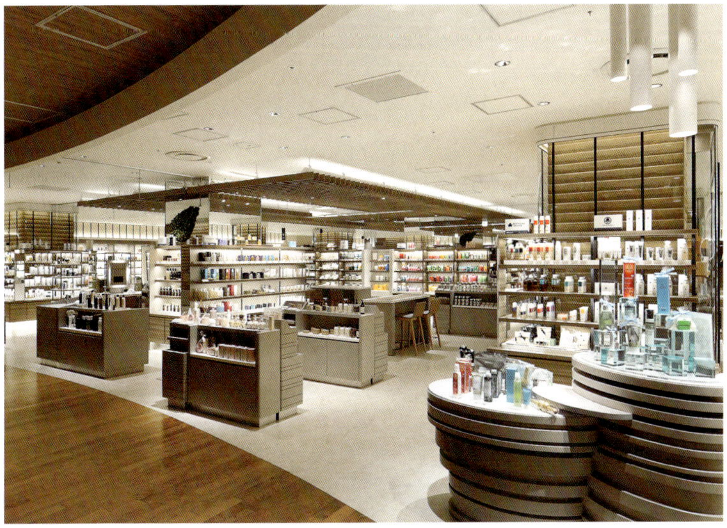

N°050
Tokyo/Japan
May 2010
AOYAMA Francfranc

「デザインとアートの隙間のような空間を作りたかった」という森田の言葉の通り、店内の中央に位置する巨大なシャンデリアは、もはやインスタレーション。倉科昌高氏とのコラボレーションによる木目のファサードは、商業施設というよりも倉庫や格納庫をイメージしたものだった。「ファッション&アート」というコンセプトに、アトリエのような空気感を付与している。屋根の上には、メタル製の旗が風に吹かれたようにはためいている。2階部分の壁面に置かれたチェアを多く用いた作品は、ディスプレイであると同時にアートでもある。その"解釈のゆとり"こそが、森田が狙っていた「抜け感」なのだ。インテリアだけでなく、カルチャー全般を発信する空間に必要な「隙間のような」遊び心が、随所に見て取れる。

The massive chandelier in the center of this store is more an installation than anything else. It perfectly demonstrates Morita's idea of bridging the narrow border between design and art. The wood grain facade is a collaborative effort with Masataka Kurashina, and simulates a warehouse or storage facility rather than a commercial building. The work adds a touch of the atelier to the concepts of fashion and art. A metallic flag flutters on the rooftop as if to signify the passing breeze. The row of chairs that lines the second-floor wall surface is both a display area and an artwork. Everything is up for free interpretation, and this openness is precisely what Morita was aiming for. The design is sprinkled with playful "in-betweens," a necessary ingredient for a space that sets the trend not only for interior items but for the entire culture.

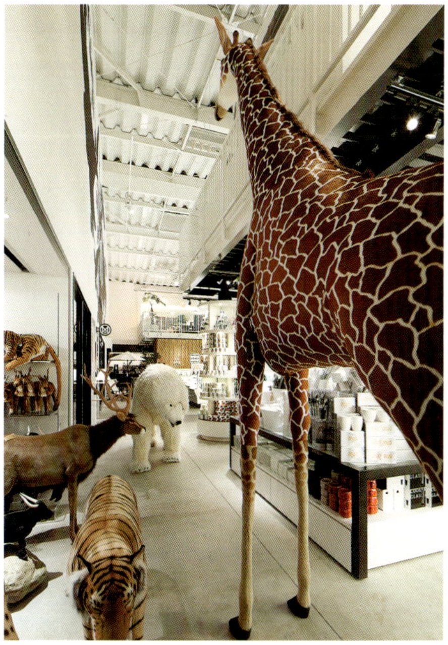

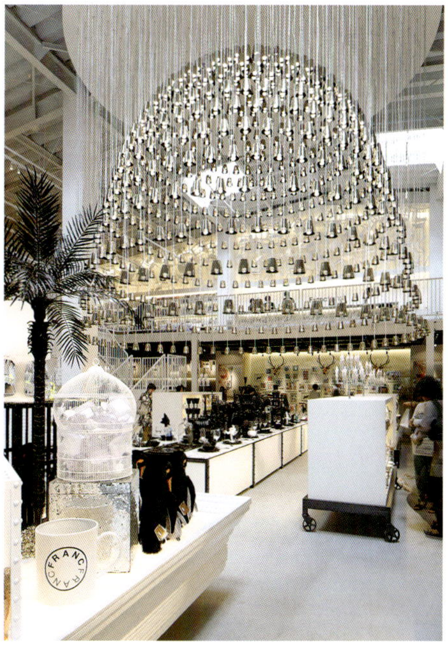

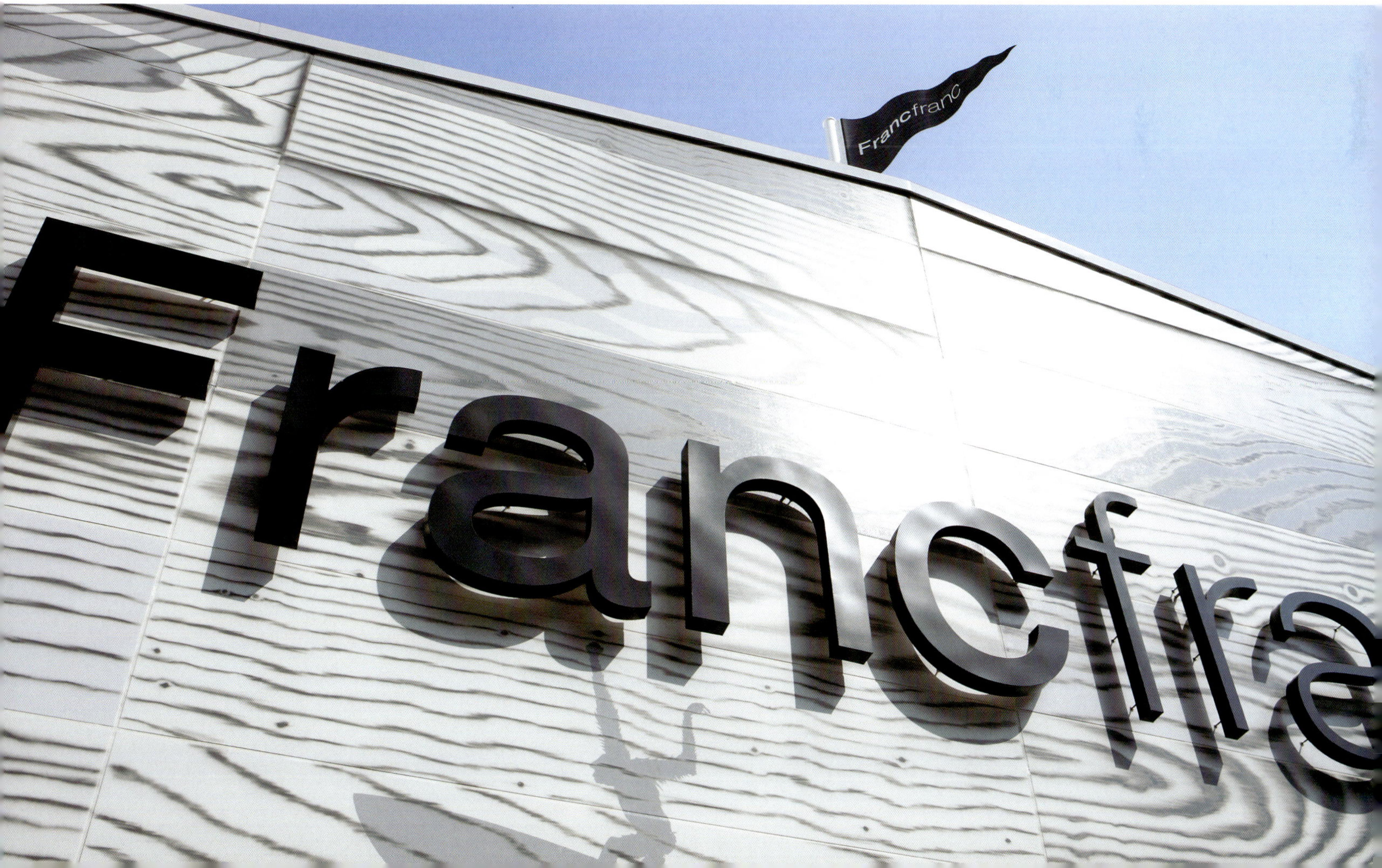
Francfranc

Francfranc

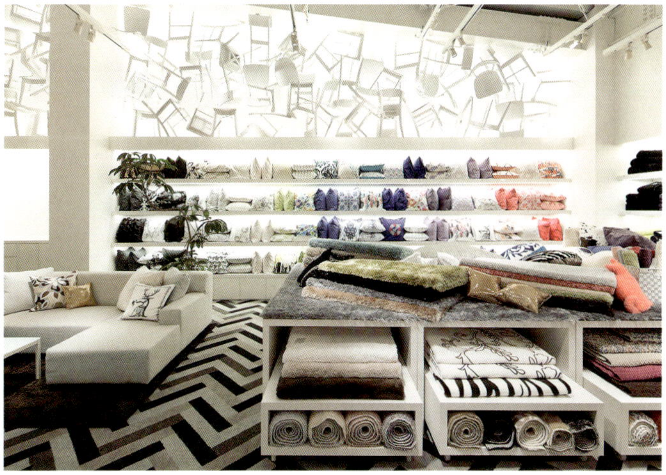

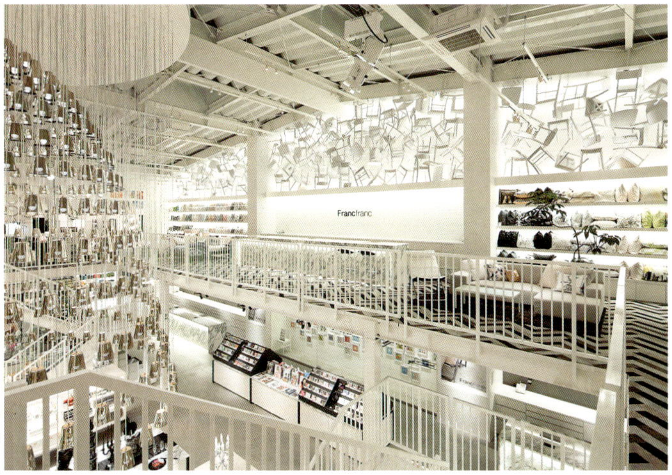
Francfranc

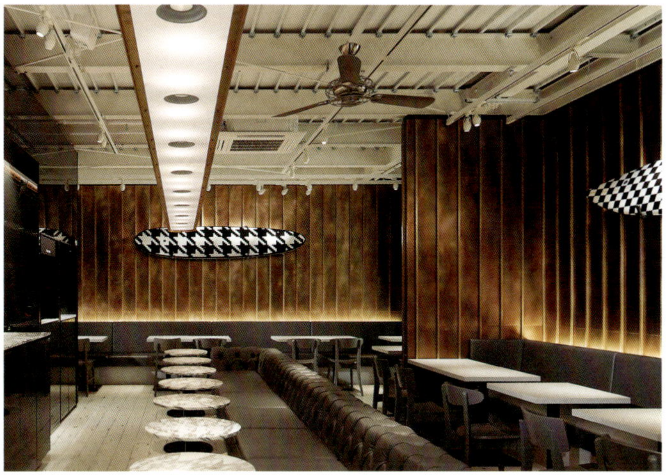

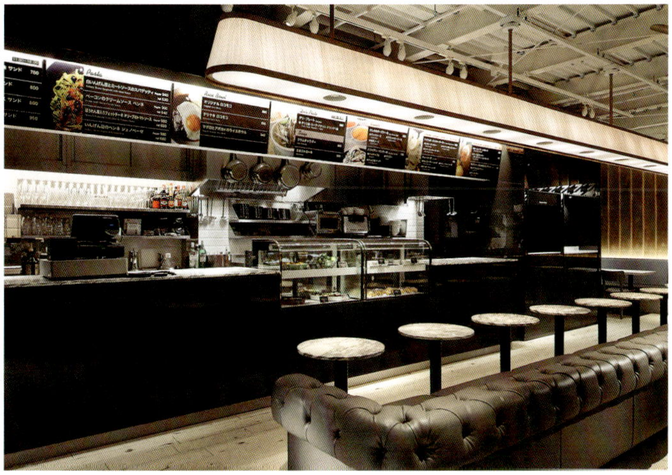

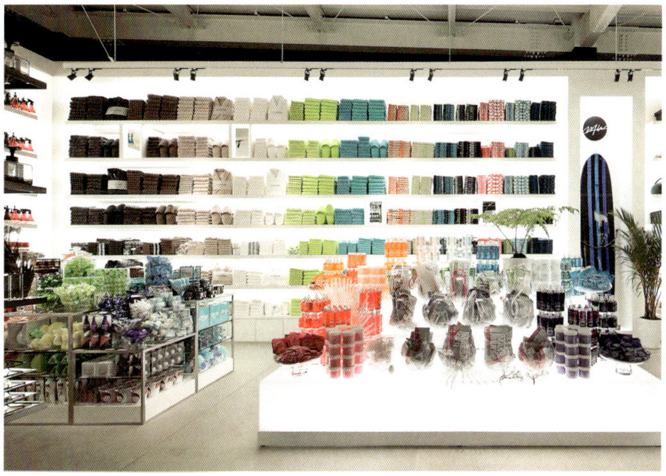

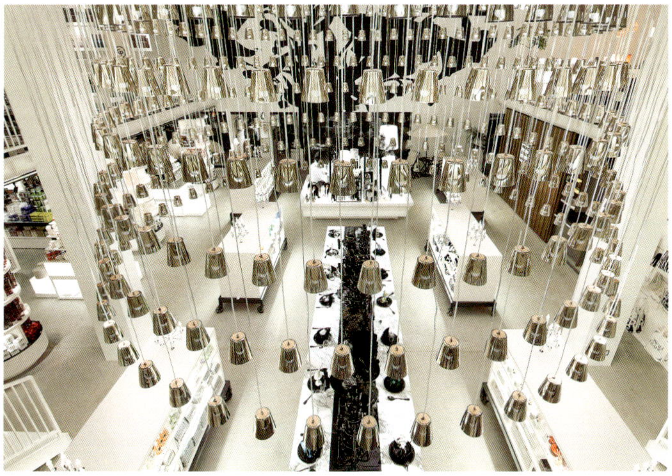

N° 051
Nagoya/Japan
Oct.2010

NAGOYA Francfranc

コンセプトは、『Lifestyle with Art』。青山店で手がけたデザインと同様に、アートが生活に溶け込み、身近に感じられる暮らしを提案するための仕掛けが施されている。ファサードには、フォトフレームから着想を得て、東京と同じく倉科昌高氏のペイント。正面にもやはり、白い羽がペイントされた巨大なシャンデリアが訪れる人を迎えている。東京と名古屋、同じくアートをテーマにしたデザインでありながら、まったく異なる表情を生み出し、名古屋はよりエレガントな雰囲気を纏っている。2階から3階へと続く吹き抜けには巨大な棚を設置してスケール感の妙を演出し、3階にはカフェスペースもデザインした。各フロアのデザインの違いが、階上へと誘う。

The concept for this project is "Lifestyle with Art." Similar to the design for the Aoyama Francfranc store, this project employs various devices to suggest a lifestyle integrated with works of art. The facade, inspired by a photo frame, was painted by Masataka Kurashina. A chandelier painted in large white feathers welcomes guests at the front entrance. Although both the Tokyo and Nagoya stores are dressed with an artistic theme, the Nagoya store takes on a more elegant atmosphere with a completely different look. In the open ceiling space connecting the second and third floors, a large shelf was built to amplify the scale, with a café space covering a portion of the third floor. The difference between each of the floors is what tempts one to keep climbing upward.

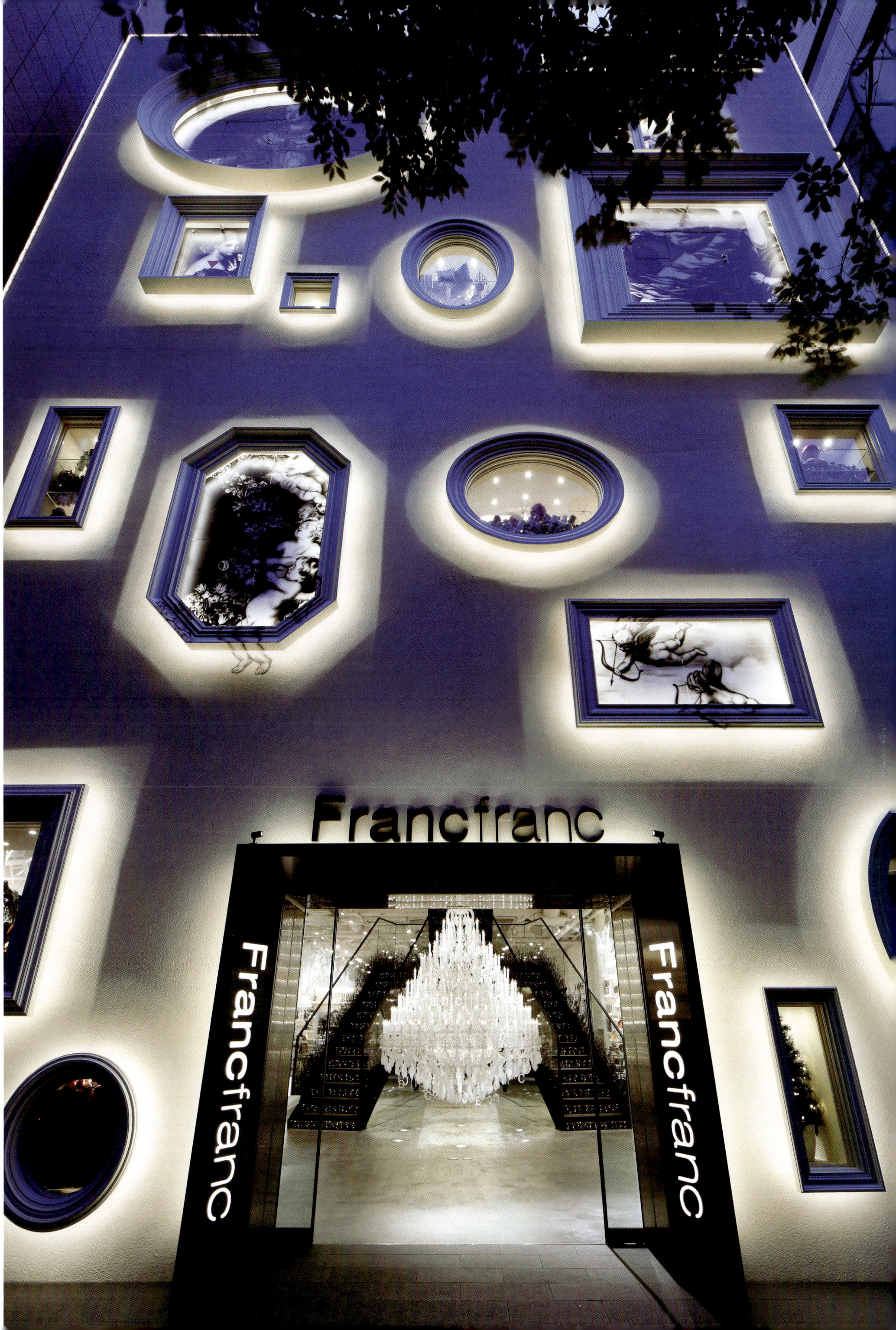
Francfranc
Francfranc
Francfranc

N°052
Seoul/Korea
Nov.2011

Samantha Thavasa
ロッテ百貨店本店

複合施設内にありながら、三方向から入ることができるアイランド区画にあったため、特に視認性を高めることが求められた。「可愛い」「キラキラ」というブランドイメージから導き出されたのは、オブジェのような「カップケーキ」の什器。どの角度からも目に留まるようにデザインされている。また、空間のデメリットとなる柱部分には、あえてリボンのデザインを施した姿見を配置。思わず自分を映してみたくなるような効果的なデザインとなっている。さらにシンプルな空間に差し色として用いたのが、ブランドカラーのひとつでもある「サマンサブルー」のキューブ什器。可動式のため、アイテムによって陳列も自由に変えることができる。

Because the project is located on an island lot with three-directional exposure inside a commercial complex, it was important for Morita to create an easily identifiable landmark. Guided by the brand's cute and glittery image, Morita found his inspiration in the cups used for baking cupcakes. The design was created to draw attention from all angles. The large supporting column is camouflaged by a mirror festooned with a ribbon motif, to entice customers for a quick look. Cubes painted in "Samantha Blue," one of the brand's signature colors, accentuate the simple space. These portable cubes can also be rearranged for various displays.

N°053
Tokyo/Japan
Aug.2010

LOVE SWEETS ANTIQUE 青山店

青山通りに溶け込みつつ、独自の色を発信するためのポップなデザイン。モチーフは、代表的なメニューである『とろなまドーナツ』だった。店内にはカラフルなチャームを使って、シャンデリアまであしらった。どこか『不思議の国のアリス』のような物語感のあるファサードにも、ドーナツがちりばめられている。派手なアクセントに眼が向いてしまうが、この店でもっとも重要なのは、店内の壁を彩る「LSAブルー」というオリジナルの青。飲食店には珍しい紫がかった青は、それだけで見れば食欲をそそるものではない。だが、ドーナツのカラフルなチャームや世界観を構築するには、なくてはならない色。「幸せな驚き」を与えることに成功している。

With a unique color, this design pops out from the backdrop of Aoyama's main street. The featured motif is the store's signature menu item, the Toronama Donut. The interior is adorned with colorful charms and finished with a chandelier. The facade is also decked with the donut motif, exuding an "Alice in Wonderland" ambience. Although the extravagant accents attract the eye, the most important aspect of this store is the "LSA Blue," a customized color specifically selected for these walls. The purplish blue is a rare choice for a food store, and the color itself is far from appetizing. However, as a backdrop for a world of donuts and colorful charms, the blue is a vital element in the overall composition. The resulting design achieves a sense of happy surprise.

N°054
Shanghai/China
Oct.2011

boutique by Shanghai Xintiandi

なぜ3倍にもスケールアウトさせた巨大な椅子をデザインに用いるのかと言えば、そこには圧倒的な存在感が宿っているからだった。ショーウィンドウからも覗くことができるその巨大な姿に、ヒトは惹き付けられてしまう。「まるでエッシャーの騙し絵のような世界観を作りたかったのだ」と森田は言う。その世界の中では、煙のエッチングを施されたランウェイにもなるビッグテーブルとステージ用のライティングが、ゲストにブティックを訪れる喜びを与えてくれる。いかに日常とは違う心地よい世界を作り出すか。極端にも思える仕掛けは、ディテールを作り込むことで説得力を宿し、時が経つほどにクラシックへと育っていく。

This gigantic chair, blown up to three-hundred-percent scale, was incorporated into the design because of its overwhelming presence. The chair attracts attention from the display window, catching the eyes of passersby. Morita wanted to create a world of visual illusions, like those found in Escher's prints. In this illusionistic world, guests are entertained by an enormous table dressed in smoke etchings, an item that also turns into a runway with theatrical lighting. The challenge was to create a comfortable world that was still out of the ordinary. These seemingly extreme devices are armed with convincing details, with margins to grow increasingly more classical over time.

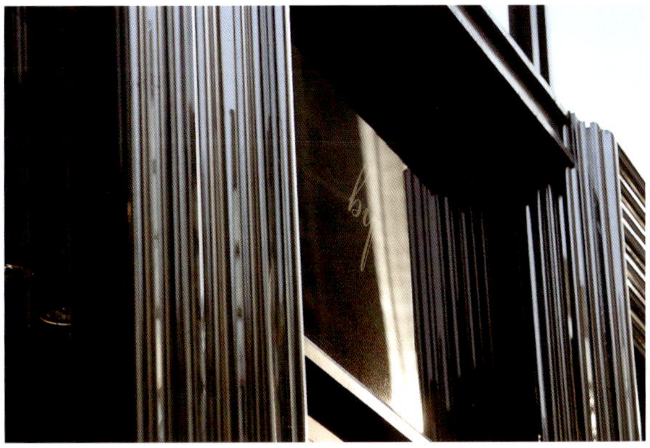
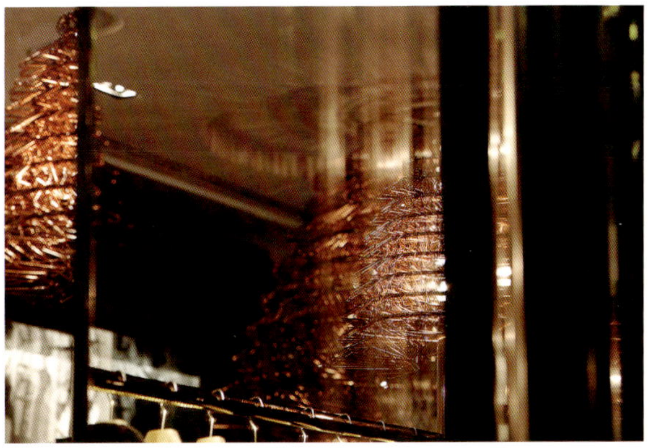
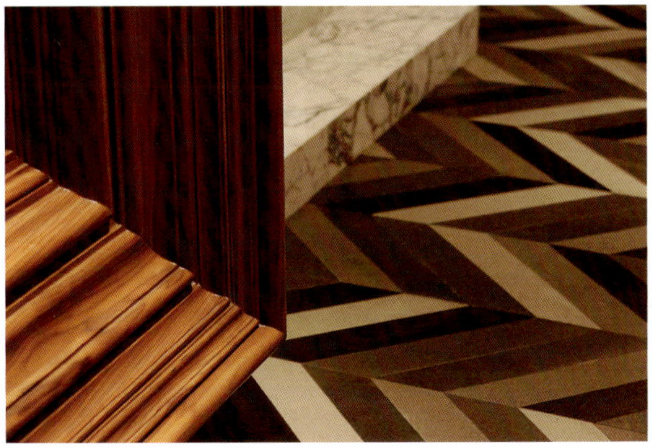
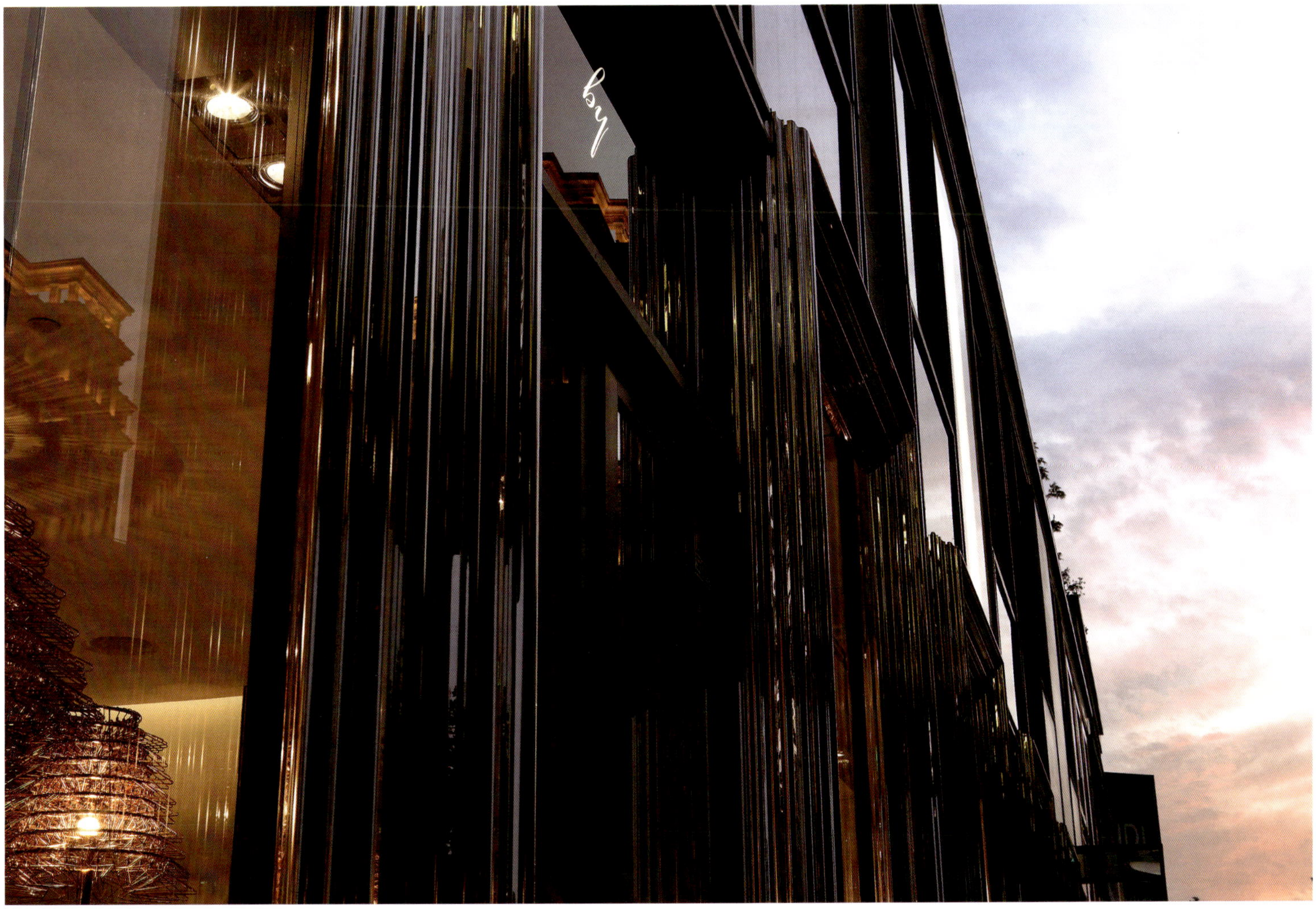

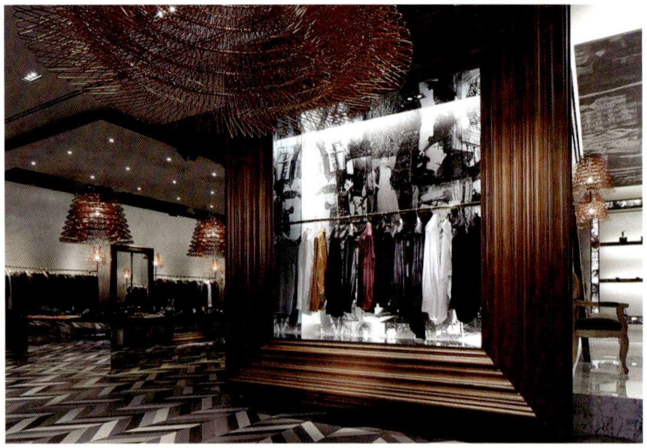

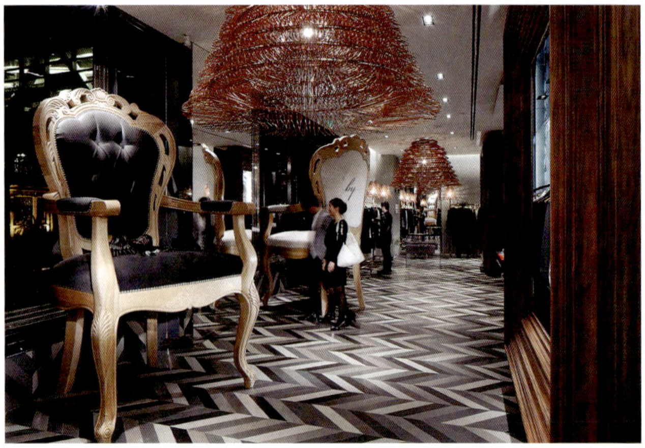

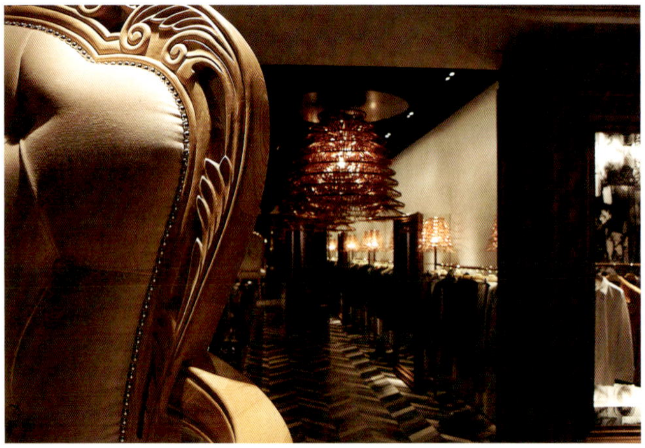

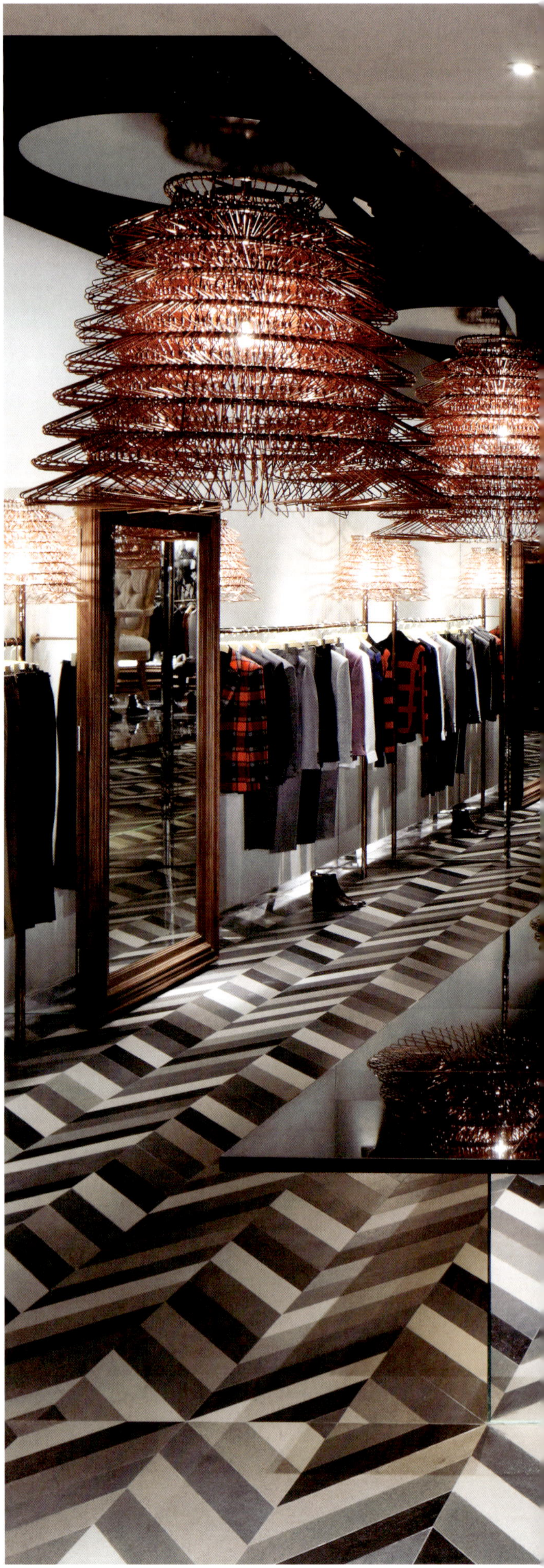

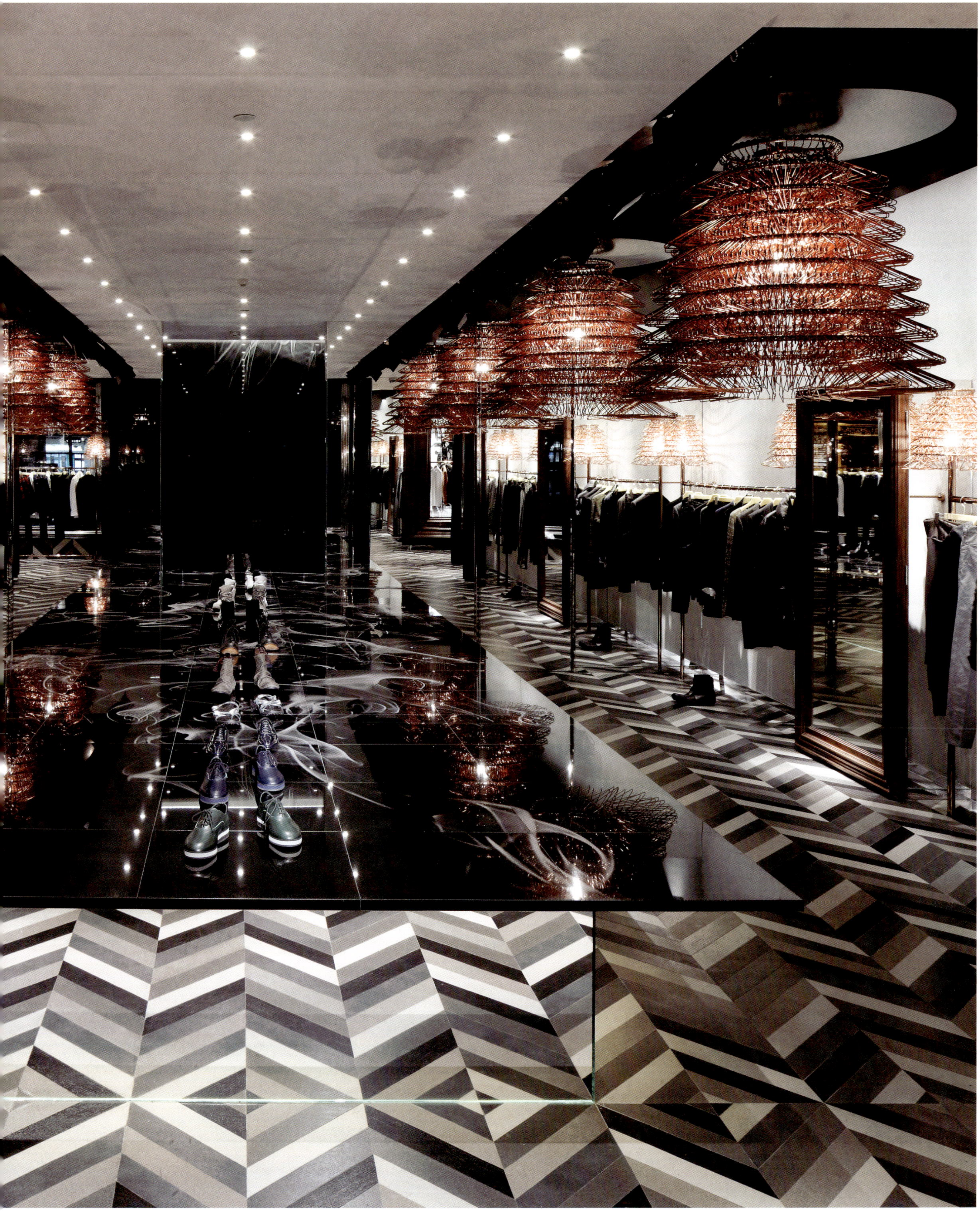

N°055
Osaka/Japan
Oct.2007

cagi de rêves

「建物内の店舗」という条件は、他の空間との差別化において、デザインの果たす役割が大きいのかもしれない。一目でどんな店舗か分かる必要があり、独立した空間であることを表現しなければならない。「cagi」とは、夢の扉を開く鍵のことだという。そして鍵とは、チョコレートのこと。森田は、店を形作る壁そのものをチョコレートで作ることにした。板状のチョコレートをモチーフとした格子組みで、建築内に四角い箱を建てる。店内が透けて見えることで圧迫感を軽減。空間内には宝石を展示するのと同様のスタイルでチョコレートが置かれている。いかに客を「もてなすか」を考え抜く森田の指示通りに、チョコレートの展示は、子どもの目線でも見ることのできる高さに設定されている。

The fact that this project was located inside a building played an important role in creating this distinctive space. The design had to clearly define the store at first glance, conveying its independence from the surrounding environment. The term "cagi" signifies the key to opening the door into a dream. This *key* is chocolate. Morita decided to use this chocolate metaphor for the walls of the store. A square box was built inside the architecture, embroidered with the chocolate bar's lattice motif, and the lattice was kept transparent to alleviate tension. Inside, chocolates are displayed like exquisite pieces of jewelry. To treat the customer, Morita made sure the chocolate display was measured just low enough for a child to take a peek inside.

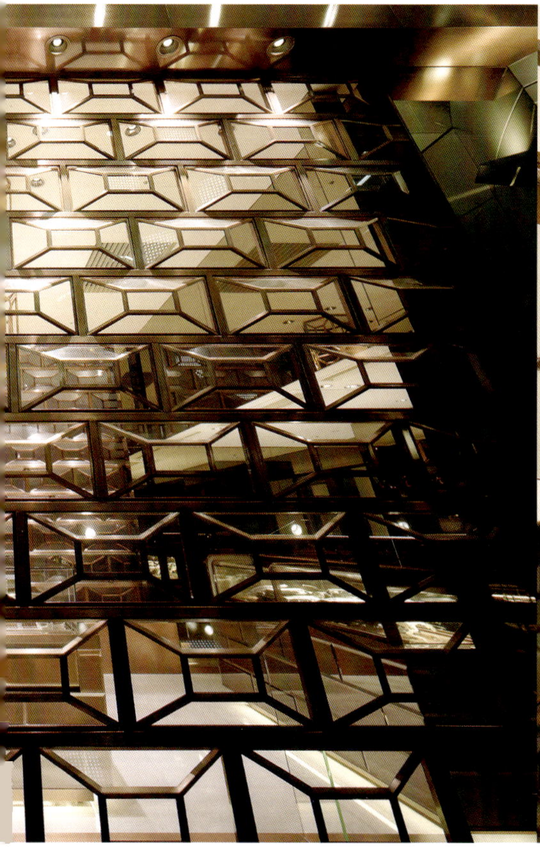

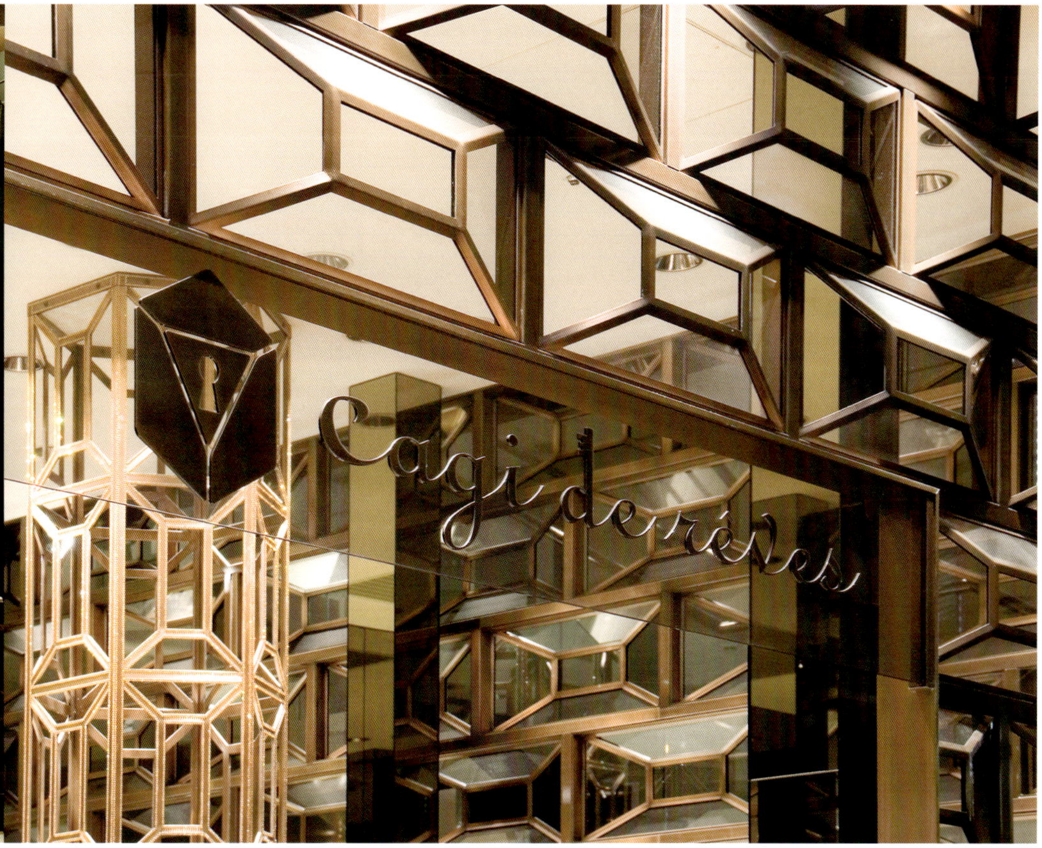
Cagi de rêves

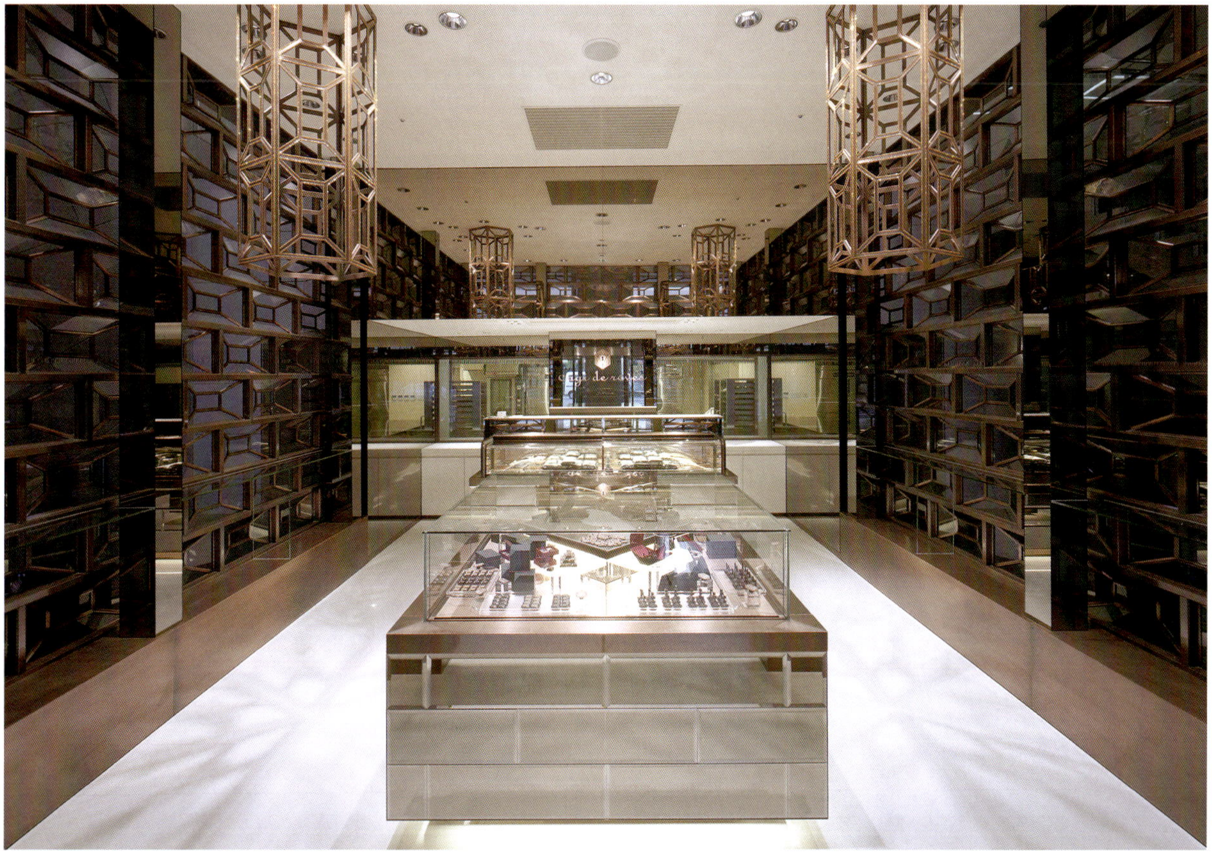

N°056
Tokyo/Japan
Jul.2007

couronne

硬質な空間である。安藤忠雄氏による設計ということもあるが、やはり扱うアイテムが時計であるということが、大きな理由のひとつ。その硬さを和らげるために森田が用いたのが、ウッド・ビーズのカーテンと、コッパーカラー。まるでカーテンのように天井から垂らされたウッド・ビーズは、光を柔らかく反射する作用もある。空間を統一するコッパーカラーを採用することでその効果はより強くなっている。フローリングとカーペットによって、空間を仕切ることなく演出を変える。スタンドのシャンデリアはエレガンスを、VIPルームへと続く壁面と柱の鏡は広がりを、硬質な素地に温もりを纏った空間に、それぞれプラスしている。

This space is unbreakable. The fact that it was designed by Tadao Ando might be one reason. That the store showcases watches and clocks, however, is another. To take the edge off this rigidity, Morita used curtains made of wooden beads with a layer of copper coloring. The beads, generously draped from the ceiling, diffuse the light into a diluted glow. The light is also intensified by the copper color that ties together the interior space. The switching from hardwood flooring to carpet naturally separates the space without the use of awkward partitions. The chandelier hints at refined elegance, and the mirrored wall surfaces and pillars leading to the VIP room expand the air. The space is characterized by a blanket of warmth layered onto a solid base.

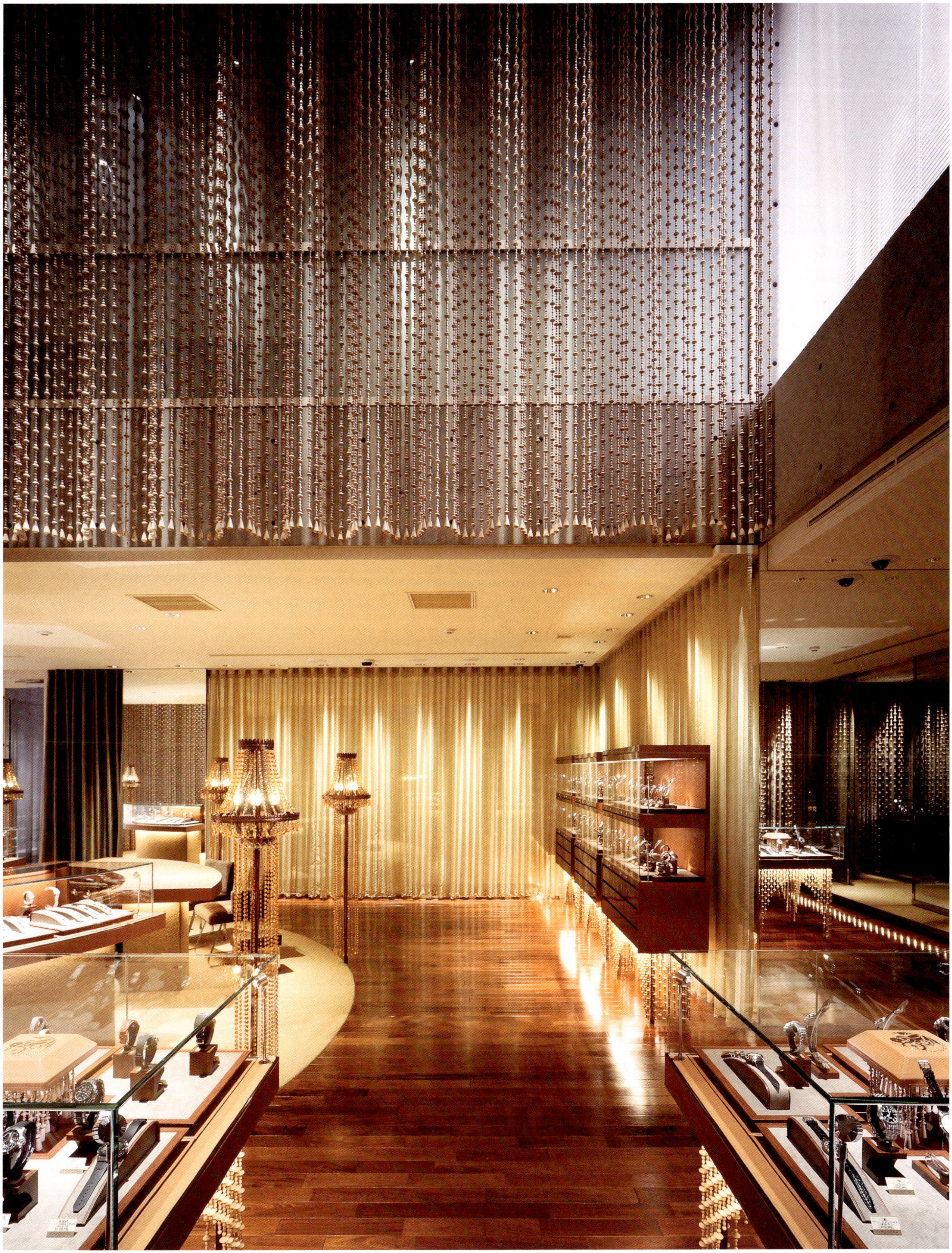

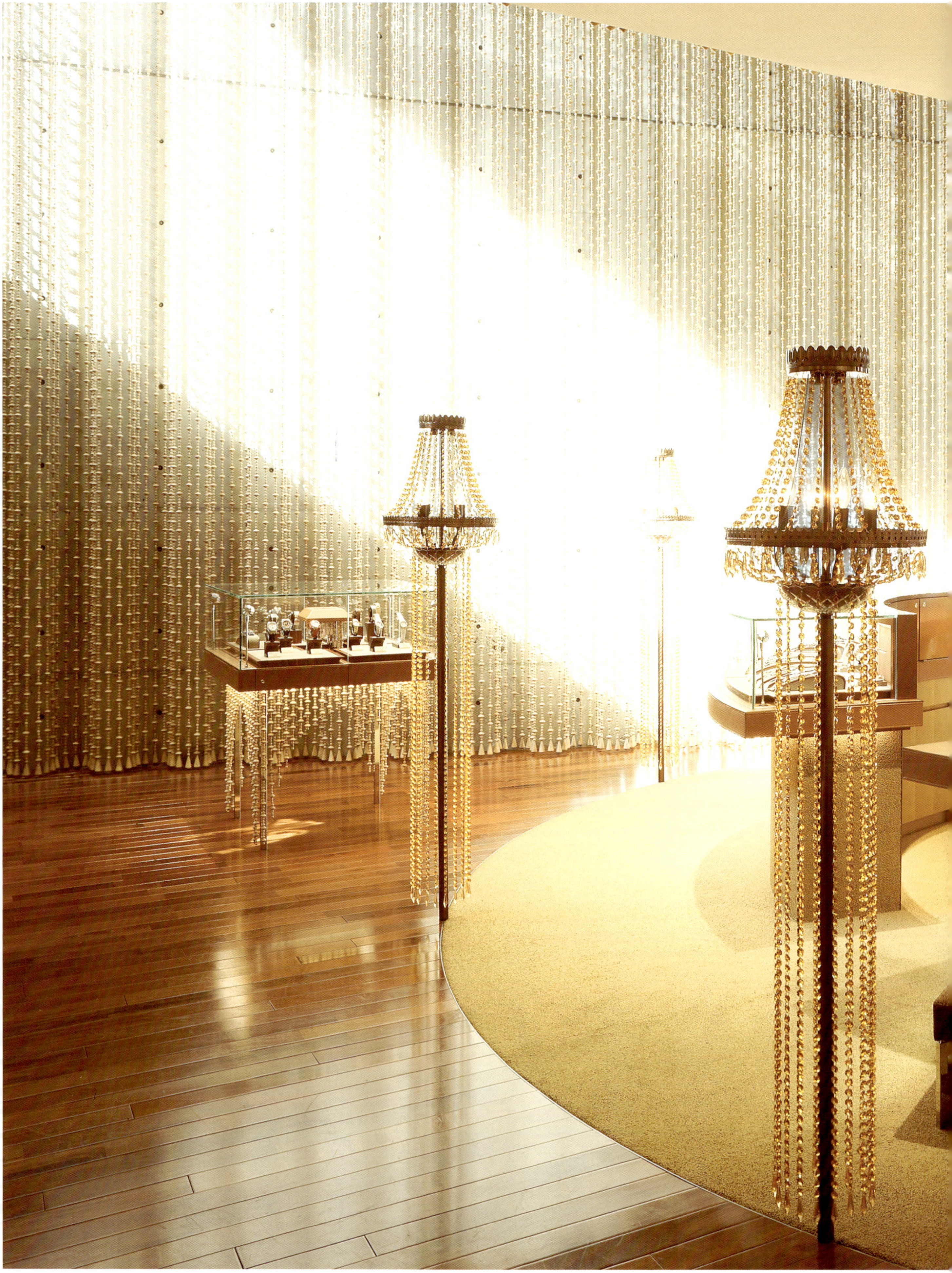

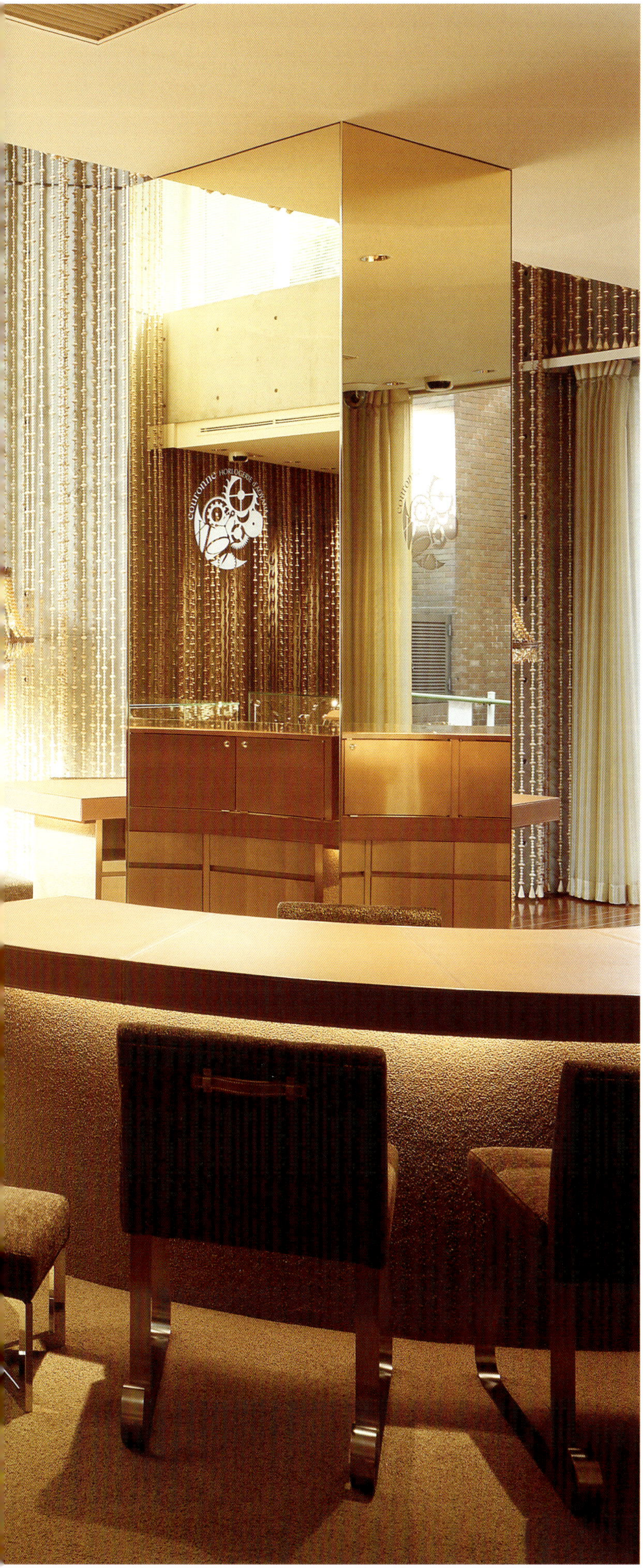

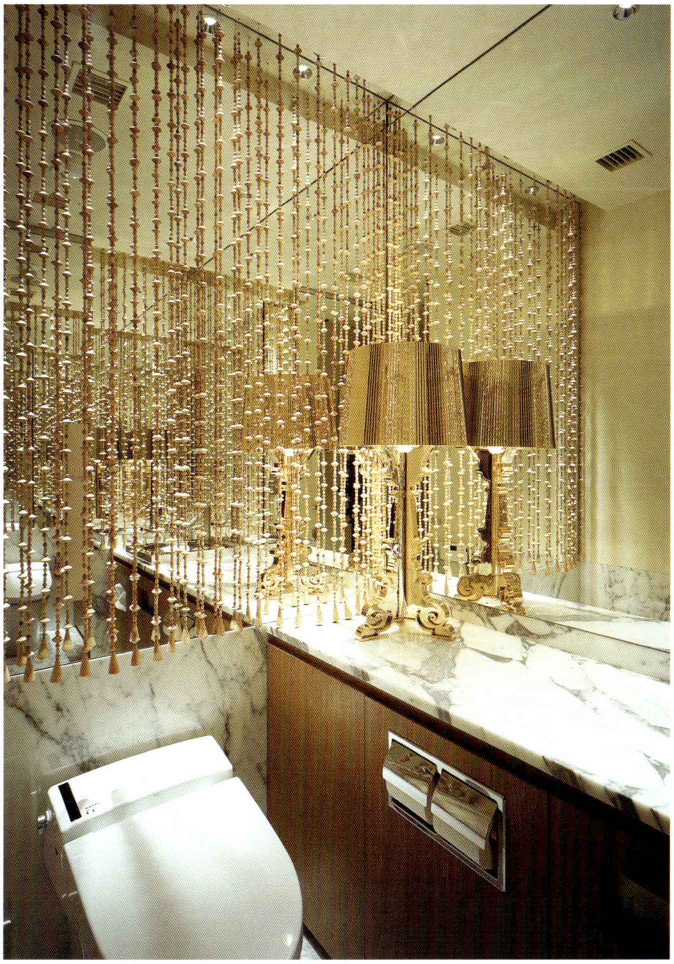

N°057
Tokyo/Japan
Jul.2007

AUDEMARS PIGUET AP TOWER

「ライティングは、言うなればメイクと同じようなもの」だと、森田はいつも口にしている。森田のデザインでもっとも重要な要素は、光なのだ。銀座7丁目という華やかな場所にありながら、街灯の白いライティングは、影をなくし硬い印象を与えてしまう。そこで打ち出したのが、通りへと溢れる、柔らかな光。周辺に競合ブティック犇めく通りで、一際強いエレガンスを演出するため、ファサードは行灯をモチーフとしている。遠近両方の視点に、それぞれ異なるデザインが浮かび上がる。近景には、時計のムーブメントをモチーフに植物へと発展させたデザインのパネルがはっきりと見え、遠景には、電球色のLEDを組み合わせた光がファサード一体に浮かび上がる。ムーブメントのモチーフは、最上階のVIPルームへと繋がり、強さと柔らかさが同居したデザインとなった。

One of Morita's favorite sayings is that lighting is "a lot like makeup." For Morita, light is the most important element of design. Despite this boutique's location inside the vibrant area of Ginza 7-Chome, the white lights of the streets create a rigid impression by taking away too much shadow. The solution was to create a radiant veil of warmth that spills onto the streets. The facade portrays motifs of paper shade lamps to elegantly outclass the competition on a street where numerous boutiques jostle with one another. The result is a layering of different designs that meet the eye at varying depths. In the foreground, the panel depicts a clock that evolves into an organic plant; in the background, LED light illuminates the facade. The motif, portraying the ticking motion of the watch, continues into the top floor VIP room, unifying both intensity and warmth in one coherent design.

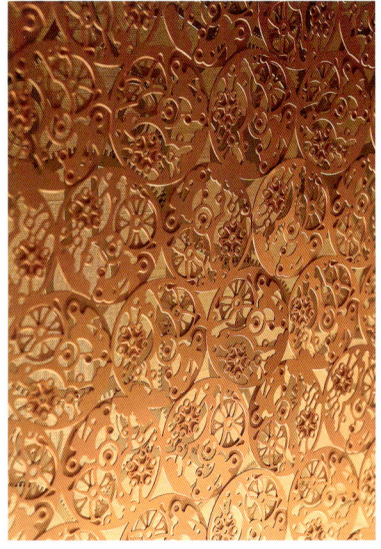

AP
AUDEMARS PIGUET
GRANDIR
JULES AUDEMARS COLLECTION
AP
AUDEMARS PIGUET

N°058
Tokyo/Japan
Apr.2007
RESONA BANK
Tokyo Midtown

デザインだけでなく、空間のあり方そのものを考えるコンサルティングに近い提案ができることも、森田が多く求められる理由かもしれない。いや、本来デザインと機能は不可分のものだからこそ、業務内容に踏み込んだ"設計"が必要になる。通常、外回りが多い銀行にあえて上質な空間を作り、客に来てもらうというコンセプトのもと、この空間は作られている。遮断する壁はなくとも、プライバシーを守るための工夫が施され、レザーの家具を多用しているのも柔らかさを表現する仕掛けのひとつ。「どんなビジネスも、エンドユーザーのリピーターがあってこそ」という森田の言葉の裏には、どの物件にも共通するオーダーメイドの思想が見える。

One of the reasons why Morita is popular among his clients is because his proposals aren't just about the design but about redefining the space itself. True design cannot be separated from practicality and function, which is why planning for each design must touch upon the very core of a business. This bank space was created for client reception, and although there are no partitioning walls, the design achieves sensible privacy, with leather furnitures for extra warmth. "All businesses must value their loyal customers," Morita says, hinting at the tailored philosophy that underlines all his projects.

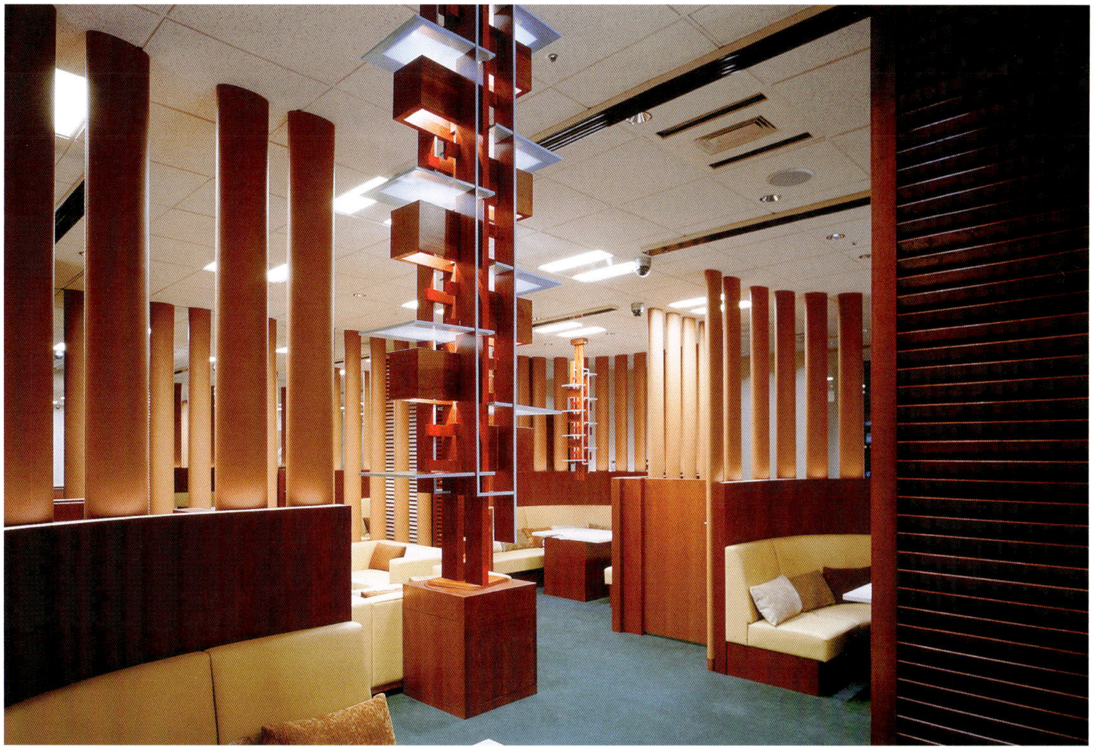
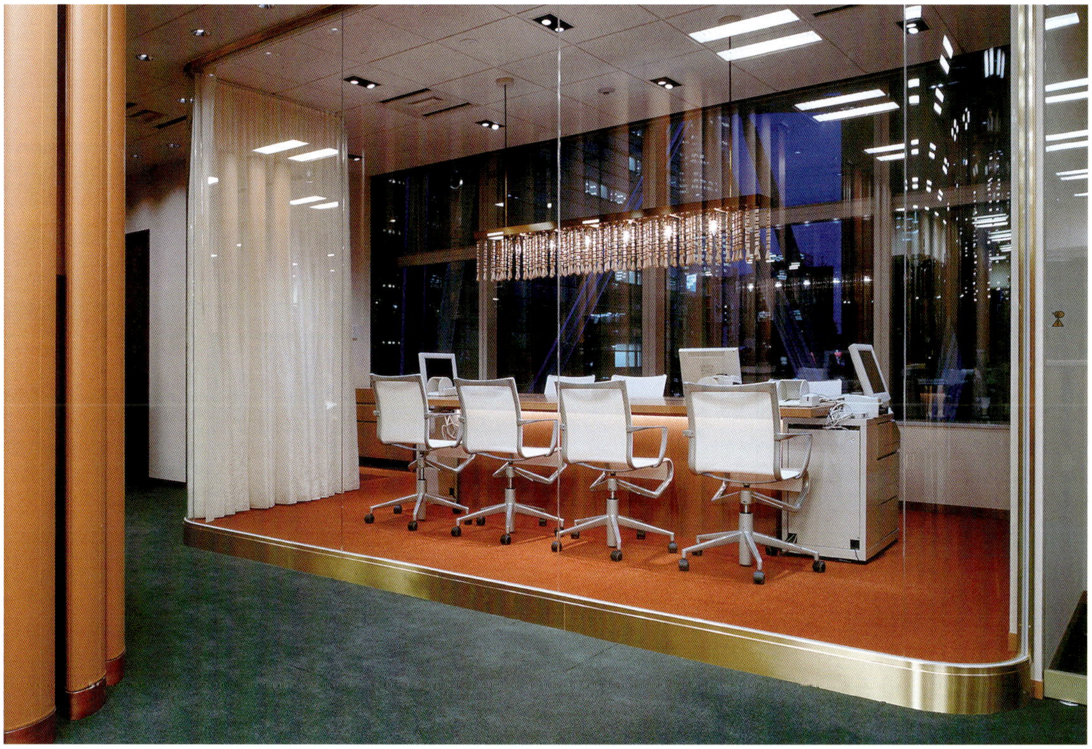

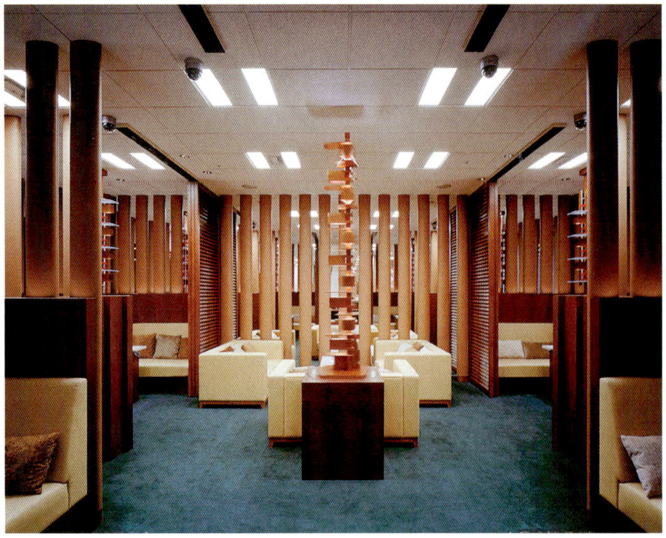

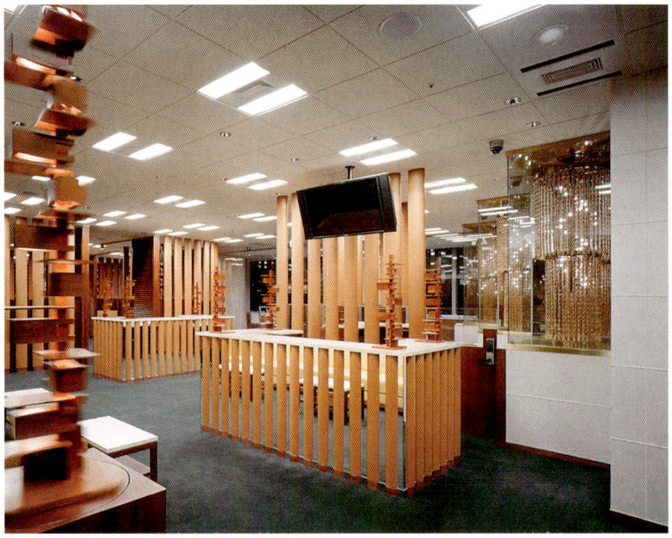

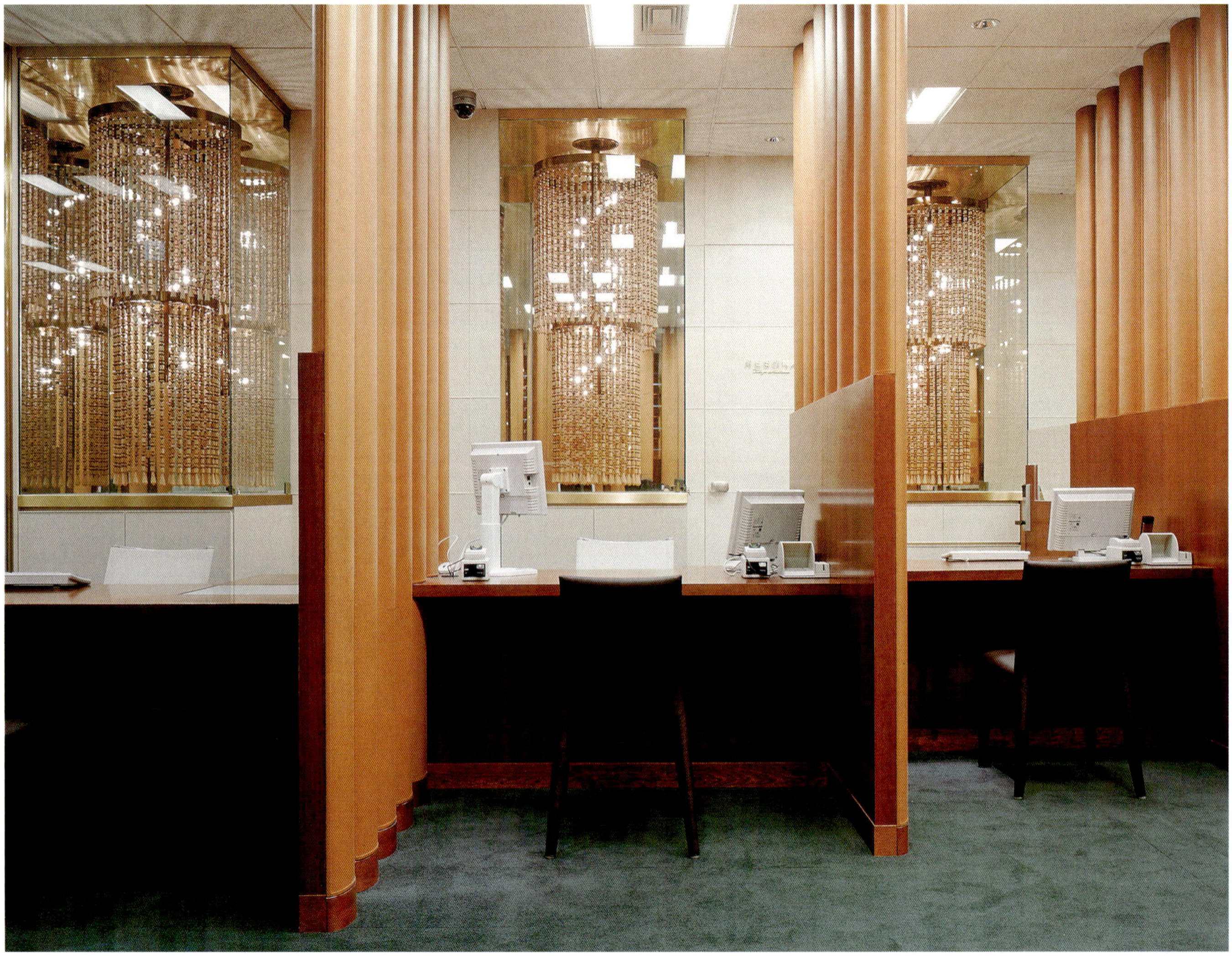

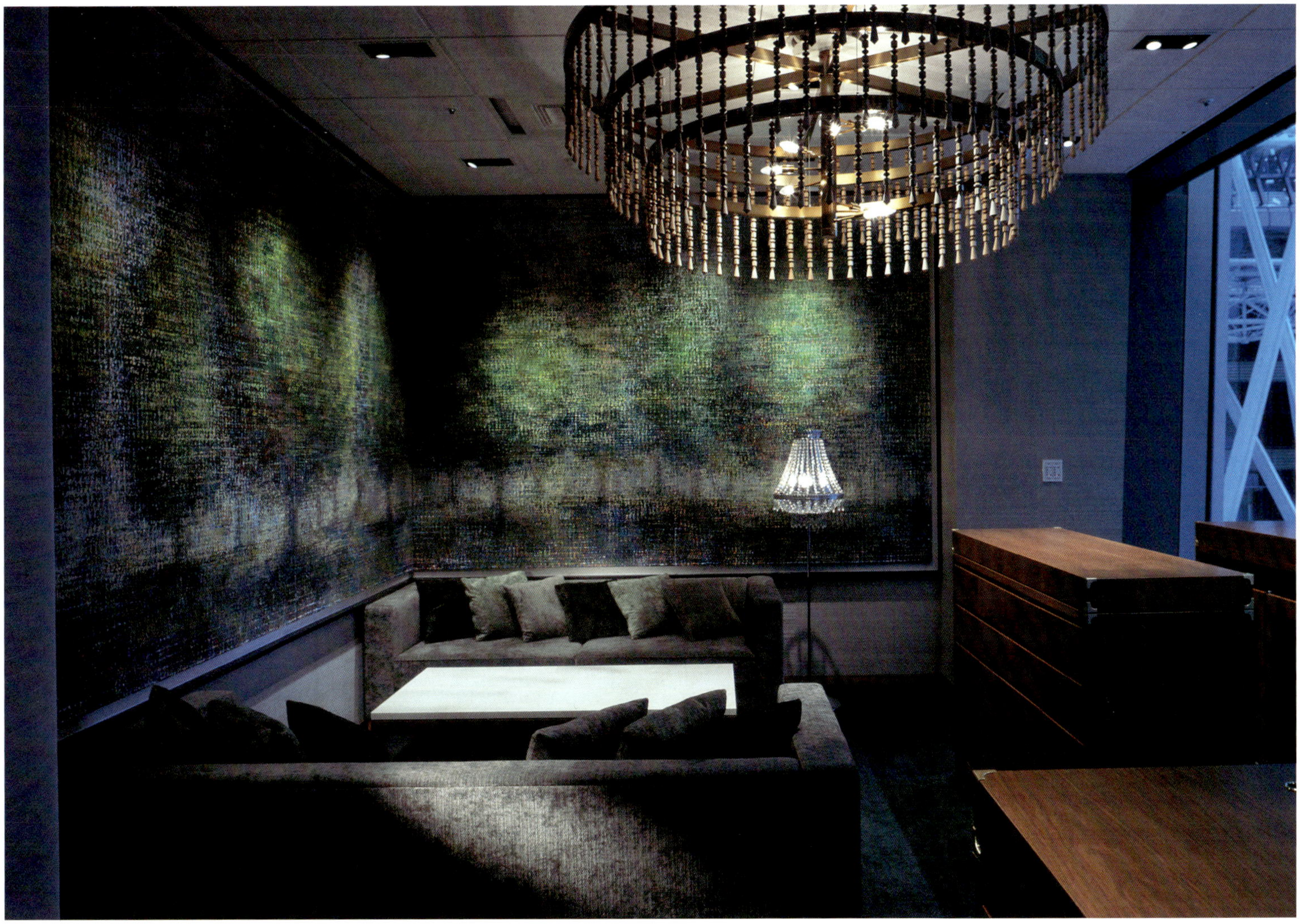

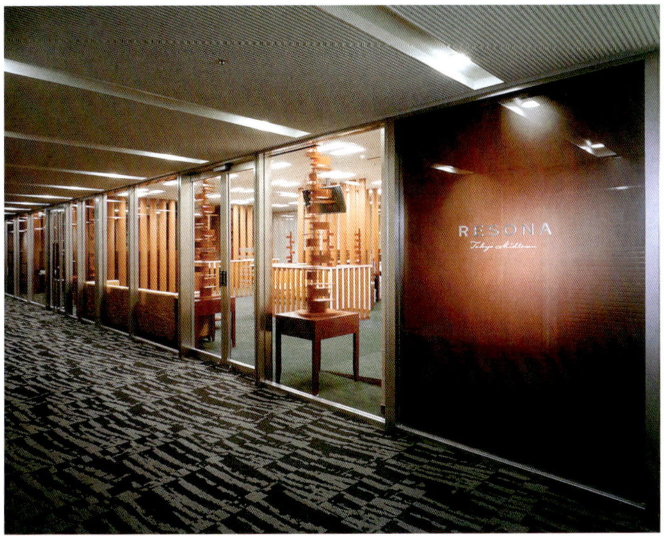
RESONA

N°059
Tokyo/Japan
Nov.2005
TOKIA

東京・丸の内にある商業施設「TOKIA」。地下エリアという特性上、縦に細長く店舗が配置される。地下街のコリドーをいかに区分けし、各テナントへと誘導するのか。歩行者が距離感を把握しやすくするために設置したのが、光の彫刻だった。3次元に展開される照明は、時に店舗のサイン機能を果たし、あるいはベンチやカウンターとしても利用できる。さらに光がコリドーの奥までも届くように設計。調光によって、地下街でありながら、時間を感じることもできる。オブジェのような照明という大胆な発想は、実に効果的だった。エレベーターや廊下など、2階、3階の共用部分にもその"光の扱い方"は通じている。無機質に感じられてしまう空間を柔らかく変化させている。

"TOKIA" is a commercial building located in Marunouchi, Tokyo. As with a typical underground area, storefronts are positioned vertically in a narrow line. The challenge was to efficiently section the underground shopping center and lead the way toward different shops. Light sculptures were placed as points of measurement to help visitors grasp the sense of distance. This three-dimensional lighting transforms into different shapes, taking the form of store signs, benches, and counters. The light also reaches far into the end of the corridor, and visitors experience a sense of time through this controlled lighting. This bold idea of turning the lighting into sculptural work proved to be quite effective. The same rule applies to the elevators, hallways, and the common spaces on the second and third floors. The air is thus relieved in an otherwise austere and inorganic space.

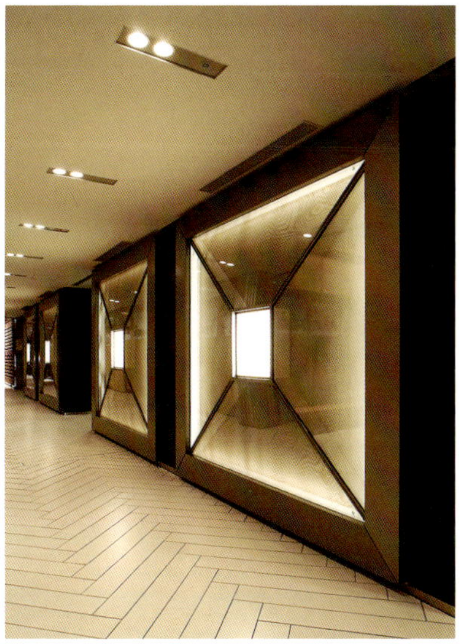
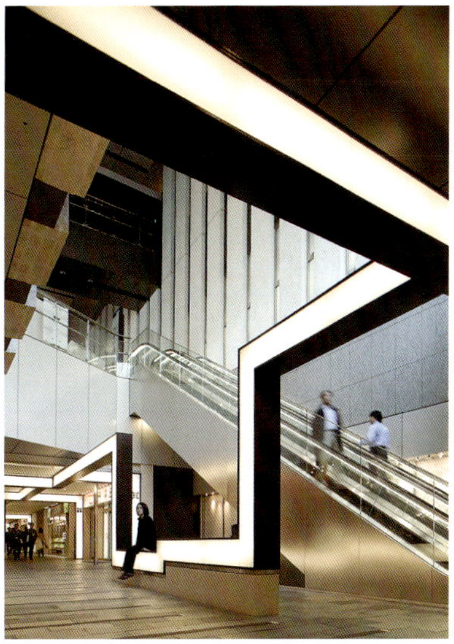
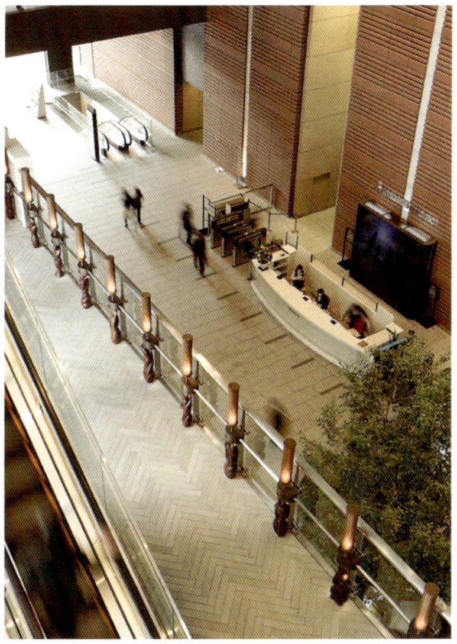
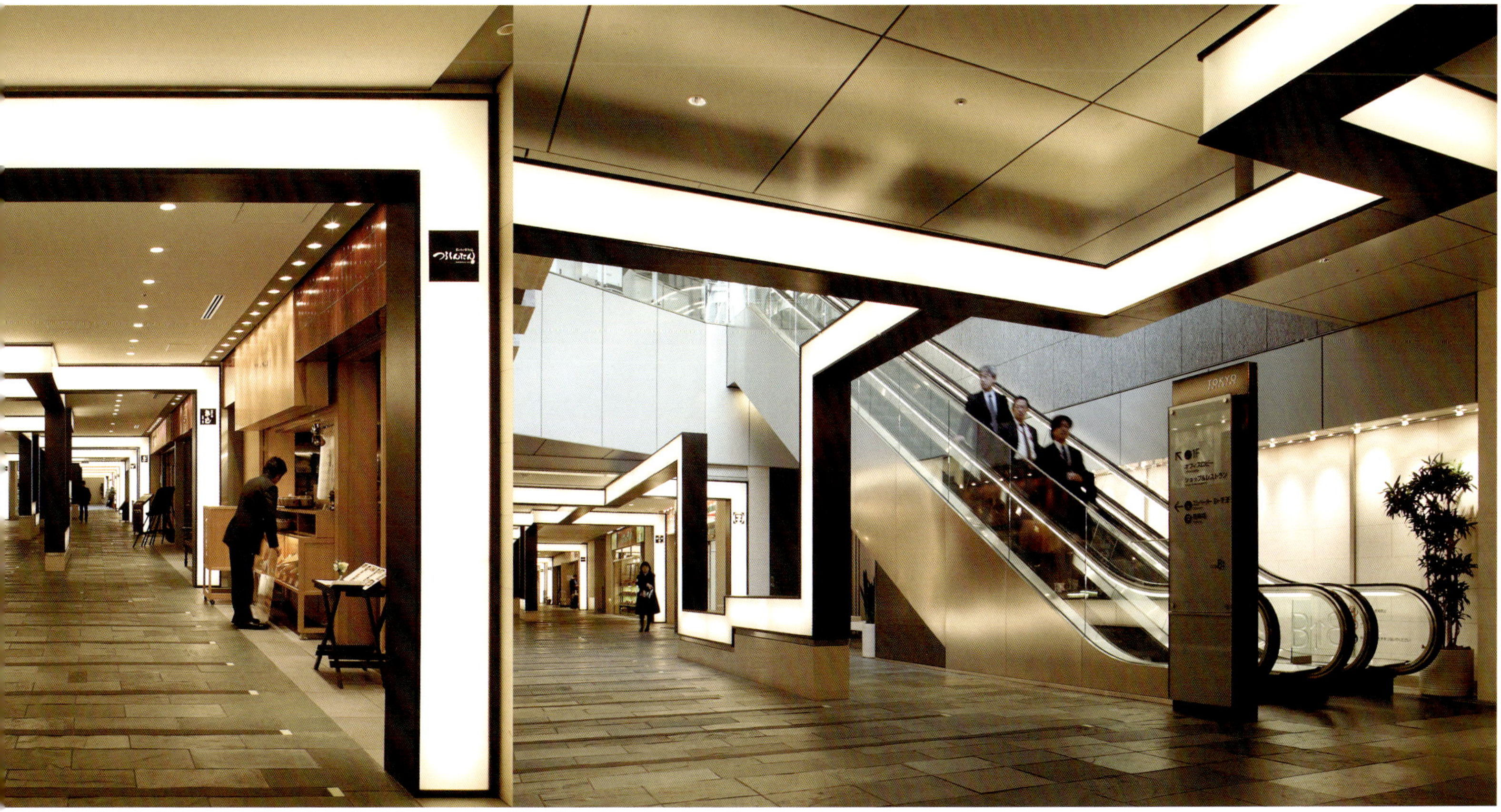

N°060
Tokyo/Japan
Nov.2007
K-two AOYAMA VADI

男性専用のトータルビューティーサロンで求められるのは、硬派でありながらサプライズのある空間だろう。床材に用いた大理石は、各ブースに表情をつけ、さらに女性をモチーフにしたモノクロのアートを間仕切りに用いることで、艶のある空間を構成している。天井まで続く壁ではなく、間仕切りによって構成することで圧迫感を軽減し、空間に広がりを生んでいる。さらに、間接照明の効果も上がる。細かなサイズの設定によって、光のこぼれ方、機能が変わってくるからだ。同様に中央に配置されたチェストは、ゲストにとっては間仕切りとして機能している。スタッフにとっては、店内を見渡せるような高さに設定している。

In this men's beauty salon, the design is meant to remain conservative while still retaining elements of surprise. The marble floor adds unique expressions to the booths, and the monochromatic female motifs are used as partitions to create an alluring space. None of the walls reach the ceiling; the space preserves its openness by using only partitions to separate each section. This also amplifies the ambience of the indirect lighting, the function and flow of which are determined by detailed sizing. A large drawer is placed in the center as another partition for the guests, measured just high enough for the staff to keep an eye on the entire space.

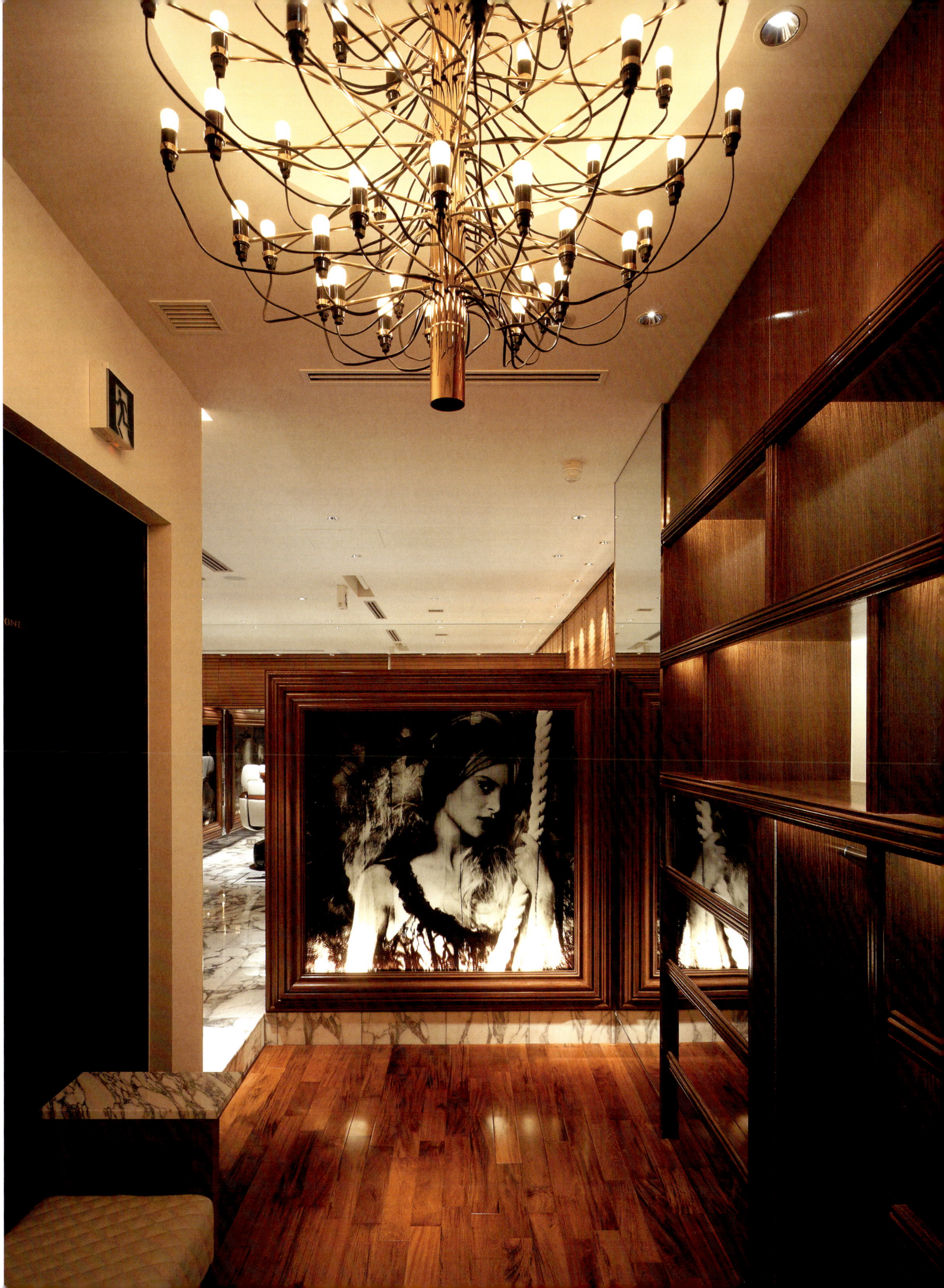

N°061
Tokyo/Japan
Nov.2007

K-two AOYAMA LU DORESS

スケールアウトしたトランクが、スタイリングミラーになっているヘアサロン。移動可能な箱として目に映るからだろう。リズミカルな印象を受ける。当然、照明もこの箱の中に仕込まれている。モノクロームの女性をモチーフとした佐竹穰氏の作品は、時に間仕切りとして用いられ、機能的な役割を担っている。3階建てのこのプロジェクトでは、各階の役割がそれぞれ異なっているが、モノクロームの女性という共通項が鏡によって反復されることで、それぞれの階を貫く同じ世界観を作り出している。また、白く清潔な空間全体のトーンを決定している。

This project was a hair salon, its centerpiece the series of portmanteau of scaled-out proportions that also function as styling mirrors. The portmanteaus look like portable boxes, giving the design a rhythmical impression. Of course, lighting is also contained inside these boxes. Joe Satake's monochromatic female motifs are used partly as partition walls. Although the three floors are defined differently, the monochromatic imagery of the women is echoed throughout the entire space, a set of mirrored reflections that color the building in a coherent world. The imagery also controls the clean white tone of the space.

N°062
Tokyo/Japan
May 2011
BRILLIAGE

「女性が持つ瑞々しさから発想した」と森田が語る、鏡面にランダムに配されたスタッズは、まるで水中に広がる無数の泡のようにも見える。屏風状の鏡面は、屋外に設置された同じく屏風状になった壁との狭間で、幾重にも反射されて奥行きを作り出している。スタッズは鏡の中に映り込み反復し、透明感を演出する。差し込む自然光の変化によって、その世界は青にもなり、ゴールドにもなる。サロンの主役である鏡面に配された"無数の泡"もやはり、光を増幅するための装置なのだ。奥に進めば、カットスペースとは対照的にベージュの抑えたグラデーションのガラスでまとめられたサロンがある。トーンの変化で、空間の表情を変えている。

Morita, who was inspired by "the dewy freshness of women," studded these mirrored surfaces to simulate the infinite bubbles of water. The mirrored screens reflect off a similar outdoor wall to create an endlessly layered illusion of expansiveness. The studs captured within the mirror exude a feeling of transparency, and with the changing of natural light, the world wavers from blue to gold. The infinite bubbles that encrust the salon's mirror are another device that amplifies light. Further inside, the salon is dressed with gradations of beige glass to contrast with the haircutting area. These spaces are defined by a change of tone.

N°063
Tokyo/Japan
Jan.2009

Takano Yuri
BEAUTY CLINIC Shinjuku

白を基調としていながらも、「プラチナ」と「ゴールド」を随所に使用し、「美を磨く空間」であることを表現している。壁面にはメッシュ加工が施され、シャンデリアの柔らかな光が溢れる設計。施術室では壁やパーテーションのモアレから、幻想的な光が浮かび上がる。ビルのガラス面に浮かび上がるシャンデリアの光と同じデザインのものが、パウダールームの鏡に使われていたり、廊下のライトが一輪挿しを兼ねていたり、シンプルな世界には実にアイコニックなモチーフが登場する。シンプルだからこそ、ラグジュアリーなエッセンスを細部に宿らせる。華やかであり、かつ柔らかい空間は、色のバリエーションとディテールの装飾によって作り上げられた。

Through the use of platinum and gold over a base of white, the space is designed specifically for personal beauty. The wall surfaces are perforated as a mesh surface, allowing the chandelier's light to flow softly. Inside the treatment rooms, ambient light emerges from the moiré of the partition walls. This simple world is filled with iconic motifs: the chandelier light, which appears on the building's glass surface, is replicated inside the mirrors of the powder rooms, and the hallway lights perform a dual function as bud vases. Because the design remains simple, the essence of true luxury is embedded in the detailing. The vibrant yet gentle interior is a result of the layering of various colors and embellished details.

N° 064
Tokyo/Japan
Dec.2011
KENZO DENTAL CLINIC

歯科医院独特の緊張感を緩和するために、自然素材を多用した。ファサードには、温かな大地をイメージしたグラデーション。大きなウッド・ビーズが流れるように光をこぼし、昼夜を問わず、通りからの外観のアイコンとなっている。さらに院内には、細かなウッド・ビーズのカーテンが壁面を飾る。照明にもウッド・ビーズを用いて統一感を生み出し、木からエネルギーを受けて再生するというイメージを強調している。狙いは素材の連続性による「統一感」と「揺らぎ」だ。ウッド・ビーズこその「揺らぎ」が、光の柔らかな変化を生み、リラックスした空気が、クリニックの中を満たしている。

To alleviate the nervous atmosphere typical of dental clinics, the design uses a variety of natural materials. The facade is a gradient of earthy warmth. Large wooden beads overflow with streams of light, a visual icon that adds character to the exterior throughout the day and night. Inside, the wall surfaces are also decked with curtains of intricate wooden beads. These beads are echoed in the lighting as well, emphasizing the image of a cycle of energy originating with trees. The aim was to achieve unity and tremor through a succession of materials. The slight trembling of the wooden beads creates a soft change of light, filling the clinic with a relaxed atmosphere.

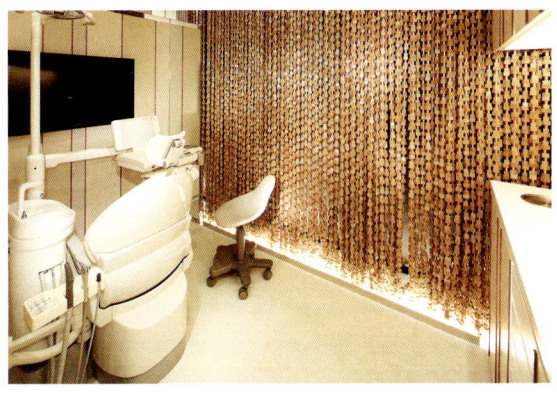

N°065
Kyoto/Japan
Oct.2002

嵐電 嵐山駅

京都・嵐山という土地柄からか、観光シーズン以外は人が少なく、駅としての機能を果たすのみの場所だった嵐山駅に、とにかく「人を集めること」が、クライアントからの依頼だった。そこで既存の駅舎のイメージを新たに展開すべく、通過する場所ではなく、駅そのものを人の集まる場所として捉え直した。ショップを含め滞在する場所としての駅をデザインしている。例えば、嵐山一帯が竹林の多い土地であることを活かし、約3000本もの竹でコンコースを埋め尽くす。さらに渡月橋をイメージした太鼓橋を構内に設置し、正面には季節によって変化をもたらすことができるように「のれん」を掛けている。また、駅は出会いと別れの場所でもあるというコンセプトのもと、ドラマティックなライティングで、京都の夜を演出している。

Due to its touristy location in Arashiyama, Kyoto, the station only attracts visitors during its peak seasons. The client therefore wished to attract as many people as possible. To redevelop the image of the existing building, Morita redefined the station as a destination rather than a transitory stop. The station, with its stores, is designed as a place for spending time. For example, the concourse is covered with over three thousand bamboo trees, a material that makes use of the Arashiyama area's bamboo forests. An arching bridge, reminiscent of the Togetsukyo Bridge, is placed inside the station, and removable *noren* curtains drape the front to reflect the changes in season. The concept also captures the station as a place for departures and encounters, with dramatic lighting to illuminate the Kyoto night.

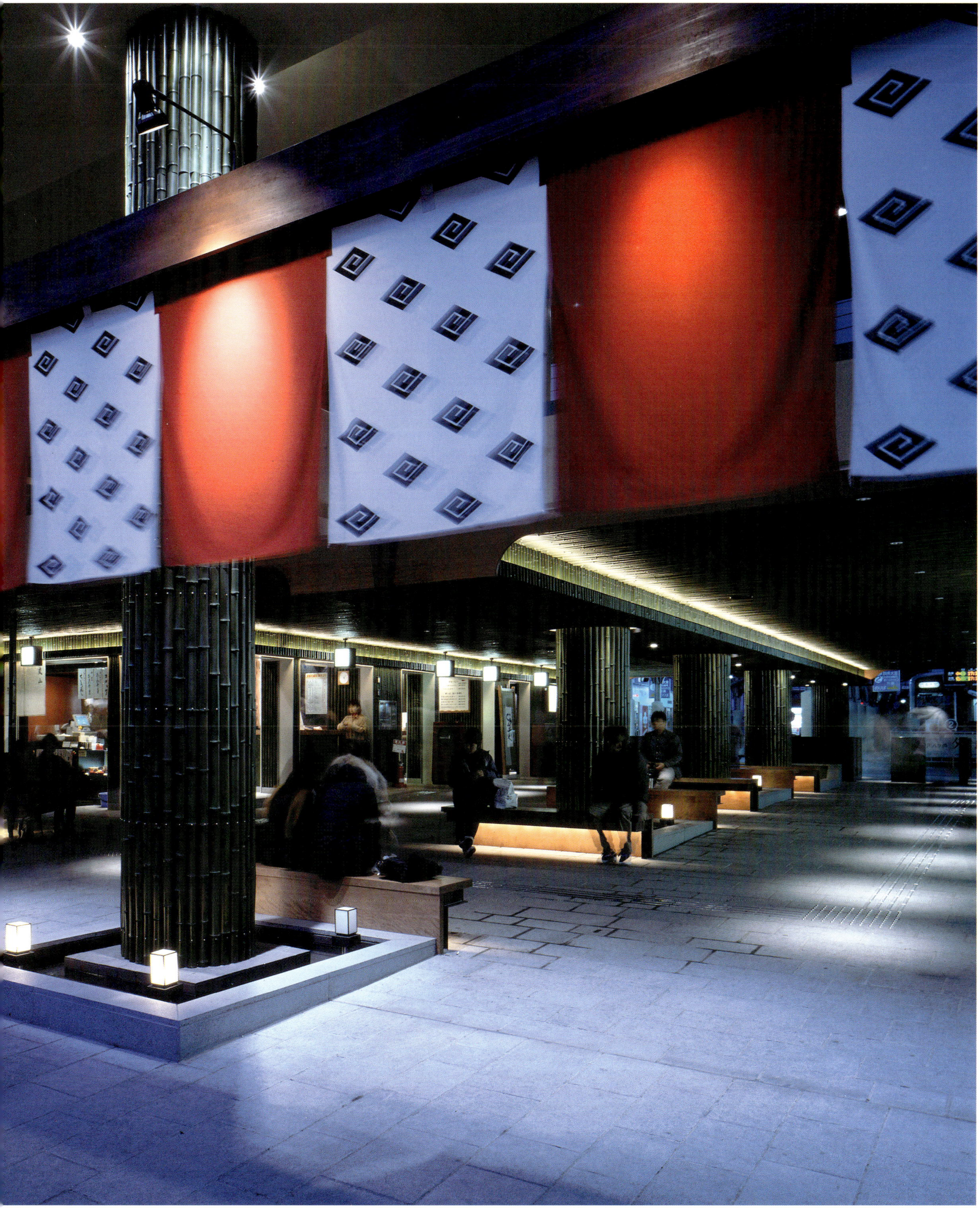

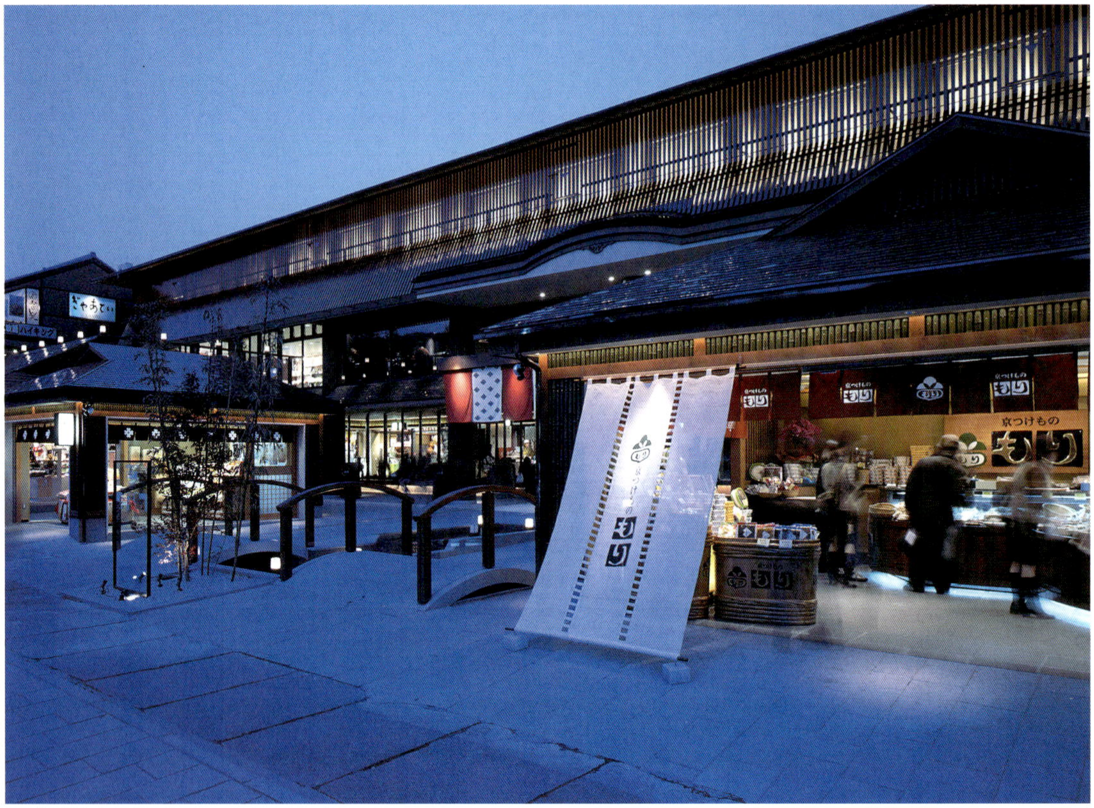
京つけもの

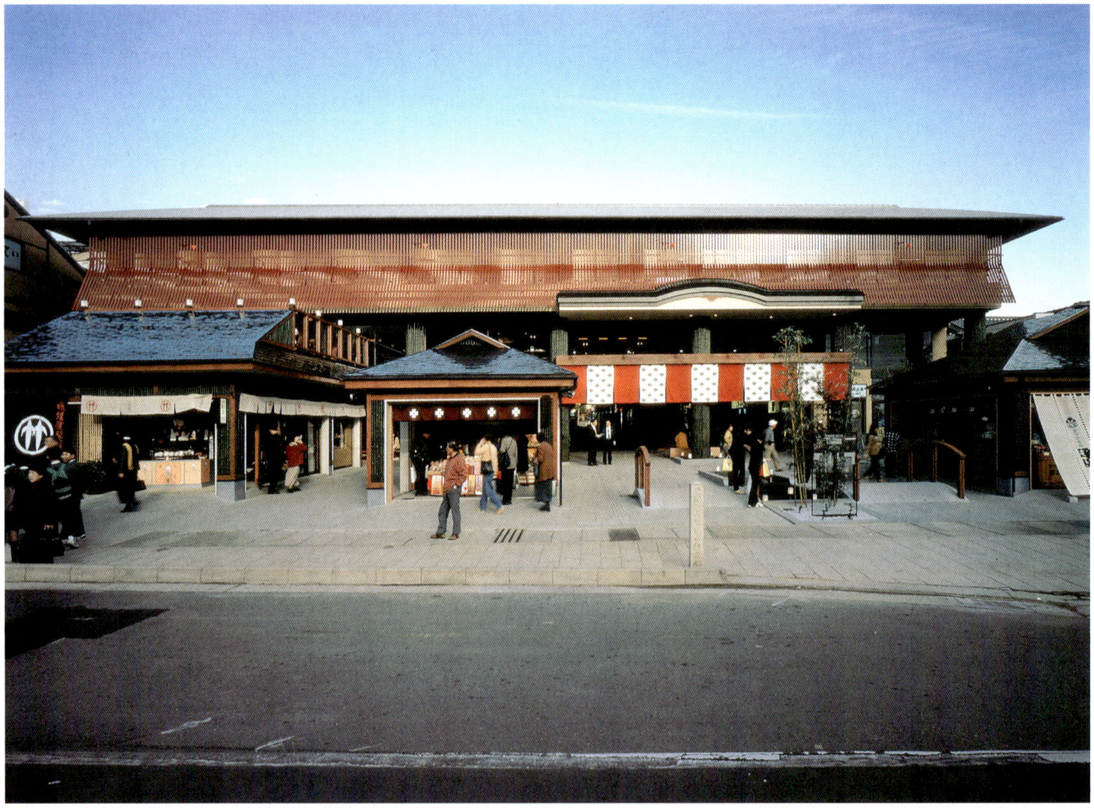

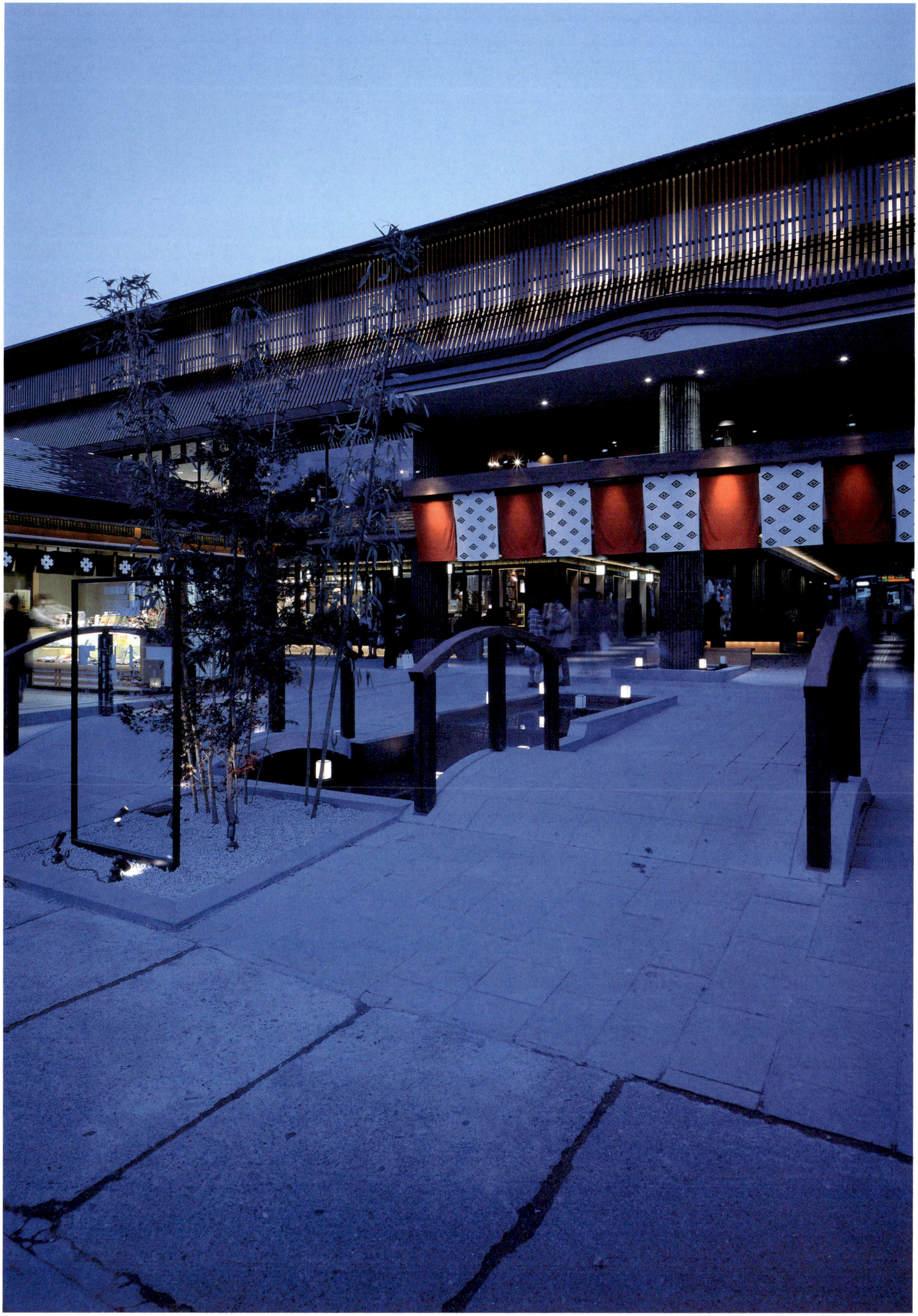

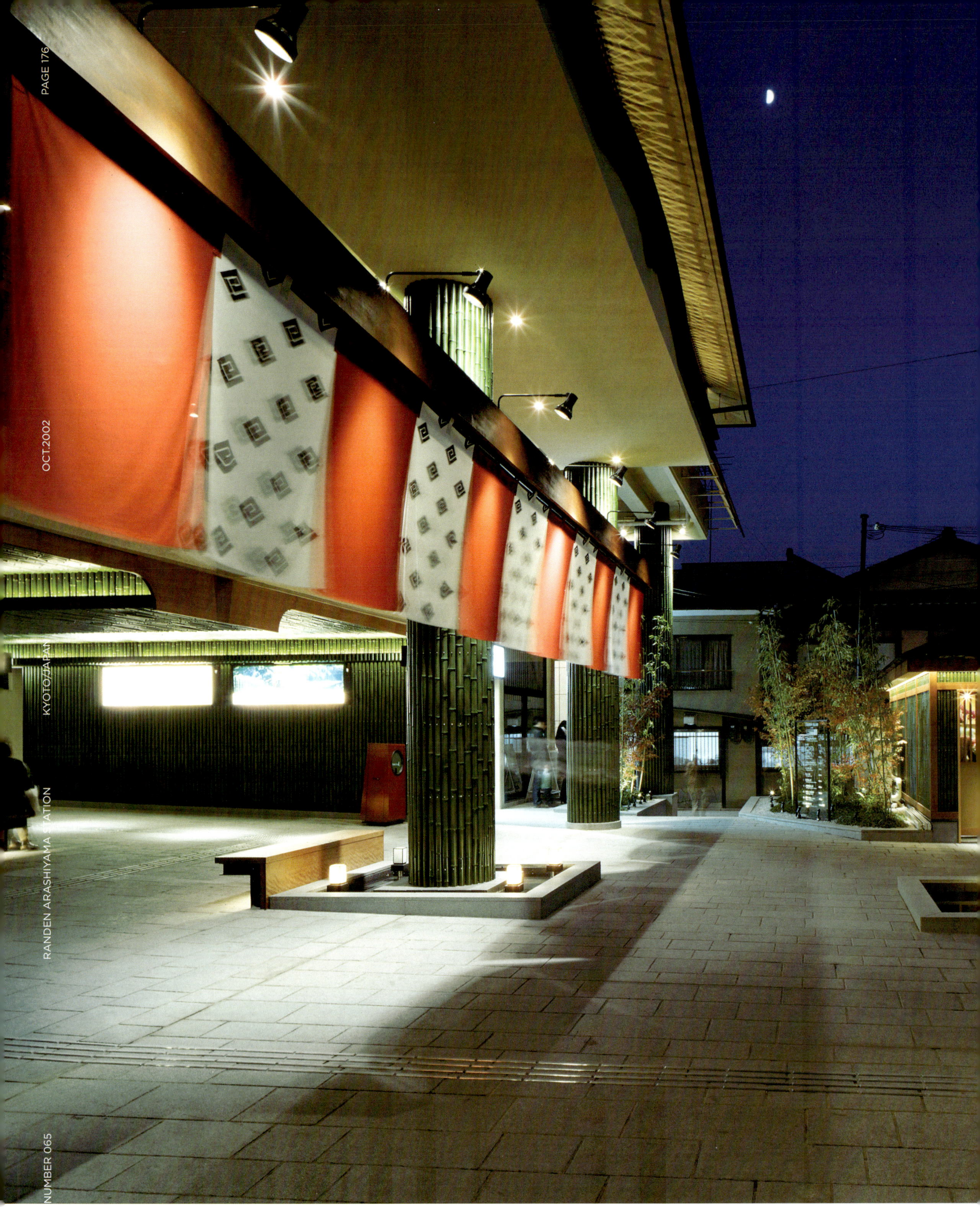

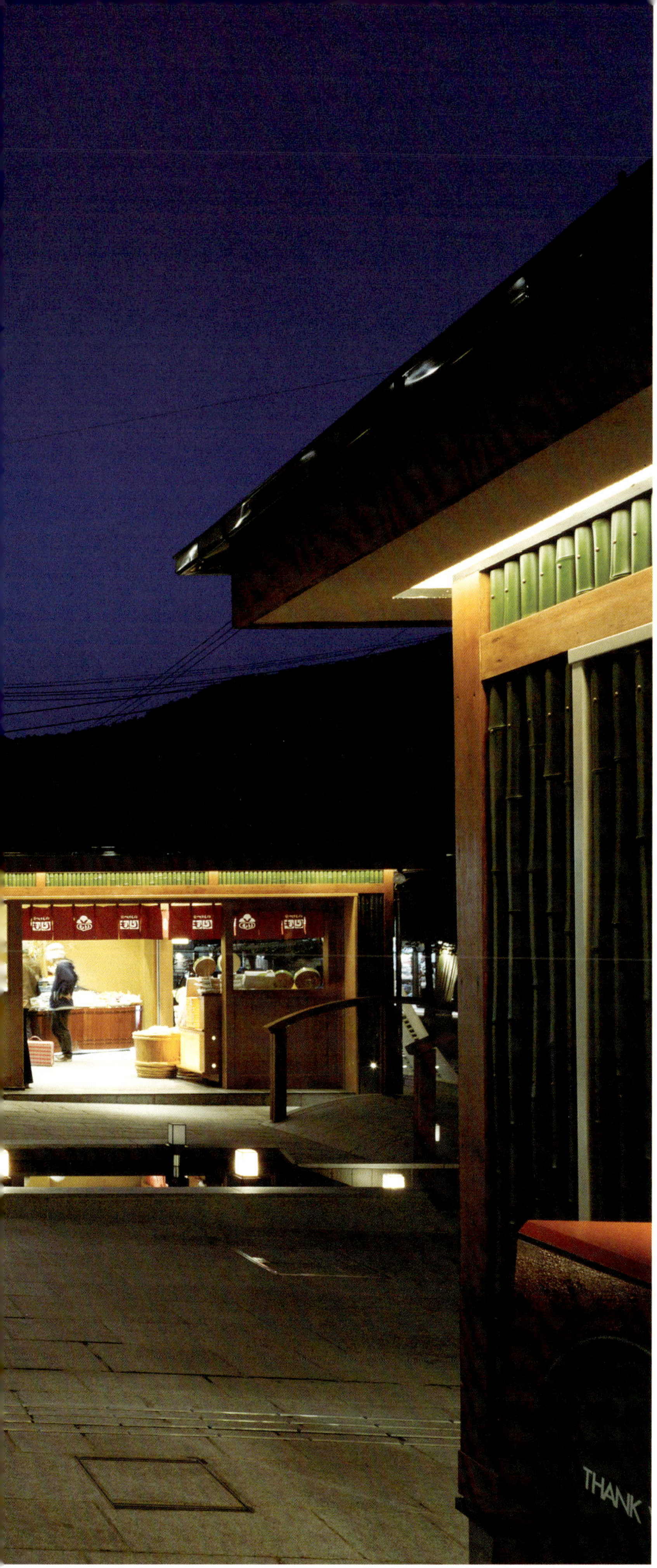
THANK

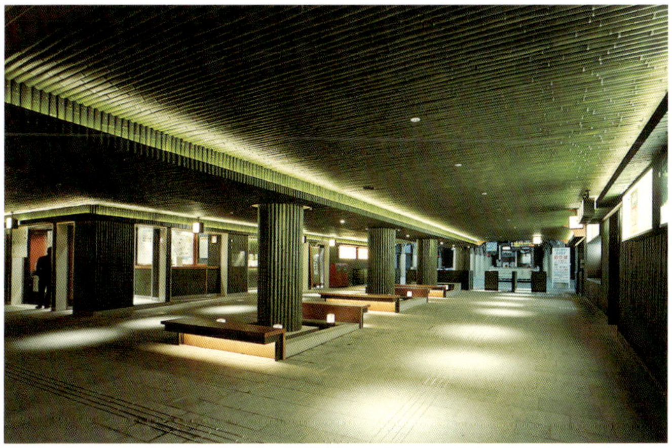

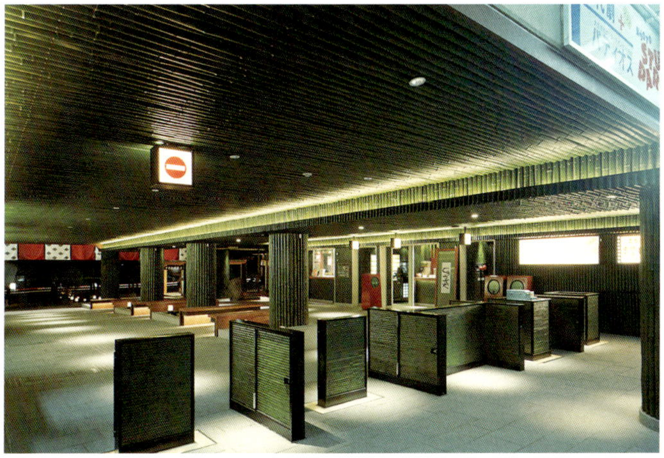

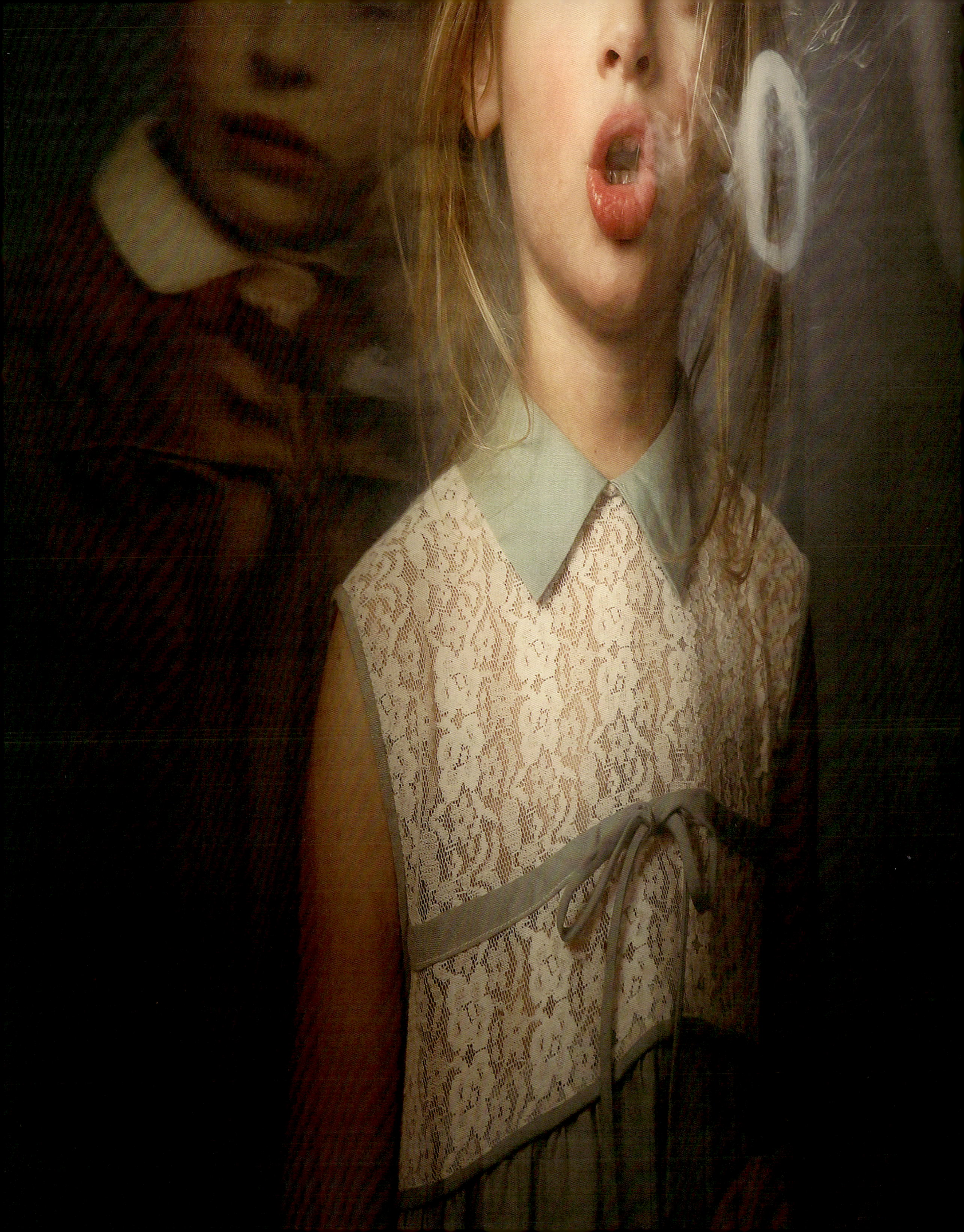

人がいるから、デザインが生まれる。

「大学生のとき、神戸の三宮には20歳くらいの子がオシャレして行けるバーがなかった。ワンコインでビールが飲めて、3000円くらいで気軽に楽しめるような場所がなかった。ある人に『NYのバーみたいな雰囲気で、そこにはいろんな業界の人が集まってきて、気がついたら人と人が繋がっているような、そんなバーがあったらいいですね』って話したら、『それだよ、森田。やってみなよ』と。そうやって始まったのが、最初の〈COOL〉というバーだった。雑誌『VOGUE』の切り抜きを大工さんに見せながら、『ここに写っている柱みたいなものを作りたいんですけど、どうしたらいいっすかね?』って。どうやったら作れるのかを夜な夜な話していた。今は写真の中にあるものではなくて、頭の中にあるものを形にしているけれど、やっていること自体はあの時から何も変わらない。

僕がやっていることは、クライアントのお金を使ってデザインしているものだから、自分の作品であるという意識はまったくない。自分のお金を使っていれば、それはアートになるのかもしれないけれど。だから僕は、手がけたものはすべて"物件"と呼んでいる。

シャンデリアの派手なイメージが強いかもしれないけれど、このアーカイブを見れば分かる通りに、"地味"と呼ぶのが正しいような、シンプルな物件も多く手がけている。だって、ゴージャスなお好み焼き屋さんって美味しくなさそうでしょう? おかんがやっているような店の方が絶対にいい。僕は、おかんから超可愛いお姉ちゃんまで、その店のストーリーに沿ってテイストを合わせることができるカメレオン。つまりは、人とクライアントの目的ありき。人とのコミュニケーションによって、デザインは生まれている。男も女も、年齢層もバラバラで、あらゆる業界の友だちたちとのコミュニケーションから、僕の仕事は成立している。そのスタンスも、昔から変わっていない」

Design is based on people.

"When I was still in school, there were no bars in Sannomiya, Kobe, for twenty-some girls to dress up and hang out in. There was no place that offered beer and some fun for a reasonable price. One day, I was talking with someone about 'a place with a New York vibe and a mixed crowd, where people connect with each other without knowing it.' And this person said to me, 'That's it, Morita, that's what you need to create. Why don't you go ahead and do it.' That's how a bar named 'Cool' started. I showed cutouts from the *Vogue* magazine to my carpenters, asking them to replicate a column-like object in the photo. We would talk for hours. Now, I've moved on from magazine cutouts to physicalizing the images in my head, but the process still remains the same.

I don't consider my designs as works of art. I'm using my client's money to design *for* them. Only when everything comes out of my own pockets, the term 'art' might become more appropriate. That's why I call my work 'projects' instead of 'art.'

People might have a glittery chandelier image of me, but as this archive shows, I also work on projects that are simple and modest. You wouldn't want to eat at an outrageously gorgeous *okonomiyaki* stand, would you? A homey store would be so much more appropriate. From pretty ladies to mamas who serve the best *okonomiyaki* in town, I'm like a chameleon who can change my taste according to the type of business. It's all up to my clients and their customers. Design comes out of communication with people, and my work is based on my conversations with friends: people from different professional fields, age and sex. And this stance towards my work remains the same, ever since I first started out as a designer."

N°066
Hong Kong/China
Jun.2006
松菱

何かに見立てることで、演出がより効果的になることがデザインの世界にはよく起こる。香港の鉄板焼きレストランでは、カウンターキッチンが能舞台となった。ゲストの目の前で披露される「パフォーマンス」によって、食はエンターテイメントとなり、そのための"舞台"を作るのが森田の役割。本物を感じさせるため、日本を婉曲的に表現している。例えば能舞台にある鏡板から着想を得て、松菱の「松」をシェフの背後に写真であしらった。あるいはシルバーでコーティングされた能面は、その分かりやすい答えかもしれない。角席が多く生まれるようにカウンターの形状をデザインし、写真を和紙に印刷し、ガラスで封印することにより光の動きを演出する。「食」を楽しむために必要な要素が、日本らしい伝統工芸をキーワードに展開されたデザインである。

In the world of design, staging becomes even more effective through visual association. For this Hong Kong *teppanyaki* restaurant, the kitchen counter was likened to a *Noh* stage. In a restaurant where dining becomes entertainment, Morita's role was to create a stage on which the performance could unfold before the guests. To convey authenticity, the concept of Japan is expressed through a degree of euphemism. For example, photographs of pine trees, taken from the restaurant's name, adorn the background walls to signify the mirror used in the *Noh* theater. The silver-coated *Noh* masks are perhaps more obvious indications of this concept. The counter shape was designed in order to create as many corner seats as possible, with glass-sealed photographs printed on Japanese paper to dynamically reflect the changing light. The necessary ingredients of a dining experience have been redeveloped into a design inspired by traditional Japanese craft.

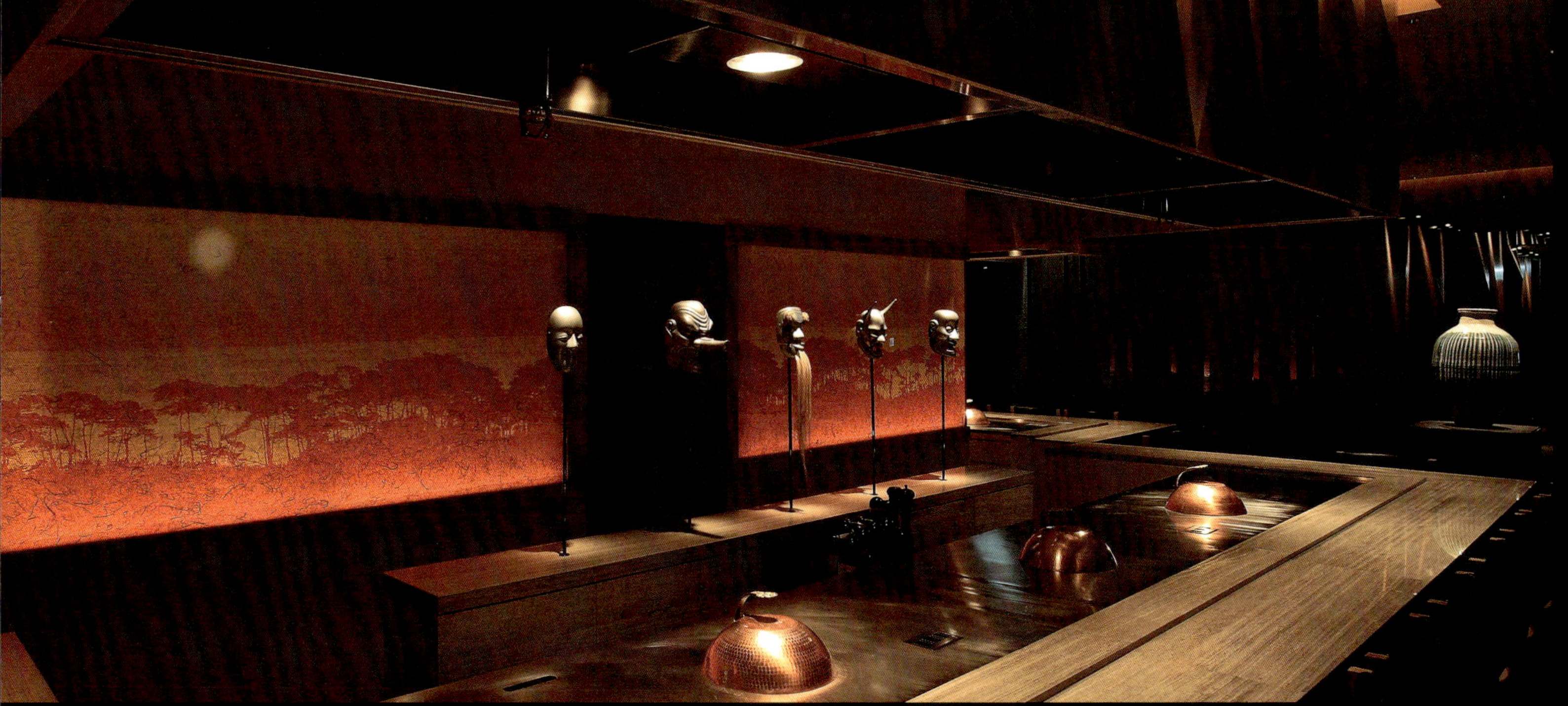

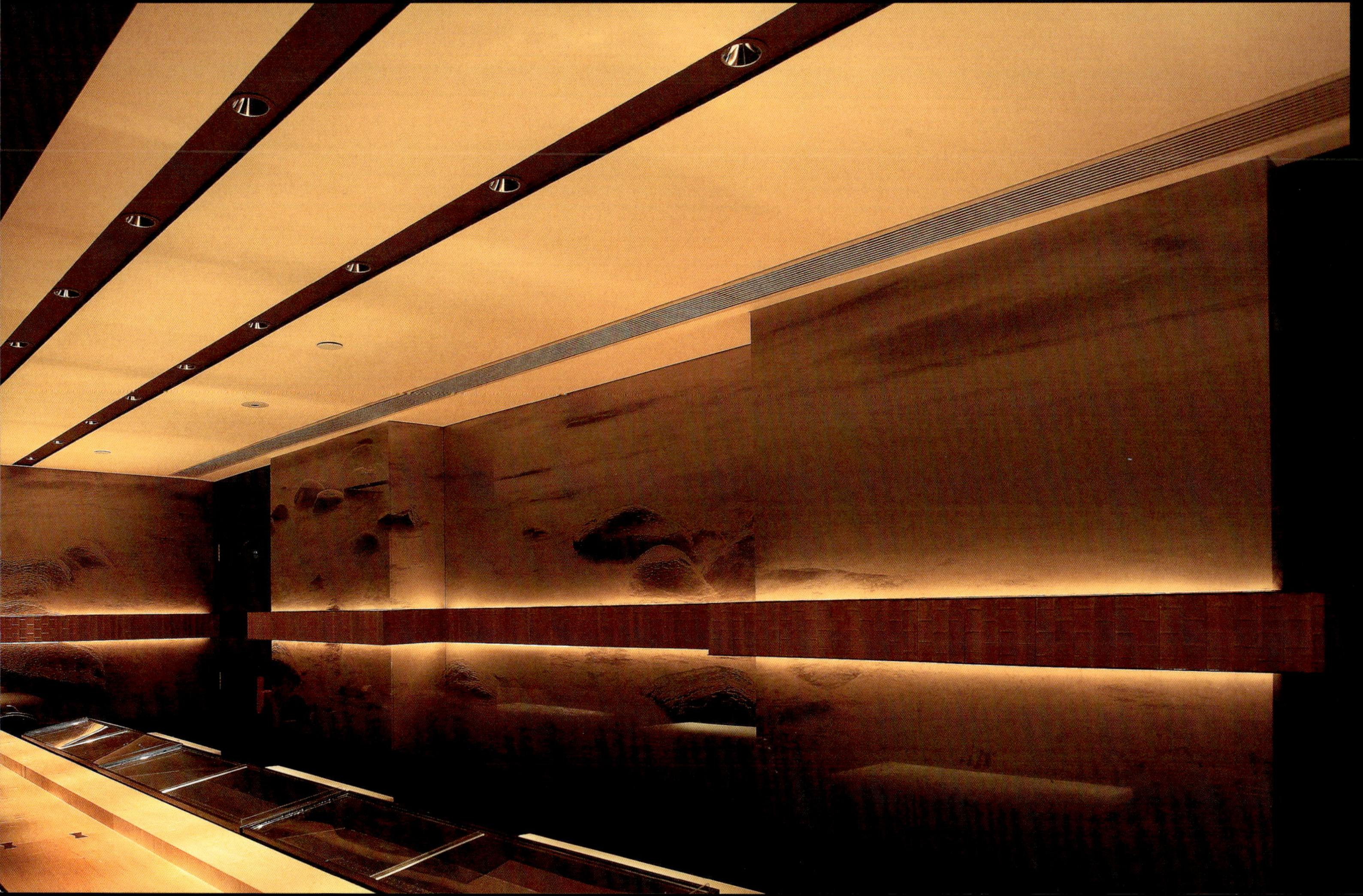

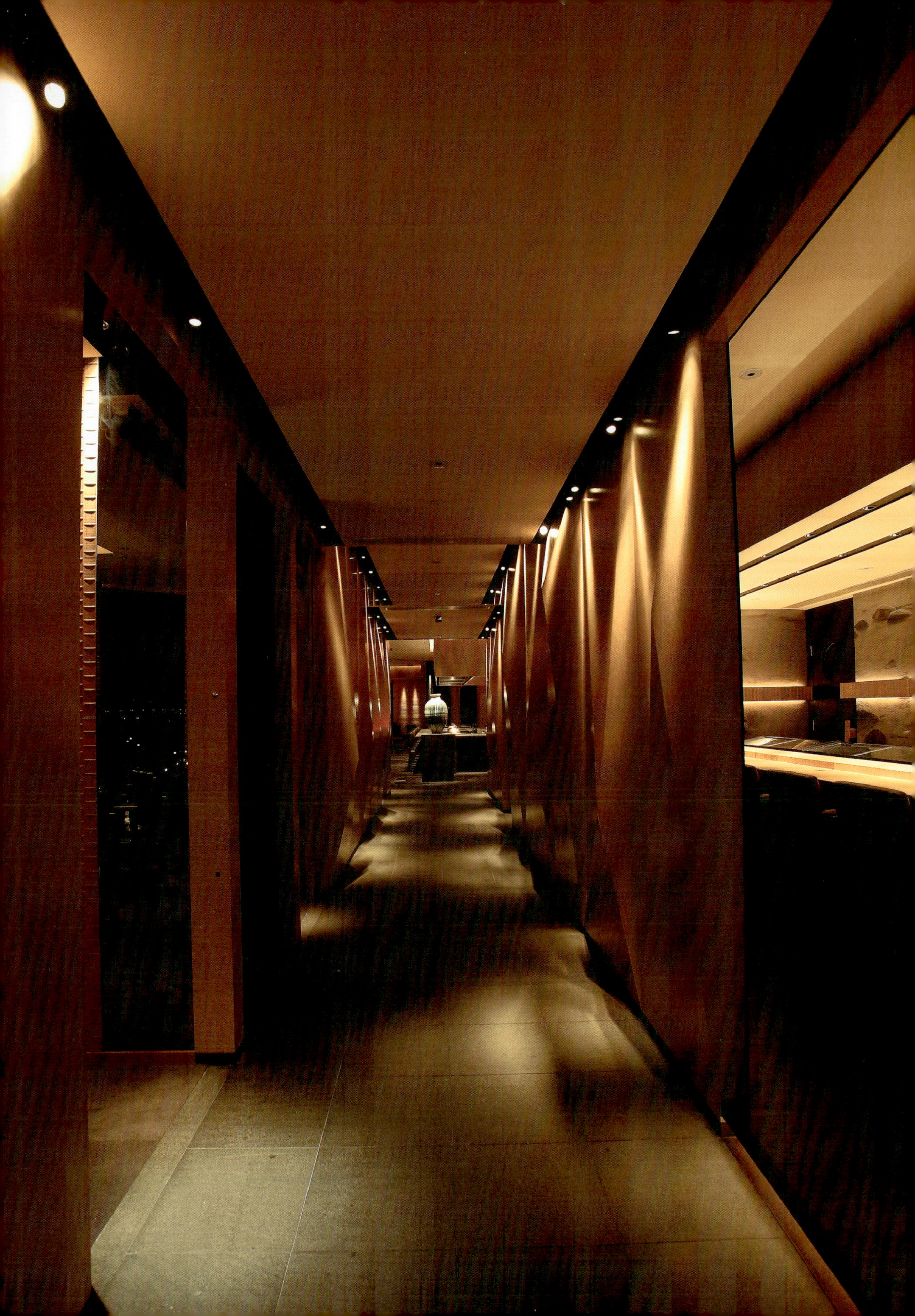

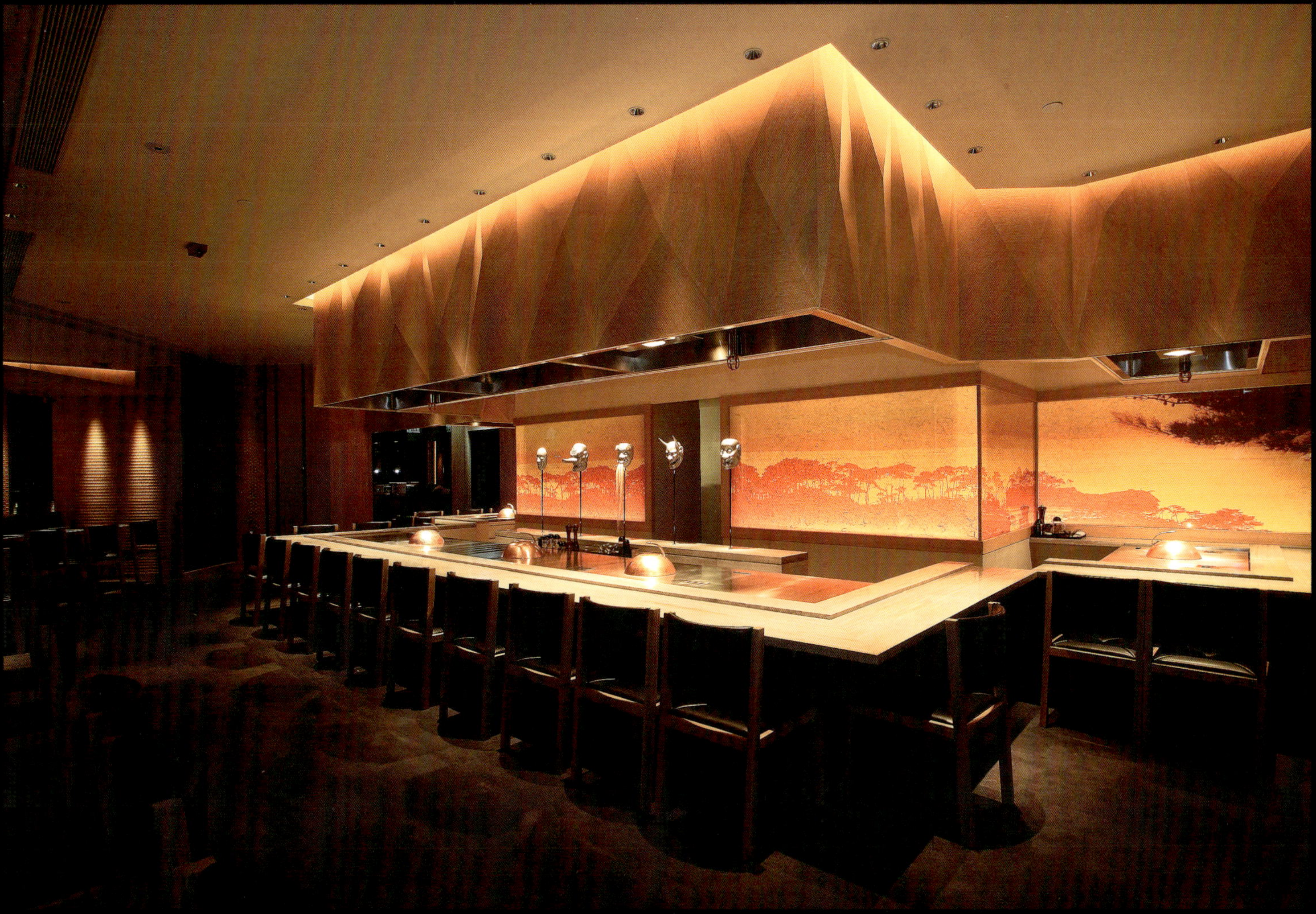

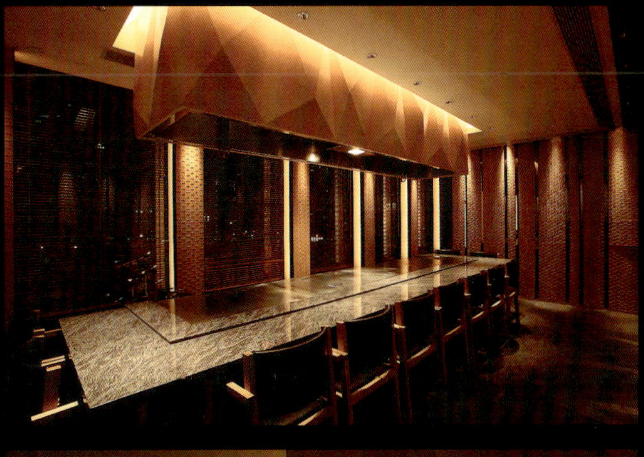

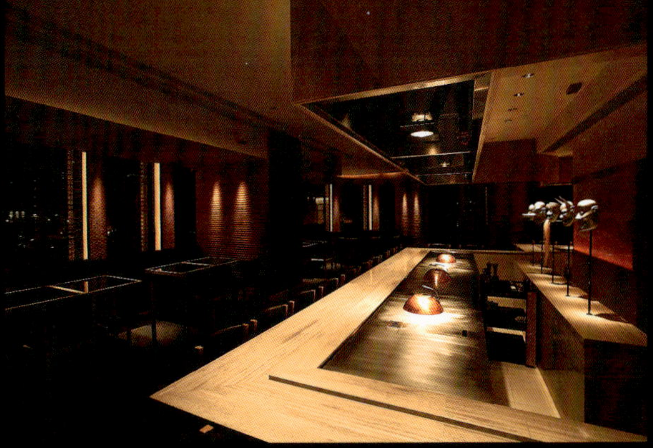

N°067
Doha/Qatar
Jun.2010
Tse Yang

カタールという中東の国で、日本人である森田が中華レストランをデザインする。その文化のミクスチャーを成功に導いたのは、やはり圧倒的な存在感を放っている、メインダイニングの真紅のシャンデリアだろう。およそ9000本ものチャイナ・タッセルを用いて天井を埋め尽くすかのように広がる様は、世界のどこにいるのかを忘れさせるほどの効果がある。壁面には天井まで続くブロンズ硝子がはめ込まれた中国格子。さらにはチャイナドレスのトルソーや、壺をモチーフにしたアートなど、圧倒的な遊び心がこの空間を成立させている。バーには、天井からウッド・ビーズが連なり、5mもの高さのワインセラーの中にはクリスタルが配されたシャンデリア。異なる空間であれ、その"ふり切った感覚"は、共通している。

The project required Morita, a Japanese, to design a Chinese restaurant in the Middle Eastern country of Qatar. This dynamic mix of cultures was successfully achieved through the use of a crimson chandelier, which exudes an overwhelming presence in the main dining area. Using over nine thousand Chinese tassels to cover the ceiling, the sweeping design shocks guests out of time and location. Chinese latticework, embellished with bronze glass, takes over the wall surfaces and reaches the ceiling. The space is completed with compelling playfulness, accented with a china dress torso and artwork of pots. At the bar, wooden beads hang from the ceiling, and a five-meter-high wine cellar is decked with crystal chandeliers. The common theme connecting the separate spaces is that of "stepping over the edge."

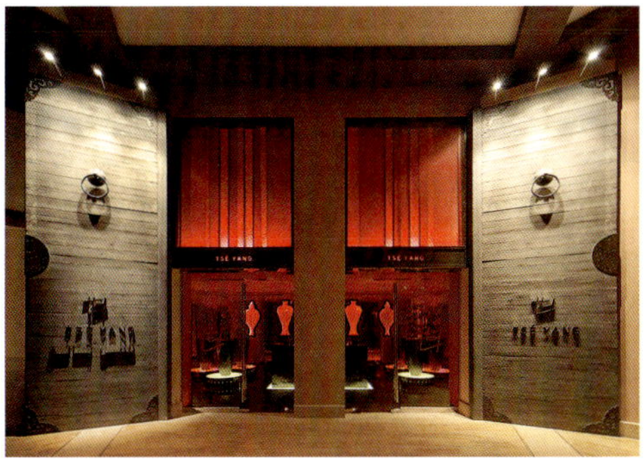
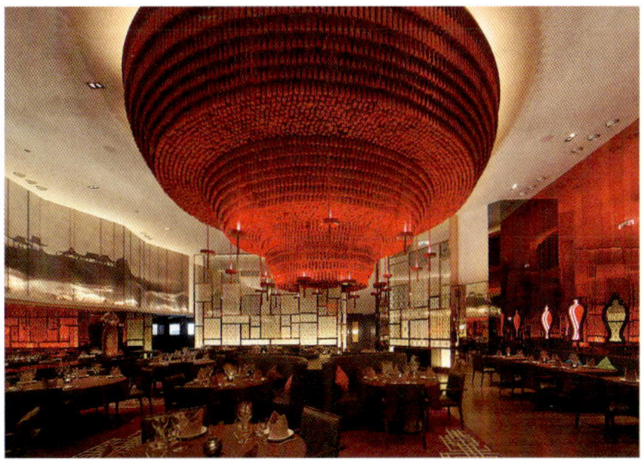
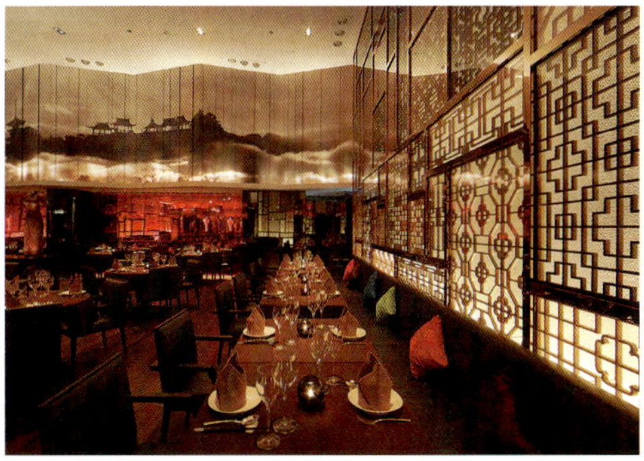
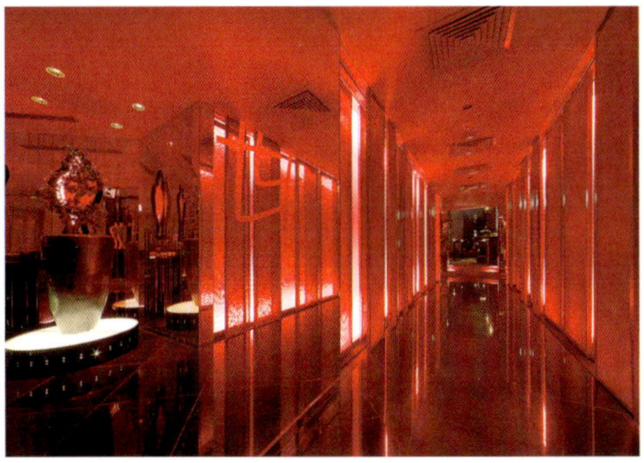
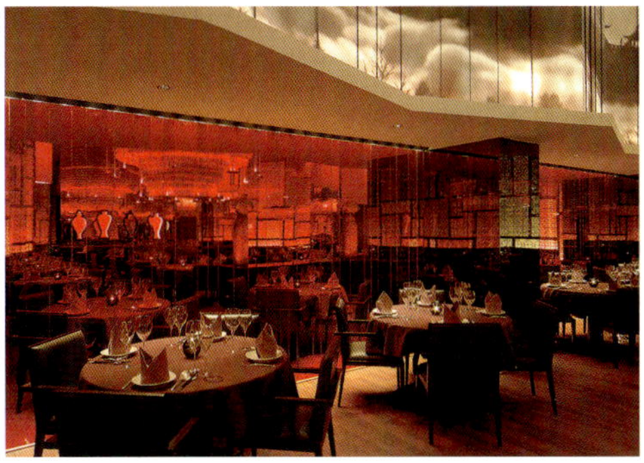
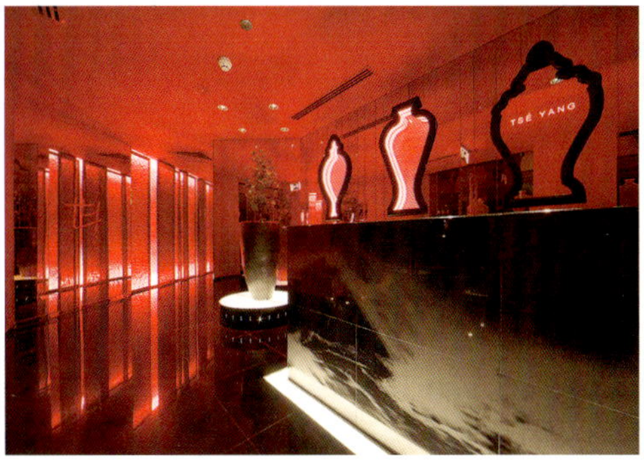
TSÉ YANG
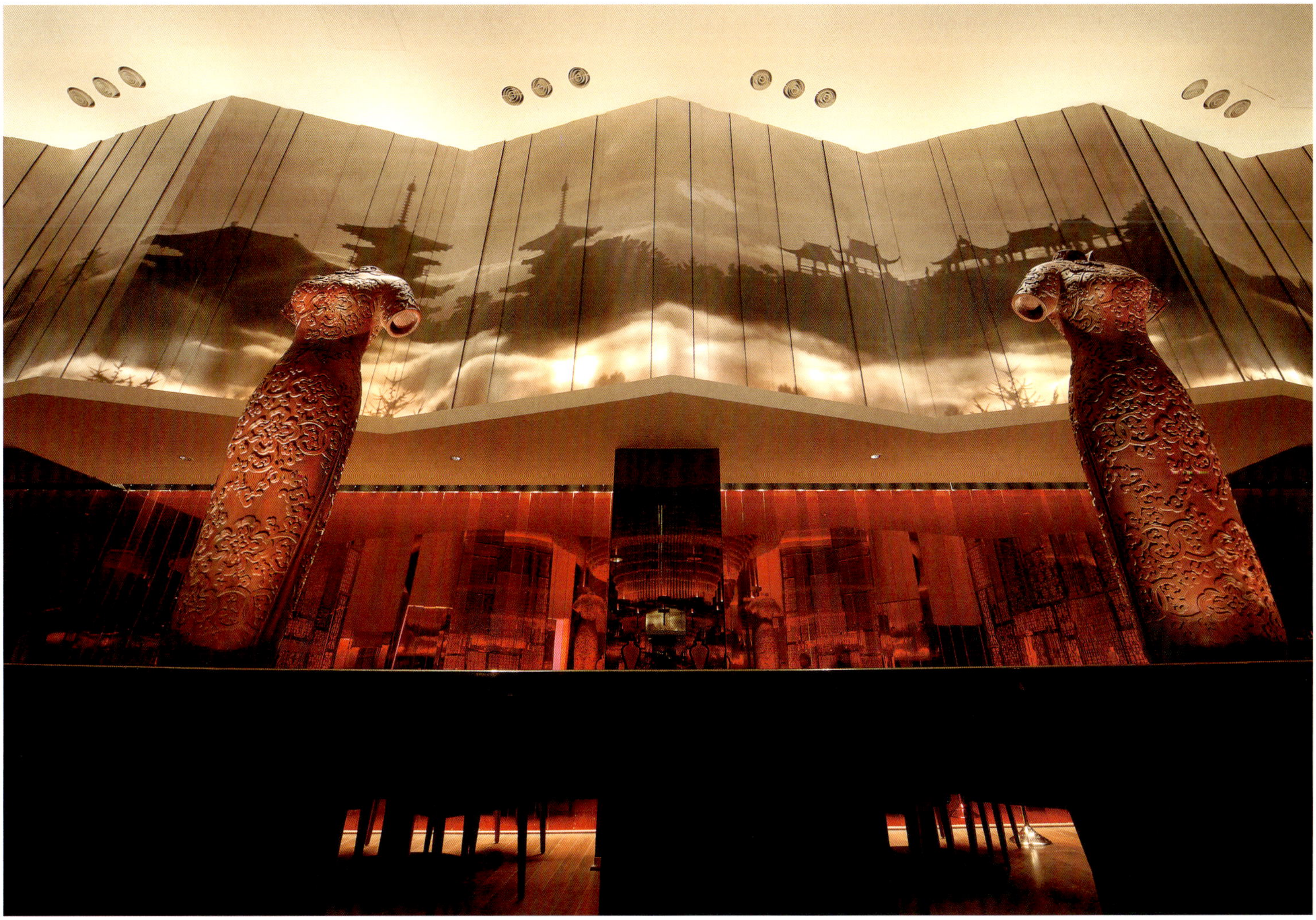

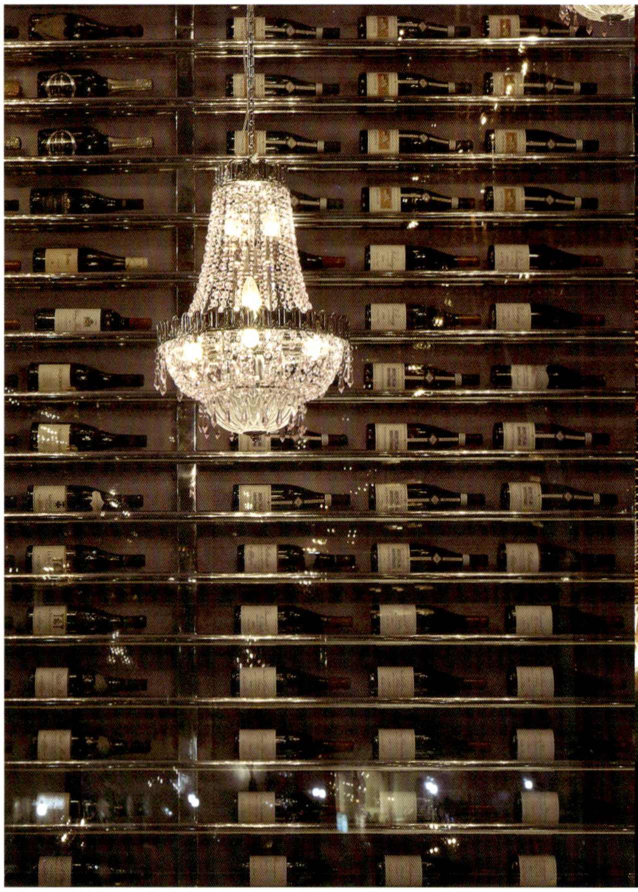

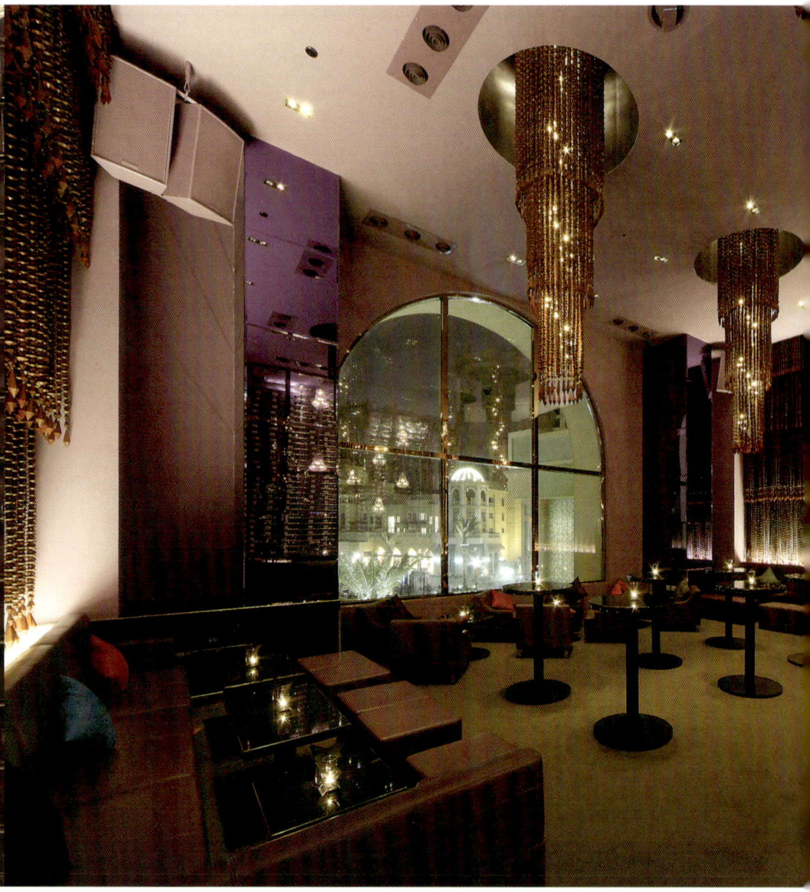

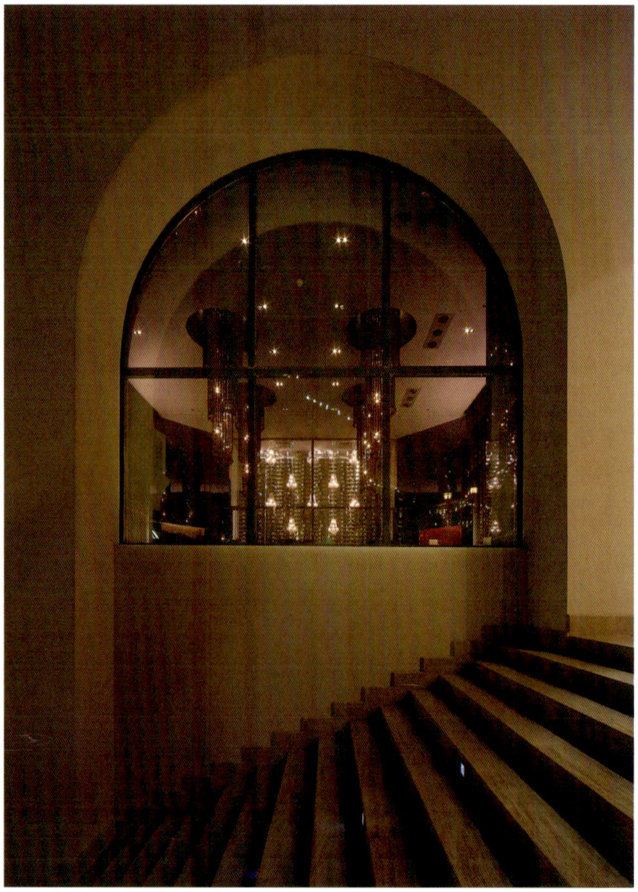

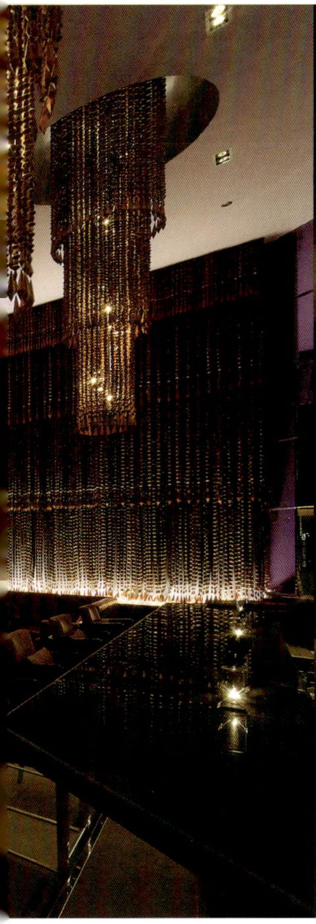
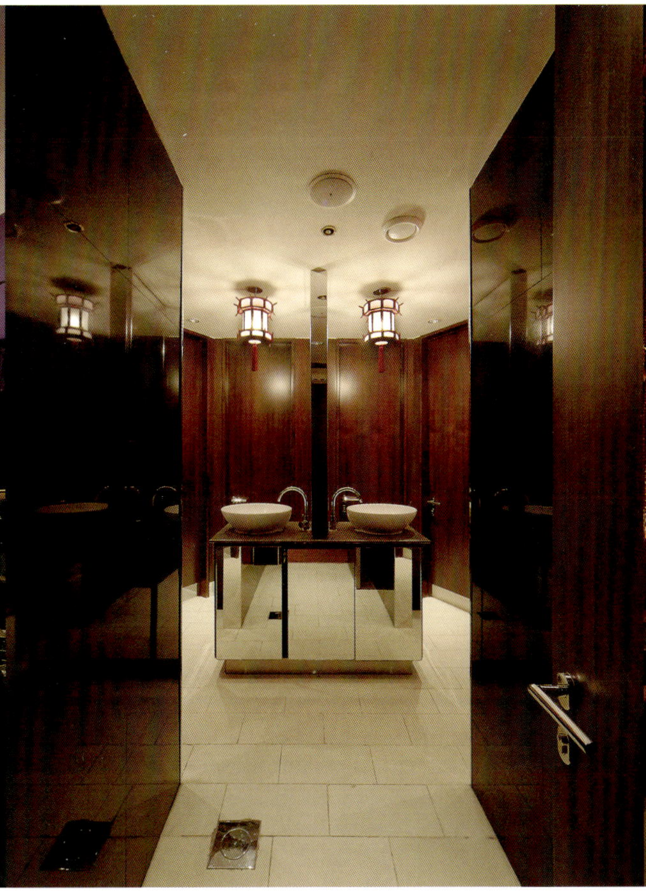
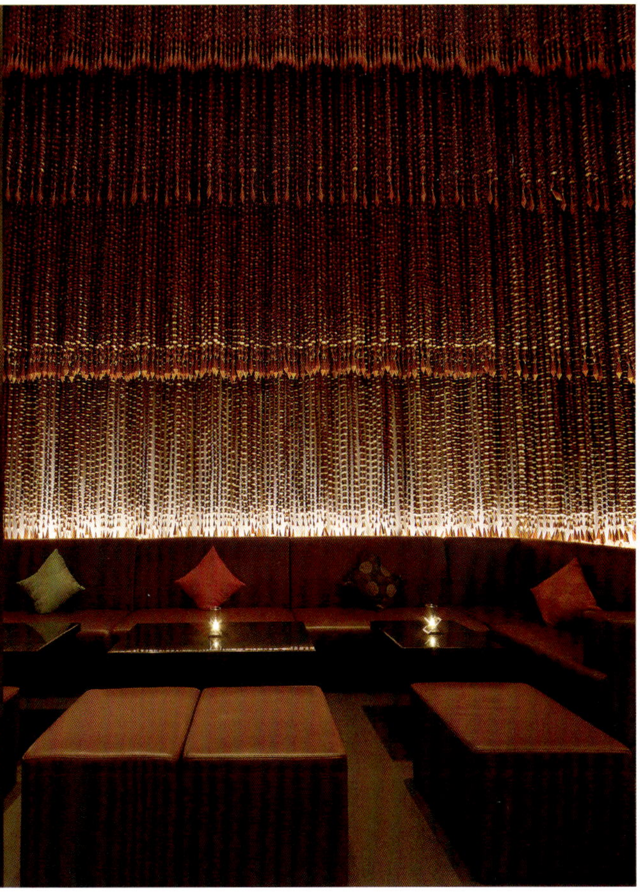
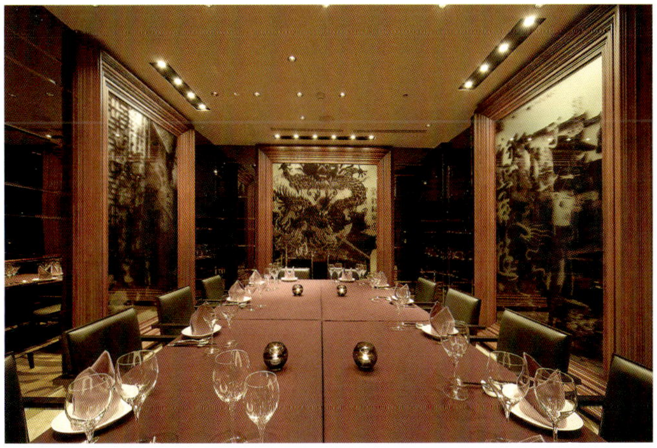
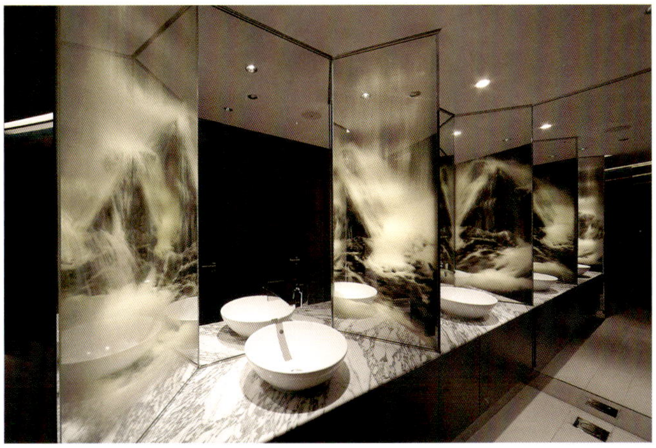
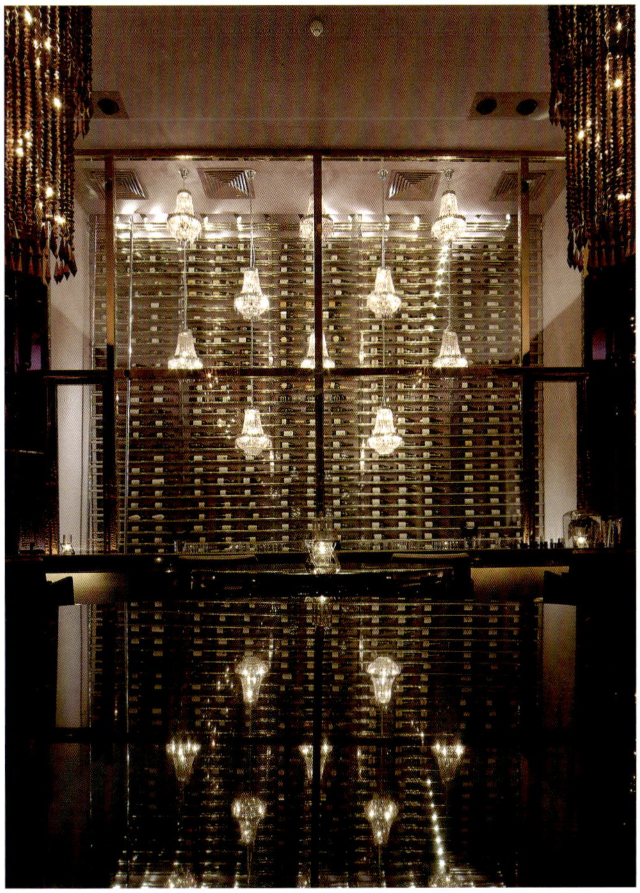

N° 068
Kagawa/Japan
Sep.2002

郷屋敷

田園風景の広がる丘陵地帯に抱かれた、寄せ棟造り茅葺き屋根の建物。築200年以上の豪農の屋敷が、会席料理に讃岐うどんを加えた料理店へと生まれ変わった。リノベーションの際に森田が依頼されたのは、使い勝手の良い空間であること。離れ座敷が回廊で繋がれ、蔵が点在する構成を変えることなく、空間をアレンジするためにはどうすればいいのか。森田が行ったのは、ディテールを変えることだった。畳を絨毯やフローリングに変えて椅子席に、ライトをオリジナルのものに、空間の仕切りを鏡へと変えることで、広がりを生み出した。建築様式をそのまま活かすことで、自然への同化という概念を引き継いだ屋敷は、地元のランドマークとしての新たな価値を纏い始めている。

The architecture for this project was that of a thatched, hip-roofed building in the hilly countryside, surrounded by a rural landscape. The two-hundred-year-old mansion of a wealthy farmer had been converted into a restaurant that serves traditional Japanese cuisine with *sanuki udon*. Morita was asked to renovate the project into a functional space that is easy to use. The question lay in how to arrange the space without having to touch the structure, a building characterized by its storehouses and a corridor running through the detached rooms. Morita's solution was to alter the details. *Tatami* mats were changed to carpeting and hardwood floors, with chairs used instead of low seating. Lighting was reverted back to its original design, and mirrors covered the partitions to create an open feel. In the preservation of its architectural style, the mansion continues the concept of blending with nature. The project is beginning to take on new meaning as a local landmark.

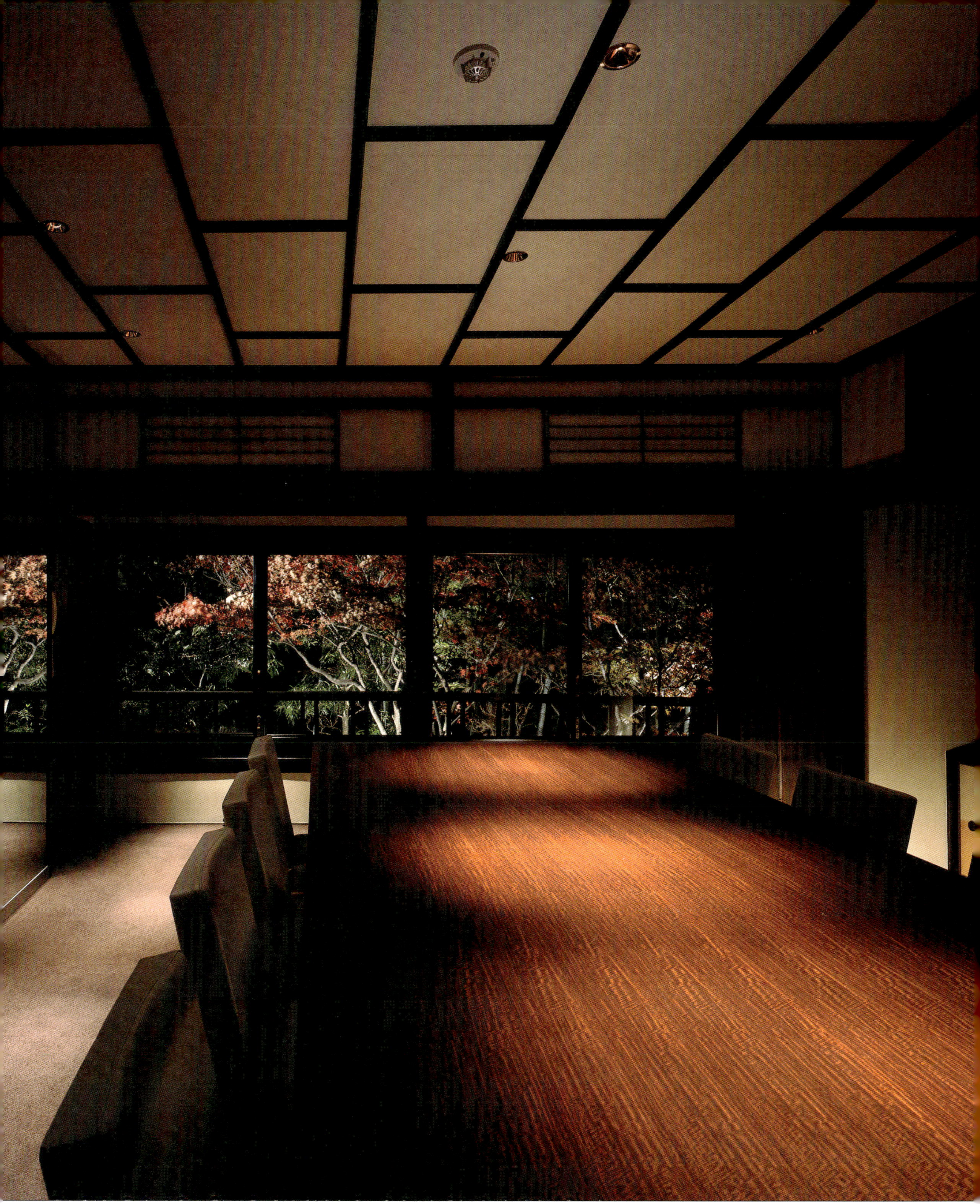

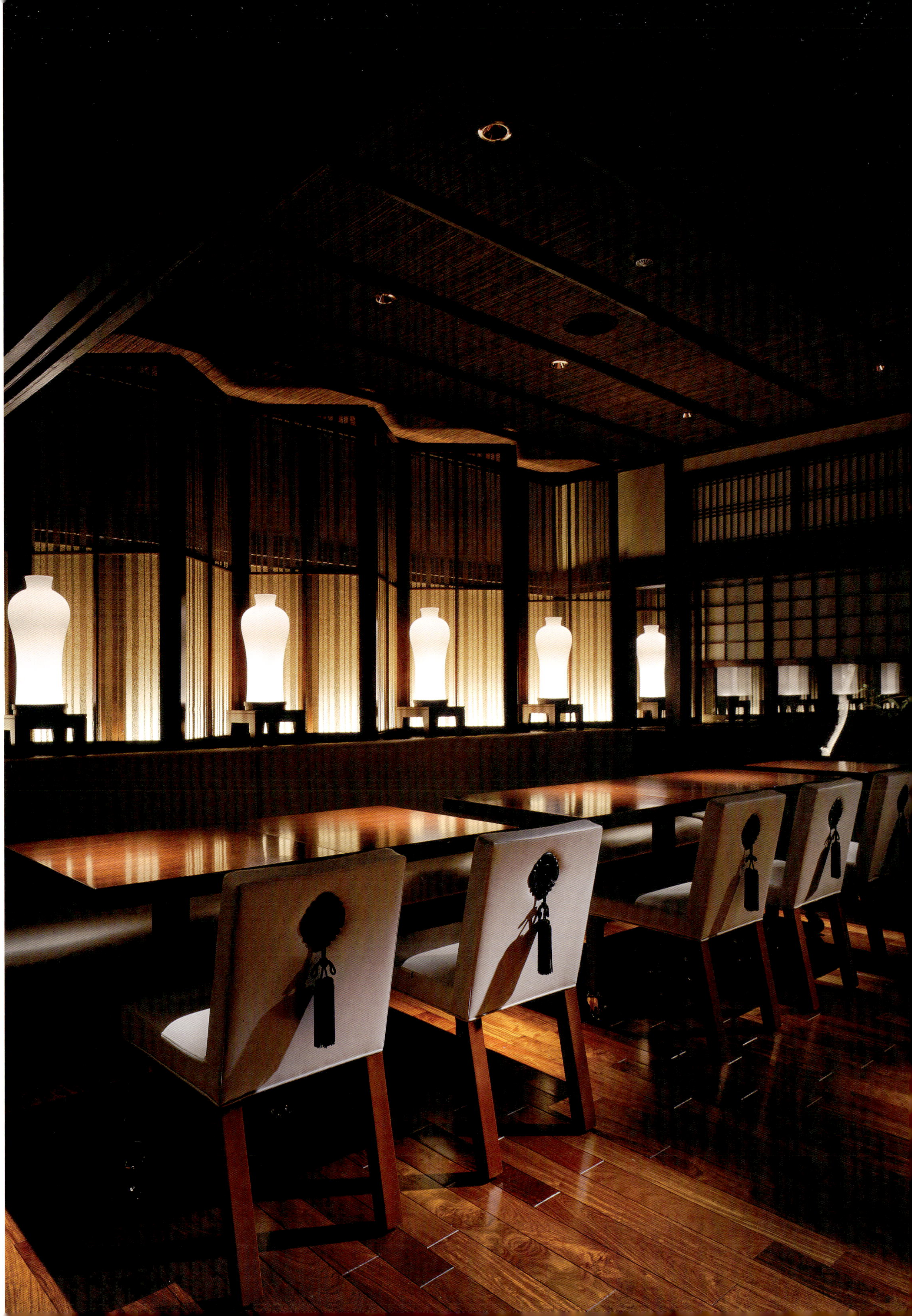

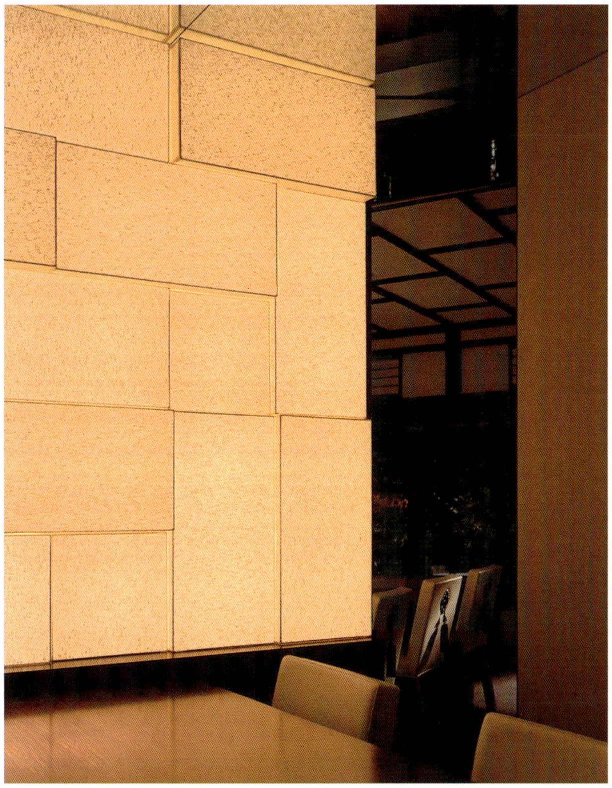
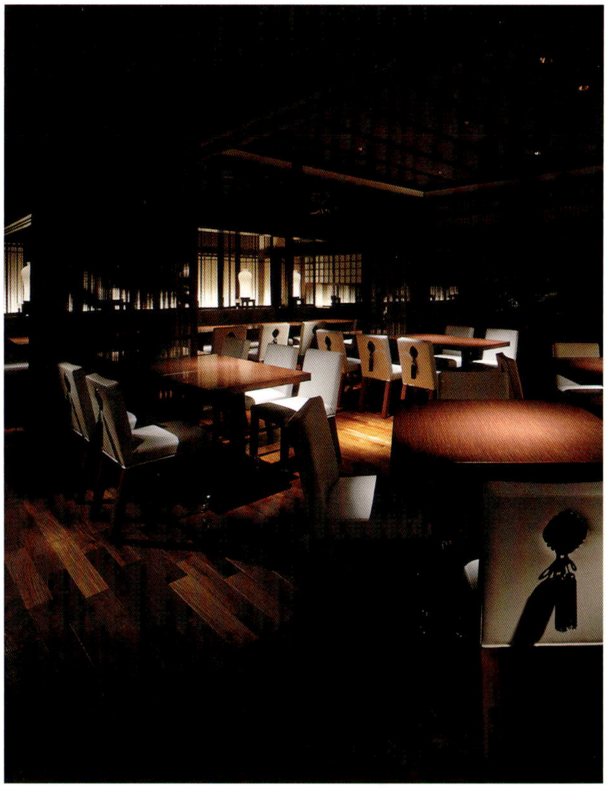
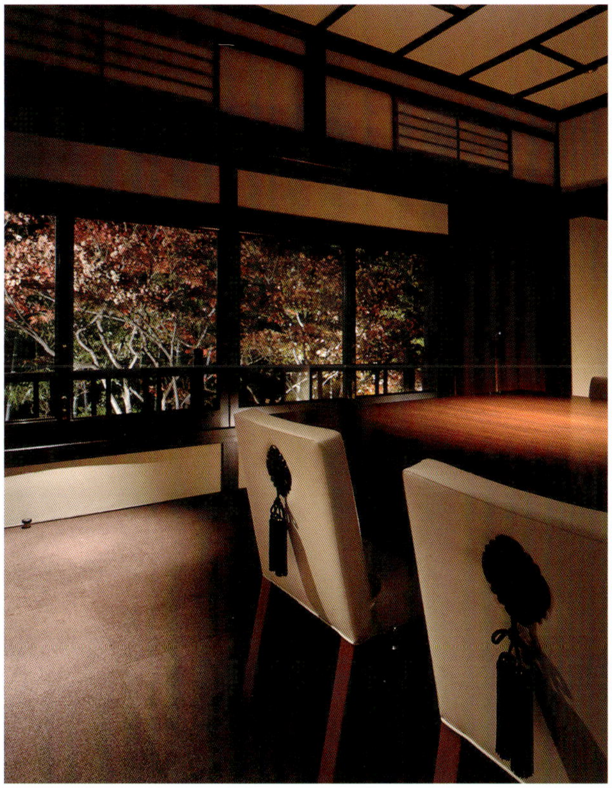
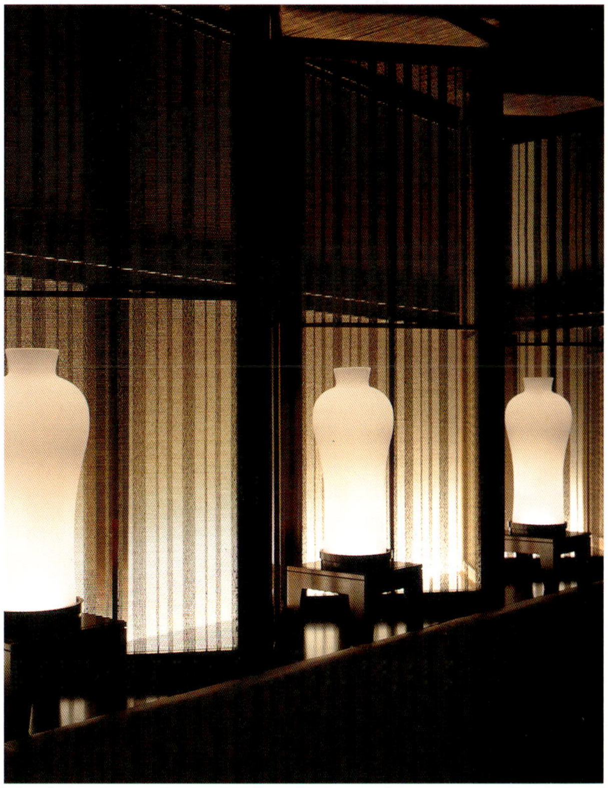

月の家

地下へと続く階段を下りると柔らかな光が迎えてくれる。ガラス壁面から、ほんのりとこぼれる店内の照明も、計算され尽くしている。幻想的な印象は、空間内に足を踏み入れた後も続いていく。カウンターを包み込むように張られた鏡によって、店内に点在する行灯が映り込み、まるで店内が行灯そのものの中に入ってしまっているかのような印象を訪れるゲストに与えている。行灯は、まさしく月をイメージしたもの。反復され増幅される、ぽっかりと宙に浮かんだような柔らかな光は、単体として存在する時よりもはるかに強く複雑な効果を生む。光と鏡の相性に精通する森田らしい、広がりを生み出すアイディアである。

Stepping down the stairs into the underground space, guests are greeted by a warm light. The interior lighting that gently spills from the glass wall surface is also meticulously calculated. This dreamy ambience continues past the entrance and into the interior, where flickering points of paper shade lamps reflect off the mirrored surfaces surrounding the counter space, immersing the guests in the illusion of sitting inside the lamp itself. The lamp is a representation of the moon, and the floating balls of light are multiplied and amplified, creating an intense and complex effect. This idea of creating a sweeping expansion is an example of Morita's mastery in the use of light and mirrors.

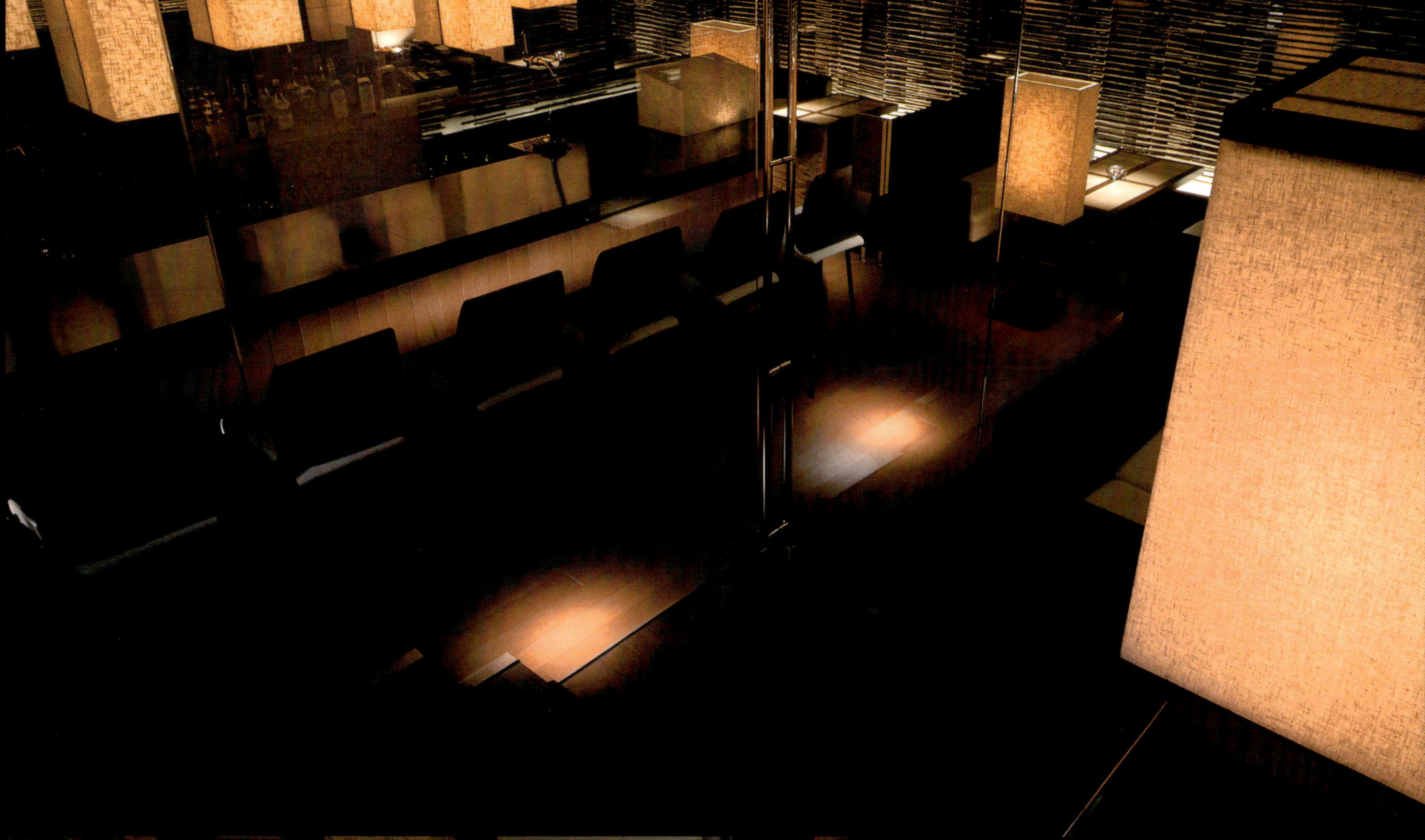
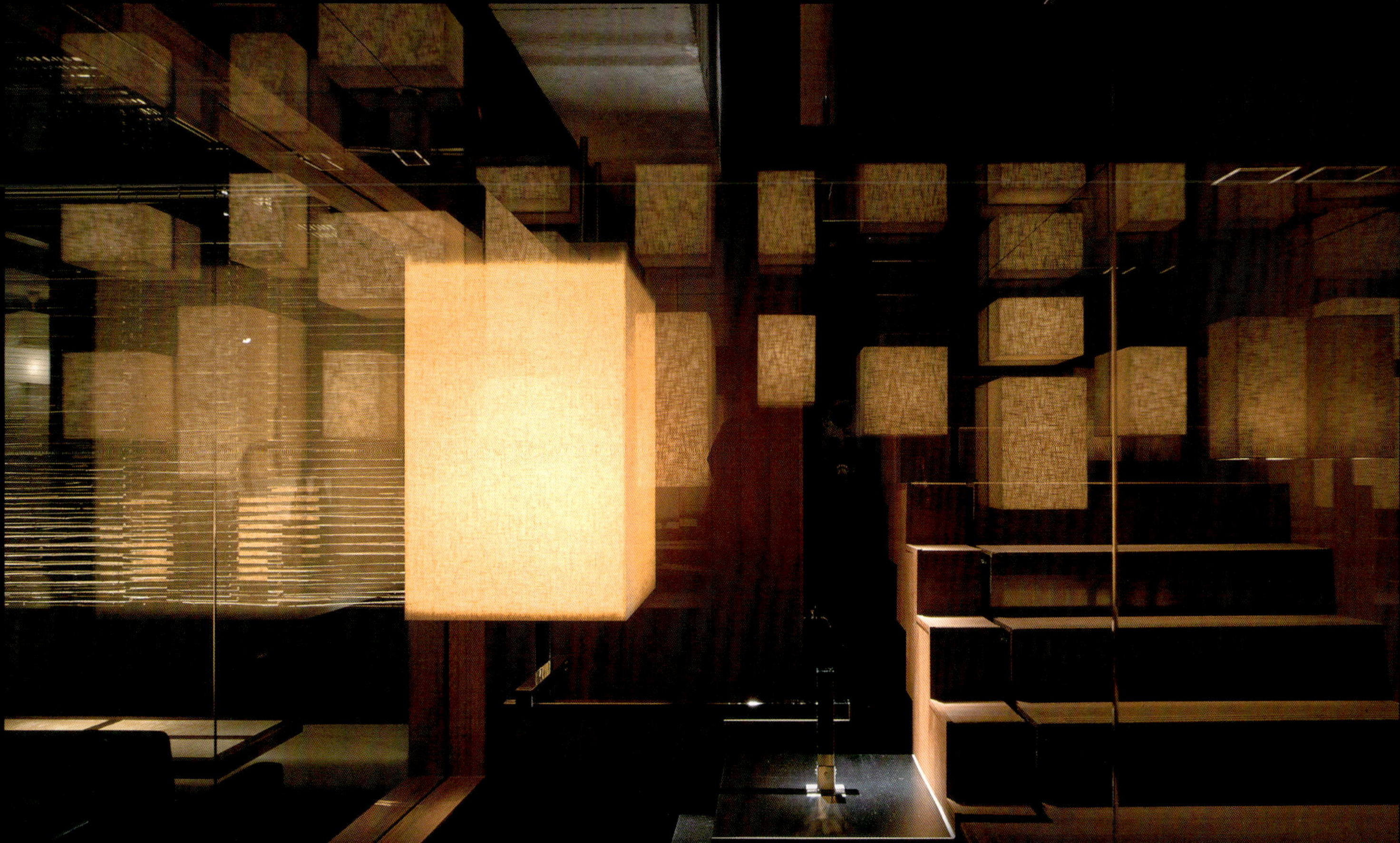

N°070
Osaka/Japan
Apr.1999
Photogenic

フィルム写真に漂うノスタルジーや贅沢な香りを店内に映し込むために森田が採用したのは、やはり本物の写真だった。ギャラリーのように壁面を写真で覆い、まるでライトボックスを覗き込んでいるかのように浮き出たネガの世界が独特の落ち着きをもたらしている。北山孝雄氏が若き頃に世界を回って切り取った風景は、モノクロームでありながら、店内を鮮やかに染める。店内奥のミラーは、一点透視のようにどこまでも続く空間を作り出すことに成功し、フィルムは写真から映画のコマへと見え方が変化していく。作り出された動きと不思議な落ち着き。そのバランスに、大胆なデザインを施すための思考の足跡がある。

To evoke the nostalgia and luxurious feel of film photography, Morita used actual prints of photographs for his design. Wall surfaces were covered with photographs to simulate a gallery, and the negative images create a uniquely relaxed atmosphere with their floating impressions. Although monochromatic, the captured landscapes vividly color the interior with scenes photographed by Takao Kitayama during his youthful days. An infinite space is achieved through a mirror placed in the back, transforming the still photographs into a single frame of a motion picture. The art of balancing artificial movement and peculiar comfort: this is where the idea for a daring design is hidden.

SAMSUNG
TV-VIDEO-FAX
McDonald's
GAP

free purpose bar
Photogenic

N°071
Kyoto/Japan
Apr.2006

お茶屋 まん

「新しい時代の空気を取り入れたい」という現役の芸妓でもあるオーナーからのオーダーで試みたのは、光の解釈によって空間を魅せること。通常よりも格子を細く組むことで導かれる光の方向を限定したり、ダウン／アップライトを多用することでラグジュアリー感を演出したり。まるで行灯のように柔らかく浮かび上がるファサードのデザインがもっとも特徴的だろう。「ライティングによって、芸妓さんや舞妓さんたちの艶のある美しさを引き立てたかった」とは森田らしい言葉ではないか。ただし、デザイン上でもっとも重要なのは「祇園の雅と凛とした品格が息づいていること」。森田の柔軟な感性が、祇園という歴史の積み重ねの上に、新しい解釈を加えている。

In response to the acting *geigi* owner's request to incorporate a modern feel, Morita experimented with different interpretations of light. The latticework was woven more tightly than usual to control the light direction, and down/uplights were applied to evoke a luxurious ambience. The facade, designed to glow softly like a paper shade lamp, is perhaps the most characteristic element of this effect. "I wanted to amplify the alluring beauty of the *geigi* and the *maiko*," says Morita. However, it was even more important for the design to convey Gion's grace and refined dignity. Morita's flexible sensibility adds a layer of new meaning to the continued history of Gion.

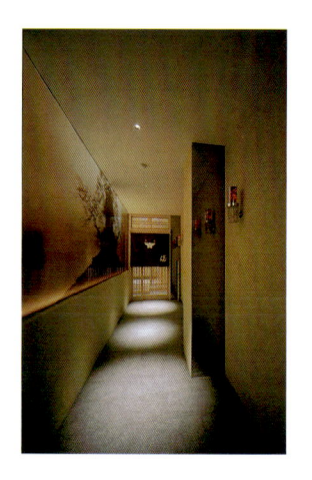

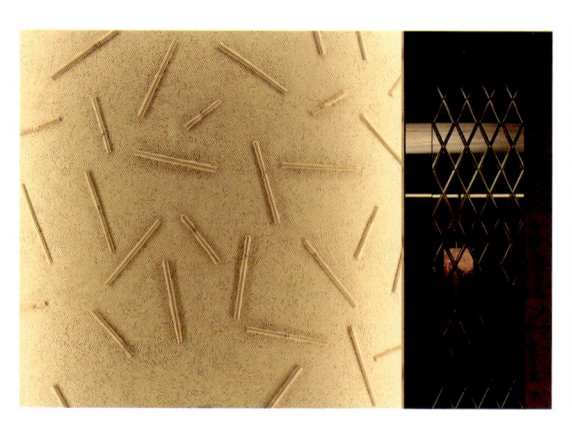

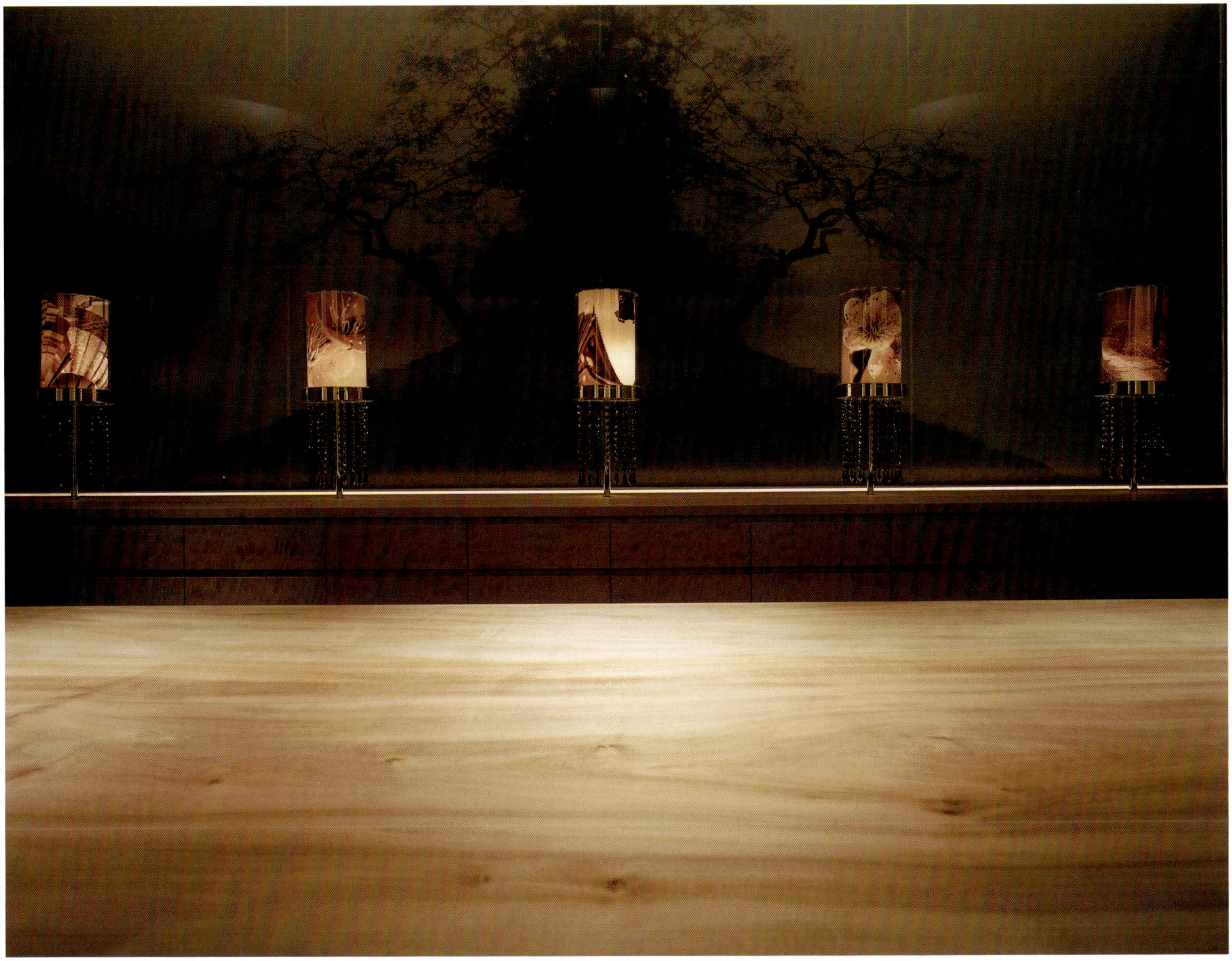

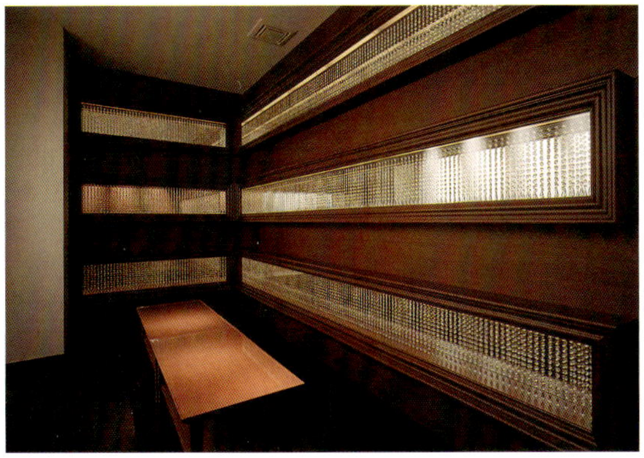

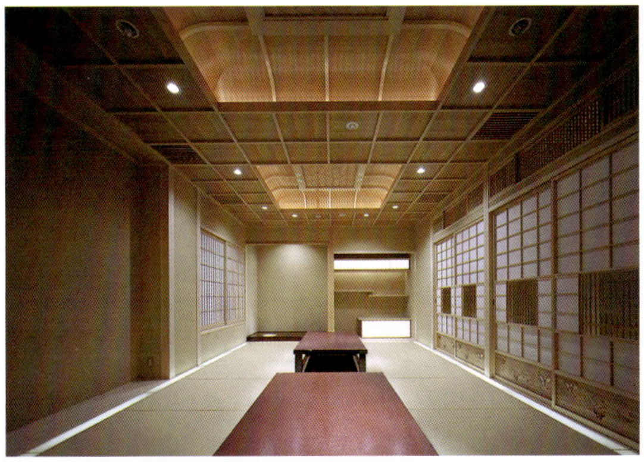

N°072
Osaka/Japan
Oct.1999
村田みつい

店内壁面を構成するのは、3500個もの一合升。連続する升は格子となり、さらに仕込まれた間接照明によって壁の印象を柔らかいものに変えている。落ち着いた店内に比べ、実はファサードには瓦が垂直に差し込まれていたり、公園で見かけるような水飲み場がトイレ内の手洗いとして設置されていたり、かなり大胆なデザインがされている。強烈な個性を放ちつつ、「おばんざい」という家庭料理を提供するお店として温かみを担保すること。相反するような目的を可能にしているのは、やはり、升という物語を繋ぐアイテムを多用しているからだ。

The interior wall surfaces of this space is composed of 3,500 square wooden *masu* boxes. The repetitive pattern of the *masu* creates a lattice, with indirect lighting to control the overall impression. Compared to the relaxing atmosphere of the interior, the rest of the design remains quite bold, with a facade planted with roof tiles and a bathroom that features a sink similar to those found in public parks. While emanating a distinct individuality, the restaurant must also offer coziness as a place for one to enjoy homey dishes. These two opposing objectives are achieved through the repetitive use of *masu*, an item that reflects the story of the restaurant.

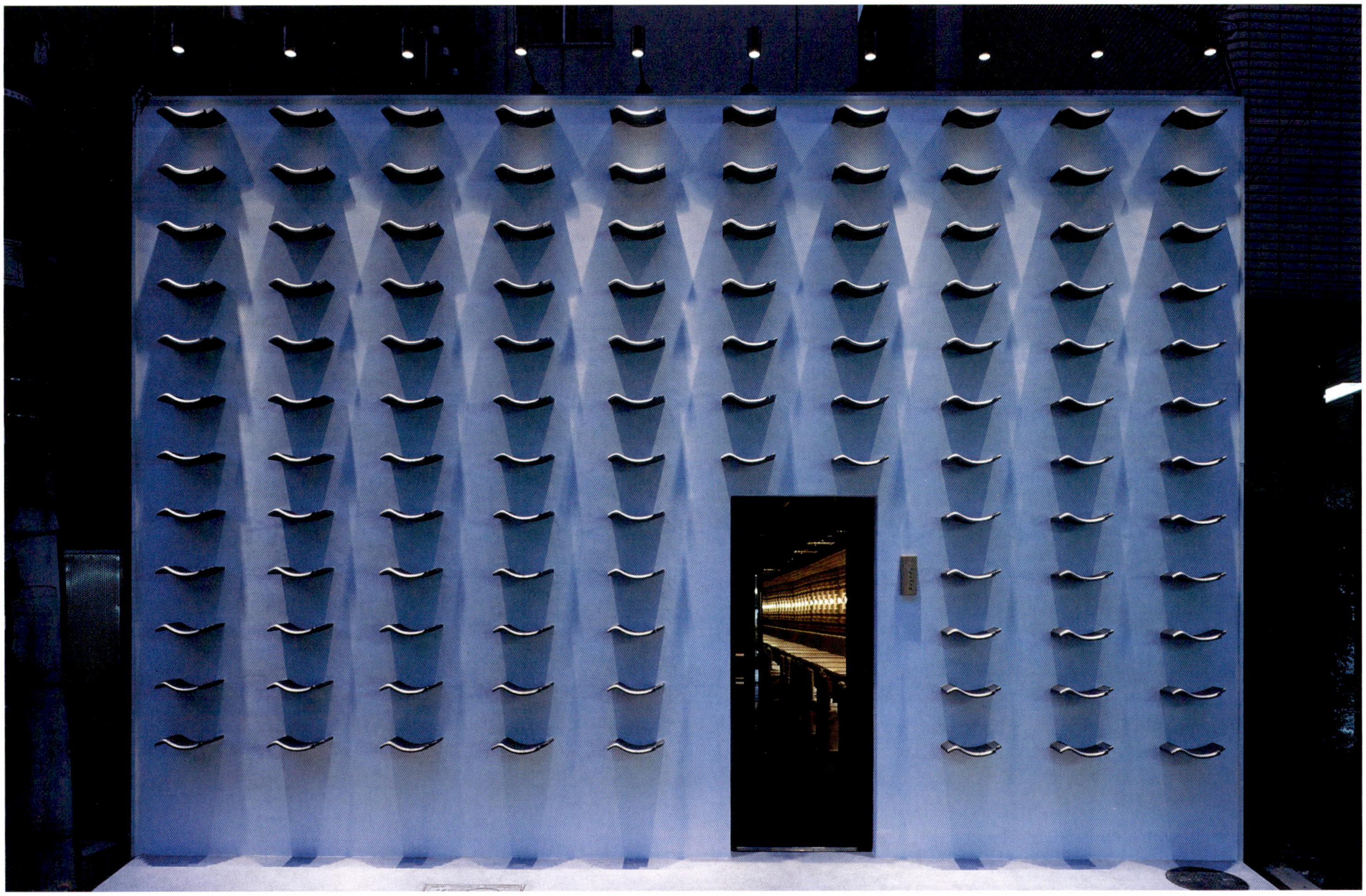

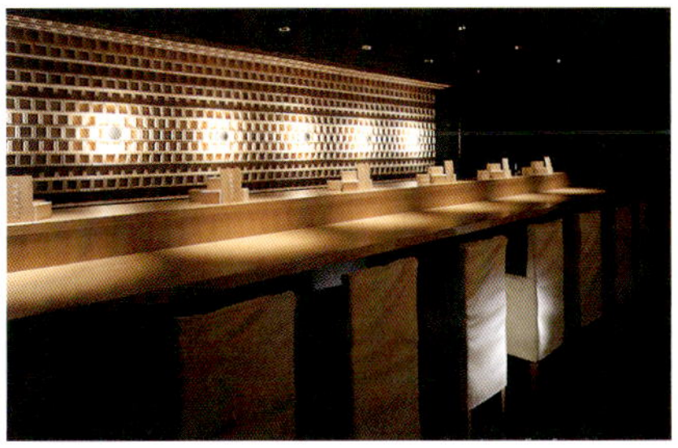

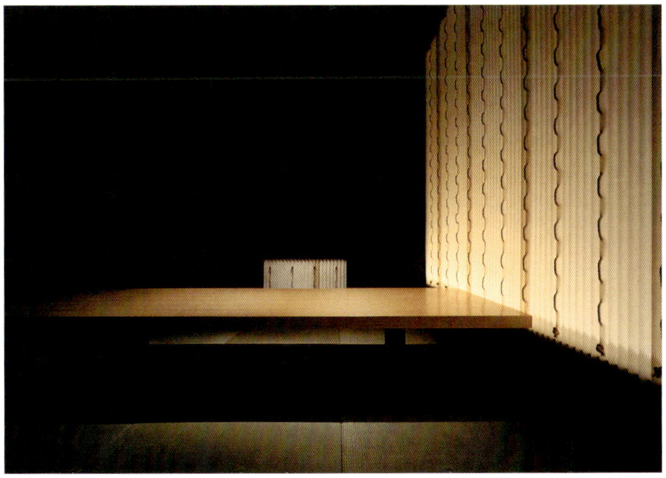

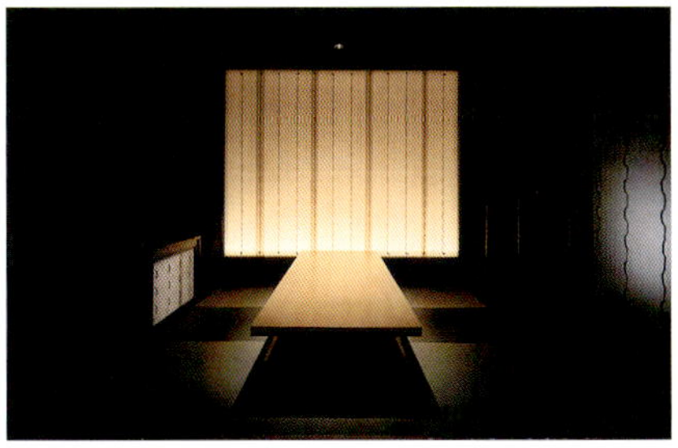

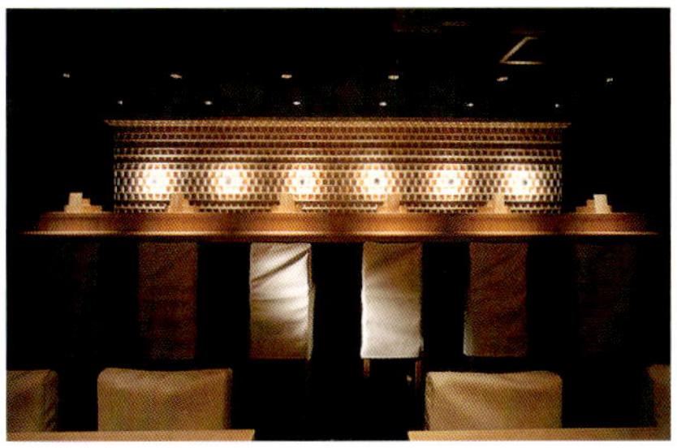

N°073
Tokyo/Japan
Nov.2009
二戀

10坪の空間にL字カウンターの10席のみ。空間は、限定されればそれだけ緊張感が増すが、この板場との距離感は、料理へと向き合うには適したもの。壁面には、京都の陶芸家、近藤髙弘氏の作品。強調された縦線に、さらにプラチナの"滴"を施すことで、板場全体を華のある場所へと進化させている。抑えたステージ感の演出は、おもてなしであることが伝わってくる。客席の背面には、リズムを生むようにと大きさ厚みの異なる木材を組み合わせた。縦のラインと抑えた横のライン。緊張感の中に、次第に寛ぎが生まれてくるのは、遊び心が宿されているからだろう。パープルの椅子が、アクセントとして効いている。

There are only ten seats around the L-shaped counter in this space, measuring only thirty-three square meters. Although strictly limiting the space's function creates an automatic nervousness, the distance between the seats and the counter allows one to comfortably appreciate the dining experience. Works of art by Kyoto's ceramist Takahiro Kondo embellish the surfaces of the wall. Strong vertical lines are treated with droplets of platinum to elevate the entire counter space in splendor. The stage is toned down in moderation, an evidence of thoughtful hospitality. Behind the seats, an assortment of wood creates a positive rhythm through varying thickness and size. With vertical lines and controlled horizontals, the design's playfulness gradually alleviates the initial nervousness. Purple chairs finish off the design with an accent.

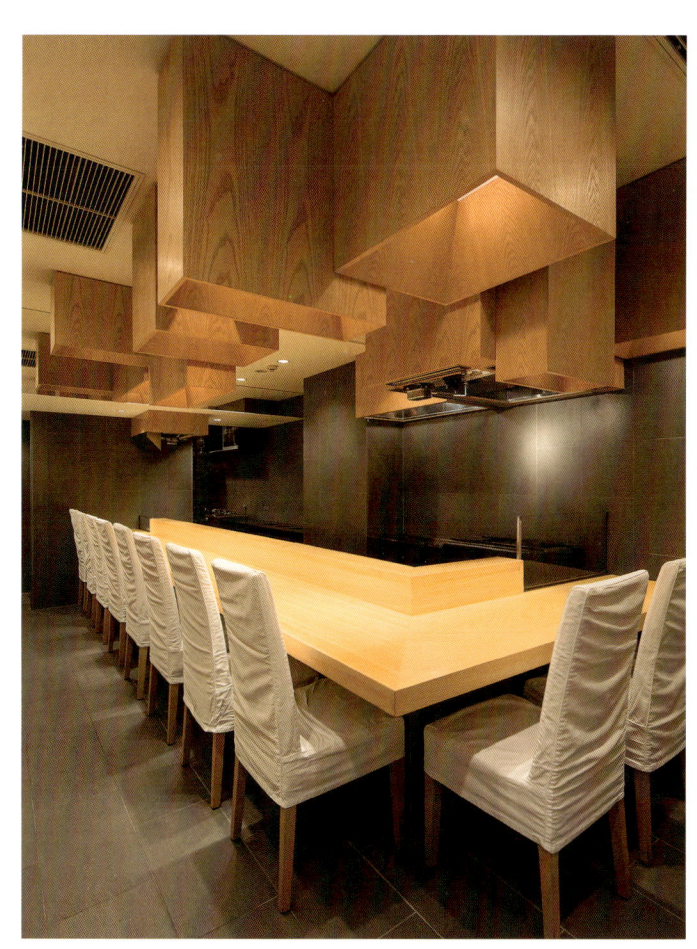

N°074
Tokyo/Japan
Apr.2013

尾崎幸隆

清廉なカウンターの上に吊されているのは、ボックス型の照明。ランダムに並べることでシンプルな空間に変化を生んでいる。ボックスで囲うことでスポットのように光を届けるのは、「フードを彫刻のようなアート作品として見せたかった」からだ。カウンター席は舞台でもあるという森田の思想が垣間見える。また、個室は同様にランダムな縦スリットによってリズムを生み出した。可動式のパーテーションを開放し、個室を連結させればその縦スリットの連続性によって繋がりがもたらされる。不規則性によって、むしろシンプルさが際立つ店内。デザインの効果がはっきりと分かる空間となっている。

Hanging over a clean counter is a series of box-shaped lighting fixtures, randomly lined to create movement within a simple space. The reason for containing the light inside these boxes was to illuminate food as artistic sculptures. The design is a reminder of Morita's philosophy, which regards the counter as a kind of theatrical stage. Private rooms are divided with vertical slits, randomly cut to create rhythm. By opening the movable partitions to connect the rooms into one large space, these vertical slits link together to create a progressive coherence. The simplicity of the design is heightened by its irregularity. The space is one that clearly exemplifies the effectiveness of its design.

N° 075
London/UK
Oct.2009

aqua london

『kyoto』『nueva』という2つのシーンからなるレストラン。まったく異なる空間を繋ぐのは、「日本の究極の美」を表現している着物の「帯」をモチーフとしたデザイン。織り、刺繍を施し、色とりどりの糸が空間に視覚的な面白さを付与している。もうひとつ、『kyoto』のプロジェクトに共通する素材が、「禅」を表現する日本らしいマテリアルである「炭」。心の浄化と静けさを表すため、天井から吊り下げられたり、若冲からインスピレーションを得て「炭の華」として設えられたり。壁面にはウッド・ビーズ、さらに木製タイルによってスペインの明るく輝く太陽を表現した『nueva』。スパニッシュデザインのシーンと『kyoto』を繋ぐ日本らしい小道。ふたつの空間は、それぞれ異なるアレンジを纏って、ひとつのカタチとなっている。

This restaurant is composed of two entirely different scenes, "kyoto" and "nueva." The spaces are linked by a design that features the Japanese *obi*, or kimono belt, the ultimate embodiment of Japanese beauty. Colorful strings of weaving and embroidery add visual depth to the space. Another element symbolic of Japanese Zen is charcoal, which is incorporated into the materials for the "kyoto" project. These pieces of charcoal are used in various ways: some are hung from the ceiling to express peace of mind; others are made into a charcoal flower, inspired by Japanese artist Jakuchu. In "nueva," wooden beads and tiles adorn the wall surfaces to portray the bright Spanish sun. A distinctively Japanese passageway connects the Spanish design back to "kyoto." The two spaces, dressed in uniquely different arrangements, are integrated into one consistent shape.

N°**076**
Kobe/Japan
Dec.1996
IT'S

ビルの5階にある小さな扉を開けると続く、白い廊下の空間。下からのライトの無機質な道を抜けると、一気に木の世界に入る。カウンター後ろの壁面から天井へとそのまま続く木と、その間に設けられた光のアーチ。さらに、同じ木材を使いながらランダムに組むことで空間に変化を生んだ照明が、スポットの光をテーブル席に当てている。隠れ家という言葉がどうしても当てはまってしまうのは、そのエントリーからの流れだけではなく、木の温もりが光のラインによって増幅されているから。大きなカウンターテーブルも、その存在感を主張するというよりも、場を構成するひとつの要素としてしっくりと収まっている。同じ素材を多用する際のバランスが、いかに難しく、大切であるかが伝わるデザインである。

A white hallway continues from a small door on the fifth floor. From an inorganic space illuminated by low lighting, the site quickly transforms into a world of wood. A row of wooden material stretches from behind the counter to reach the ceiling, sandwiched by arches of light. The same materials are further arranged in random combinations to create dynamic lighting, shedding spots of illumination on the table. The place is inevitably a hidden gem, not just because of its flow from the entry, but because the warmth of wood is amplified by lines of light. The large counter is comfortably integrated into the composition without being too disruptive with an overwhelming presence. The design is an example of how difficult and important it is to maintain a thoughtful balance in the repetitive use of a singular material.

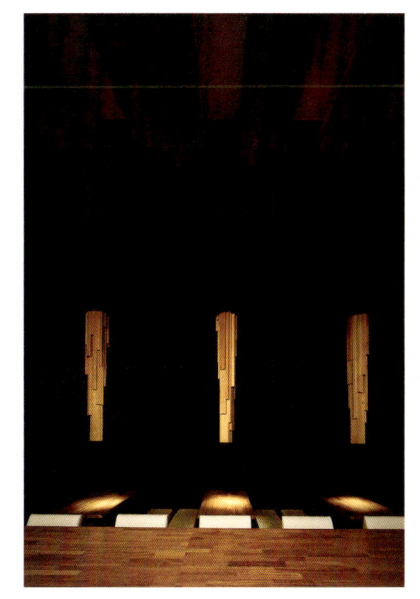

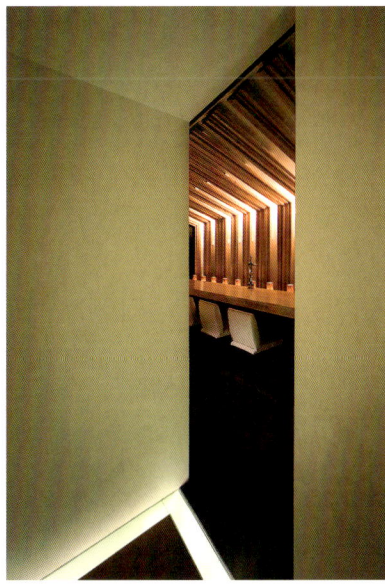

N°077

Tokyo/Japan

Jan.1998

KEN'S DINING NISHIAZABU

西麻布という多国籍な土地柄、あるいは壁面に書かれた多様な国の文言でも分かる通り、和洋折衷、シノワズリの世界が店のコンセプト。クリアミラーに埋め込まれた宙に浮いたような半分の壺は、その浮遊感によって未知の世界を演出している。未知であることは興味を喚起すると共に、不安をあおりかねない。では、どうすればよいのか。レストランにおいては、料理を美味しく見せるライティングに力を注ぐことが、ひとつの回答だった。さらに反射によって表情が華やかに映るように設計する。未知と既知のバランスもまた、森田が世界観を構成する上で重要なファクターになっている。

As indicated by the multicultural neighborhood of Nishi-Azabu, and the wall surfaces engraved with writings in multiple languages, the concept of this project is Chinoiserie. The floating piece of jar half embedded into a clear mirror projects the idea of a strange and unknown world. While the unfamiliar incites curiosity, it can also become the source of anxiety. How, then, does one solve this problem? In this restaurant, the solution was to pour all effort into illuminating the dishes with careful planning. Reflection was used to irradiate facial expressions. The balancing of the unknown with the known is another important factor that helps Morita in composing his signature style.

A delicate blend of skill, innovation, and creativity that's the mark of Kenichiro Okada's cuisine.

Un délicieux mélange de dextérité, d'innovation et de créativité est la marque de la cuisine de Kenichiro Okada.

La cucina di Kenichiro Okada, una delicata fusione di esperienza, innovazione e creatività.

N° **078**
Osaka/Japan
Oct.2005

Salon á dîner Galerie

アートをデザインに用いる理由は、そのアートが持つ力を空間に宿らせるためであることがほとんどだが、このサロンでは、名前の通りアートが主役になっている。手彫りのオブジェを眺めるためのインテリアデザイン。いや、眺めるという行為と寛ぐという行為が、空間で一体となるように仕掛けられている。キャメルブラウンのレザーソファに、木目の美しいブビンガ材の一枚板カウンター。重厚感のあるブラックステンレスを開くと現れる直線的な通路からのエントリーは、期待感をあおるという意味において、ギャラリーのそれと共通するものがある。カラオケルームさえ完備したギャラリー。その矛盾に満ちた存在は、森田のインテリアデザインがさまざまな条件を呑み込んでいることの証である。

Art is often incorporated into design so that one can borrow its power. For this salon, however, art was not borrowed; it was made into a centerpiece. This interior design was planned specifically to allow guests to appreciate the hand-carved objects. In fact, the space was designed so the act of viewing is blended with the act of relaxing. Furnishing elements include caramel brown leather sofas and a solid bubinga wood counter with an intricate grain. The entry stems from a linear passage that appears behind stately black stainless steel, with as much excitement and anticipation as can be found in an actual art gallery. A gallery, with a *karaoke* room. This contradiction is the proof that Morita's interior design flexibly accommodates a variety of conditions.

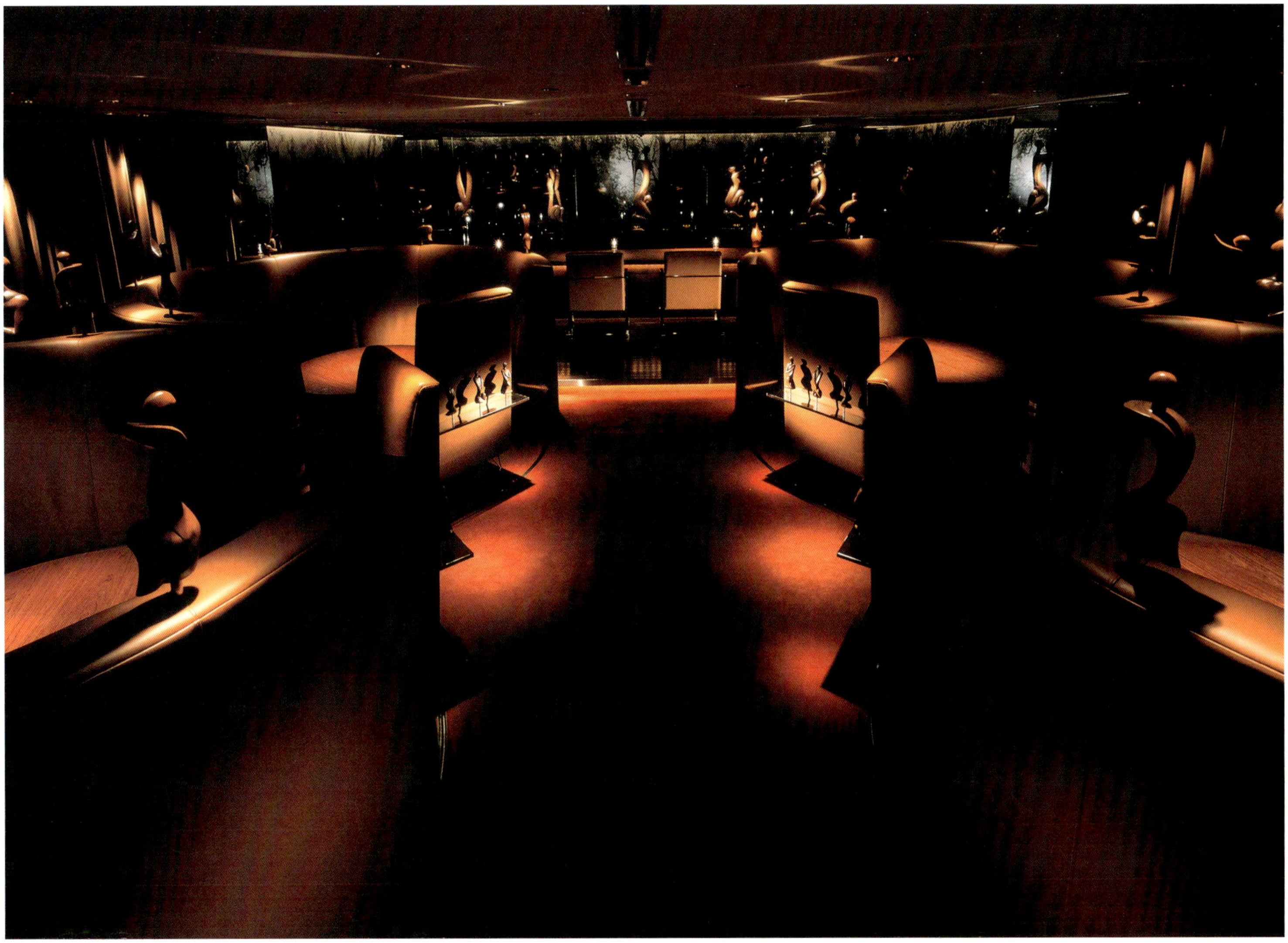

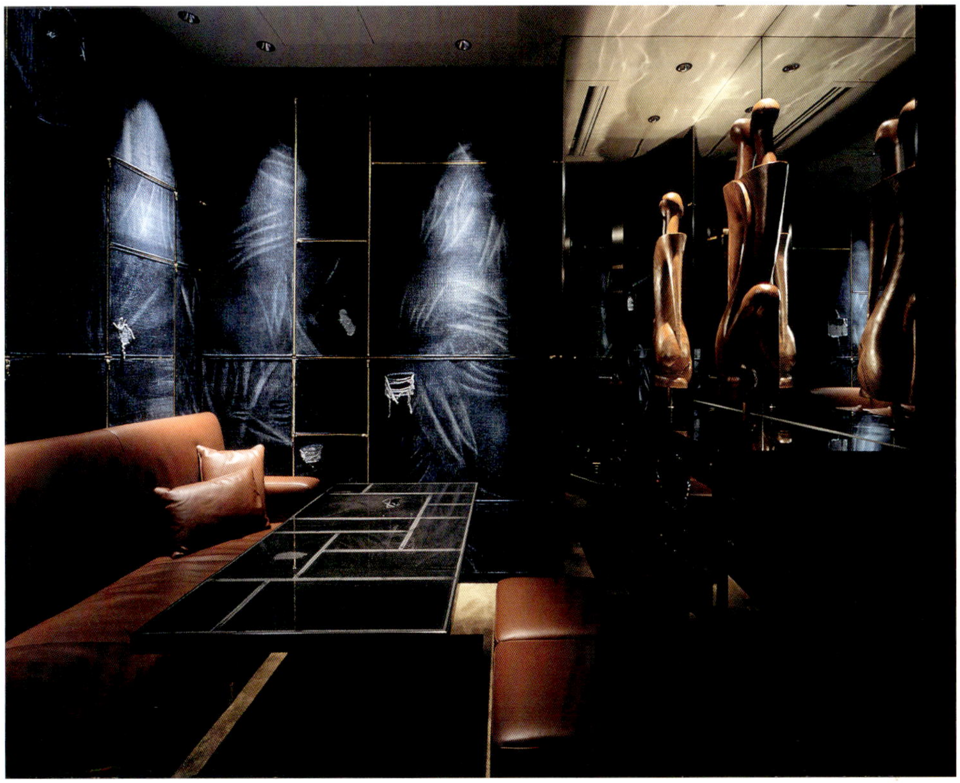

N° 079
Ashiya/Japan
May 2005
NAMISUS

会員制バーと老舗のすし屋のコラボレーションという異なる業態の店舗を入口は違えど、ひとつの敷地内に成立させるためには、共通の空気感を作り出すことが必要となる。無垢の木を削り出して作ったウッド・ビーズが、"波"のようにカウンターを囲むすし屋に対して、わずか8席の石庭を眺めるクロコダイル本革のカウンター・バー。「落ち着いている」という言葉だけでは説明しきれない、カウンターに座った際のステージ感や視線を導く方向、あるいは計算された経年変化など、トーンと呼ぶべきものでふたつの店舗は繋がっている。ちなみに、バーの店名『NAMISUS』とは、すし屋の店名『すし萬』を反対から読んだものだとか。

Although this collaboration between an exclusive bar and a sushi restaurant is equipped with separate entrances, a sense of shared ambience was vital for the project's success. In the sushi restaurant, beads carved from bare wood surround the counter with undulating waves, whereas the bar is made of only eight seats, with a crocodile leather counter and a view of the rock garden. The common link between the two spaces is the tone—an atmosphere that is more than just relaxing but is characterized by the theatrical staging of the counter, the cunningly directed gaze, and the calculated margins for the space to age and mature. By the way, the name of the bar, NAMISUS, is the name of the sushi restaurant spelled backwards.

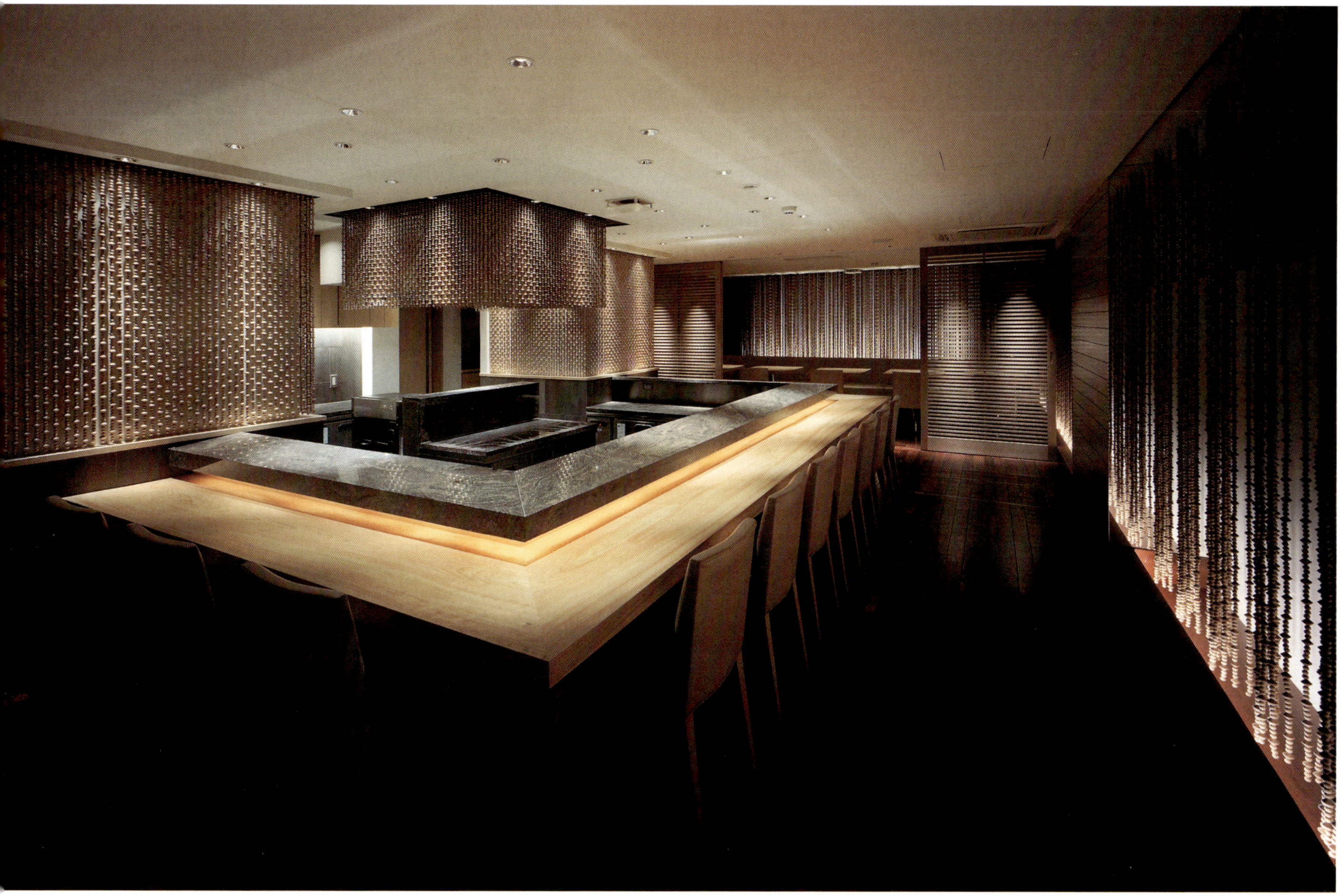

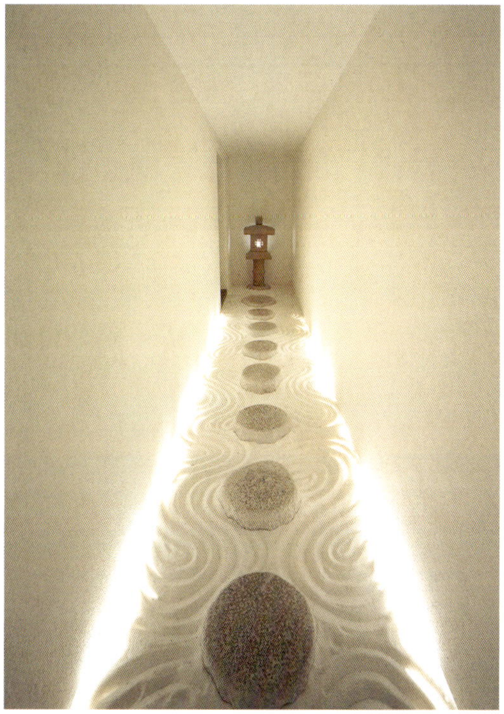

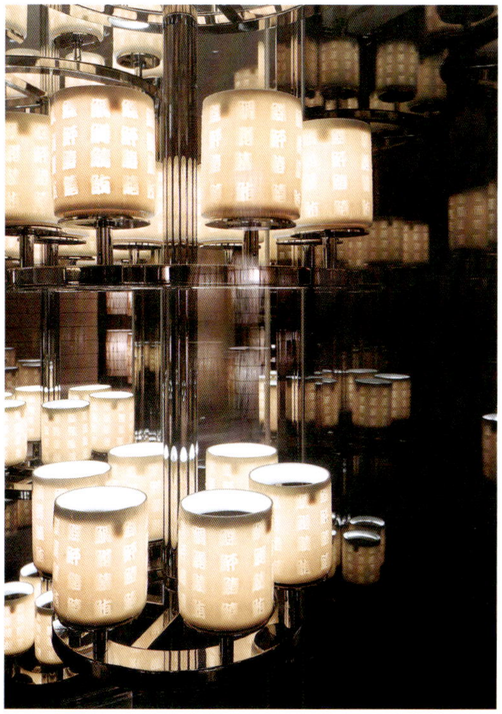

N°080
Tokyo/Japan
Apr.2013
1967

例えば鏡に映ったシルクハットとヒゲ、あるいはブロンドの髪に口元のほくろ。つい自分の顔を当てはめてみたくなるような、遊び心に満ちている。森田ほか、1967年生まれの"大人"たちによって仕掛けられたスペースには、楽しむための仕掛けが随所に施されている。4つの個室はコンラッド・リーチやカルロ・ピエローニ、メルビン・ソコルスキー、佐竹穰といった、それぞれテイストの異なるアーティストの作品が飾られ、違う空気を生み出している。さらに夜になるとシャッターが開かれて現れるひな壇状のスペース。親密な社交場としてのラグジュアリーなデザインが施されている。圧倒的な存在感を放つミラーボールとシャンデリアの組み合わせが空間を統べ、店舗の半分近くを占めるガーデン・ラウンジが開放感をもたらしている。

With the top hat and beard that appear in the mirror, or the blond hair and beauty mark, this design is filled with engaging humor. The space, which was created by Morita and a group of 1967-born "adults," has been treated with numerous fun and humorous devices for play. The four rooms are decked with works by Conrad Leach, Carlo Pieroni, Melvin Sokolsky, and Joe Satake to differentiate each space through distinct tastes. In the evening, the shutters are opened to reveal a tiered area, luxuriously designed for intimate socialization. The mirrored ball and chandelier dominate the interior with a powerful presence, and the garden lounge, which takes over almost half of the space, emphasizes this open feel.

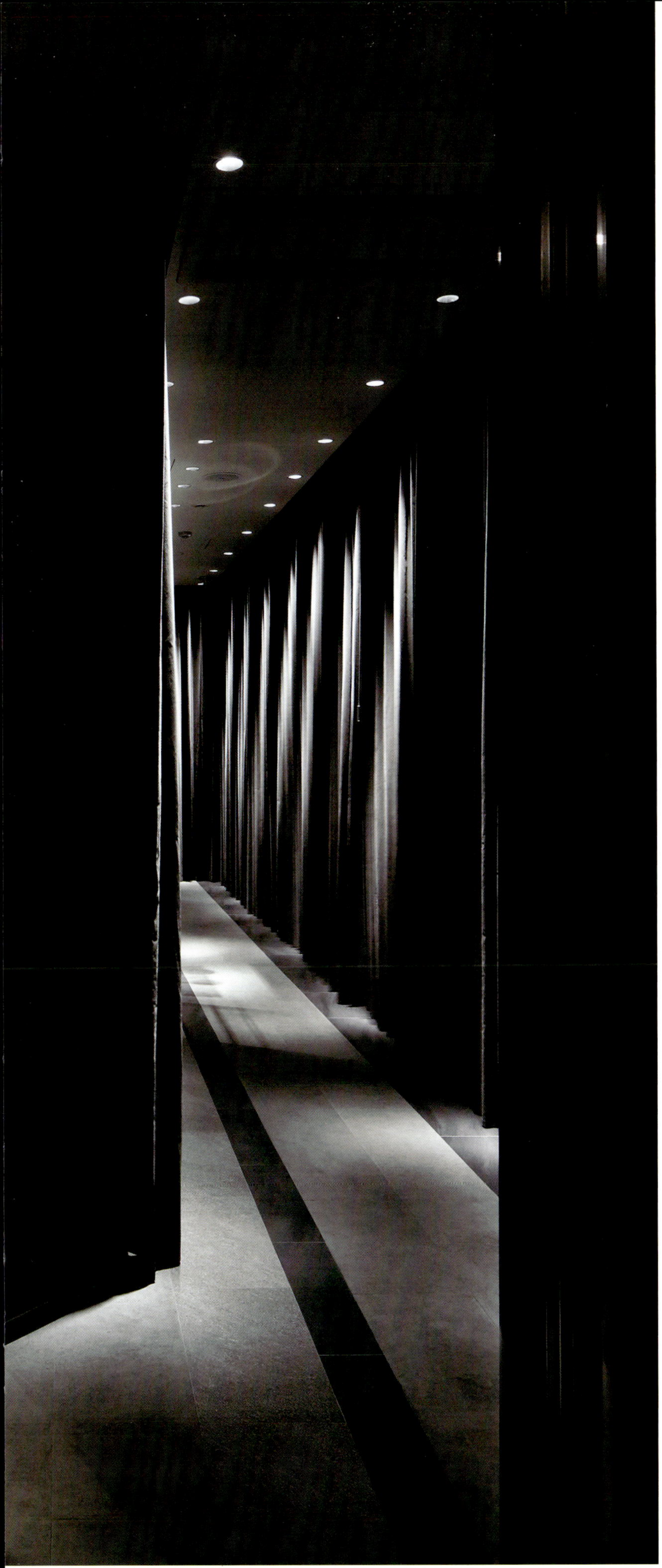

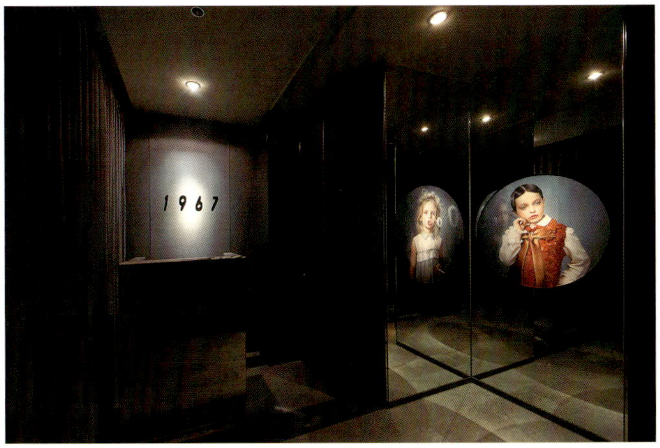
1967

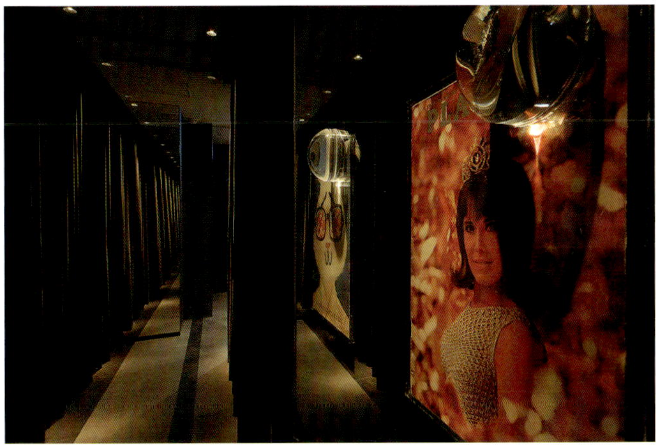

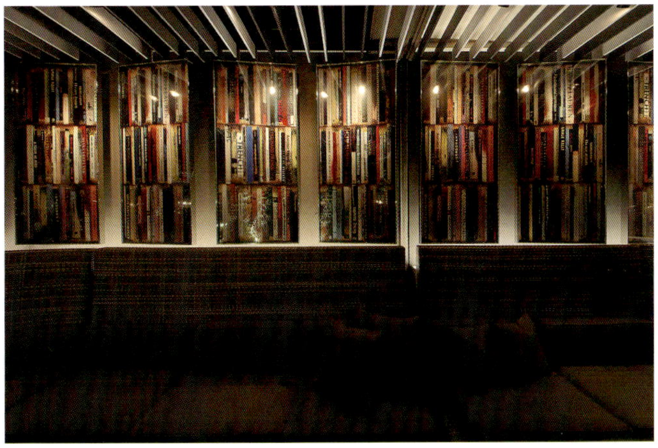

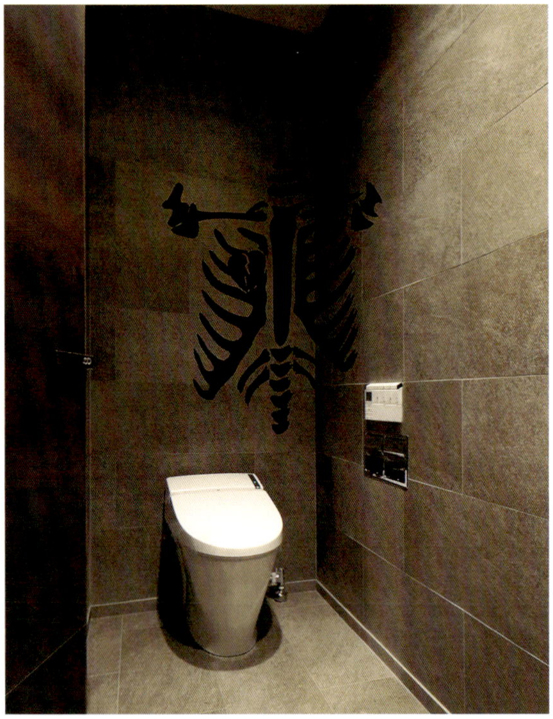

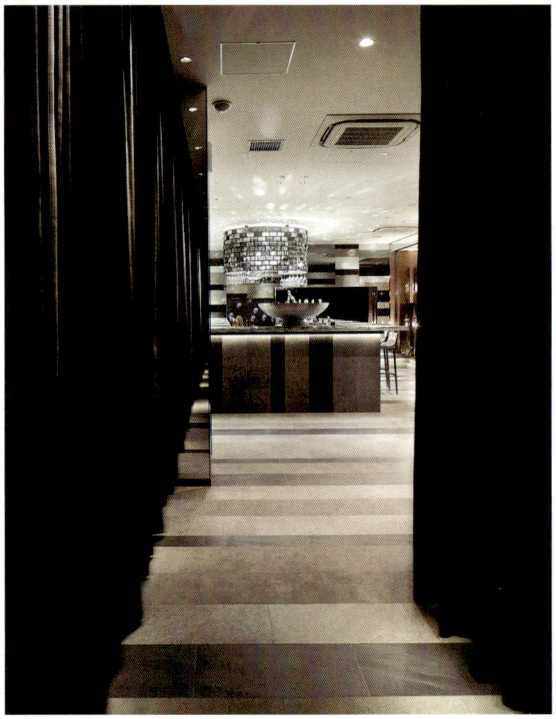

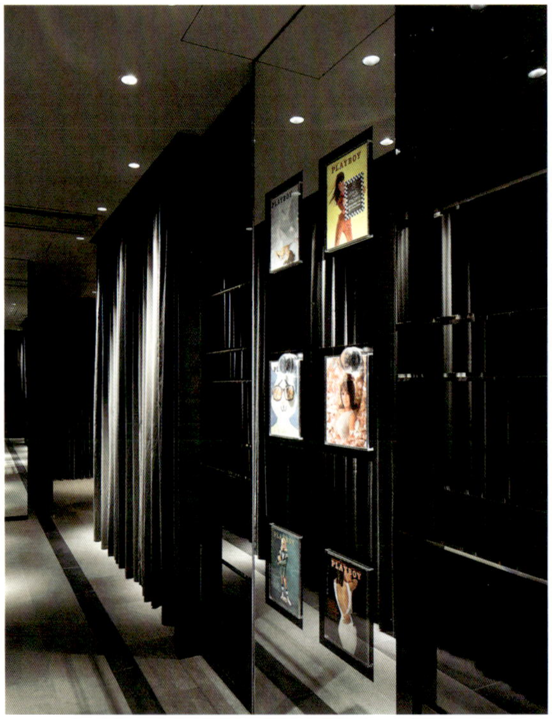

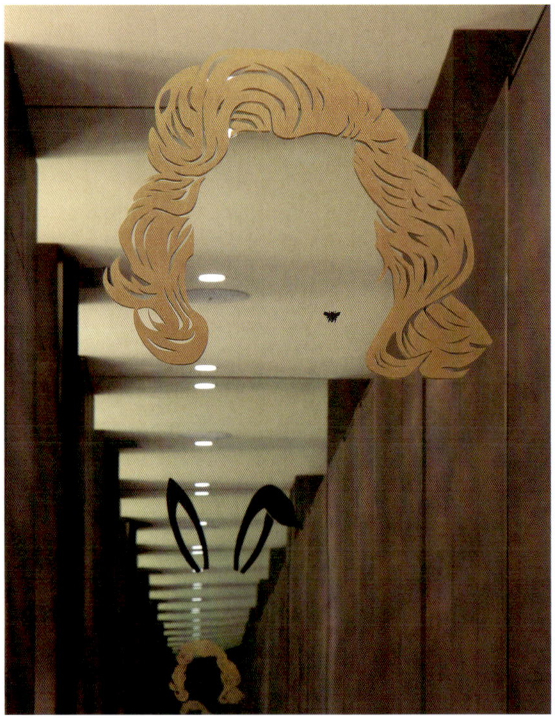

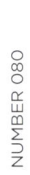

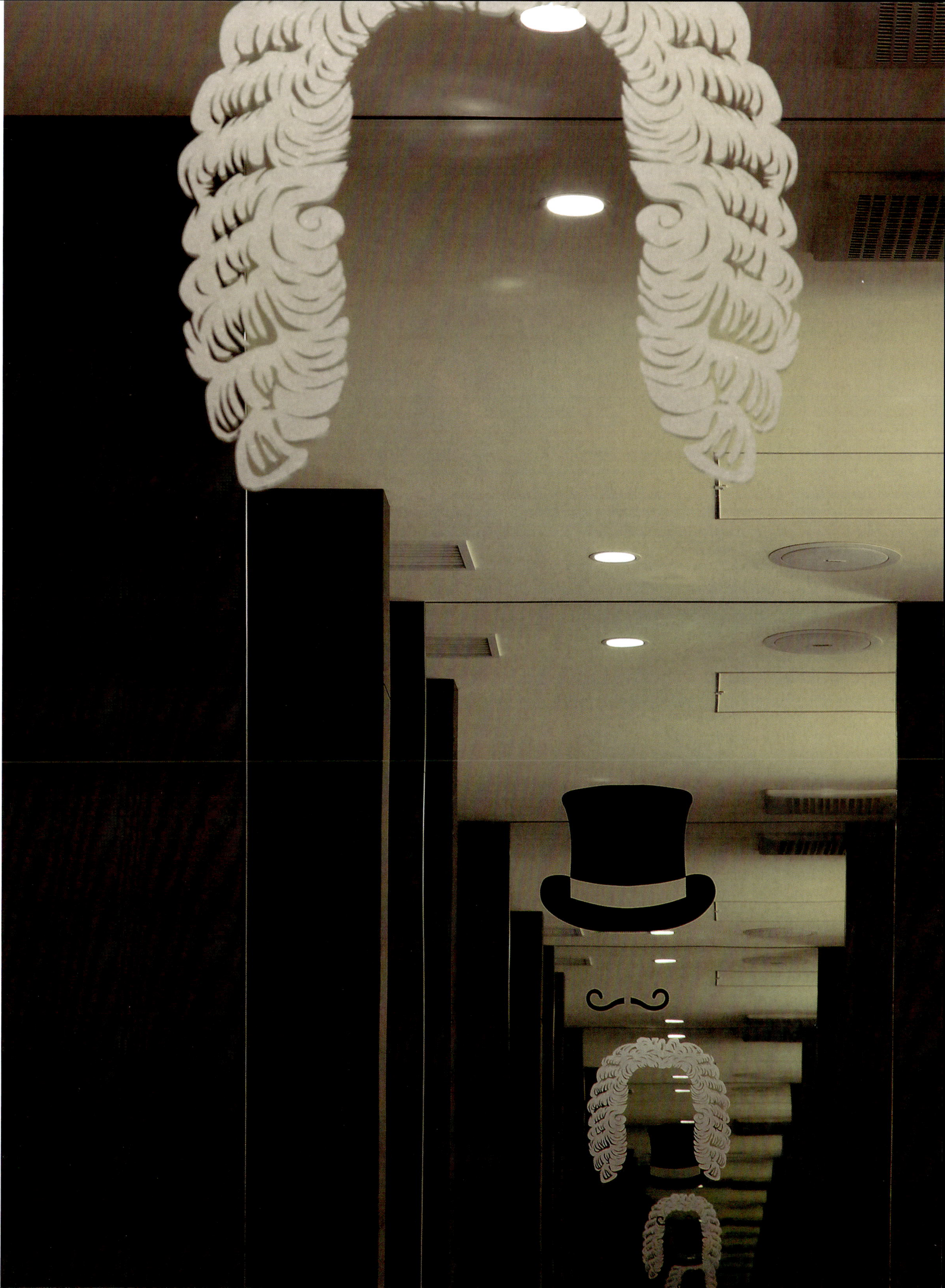

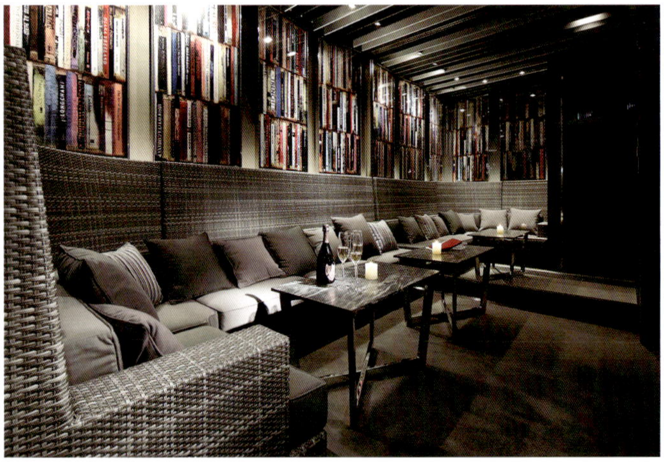

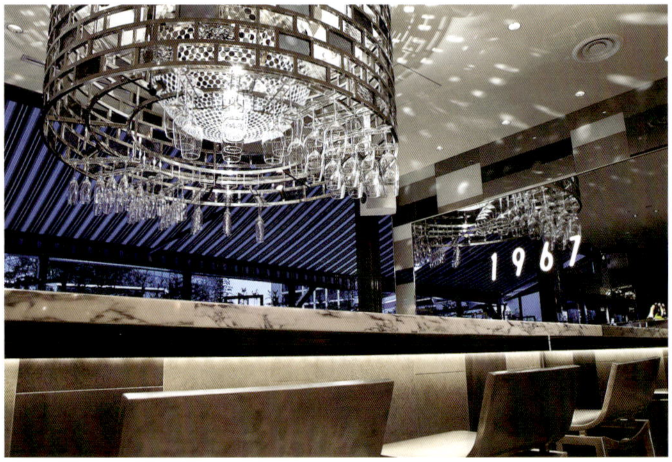
1967

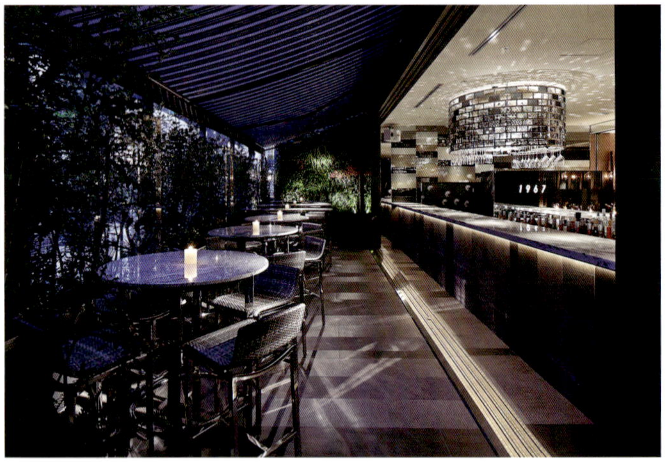
1967

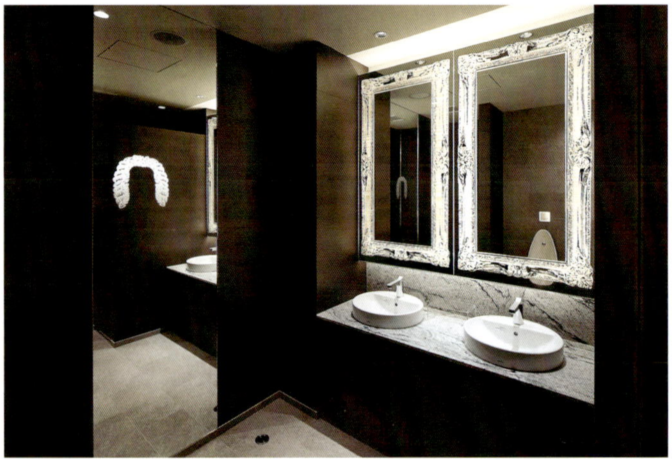

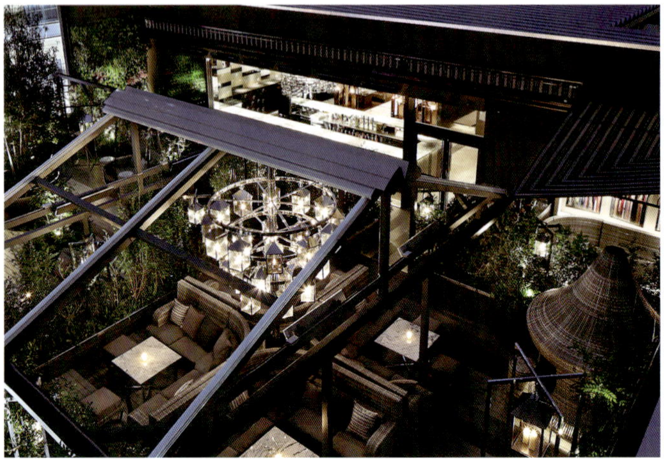

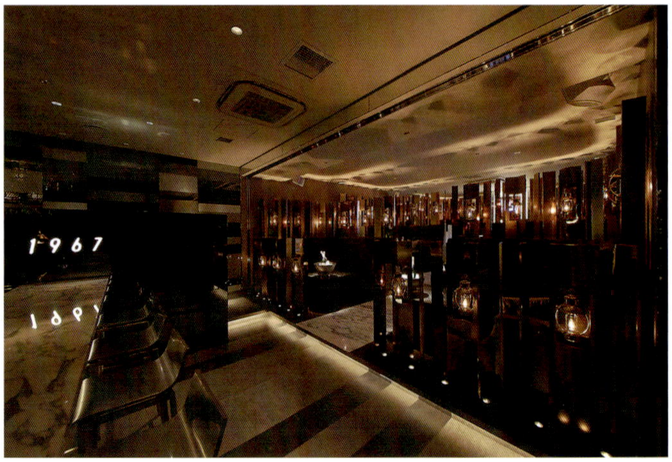
1967

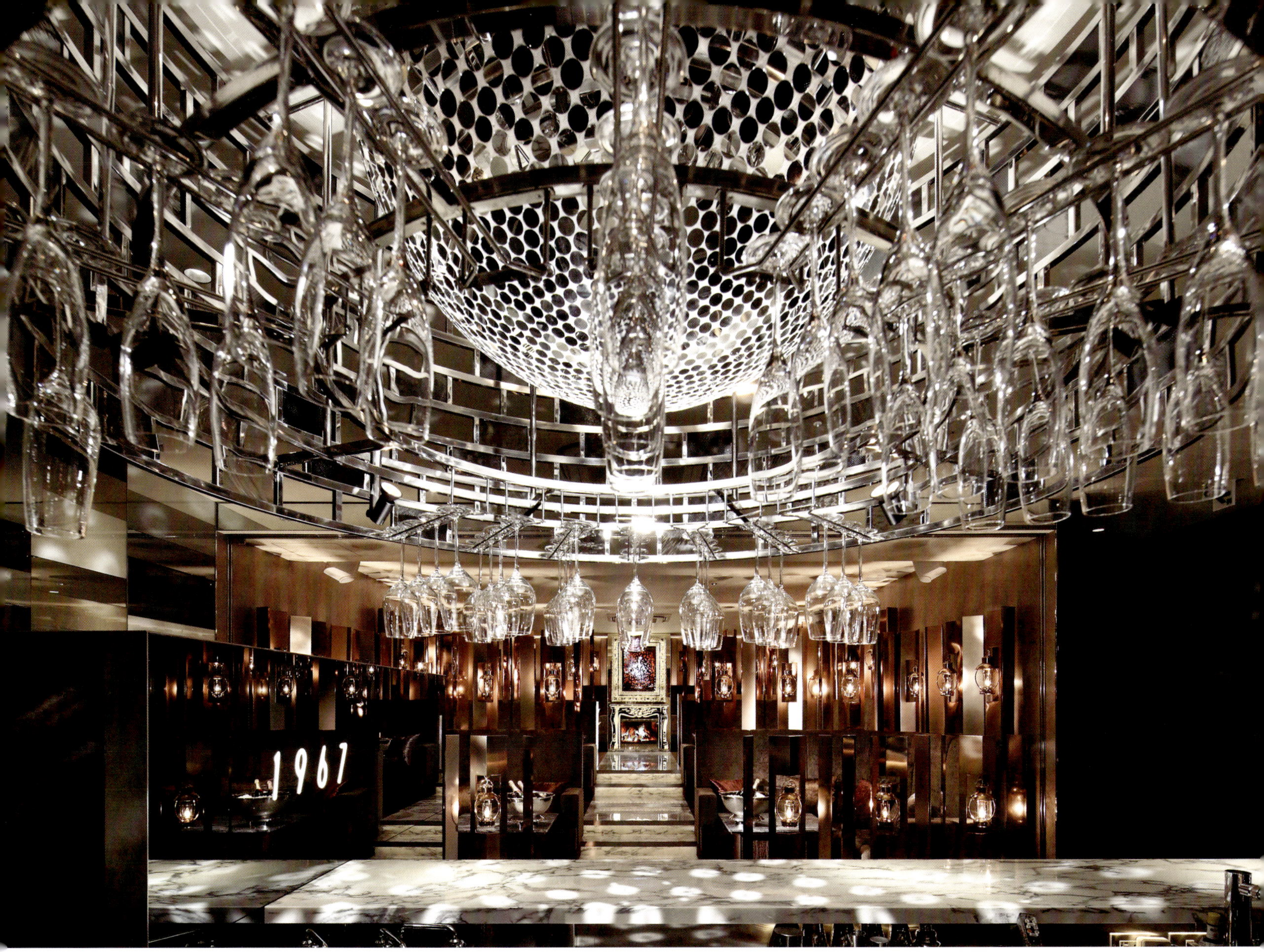
1967

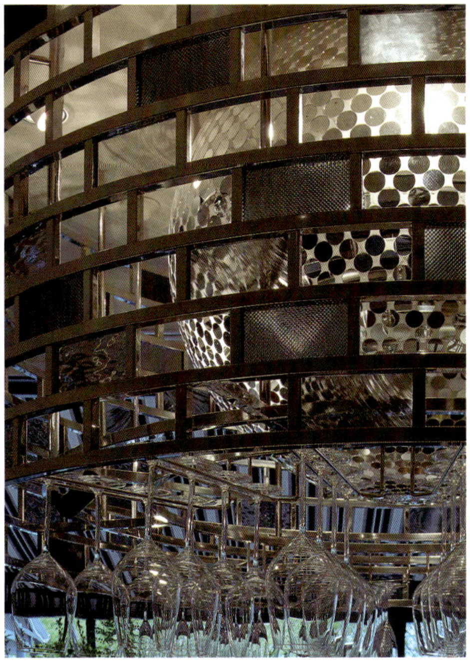

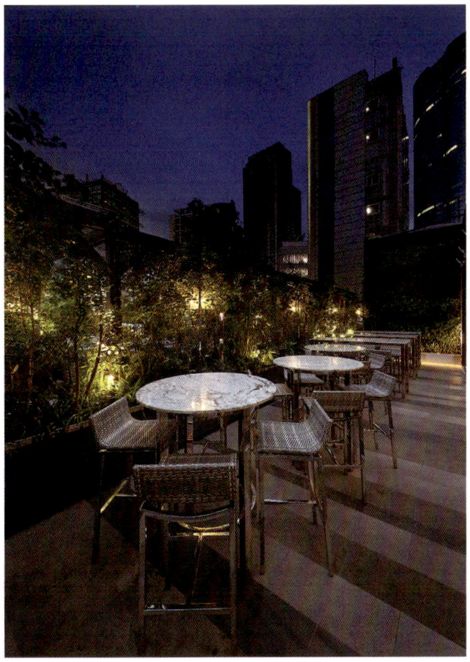

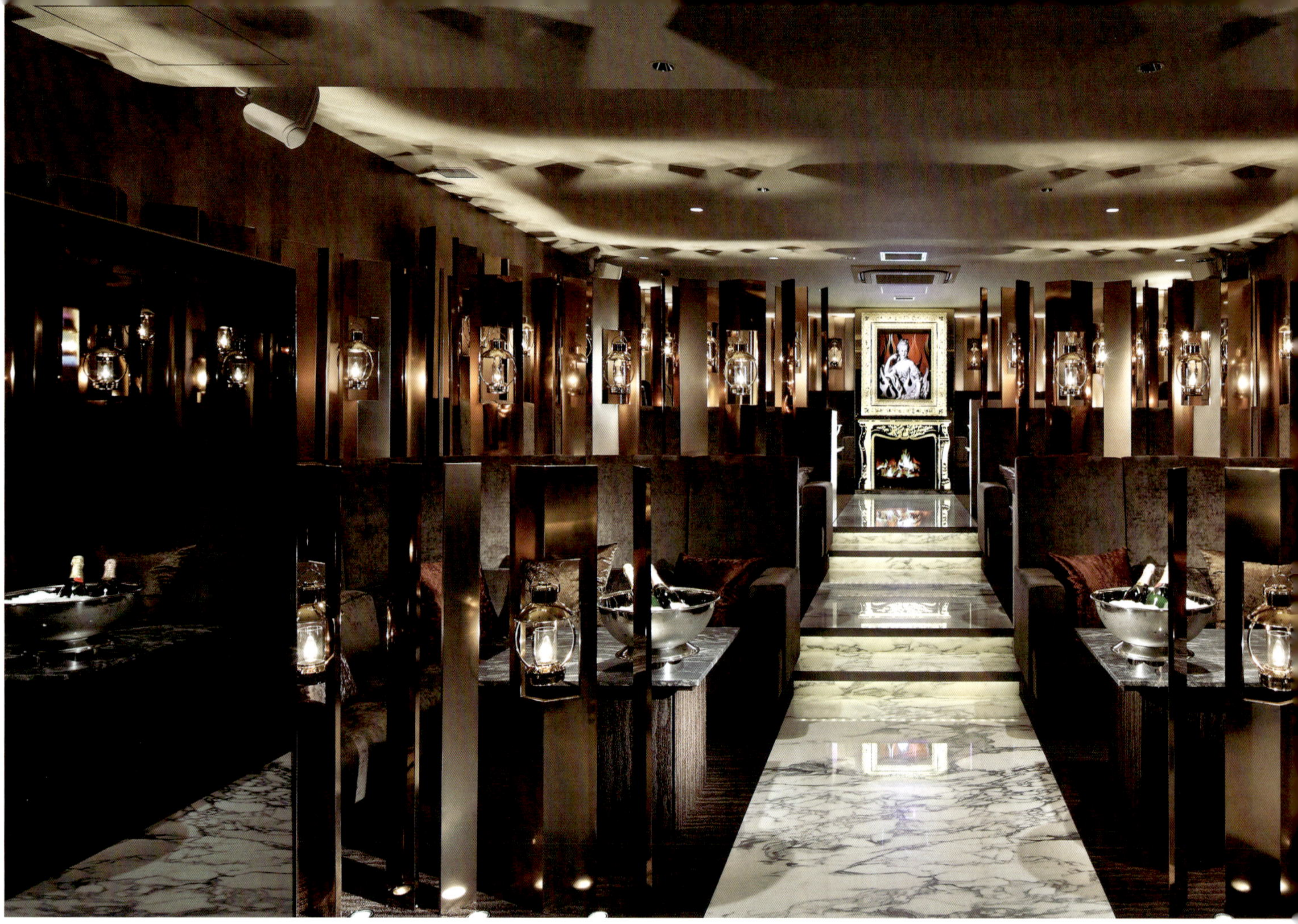

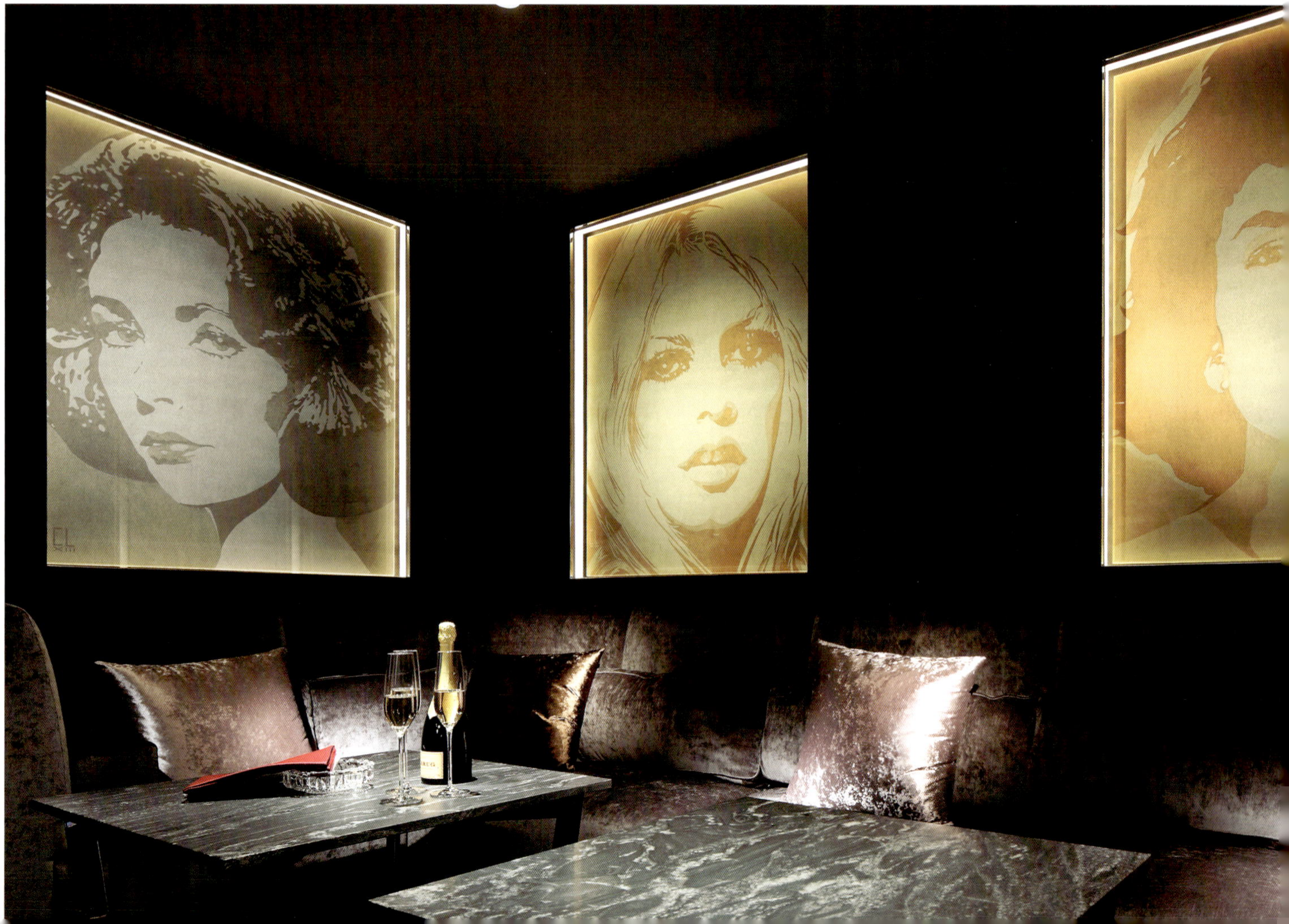

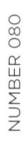

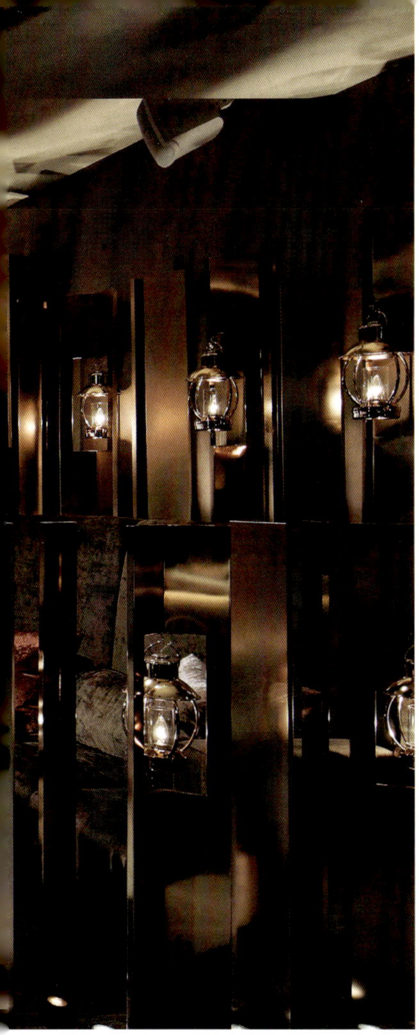
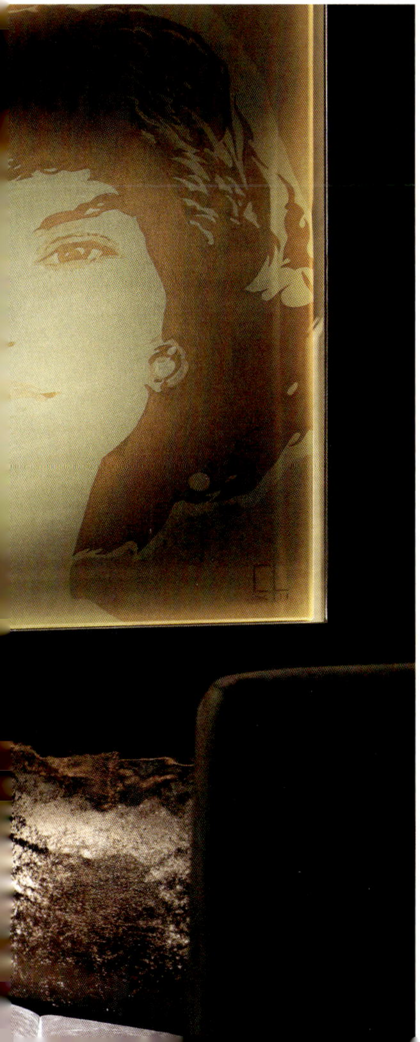
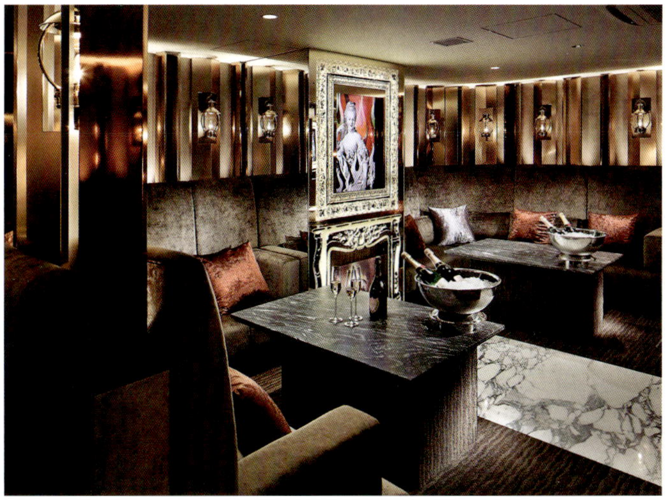
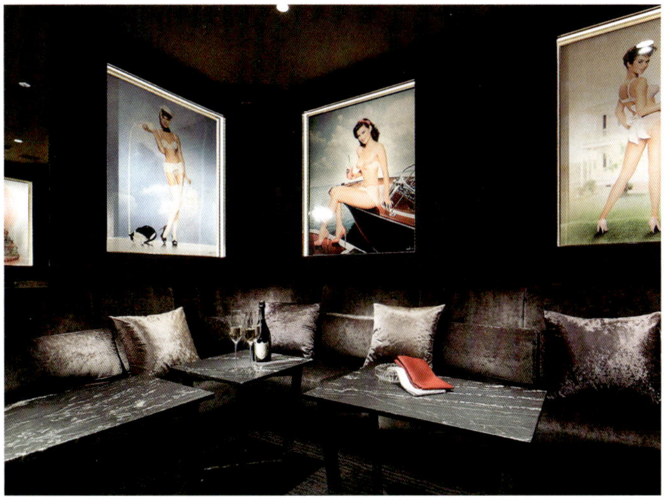
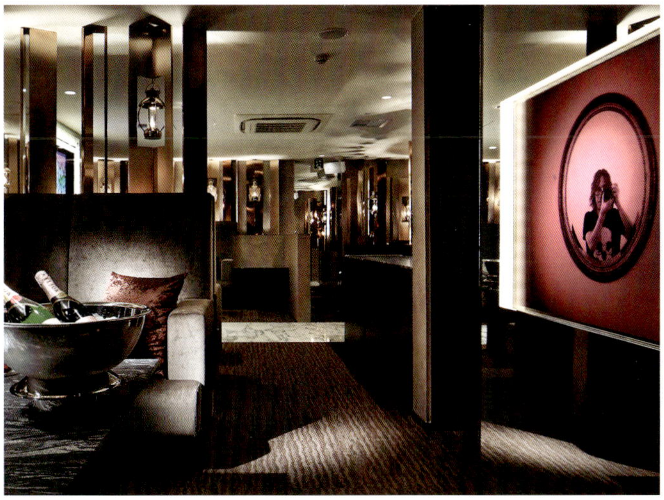

N°	Name	Location	Type	Date
N°001	MEGU New York	New York/USA	Restaurant	Mar.2004
N°002	MEGU Midtown	New York/USA	Restaurant	Apr.2006
N°003	GLAMOUROUS192	Nagoya/Japan	Club	Mar.2005
N°004	CLUB BACH	Osaka/Japan	Club	Apr.2009
N°005	COTTON CLUB	Tokyo/Japan	Lounge	Nov.2005
N°006	clotho	Tokyo/Japan	Bar	Sep.2007
N°007	WYNDHAM the 4th	Hong Kong/China	Bar	Jan.2012
N°008	D	Tokyo/Japan	Bar	Jan.2012
N°009	club TSUKI	Tokyo/Japan	Lounge	Dec.2007
N°010	HARRY'S BAR	Kobe/Japan	Bar	Aug.2001
N°011	Sonoma Wine Garden	Santa Monica/USA	Bar	Aug.2010
N°012	W Hong Kong	Hong Kong/China	Hotel	Aug.2008
N°013	ANA CROWNE PLAZA KYOTO	Kyoto/Japan	Hotel	Dec.2012
N°014	CHAPELLE DES ANGES	Nagoya/Japan	Chapel	Mar.2009
N°015	ARFERIQUE SHIROGANE	Tokyo/Japan	Banquet	Jan.2011
N°016	O.M.CORPORATION	Osaka/Japan	Office	Apr.2006
N°017	Future Plaza of Fantasia	Chengdu/China	Commercial Complex	Oct.2012
N°018	Residence "S"	Hyogo/Japan	Residence	Aug.2011
N°019	Residence "M"	Tokyo/Japan	Residence	Jul.2007
N°020	Residence "CT"	Hong Kong/China	Residence	Jan.2012
N°021	Brillia ARIAKE Sky Tower	Tokyo/Japan	Residence	Mar.2011
N°022	FIELDS Office Lobby	Tokyo/Japan	Office	May 2012
N°023	SAN-EI Faucet Osaka Showroom	Osaka/Japan	Showroom	Mar.2004
N°024	INITIAio Nishiazabu	Tokyo/Japan	Residence	Mar.2012
N°025	SELLTS LIMITED Office	Tokyo/Japan	Office	Nov.2012
N°026	SUNRISE	Osaka/Japan	Office	Apr.2007
N°027	Residence "T"	Osaka/Japan	Residence	Mar.2007
N°028	GLAMOROUS co.,ltd.	Tokyo/Japan	Office	Jan.2011
N°029	LA FÊTE HIRAMATSU	Osaka/Japan	Restaurant	Dec.2012
N°030	OCEAN ROOM	Sydney/Australia	Restaurant	Sep.2009
N°031	Shato hanten	Tokyo/Japan	Restaurant	Sep.2012
N°032	THE ST.REGIS OSAKA La Veduta	Osaka/Japan	Restaurant	Oct.2010
N°033	THE ST.REGIS OSAKA Rue D'or	Osaka/Japan	Restaurant	Oct.2010
N°034	HAJIME	Tokyo/Japan	Dining	Feb.2002
N°035	SAVOY	Tokyo/Japan	Dining	Apr.2013
N°036	sinamo	Kyoto/Japan	Dining	Apr.1999
N°037	NETSURETSU SHOKUDO, HEP NAVIO	Osaka/Japan	Dining	Jul.1996
N°038	Hitsumabushi Nagoya Bincho, Ikebukuro PARCO	Tokyo/Japan	Dining	Nov.2011
N°039	Kobe Rokkomichi Gyunta, Shinjuku Lumine 1	Tokyo/Japan	Dining	May 2012
N°040	Hamac de Paradis Kambaikan	Kyoto/Japan	Dining	Mar.2004
N°041	HECHIMA	Osaka/Japan	Dining	Sep.1995
N°042	Château Restaurant Joël Robuchon	Tokyo/Japan	Restaurant & Bar	Dec.2004
N°043	LE CAFÉ de Joël Robuchon	Tokyo/Japan	Café	Apr.2004
N°044	DBL	Osaka/Japan	Café	Mar.2008
N°045	DEAN & DELUCA AOYAMA	Tokyo/Japan	Café	Dec.2005
N°046	ISLAND VEGGIE Hawaiian Veggie Style	Tokyo/Japan	Dining	Oct.2011
N°047	CHOiCE!	Tokyo/Japan	Dining	Apr.2010
N°048	The central restaurant at the center of the Diet building	Tokyo/Japan	Dining	Jun.2012
N°049	Redevelopment of ISETAN Shinjuku main store	Tokyo/Japan	Department Store	Mar.2013
N°050	AOYAMA Francfranc	Tokyo/Japan	Retail	May 2010

N°051	NAGOYA Francfranc	Nagoya/Japan	Retail	Oct.2010
N°052	Samantha Thavasa, Lotte Department Store	Seoul/Korea	Retail	Nov.2011
N°053	LOVE SWEETS ANTIQUE AOYAMA	Tokyo/Japan	Retail	Aug.2010
N°054	boutique by Shanghai Xintiandi	Shanghai/China	Retail	Oct.2011
N°055	cagi de rêves	Osaka/Japan	Retail	Oct.2007
N°056	couronne	Tokyo/Japan	Retail	Jul.2007
N°057	AUDEMARS PIGUET AP TOWER	Tokyo/Japan	Retail	Jul.2007
N°058	RESONA BANK Tokyo Midtown	Tokyo/Japan	Bank	Apr.2007
N°059	TOKIA	Tokyo/Japan	Commercial Complex	Nov.2005
N°060	K-two AOYAMA VADI	Tokyo/Japan	Salon	Nov.2007
N°061	K-two AOYAMA LU D0RESS	Tokyo/Japan	Salon	Nov.2007
N°062	BRILLIAGE	Tokyo/Japan	Salon	May 2011
N°063	Takano Yuri BEAUTY CLINIC, Shinjuku	Tokyo/Japan	Salon	Jan.2009
N°064	KENZO DENTAL CLINIC	Tokyo/Japan	Clinic	Dec.2011
N°065	RANDEN Arashiyama Station	Kyoto/Japan	Station	Oct.2002
N°066	Matsubishi	Hong Kong/China	Dining	Jul.2006
N°067	Tse Yang	Doha/Qatar	Restaurant	Jun.2010
N°068	Goyashiki	Kagawa/Japan	Restaurant	Sep.2002
N°069	Tsuki no Ie	Kobe/Japan	Dining	Aug.2000
N°070	Photogenic	Osaka/Japan	Dining	Apr.1999
N°071	Ochaya Man	Kyoto/Japan	Restaurant & Bar	Apr.2006
N°072	Murata Mitsui	Osaka/Japan	Dining	Oct.1999
N°073	Nico	Tokyo/Japan	Restaurant	Nov.2009
N°074	Ozaki Yukitaka	Tokyo/Japan	Restaurant	Apr.2013
N°075	aqua london	London/UK	Restaurant	Oct.2009
N°076	IT'S	Kobe/Japan	Bar	Dec.1996
N°077	KEN'S DINING NISHIAZABU	Tokyo/Japan	Dining	Jan.1998
N°078	Salon á dîner Galerie	Osaka/Japan	Lounge	Oct.2005
N°079	NAMISUS	Ashiya/Japan	Dining	May 2005
N°080	1967	Tokyo/Japan	Lounge	Apr.2013
N°081	COOL	Kobe/Japan	Bar	Sep.1987

森田 恭通
デザイナー / GLAMOROUS co.,ltd. 代表

1967年大阪生まれ。学生時代より現場で経験を積みながら、フリーの立場でデザインの基礎を身体で覚えていく。2000年6月に〈GLAMOROUS〉設立。国内はもとより、香港、ニューヨーク、ロンドン、カタールなど、世界各国でプロジェクトに携わる。豪奢な内装のイメージがあるが、「オートクチュール」なデザインを信条とし、現在ではプロダクトなども手がけている。

主な受賞歴
The International Hotel and Property Awards 2011
China Best Design Hotels Award Best Popular Designer
The London Lifestyle Awards 2010
The Andrew Martin Interior Designers of the Year Awards

Yasumichi Morita
Designer / CEO of GLAMOROUS co.,ltd.

Born in Osaka, JAPAN in 1967. Starting with a project in Hong-Kong in 2001, his work has been successfully expending globally to cities including New York, London and Shanghai. His creative activities have expanded into graphic and product design beyond his original career in interior design.

Awards;
The International Hotel and Property Awards 2011
China Best Design Hotels Award Best Popular Designer
The London Lifestyle Awards 2010
The Andrew Martin Interior Designers of the Year Awards

N° 081
Kobe/Japan
Sep.1987
COOL

「すべてはここから始まった」と森田が遠い目をして語る、18歳で手がけた人生で最初の物件。「ソウルミュージックが流れるニューヨークの地下倉庫のようなバー」を作るため、デザインも未経験で、図面を書くこともできなかった森田が、「VOGUE」や「ELLE」といった雑誌からイメージカットを切り抜き、内装業者と共に夜な夜な施工に取り組んだ。自らイラストを描いたり、有刺鉄線でオブジェを制作したり、「いろいろな業種の人が集まる」ことを目標にデザインに取り組んだ結果、空間が人の流れを作り、感情を動かすことを知った現場でもある。現在も内装が変わることなく、多くの人に愛され続けるバーである。

"This is where it all started," says Morita, remembering his very first project, which he took on at the age of eighteen. To create a New York underground bar with blaring soul music, Morita, who at the time had absolutely no design experience, worked day and night with the interior contractors, explaining the image in his mind with cutouts from magazines like Vogue and Elle. With the intent to bring together people from all different fields, Morita worked on the design by drawing illustrations and creating objects out of barbed wire. The project turned out to be an important learning experience, where Morita discovered how space can be used to control flow and evoke emotion. The interior of this project still remains the same, continuing its history as a beloved bar.

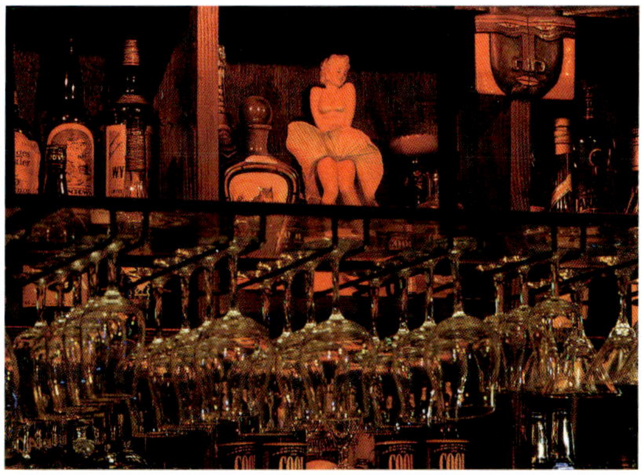

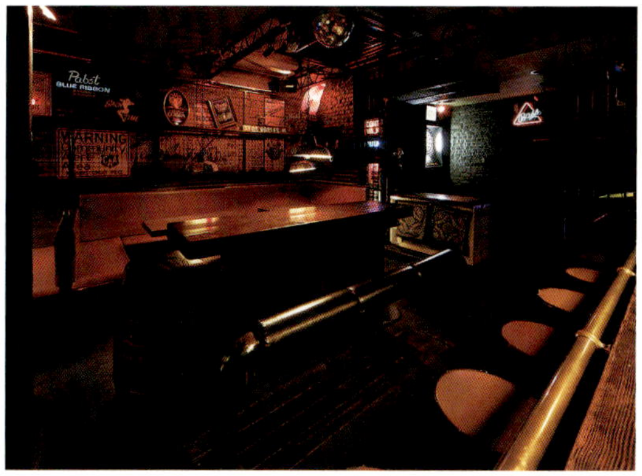

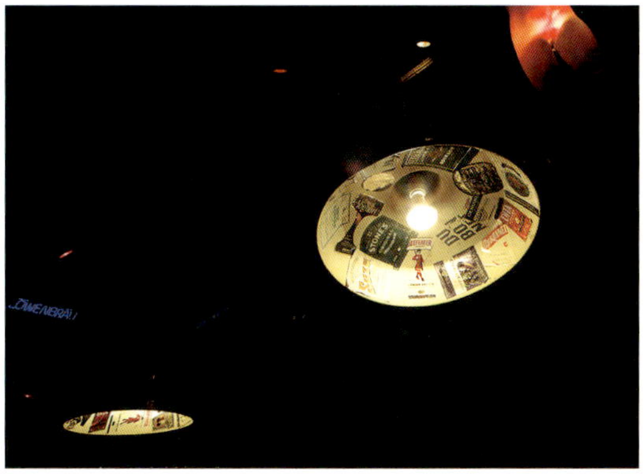

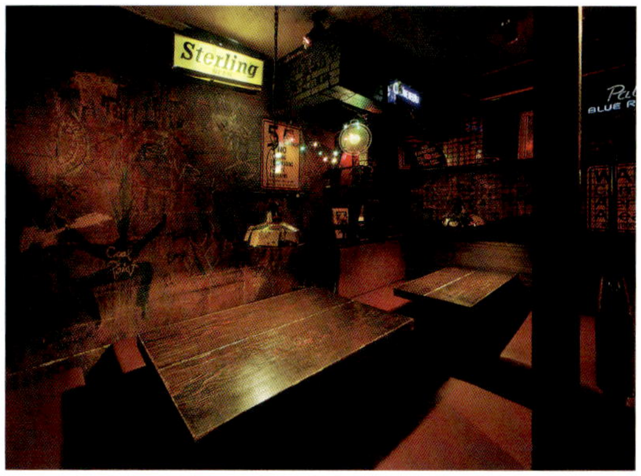
Sterling

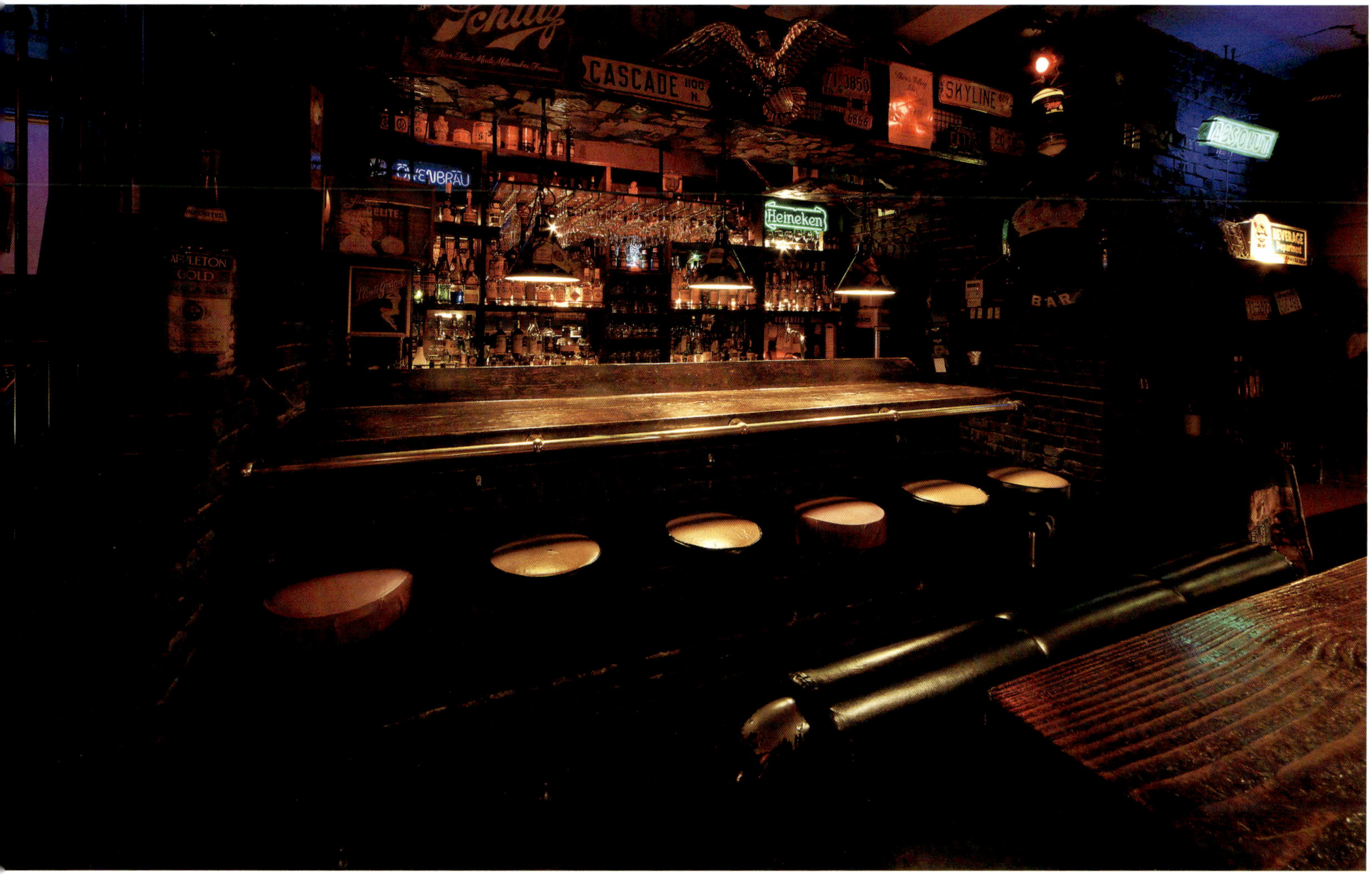
CASCADE
SKYLINE
Heineken
ABSOLUT
BAR

N·Y FEELING SPACE
COOL
SHOT BAR

MINES DANGER

GLAMOROUS PHILOSOPHY NO.1
森田 恭通

アートディレクション・デザイン: 関口 修男 | PLUG-IN GRAPHIC
デザイン: 野村 衛 | PLUG-IN GRAPHIC
編集・文章作成: 村岡 俊也
翻訳: 坂井 絵理加 | NUANCE TRANSLATION
竣工写真: Nacasa & Partners inc.
  SEIRYO STUDIO
  LIBERO CREATIVE
  iMAGE28
  須佐 一心
  Jimmy Cohrssen
  Sharrin Rees
写真: 阿部 健
プリンティングディレクション: 佐々木 陽介 | アベイズム
プリンティングコーディネート: 羽村 舞子 | アベイズム
制作: 多田 綾 | GLAMOROUS co.,ltd.
  中野 響平 | GLAMOROUS co.,ltd.

発行日: 2013年11月5日 初版／第一刷発行

発行人 山崎 浩一
制作統括 後藤 哲也
発行所 株式会社パルコ
  エンタテインメント事業部
  東京都渋谷区宇田川町15-1 〒150-0045
  tel: 03-3477-5755
  www.parco-publishing.jp

印刷・製本 アベイズム

©GLAMOROUS co.,ltd.
©PARCO co.,ltd.
All rights reserved.

無断転載禁止
ISBN978-4-86506-008-9 C0072
Printed in Japan

GLAMOROUS PHILOSOPHY NO.1
Yasumichi Morita

Art Direction & Book Design: Nobuo Sekiguchi | PLUG-IN GRAPHIC
Design: Mamoru Nomura | PLUG-IN GRAPHIC
Editing & Writing: Toshiya Muraoka
English Translation: Erica Sakai | NUANCE TRANSLATION
Architecture Photo: Nacasa & Partners inc.
  SEIRYO STUDIO
  LIBERO CREATIVE
  iMAGE28
  I.Susa
  Jimmy Cohrssen
  Sharrin Rees
General Photo: Takeshi Abe
Printing Direction: Yosuke Sasaki | Abeism
Printing Coordination: Maiko Hamura | Abeism
Production: Aya Tada | GLAMOROUS co.,ltd.
  Kyohei Nakano | GLAMOROUS co.,ltd.

First Printing: Nov 5, 2013

Publisher Koichi Yamazaki
Producer Tetsuya Goto
Publishing House PARCO co.,ltd.
  Entertainment Department
  15-1 Udagawa-cho, Shibuya-ku, Tokyo 150-0045
  tel: +81-3-3477-5755
  www.parco-publishing.jp

Printed by Abeism

©GLAMOROUS co.,ltd.
©PARCO co.,ltd.
All rights reserved.

No reproduction without written permission.
ISBN978-4-86506-008-9 C0072
Printed in Japan